Schumpeter's Market

Also by David Reisman

Adam Smith's Sociological Economics
Alfred Marshall: Progress and Politics
Alfred Marshall's Mission
Anthony Crosland: The Mixed Economy
Conservative Capitalism: The Social Economy
Crosland's Future: Opportunity and Outcome
The Economics of Alfred Marshall
Galbraith and Market Capitalism
The Institutional Economy: Demand and Supply
Market and Health
The Political Economy of Health Care
The Political Economy of James Buchanan
Richard Titmuss: Welfare and Society
State and Welfare: Tawney, Galbraith and Adam Smith
Theories of Collective Action: Downs, Olson and Hirsch

Schumpeter's Market

Enterprise and Evolution

David Reisman

Edward Elgar
Cheltenham, UK • Northampton MA, USA

Published by
Edward Elgar Publishing Limited
Glensanda House
Montpellier Parade
Cheltenham
Glos GL50 1UA
UK

Edward Elgar Publishing, Inc.
136 West Street
Suite 202
Northampton
Massachusetts 01060
USA

A catalogue record for this book
is available from the British Library

Library of Congress Cataloguing in Publication Data
Reisman, David A.
Schumpeter's market : enterprise and evolution / David Reisman.
p. cm.
Includes bibliographical references and index.
1. Schumpeter, Joseph Alois, 1883–1950. 2. Economists—United States—Biography. 3. Entrepreneurship. 4. Capitalism. 5. Equilibrium (Economics) 6. Evolutionary economics.
I. Title.

HB119.S35R44 2004
330'.092—dc22

2003049435

ISBN 1 84376 164 5

Printed and bound in Great Britain by MPG Books Ltd, Bodmin, Cornwall

Contents

Acknowledgements

The publishers wish to thank the following who have kindly given permission for the use of copyright material.

HarperCollins Inc. for excerpts from: *Capitalism, Socialism and Democracy* by Joseph A. Schumpeter, 3rd edition, 1942, 1950.

Harvard University Press for excerpts from: *The Theory of Economic Development: An Inquiry into Profits, Capital, Credit and Interest in the Business Cycle* by Joseph A. Schumpeter, translated into English by Redvers Opie, Cambridge, MA: Harvard University Press, Copyright © 1934 by the President and Fellows of Harvard College, Copyright © 1962 by Redvers Opie.

The McGraw-Hill Companies for excerpts from: *Business Cycles* by Joseph A. Schumpeter, 1939.

Princeton University Press for excerpts from: *The Economics and Sociology of Capitalism* by Joseph A. Schumpeter, edited by Richard Swedberg, 1991.

Routledge (Unwin Hyman) for excerpts from: *Capitalism, Socialism and Democracy* by Joseph A. Schumpeter, 3rd edition, 1942, 1950.

Transaction Publishers for excerpts from: *Essays on Entrepreneurs, Innovations, Business Cycles, and The Evolution of Capitalism* by Joseph A. Schumpeter, 1951, 1989.

Every effort has been made to trace all the copyright holders but if any have been inadvertently overlooked the publishers will be pleased to make the necessary arrangements at the first opportunity.

1. Introduction

Schumpeter knew that economics was a labyrinth of concepts. Deprived of its mental images it would be no more than a tool-kit of discrete *how tos* struggling for hegemony with the showy pirouettes of mathematical abstraction. It is the ideas and the perspectives that rescue the Good Life from the instrumental and the formal. Schumpeter's economics is an intellectual's attempt not to draw narrow advantage from the wealth of nations but rather to satisfy a deep-seated personal curiosity about the origins and functions of man's material aspirations. Market, enterprise and evolution are the three irreducible constructs which give consistency to his whole life's work. Linked together, they form the synthesis that interprets the facts and the tendencies through the paradigm of a sophisticated world-view.

The market is supply and demand. Seen as statics, it is a gravitational field that produces an equilibrium price as if guided by an omniscient auctioneer. Seen as dynamics, it is a voyage of discovery that, powered by profit or driven on by challenge, need never arrive at its final point of rest. The market is a mechanism that inputs the signals, diffuses the information and outputs the allocation. The market is also a process, a motorway, a laboratory and a framework for discourse without end.

Enterprise is restless transformation. It is the way in which the market delivers change and the reason why evolution continues to grind out new surprises. The entrepreneur is a person who implements innovations in order to make his undertaking a success. Entrepreneurship is the propensity to pioneer new initiatives behind a veil of unknowledge so thick that it conceals the competition, the bad luck and the shipwreck. The propensity, separate from the person, can survive in the balanced teams of corporate organisation, but it can also be put at risk by the stifling repetitiveness of self-reproducing bureaucracy. Private sector or public sector, creative destruction is not for all seasons.

Evolution is institutional mutation. It is matter in motion as one historical uniqueness gives way to the next unintended consequence. It is also memory embedded where ideologies filter, atavism brakes and tacit knowledge hands on a once-was template that has been made an irrelevance by events. Perfect competition gives way to monopoly which endogenises the technological economies of breakthrough and scale. Accommodation and merger take the place of the same-side rivalries that used to keep the pricing keen.

Depersonalised capitalism is crowded out by the depersonalised State. Planned socialism takes over. The voyage through uncertain markets into predetermined centralism is guided by an invisible hand that will not compromise on the stages of growth.

Schumpeter's economics is the mix of his three irreducible constructs. This book, *Schumpeter's Market: Enterprise and Evolution*, seeks to trace out his logic and make sense of his system. Chapter 2 deals with Schumpeter's life, his intentions and ambiguities, his ongoing dialogue with the economics of Karl Marx. Chapter 3 is concerned with tendencies, visions, academic disciplines and the need to think big. Chapter 4 is about the flashes of insight of the forceful entrepreneur, Chapter 5 about the large corporation which inherits his supremacy and perhaps also his role. Chapter 6 turns to the sociology of class, imperialism and motivation in the capitalist society which is coming to an end. Chapter 7 examines the inexorable bureaucratisation that has to lead to State control, Chapter 8 the productive and allocative efficiency of a socialist plan that may or may not be able to keep the dynamic alive. Chapter 9 shows that national character and cultural values ensure that even under socialism there is much in economic sociology that will remain the same.

Chapter 10 explains that capitalism is in decay because of internal contradictions that rationalise the loyalties and break up the dynasty. Chapter 11 questions the influence of the intelligentsia and suggests that even corporate capitalism might command widespread support. Chapter 12 says that growth, full employment and price stability are normally safe in the market economy. Chapter 13 on the cycle as a salutary spring clean continues the analysis of macroeconomic good performance. It shows that, although capitalism in Schumpeter's view was doomed, it was not the volatility of crises that would bring about its unavoidable decline and fall.

The book concludes by stating the obvious – that Schumpeter made a number of assertions that are unlikely to stand the test of time. The whole, however, is more than the sum of the parts. Schumpeter's synthesis is the manifesto of an evolutionary economics that refuses to accept its market or its enterprise save where each is situated in its context. Everything leads to everything else. It is true in Schumpeter's economics. It is true in life.

2. Schumpeter's vision

Malthus means population. Marx means revolution. Keynes means unemployment. Schumpeter means entrepreneurship. Wolfgang Stolper is right to warn against such context-less selectivity that tears the piece from the puzzle that alone gives it sense: 'What matters is not merely the one or the other idea, however great, however significant. What matters is the place of the idea in the "vision" of the genius, the theory in the literal sense: the view of things as a whole.' (Stolper, 1951:102). Schumpeter's *Weltanschauung* is Schumpeter's *Gedankengebäude*. It is not one brick in the Colosseum. It is the *sui generis* of the overarching Colosseum itself.

Schumpeter's vision is not a sequence of higgledy-piggledy *ad hoc*s. Instead it is a single story that its author released in instalments in the space of four decades and more. It is the envelope of two concentric circles. The inner circle is the *system*, made up in market capitalism of 'independent quantities ... mutually determining one another' (Schumpeter, 1928:50). The outer circle is the *order*, the 'cultural complement' (Schumpeter, 1942a:121) of ideas, values, polity, society that in present-day conditions may be called the 'civilization of capitalism' (Schumpeter, 1928:49). A downswing is a crisis in the *system*: temporary, passing, it is not a threat to the survival of the process but the precondition for it to succeed. Rationality, democracy, 'Gladstonian liberalism' (Schumpeter, 1942a:126), individualism are the real enemy at the gate: a crisis in the *order* and not in the Walrasianism, it is institutional factors such as these that explain the historical transformation of the social economy from one set of interdependences to another social language, coherent and unique.

The consistency both in the bricks and in the structure is remarkable. There cannot be many great thinkers who in 9 major books, over 200 papers, over 90 book reviews, have deviated so little from their theme. Clemence and Doody, while Schumpeter was still making additions to his edifice, commented that no tenet of any significance had been changed since Schumpeter was a new talent in his twenties: 'His youthful vision, first reduced to a comprehensive model in 1911, has since been elaborated and refined, but it has been altered in no essential respect to the present day. Such extraordinary consistency is almost unique in our science.' (Clemence and Doody, 1950:1). Stolper, looking back over the unfolding of the interdependent synthesis, reached the similar conclusion that somehow the components all added up to a car: 'In rereading

Schumpeter's work, the reader gradually and at an accelerating pace becomes filled with the insight of an almost miraculous unity of thought.' (Stolper, 1951:105). The Pareto of the *Manual* was not the Pareto of the *Treatise*. Schumpeter, on the other hand, was all of one piece. Almost unique in economic science, he had no apprentice years and seldom changed his mind. The vision of the *Wesen* is the vision of the *Cycles*.

This chapter, complemented by the next, is concerned with the underlying vision that gives unity to the disparate insights. Section 1, Schumpeter and his books, situates the publications in the framework of Schumpeter's life and times. Section 2, Intentions and objectives, asks what Schumpeter sought to achieve when he investigated and wrote. Section 3, Schumpeter and Marx, explores the nature of the 'permanent dialogue with Marx' (März, 1991:21) that made Schumpeter so unusual a non-Marxian economist.

2.1 SCHUMPETER AND HIS BOOKS

Newness is the leitmotiv. There is not a single topic in the whole of Schumpeter's economics that is not a function of the never-contented quest for challenge and change. Schumpeter admired the businessman on the barricades for the same reason that Hegel admired the Napoleon on horseback – because the man of ideas always admires the man of action who can get things done. Yet there is something more. Schumpeter himself was de facto an entrepreneur. Throughout his long career, in the body of his prolific output, he demonstrated that he was able to produce an intellectual synthesis radically different from that of mentors like Menger and Marshall who had guided him to the trail that he was to blaze.

Josef Alois Schumpeter was born (an only child) on 8 February 1883 in Triesch (now Třešt), Moravia. His father, a small factory owner, died when he was four and, in 1893, his mother married Lieutenant Field Marshall Sigismund von Kéler. This translation from the middle to the upper class made possible Schumpeter's schooling at the elite Theresianum in Vienna. Schumpeter at Austria's Eton must have been aware that he did not really fit in with the young aristocrats who were being groomed to administer the Austro-Hungarian Empire.

From 1901–1906 Schumpeter studied law and economics (also attending lectures on statistics, mathematics and politics) at the University of Vienna. It was a centre of the marginal utility approach which had been pioneered in 1871 by Menger and further developed by his disciples Wieser, Böhm-Bawerk and Philippovich in the *Methodenstreit* with the inductivists like Schmoller of the German Historical School. Obtaining his doctorate (Dr Juris) in law in

1906, Schumpeter travelled to Berlin to attend a seminar and then on to England. There he spent a year as a research student at the newly-founded (in 1895) London School of Economics. In the round Reading Room of the British Museum, immersing himself in the great classics of world economics, Schumpeter made notes in several languages that were to last him a lifetime. While in England he met Gladys Seaver, whom he married in 1907. They separated in 1913.

From 1907–1908 Schumpeter practised law (with an Italian law-firm) at the International Mixed Tribunal in Cairo, Egypt. He also gave advice on personal finance and business administration. In the evenings he found time to write a major book of over 600 pages. *Das Wesen und der Hauptinhalt der Theoretischen Nationalökonomie (The Nature and Principal Content of Economic Theory)* was published in 1908. A treatise on methodology that sought to reconcile the abstract subjectivists with the empiricist fact-gatherers – 'The only difference lies in the interest in different problems' (Schumpeter, 1908:7) – its erudition and perspicuity were all the more striking when one recalls that the intellectual maturity was that of a young author, still only 25. Schumpeter, as Spiethoff says, was Schumpeter from the very start: 'Josef Schumpeter was never a beginner but a precocious genius; he entered the scientific arena a full-fledged master' (cited in Stolper, 1951:105).

In 1909, back in Vienna, he secured his Habilitation through the *Wesen*. He was the youngest economist in Austria to have done so. Despite his obvious brilliance, he was never offered an academic appointment at the University of Vienna. Schumpeter began his teaching career at the University of Czernowitz (now Chervotsky, in the Ukraine), where he served as *Ausserordentlicher* (Associate) Professor of Economics from 1909 to 1911. It was at Czernowitz that he first formulated the interpretation of entrepreneurship and cycles, innovation and progress, that was to be the bedrock for his subsequent work and his reputation.

The Theory of Economic Development appeared in 1911. Officially it was published in 1912. The English translation of 1934 relies on the 1926 (abridged) edition. The main change made in the 1926 edition is that the author rewrote large sections of Chapter 2 ('The fundamental phenomenon of economic development') and Chapter 6 ('The business cycle'). He omitted altogether the text of his earlier Chapter 7 on 'The economic system seen as a whole'. Introducing Chapter 7 with the warning that 'we are going to change course a bit', reflecting that Chapters 1 to 6, 'in terms both of method and of content ... constitute a unified whole', he clearly believed from the start that his long sections on meaningful interaction and class consciousness were an add-on, out of keeping with the closed system of 'closely-related economic phenomena' (Schumpeter, 1912a:463) that made up the rest of the book. The technique became more sharply focused. The broader picture, however, lost much in the trim. Schumpeter writes that 'there is no purely economic development, just development itself, in all areas of the life of the nation' (Schumpeter, 1912a:470). The omission of Chapter 7 did little to support his contention that the economy could not be understood on its own.

From 1911 to 1921 he was Professor at the University of Graz. The appointment owed much to the patronage of Böhm-Bawerk. In 1913–1914 he spent a year as Visiting Professor at Columbia University in New York City: he also received an honorary doctorate from Columbia. His *Epochen der Dogmen und Methodengeschichte (Economic Doctrine and Method)* appeared in 1914. A short history of economic thought, it had been commissioned by Max Weber for a series he was editing on social economics. *The Crisis of the Tax State* was published in 1918, the important essay on 'The Sociology of Imperialisms' in 1919.

Schumpeter was exempted from military service because of his prestigious academic post. Sarajevo and beyond nonetheless left him with a profound sense of personal loss. The First World War destroyed forever the cultured idyll of aristocracy, monarchy and Austro-Hungarian leadership. The only home that Schumpeter ever knew, the passing of the old Empire made him a rootless intellectual whose social and political coordinates had withdrawn into history and would not be coming back.

Schumpeter in 1918–1919 was a member of the German Socialisation Commission in Berlin. The working group had been set up to advise on the State takeover of basic industries such as coal. Most of the members were socialists: Rudolf Hilferding, Emil Lederer, Karl Kautsky, Eduard Heimann. Schumpeter, a non-Marxist and a votary of the entrepreneur, did not find the ideological mix a problem.

Further collaboration with socialists followed. In March 1919 a socialist government was formed in Austria. It was led by Karl Renner. Otto Bauer, the new Foreign Minister, advised Renner that Schumpeter should be made Finance Minister (a post that Böhm-Bawerk had held on three previous occasions). The attachment, on leave from Graz, only lasted seven months. Schumpeter was dismissed because he put great emphasis on the inflow of foreign capital and because of his opposition to the closer contacts with Germany (extending even to *Anschluss*) that had been written into the 1918 Constitution.

From 1921 to 1924, leaving academic life behind him, Schumpeter became President of the Biedermann Bank, Vienna. He used his personal credit-line to invest in outside speculations which he hoped would fund his expensive tastes. The crisis of 1924 put paid to that. Not only did the bank itself fail but Schumpeter was saddled with a huge burden of debt which it was to take him eleven years to clear. Desperate for money, he contributed occasional pieces to non-academic journals such as *Der Deutsche Volkswirt* as well as more scholarly articles to *Schmollers Jahrbuch*, the *Archiv für Sozialwissenschaft und Sozialpolitik* and the *Economic Journal*. Many of these early papers have been reprinted in *Aufsätze zur Ökonomischen Theorie* (1952) and *Aufsätze zur Soziologie* (1953), edited by E. Schneider and A. Spiethoff, *Aufsätze zur Wirtschaftspolitik* (1985) and *Aufsätze zur Tagespolitik* (1993), edited by W. Stolper and C. Seidl. Wolfgang Stolper was Schumpeter's student in Bonn and later at Harvard. His father, Gustav Stolper, had been the editor of *Der Deutsche Volkswirt*.

In 1925–1932, a theoretician in the homeland of the historical school, Schumpeter was Professor of Economics at the University of Bonn. His teaching (reflecting, perhaps, his practical experience) was weighted towards public finance. His research, as always, was wide-ranging and quintessentially his own. The seminal papers on 'Social classes in an ethnically homogeneous environment' (1927), 'The explanation of the business cycle' (1927) and 'The instability of capitalism' (1928) all date from his years in Bonn. The publication of Keynes's *Treatise on Money* in 1930 caused him to abandon his own proposed book on the subject. An unrevised draft was found after his death. It was published in 1970 as *Das Wesen des Geldes*.

At the same time as his move, in 1925, he married Annie Reisinger. Twenty years his junior, his second wife was the daughter of his mother's concierge. His new-found happiness was not to last long. His mother died in June 1926. His wife died in childbirth in August of the same year. His son – named Josef Schumpeter – lived less than four hours. Schumpeter, already profoundly depressed by the end of the Hapsburg peace, the collapse of the Biedermann Bank, his own personal debts, his inability to show leadership in politics, never recovered from the loss. He copied and re-copied passages from his late wife's diaries (sometimes imitating her handwriting) and addressed prayer-like invocations to '*Die Hasen*', his wife and mother whom he made his personal cult. Pessimistic and resigned, he buried himself in work, calling it 'my only interest in life' (cited in Swedberg, 1991:109). Schumpeter once wrote in his diary that 'only the sick oyster produces pearls' (cited in Swedberg, 1991:204). One wonders if it was himself that he had in mind.

In 1927–1928 and again in 1930 he was Visiting Professor at Harvard University. While there he was a founding member (with Ragnar Frisch, Irving Fisher and others) of the Econometric Society. It was established in 1930 to bridge the gap between statistics and economic theory. Schumpeter was to be the Vice-President of the Society for 1938–1939 and its (fifth) President for 1940–1941. Returning to Europe in 1931, he spent some time in Japan as Visiting Lecturer at the Tokyo College of Commerce. Later named the Hitotsubashi University, it now holds 3500 books, periodicals and pamphlets from Schumpeter's private collection.

In 1932 Schumpeter accepted a permanent professorship at Harvard and made a clear break with his old life abroad. In 1948 he was made President of the American Economic Association. He was the first President of the AEA not to have been born in North America. In 1939 he became an American citizen. In 1937 he married Elizabeth Boody Firuski. A Radcliffe economist, she created the quiet home he needed to do his research and helped him to keep his self-destructive sense of failure under control. It is not known if the childless Schumpeter still wanted to found a dynasty. Elizabeth at any rate was unable to have children.

Schumpeter at Harvard taught courses on theory, money, cycles, thought and made some of his most lasting contributions to economics. He did this in an environment which cannot have done much for his psychological equilibrium.

The rise of Hitler in 1933 did not worry him: he appears to have advised former colleagues in Bonn to join the Party and argued openly that Germany had been badly treated at Versailles. What did worry him was the perception that his fellow Americans were so besotted with liberal democracy that they did not appreciate the value of strong leadership and well-disciplined order. Capable of denying that six million Jews had been killed in the Holocaust (he put the total at no more than two million), able to praise Franco's dictatorship because it got things done, Schumpeter (and, separately, Elizabeth) were investigated by the FBI for suspiciously pro-Fascist leanings. Nothing incriminating was ever found and Haberler puts the tendencies down to an extraordinary political *naïveté*, 'Needless to say he had no sympathies with the Nazi regime … . But most of his friends thought that he underestimated the dangers, the aggressive power, the intentions of Hitlerism.' (Haberler, 1951:38). What he did not underestimate was the devastation that in the war reduced Europe to a pile of rubble. The *Anschluss* in 1938 swallowed up his homeland. The streets where he grew up were Allied-bombed and Four-power-occupied. Acquaintances like Hilferding and close companions like Mia Stöckel lost their lives in the carnage. A lapsed European like Schumpeter cannot have taken much pleasure from the strafing of Cologne or the fire-storm at Dresden.

Schumpeter as late as 1944 believed that Hitler could still win the war or at least establish a lasting bloc for himself in Western Europe. He played with the idea that the Great Powers of the post-war world would be Germany, Russia, (Anglo-) America and Japan. By the end of the war he was convinced that Stalin's Bolsheviks were the real enemy and that the real victor, given Western appeasement, would be Soviet imperialism. There is much about the communists but hardly a word about the Nazis in Schumpeter's

Capitalism, Socialism and Democracy despite the fact that the book was begun in the year of Munich and completed at the time of Pearl Harbour. Schumpeter believed that American involvement in the foreign war would be a mistake.

At home as well as abroad, there were circumstances that must have taken their toll on Schumpeter's sprits. Harvard students, wanting formal economic theory, had limited time for Schumpeter's encyclopaedic erudition and his wide-ranging philosophical concerns. His macroeconomics was being eclipsed on the campuses by the *General Theory* and the rising sun of Keynes. His Harvard colleagues Schumpeter believed to be so mediocre and so shallow that he seriously considered an offer from Yale. He regretted the decision of Harold Burbank as Chairman of the Economics Department not to appoint the young Paul Samuelson. He suspected (others agreed) that Burbank was attempting to keep down the number of Jews on the staff. Schumpeter had mixed feelings about the Jews. On the one hand he was the closet anti-Semite who could write in his diary in 1938 that 'we must have either Hitler or else the Jews' (cited in Allen, 1991:II, 66). On the other hand he aided German–Jewish academics to emigrate. In the case of Samuelson, Jew or non-Jew, Schumpeter clearly wanted justice to be done.

In terms of national politics, the New Deal had not rescued American capitalism. The Soviets were boasting that scientific planning had secured them full employment. Unemployment in the United States, in sharp contrast, still stood at 14.6 per cent in 1940 – and this despite the Public Works Administration and the stimulus of the accelerating mobilisation. The uncapping of public expenditure had if anything undermined rather than rescued the free enterprise economy. It had allowed Roosevelt, a four-term President in the shadow of 'Buddy, Can You Spare a Dime?', to pave the way for socialism through his tax policies and his wage controls. As the 1930s became the 1940s, as Prague and Budapest disappeared behind the Iron Curtain, as fiscal permissiveness came to be seen as the bulwark against a future Depression, so Schumpeter must have found in the world around him external reinforcement for the feelings of failure and frustration that he was experiencing within.

The world that he knew, as well as his own personal time on earth seemed to be drawing to a close. In spite of the unhappiness and the pessimism the output was prodigious. It was in those 18 final years at Harvard that Schumpeter did some of his best and most creative research. Papers from the American years (augmented by scholarship dating back to Austria and Germany) were later assembled in three collections: *Essays* (1951), edited by R.V. Clemence, *Ten Great Economists* (1951), edited by E.B. Schumpeter and *The Economics and Sociology of Capitalism* (1991), edited by R. Swedberg. Even more influential than the journal articles and the public lectures were, however, the three major books in which a major thinker was summing up the vision that shaped his career.

Business Cycles, his first important book since 1911, was published in 1939. Its subtitle – *A Theoretical, Historical and Statistical Analysis of the Capitalist Process* – reveals just how far Schumpeter was looking beyond bounded macro-analysis to quantify the evolutionary trends in the institutional structure itself. The book uses charts and tables (but not econometrics) to show that its conjectures are borne out by the evidence.

Capitalism, Socialism and Democracy, about the decline of enterprise just as *Development* had been about its life-force and *Cycles* about its ups and downs, came out in 1942. A second edition appeared in 1947 and a third in 1950. The 1950 edition, published just after Schumpeter's death, was augmented by the late author's uncompleted paper on 'The march into socialism'. It had been delivered, from notes, to the American Economic Association in December 1949. The long Part II of *Capitalism* – 'Can capitalism survive?' – owes much to a lecture that Schumpeter gave in 1935 to the United States Department of Agriculture. That lecture in turn revisits the themes explored in 'The instability of capitalism', Schumpeter's paper of 1927 (published in 1928) to Section F of the British Association which he wrote when the triple loss less than a year before was still fresh in his mind.

Capitalism, Socialism and Democracy, written between 1938 and 1941, had been begun as a form of relaxation after the rigours of *Business Cycles*. Elizabeth recalled that 'he regarded it as distinctly a "popular" offering that he expected to finish in a few months' (E.B. Schumpeter, 1954:xi). Schumpeter, Galbraith has said, never really liked it very much: 'Schumpeter ... once told me that among his books this one inspired his special loathing. It lacked, he said, scientific depth and precision.' (Galbraith, 1977a:74).

Capitalism, Socialism and Democracy clearly lacked the formal pyrotechnics that would recommend it to the professional elite. It was, on the other hand, its very accessibility, its current-affairs topicality, its ability to force its readers, academic and secular alike, to question their most reassuring assumptions, that ensured it would continue to be read and discussed by a heterogeneous public that finds the economy exciting but the textbook catechism dull. Joan Robinson, reviewing Schumpeter's *Capitalism* for the *Economic Journal*, was quick to praise the thoughtful iconoclast for taking nothing on trust: 'No matter whether it convinces or not, this book is worth the whole parrot-house of contemporary orthodoxies, right, left, or centre.' (Robinson, 1943:383). Warren Samuels, 40 years on, said that he regarded it as 'one of the truly profound analytical and interpretive works of the twentieth century. It is one of the few books in economics – are there more than a dozen? – with which every aspiring economist must come to grips.' (Samuels, 1985:60). It remains the best remembered of Schumpeter's landmark works.

History of Economic Analysis, edited by Schumpeter's widow from an uncompleted manuscript, was published posthumously in 1954. It combines a magisterial knowledge of many authors in many languages with a philosopher's curiosity about the ideological and institutional underpinnings of wealth creation and price.

Joseph Schumpeter died on 8 January 1950. The cause was a cerebral haemorrhage to which the melancholia and the overwork may well have made a contribution. He was 66.

2.2 INTENTIONS AND OBJECTIVES

Self-image is the alpha and omega of the intellectual production function. Schumpeter saw himself as a detached observer who wanted only to discover how the economic system actually functions and develops. The *Kathedersozialist* Schmoller had used his chair to propagandise for welfare reform. The free-trade Ricardo had inserted restrictive assumptions to support his case for *laissez-faire*. Schumpeter was sharply critical of crypto-philosophers such as these: 'Those who profess to be engaged in the task of widening, deepening, and "tooling" humanity's stock of knowledge ... fail to fulfil their contract if, in the sheltering garb of the scientist, they devote themselves to what is really a particular kind of political propaganda.' (Schumpeter, 1954:805). Schumpeter was a man of the world who was entirely comfortable in the peaceful arcadia of the ivory tower: 'Schumpeter shied away from the practical attitude. By conviction, as well as temperament, he was a thinker rather than a doer.' (Leontief, 1950:109). He himself was convinced, as Allen writes, that he had made it his practice to put investigation before recommendation in all that he had said and done:

> An important fact to remember about Schumpeter is that he was a scientist. In his analytical work, he sought to know how things worked, be it a market, the process of capitalist development, how people change their thinking under the barrage of goods capitalism makes available, or the potential efficiency of socialism. As a scientist, he did not 'believe' in much of anything. He fully accepted no theories, not even his own. To Schumpeter everything was tentative, subject to change. (Allen, 1991:II, 134).

Schumpeter saw himself as an impartial investigator who wanted only to understand the *what is*. The same chemicals that kill a rat can also kill a king. Schumpeter believed that even when writing of growth it was vital not to say whether the new state was a betterment of condition or a step backward into the dark: 'We are taking great care not to speak of overall "progress" when we mean "development". We are describing facts. We are not making value judgements.' (Schumpeter, 1912a:466). He returned repeatedly to the statement of belief that theoretical extrapolation and empiricist fact-gathering must not fall victim to the party-political ideologies of ill-advised academic pedlars: 'Every teacher who uses his chair to preach is disloyal to his scientific obligations .... We must philosophise less in order the better to do our job as economists.' (Schumpeter, 1932:601, 603). In a paper in Japan in 1931 he reassured his listeners that disinterested scientists employing an unbiased methodology were likely to converge on a single, consensual view: 'This is as it should be. There is no truth which is only true for socialists. It is either true for both socialists and nonsocialists or wrong for both.' (Schumpeter, 1931a:293–4). In his Lowell Lectures in 1941 he argued strongly that the economist should spotlight efficient input-combinations but should not press for specific policies or impose his choices: 'I don't presume to judge ends. As an economist I am a technician .... I have only means.' (Schumpeter, 1941:369). In 'The march into socialism' he stated in 1949 that he could not and would not be drawn into the normative vortex: 'I do not advocate socialism. Nor have I any intention of discussing its desirability or undesirability.' (Schumpeter, 1950b:422). Schumpeter set out to distance his positive predictions from his personal ideals. He made clear that he did not intend to take sides.

Schumpeter saw himself as a scholar who wanted to learn. He also saw himself as an educator who wanted to teach. In his farewell address to the University of Bonn he said in 1932 that he had made it his mission to make people think: 'If I have a function, then it is to open doors, not to close them.' (Schumpeter, 1932:600). In 1946, returning to the topic of what made him tick, he reiterated that he was a disequilibrating gadfly who had come to stimulate controversy and re-open debate:

> We always plan too much and always think too little. We resent a call to thinking and hate unfamiliar argument that does not tally with what we already believe or would like to believe. We walk into our future as we walked into the war, blindfolded. Now this is precisely where I wanted to serve the reader. I did want to make him think. (Schumpeter, 1942a:413).

Schumpeter wanted to badger lazy minds into motion. It was his self-image that he wanted both to discover the truth for himself and to assist others to move on from the risk-averting familiarity of an unquestioned status quo.

Schumpeter wanted at once to learn and to teach. Communication, however, stood in his way. Schumpeter's economics, on the surface so straightforward, presents real problems for the reader who stops to think. Whatever his intentions, Schumpeter did not entirely attain his objectives because his meaning was not always clear.

Schumpeter's literary style often gets in the way of his message. He puts forward assertions without giving his evidence. He exaggerates his contentions in order to electrify the complacent. He cites few other authors and only exceptionally includes a bibliography. He expresses himself, moreover, in a manner that Haberler has correctly described as 'baroque': 'Schumpeter's rather complicated style of writing and theorizing makes the interpretation of his findings difficult. His style is characterized ... by long sentences, numerous qualifying phrases, qualifications of qualifications, careful or even pedantic definition of terms, and casuistic distinctions of meanings.' (Haberler, 1981:71). Schumpeter's convoluted constructions (a feature of his journalism and not just of his *History*) meant that even his more popular *Capitalism* would be difficult for a non-specialist audience to understand. As for university economists, his oblique and condensed reasoning was bound to frustrate careful scholars, unaccustomed to finding important steps buried or half-buried between the lines. The concessions that Schumpeter makes to the needs of his readers are not generous. The language is for all that no more of an entry-barrier that self-selects the initiates than one would expect from an elitist and a snob who liked silk shirts, once owned a race-horse, was often described as arrogant and knew that he was good.

The coverage itself presents a further problem. Schumpeter wrote on all the big issues that even the non-academic public found relevant and wanted to discuss. His sweeping panorama takes the traveller to a plethora of exciting destinations: entrepreneurship, innovation, organisation, bureaucracy, evolution, property rights, socialist planning, inflation, unemployment, cycles, leadership, belief. Strong on breadth, the great sequence of topical actualities is, however, too frequently weak on the organic interdependence of the parts. The author said as much when he confessed that his principal themes, 'though not independent', had in the event been left as 'almost self-contained pieces of analysis' (Schumpeter, 1942a:409). Schumpeter devoted his life to an epic novel but then allowed it to be read as a compendium of short stories. Every reader senses that there are connecting threads. The problem is that Schumpeter did not always make it easy for the student to uncover the hidden links.

Methodological ambiguities make the broad picture that much more difficult to see. Tendency laws that fall back upon a *ceteris paribus* may or may not yield good predictions. Different 'visions' necessitating different starting-points must produce different interpretations. Economics artificially abstracts an isolated dimension of a phenomenon that is not visible save in a multi-strand whole. Failing so frequently to integrate the separate and to clear up the blurred, Schumpeter's world view is more manageable but less satisfying that it would have been had Schumpeter been a salesman, determined to persuade. There is no unifying textbook. The reader who wants to see the model fully assembled is obliged to undertake the task of assembling it for himself.

Schumpeter's disciples in the normal run of things would have filled in the gaps. Marx had Engels and later Kautsky while Keynes had Kahn and Joan Robinson, Hansen and Harris. Even the early reviews of the *General Theory* such as those by Modigliani and Hicks helped to open out the hidden parentheses of Keynes's system. Schumpeter, on the other hand, was a one-man band, a self-contained individualist who neither solicited converts nor secured them. He always disapproved of the divisiveness of schools: 'I have never tried to bring into being a Schumpeter school. There is none and there never will be .... There can be no schools in our subject.' (Schumpeter, 1932:600, 603).

Schumpeter's vision does not in any case lend itself easily to adoption by followers. Entrepreneurship is the central tenet not just of Schumpeter's economics but of every other teleology that sees the human condition as the matrix of purposive action. There is no canonical text like Marshall's *Principles* that codifies the uniquely *Schumpeterian* gospel. Wide reading itself diluted Schumpeter's message: it meant that he could argue both sides of a case. His desire to stimulate thought even at the cost of settling the issues cannot have done much to attach to him narrow-minded acolytes educated exclusively in the yes/no economics of multiple choice: 'He is sometimes playful', Allen writes, 'presenting, for example, elaborate arguments in favor of a position he does not necessarily agree with and sometimes leaving the reader in doubt about his own position.' (Allen, 1991:II, 271). Schumpeter wanted to open doors. An inveterate questioner and a *provocateur*, the end result is that he opened so many doors that potential followers were condemned to select different turnings in the maze.

Schumpeter's economics was too bookish and too tentative to appeal to young people, not least to the practical young Americans of his new, adopted homeland. Keynesianism and interventionism by the 1930s were in the ascendant. Geometry and calculus were crowding out the sociological and the historical. Even if Schumpeter had wanted disciples, disciples would not have been easy to attract. Whatever the reasons, Schumpeter remained a one-off. He had no spiritual children to carry further his vision, no critical mass to perpetuate his exegesis. In that respect he recalls Pareto, of whom he once wrote tellingly as follows: 'His towering figure stood almost alone. Pareto cannot be pigeonholed. He paid court to no "ism". No creed or party can claim him as its own.' (Schumpeter, 1952a:111). Pareto, he observed sadly, had 'little chance of being popular': 'By now he is a figure of the past.' (Schumpeter, 1952a:112).

Schumpeter as a communicator encountered yet another obstacle in getting his ideas across. A transplant, an exotic, a foreigner and a throwback, he was, and was perceived to be, an outsider in time and space who did not quite belong. His socialisation and culture situated him in the stable Hapsburg order that had gone away and left him behind: 'An important component of Schumpeter's political philosophy was precisely his longing for the world that had existed before the First World War.' (Swedberg, 1991:146). That spiritual homeland levelled to the ground, even in pluto-democratic Vienna he did not really fit in: 'With the disappearance of that world, he became completely qualified to play the important sociological role of the alienated stranger.' (Samuelson, 1951:48). The move from Europe to America, as Samuelson recalls, only added a second layer of distance to an already existing estrangement: 'The America of Mickey Rooney and coca-cola he knew almost nothing about; in 1913, whilst at Columbia, he first saw a football game, and that was enough to last him the rest of his life.' (Samuelson, 1951:48). Schumpeter was in America but not of America, of Europe but also in the past. The fact that two continents were struggling within him for his world view means that his published social science was bound to come across as a mix.

Reflecting that no American scholar had ever lavished so much praise on the aristocracy or understood so well the iron law of bureaucracy, Daniel Bell, always perceptive, has this to say about the two Schumpeters wrapped up in a single psyche:

> Schumpeter talks of 'capitalism' rather than, like Keynes, of 'economies'. *He does not talk, however, of concrete capitalist societies*. It was thus not easy to notice that in his analyses he selected the economics of American industry and the sociology of European society and derived his justifications for capitalism from the first and his apocalyptic visions as to its fate from the second. (Bell, 1965:84).

Schumpeter's books would have been more widely read and more influential if he had opted for a single universe of discourse or one more accessible to the great majority even of his university-educated readers.

As with the intellectual baggage, so with the ideological affiliation: Schumpeter said that he was detached and impartial but everyone knew that he cared. Schumpeter identified a strong tendency towards socialism, insisted that centralism would be economically efficient, conceded that the change had 'a dignity all its own that is both intellectual and moral' (Schumpeter, 1942a:305), and then concluded that he did not like the new developments very much: 'These are inferences from facts that could be fully established but in no sense expressions of my personal preferences. Personally, I prefer other cultural patterns.' (Schumpeter, 1942a:418). There is all but unanimous agreement that Schumpeter, whatever he may have preferred, certainly did not prefer what was happening: he had 'an ingrained dislike for socialism' (Haberler, 1951:45), he had 'little love for socialism, and none at all for socialists' (Robinson, 1943:381), he 'always detested socialism' (Swedberg, 1991:146). Where the consensus dissolves into incomprehension relates to his surprising passivity while travelling down the slippery slope. A tendency is not a fait accompli. Something could have been done to arrest the momentum or to alter the trajectory. Schumpeter consistently refused to be the Hayek or the Mises who had a tool-kit that could bend back the bent rod: 'I have no pills to hand out; no clearcut solutions for any practical problems that may arise.' (cited in Swedberg, 1991:136).

Sometimes Schumpeter does give his own opinion. Thus, talking about the Labour Party's proposal for the nationalisation of land, he says 'this is no place for airing personal preferences' and then quickly squares off beyond the boundaries of professional duty: 'Nevertheless ... were I an Englishman, I should on the contrary oppose [that proposal] to the best of my ability.' (Schumpeter, 1942a:231n). Most of the time he keeps his normative position to himself: 'This is not a political book ... I did not wish to advocate anything.' (Schumpeter, 1942a:412–3). It is a curious posture for a political economist to adopt. Policies have consequences: high taxes attack incentives and price controls discourage entrepreneurs. Markets cause change: it is market freedom and not socialist idealism that produces the endstate evolution. Aware that institutions matter and that decision makers make choices, Schumpeter nonetheless stands aside to let the juggernaut of history crush his personal preferences beneath its wheels. That is just the problem. Few readers have been willing to take the provocative Schumpeter at his word. Schumpeter is a difficult author not least because the reader always wonders if the committed anti-socialist who was also a yes-but determinist was being entirely frank about the extent to which timely action could stave off the maybe-yes transition.

There is a final reason why Schumpeter the communicator may not have been entirely successful in the diffusion of his own core message. This returns the discussion to his personal life and temperament. Schumpeter, wanting to be liked, 'often told people what they wanted to hear' (Swedberg, 1991:56). Karl Kraus called him a 'well-known opportunist' and an 'exchange professor in convictions' (cited in Swedberg, 1991:60). Others have repeated the joke that Schumpeter only gave As to three classes of students (women, Jesuits, all others) to suggest that he had an above-average need to be popular. Much that passes for evasiveness or inscrutability in his work might only be a wish to paper over the controversial so as not to alienate his public. Besides that, there had been the failures in the past which, in Galbraith's view, made Schumpeter more guarded and cautious than he would have been had he remained in public life: 'His political and business misfortunes left him with a deep distaste for practical affairs. ... He condemned as intellectually debased economists who presumed to advise on practical questions.' (Galbraith, 1981:48). Schumpeter by the time he did his greatest work can evidently be regarded as a man who had made a conscious choice to conceal himself in science.

Swedberg rightly states that 'Schumpeter's personality is very much present in everything he wrote' (Swedberg, 1991:3). Nowhere is this tendency more strikingly in evidence than in the anxiety and pessimism of Schumpeter's great book on the end of days. Heroes are being crowded out by dwarfs. Adventure is being throttled into routine. Mould-breakers are giving way to cogs in the wheel. Market devolution is under assault from political control. *Capitalism, Socialism and Democracy* is a sad book. It is imbued with the nostalgia, with the sense of an ending, of Schumpeter's final decade. Schumpeter's *Götterdämmerung* could have been begun but could not have been finished by the flamboyant womaniser of the early 1920s. Its hidden message is that the traveller had come very far and not much liked what he had seen. Schumpeter would have been a more balanced expositor of his scholarly case if he had not allowed his sombre personality to blot out the light.

2.3 SCHUMPETER AND MARX

Schumpeter took Marx seriously at a time when few other non-Marxians, especially in the United States, were willing to do so. Only Sweezy's *Theory of Capitalist Development*, published in the same year as Schumpeter's *Capitalism*, made as heroic an attempt to reinforce Marx's standing as an academically-respectable economist. Schumpeter had lived in red Vienna at a time when Marxism was widely debated. He had been shaken as a bourgeois by the 1917 Bolshevik October, the communist revolutions in Munich and Berlin, Bela Kun's Hungarian Soviet in 1919. He had survived the Great Depression when only Stalin's Russia seemed to have been spared the *Endkrise*. Schumpeter's world was a Marx-intensive world. His life and times no doubt shed much light on his desire to explain himself to Marx, to take the Marxian message as his benchmark, to give voice to a 'non-Marxist's belief in the unique importance of that message, an importance that is completely independent of acceptance or rejection' (Schumpeter, 1942a:409). A showman's wish to shock may be a reason why he stated so frequently that the prophet of sequestration was uppermost in his thoughts. So, more significantly, were the obvious affinities between the two wide-ranging socio-political economists.

Schumpeter and Marx had much in common. Both were German-educated outsiders living in market freedom's vanguard state. Each used a mix of theory and fact to construct a complex intellectual system, 'all parts of which complement and explain one another' (Schumpeter, 1942a:9). Both may be described as bookish, learned, ambitious, curious: whether the *Theories of*

Surplus Value or the *History of Economic Analysis*, the author may rightly be termed 'a voracious reader and an indefatiguable worker' (Schumpeter, 1942a:21). Each was open to social facts and social institutions that made of economics a multidisciplinary synthesis of property, contract, law, revolution, class, ideology, perception even as it was a free enterprise of disembedded Ricardians and rootless Walrasians allocating scarce goods and services through decentralised exchange.

Most of all there was the process of change. Karl Marx, Schumpeter writes, 'was the first economist of top rank to see and teach systematically how economic theory may be turned into historical analysis and how the historical narrative may be turned into *histoire raisonnée*' (Schumpeter, 1942a:44). Marx in *Capital* said that he wanted to understand development and not merely prices: 'It is the ultimate aim of this work, to lay bare the economic law of motion of modern society.' (Marx, 1867:20). Schumpeter, unwilling to settle for stationary equilibrium and comparative endstates when the real economics is the unremitting dynamic, set himself the same history-dominated objective: 'This idea and this aim are exactly the same as the idea and aim which underlie the teachings of Karl Marx.' (Schumpeter, 1937:151).

Marx not only situated productive activity within the rubric of continuing change, he also entertained a determinist's vision of 'economic evolution as a distinct process generated by the economic system itself' (Schumpeter, 1937:160). His expectation that the basis would grind out the superstructure is encapsulated in the following passage: 'The mode of production of material life conditions the general process of social, political and intellectual life. It is not the consciousness of men that determines their existence, but their social existence that determines their consciousness.' (Marx, 1859:423). As we work, so we are. It was a facet of creative destruction that made the productive sector high-powered and history-shaping. Schumpeter describes Marx's rigorous employment of the materialist method as 'one of the greatest individual achievements of sociology to this day' (Schumpeter, 1942a:10).

Schumpeter, like Marx, treated the economy as an architect and a builder. In the *Theory of Economic Development* he argued that entrepreneurship was the economic endogeneity that propelled the transformation from one rest-stop to another without waiting for unreliable randomness to provide the external shock: 'Every step outside the boundary of routine has difficulties and involves a new element. It is this element that constitutes the phenomenon of leadership.' (Schumpeter, 1912b:84). In *Capitalism, Socialism and Democracy* he demonstrated that epoch-specific corporate capitalism was taking the course of events in tow: 'Not only the modern mechanized plant and the volume of the output that pours forth from it, not only modern technology and economic organization, but all the features and achievements of modern civilization are, directly or indirectly, the products of the capitalist process.'

(Schumpeter, 1942a:125). The economy is the productive platform for goods and services. The economy is also the root cause of the economic future itself.

That future is collectivism. Both Schumpeter and Marx admired the achievements of the capitalist transitional stage. As historians, however, they also expected that internal contradictions would cause mature capitalism to self-destruct in the face of a limit that only post-private property would be able to transcend. Like Schumpeter, Marx, 'independent of our love or hate' (Schumpeter, 1942a:3), independent of 'human volition or of desirability' (Schumpeter, 1942a:56), made the forecast that the new order would take over exclusively because the old order had imploded. Like Marx, Schumpeter, a scientist and not a utopian, as passionately opposed as the socialist was passionately in favour, 'pretended no more than to speak the logic of the dialectic process of history' (Schumpeter, 1942a:7). Capitalism had sounded the death knell of the farming-feudal order. Socialism, given time, would do no less for big business and the centralisation of scale.

They agreed on history. They disagreed on economics. Schumpeter was never a Marxist because, surplus value 'untenable' (Schumpeter, 1942a:27), the labour theory 'dead and buried' (Schumpeter, 1942a:25), the organic composition not certain to rise, the rate of profit not likely to fall, progressive immiseration demonstrably contradicted by working-class affluence, there was hardly a prediction in the whole of Marxian economics that made any sense to him.

Marx imputed class consciousness to the owners of labour power. Schumpeter, rejecting the psychological underpinnings of conflict, struggle and revolution, asserted that what the proletarian really craves is 'to become a small bourgeois and to be helped to that status by political force' (Schumpeter, 1942a:7). Marx made the capitalist a risk-taking property owner who relied on self-denial and the exploitation of his menials to build up his asset stock. Schumpeter, emphasizing innovativeness where Marx had talked of registered title, made credit creation an integral part of business expansion and joint-stock dispersion a democratic alternative to the capital–labour dialectic.

Marx expected that mechanisation and labour-displacement would ensure a reserve army of the unemployed. Schumpeter saw idle capacity as the exception, Say's Law as the rule, the cyclical downturn as a cleansing shake-out. Marx predicted that mental mutilation would be the consequence of division of labour. Schumpeter showed little interest in alienating dehumanisation experienced at the place of work. Marx said that cynical plutocrats hold the apparatus of State in the palm of their hand. Schumpeter contended that the rich cannot buy the State since the bureaucrats and the politicians have estate partialities all their own. Marx did not describe socialism but looked forward to the flat plain of classlessness. Schumpeter did describe socialism and anticipated that meritocracy would mean the continuance of – circulating – inequality. In ways such as these Schumpeter showed that his economic model was different from that of Karl Marx.

Most different of all was the image of the end. Marx said that capitalism would collapse because the system was programmed to fail. Schumpeter, on the other hand, felt that capitalism would collapse *despite* its astounding and sustained success. Marx's 'economic theory of the future' (Schumpeter, 1942a:43) was flawed because it concentrated on objective magnitudes when the real threat was social–psychological and not the economic basis. Economic success is eroded by the *order* and not by the *system*. As Leontief has explained it, the final failing is *malaise*: 'To Schumpeter, the patient is dying of a psychosomatic ailment. Not cancer but neurosis is his complaint. Filled with self-hate, he has lost the will to live. In this view, capitalism is an unlovable system, and what is unlovable will not be loved.' (cited in Allen, 1991:II, 170). Capitalism is dying of ennui and disgust. Marxism nonetheless has no body of theory that would enable it to diagnose the disease.

3. The prediction of change

Matter is in motion. There is not a great deal the moral philosophers can do about that: 'Things economic and social move by their own momentum .... The ensuing situations compel individuals and groups to behave in certain ways whatever they may wish to do.' (Schumpeter, 1942a:129). Schumpeter's economics is in that sense not about optimality but about constraint: 'Mankind is not free to choose.' (Schumpeter, 1942a:129). It is not desirability but determinism that makes the productive sector what it is: 'If this is the quintessence of Marxism then we all of us have got to be Marxists.' (Schumpeter, 1942a:130).

Things are taking their course. This chapter is about the meaning and significance of their history-to-come. Section 1, Tendencies and tendency laws, interprets the combinations and probabilities that light the way to the socialist plan. Section 2, Ideology and science, discusses the pre-empirical pre-judgements that steer the fact-finding and the forecasts by the compass of belief. Section 3, The social economy, shows that Schumpeter wanted to enrich his pure theory with statistics, with sociology and, linking together the sub-fields, with economic history in order to put changing disequilibrium back in.

3.1 TENDENCIES AND TENDENCY LAWS

Schumpeter was much impressed by Marx's attempt to use economics to map out the multi-period scheme:

> Through all that is faulty or even unscientific in his analysis runs a fundamental idea that is neither – the idea of a theory, not merely of an indefinite number of disjointed individual patterns or of the logic of economic quantities in general, but of the actual sequence of those patterns or of the economic process as it goes on, under its own steam, in historic time, producing at every instant that state which will of itself determine the next one. (Schumpeter, 1942a:43).

A microeconomist from the school of small utilities, Schumpeter had also read Hegel on the owl of Minerva that will fly at dusk, List and Schmoller on the stages of economic development that follow one another as predictably as the night that follows day. It was in the circumstances a big step but not a *very* big step for Schumpeter to extend his economics beyond market economising in the sense of Walras to bring in historical evolution in the sense of Marx. Marx had been able to situate 'disjointed individual patterns' within a single intellectual framework. Marx had been able to explain the 'actual sequence of the economic process' using a theory of cumulative causation. In both of these ways Marx had made a major contribution to the economic analysis of systems and orders that change.

Marxism is an intellectual framework and a moving picture of path-dependence. Stricter still, it is the basis-superstructure imputation that technology and its applications take the lead, cultural perceptions and stratified relationships fit in and adapt. Schumpeter reduces the economic interpretation of historical causality to the core proposition that 'the forms or conditions of production are the fundamental determinant of social structures which in turn breed attitudes, actions and civilizations' (Schumpeter, 1942a:12). His *Capitalism, Socialism and Democracy* is often taken to be a clear demonstration that Schumpeter too, like Marx, believed that economic determinism was making inexorable socialism the only name on the ballot.

In the preface of the first edition he set out his stall: 'A socialist form of society will inevitably emerge from an equally inevitable decomposition of capital.' (Schumpeter, 1942a:409). Explaining his *Capitalism*, he stated bluntly that his forecast was of *what has to be*, of a 'predictable' (Schumpeter, 1942a:375) new order that was already on its way. Schumpeter, using words like 'inevitable' and 'predictable', gives the impression that the future will be socialist just as summer must follow on from spring. The invisible hand arranges things to suit itself. There is not a great deal the moral philosophers can do about that.

Schumpeter in places seems to be confident and certain. In other places, however, countervailing forces make his tight causal nexus into a loosely-defined *dim sum* of possibilities. As his argument becomes more hesitant and tentative, so the reader begins to wonder if the alleged progression from capitalism to socialism is really to be expected at all.

In 1949, in 'The march into socialism', Schumpeter contended that it had never been his intention to be other than unbiased and open-minded: 'I do not advocate socialism. ... I do not "prophesy" or predict it. ... Factors external to the chosen range of observation may intervene to prevent that consummation.' (Schumpeter, 1950b:422). Schumpeter in 1949 said that 'the capitalist order *tends* to destroy itself', that 'centralist socialism is ... a *likely* heir apparent', that '*most* observable tendencies ... stop short of *complete* achievement' (Schumpeter, 1950b:422, 423, emphasis added). In 'The march into socialism' Schumpeter presented himself not as an omniscient futurologist but as an uncommitted student of scenarios. His aim, he said, was not to reconfirm his prejudices but merely to 'diagnose observable tendencies and to state what results would be, *if* these tendencies should work themselves out according to their logic' (Schumpeter, 1950b:422, emphasis added). The 'tends', the 'likely', the 'most', the 'complete' and the 'if' are more modest than the 'predictable' and the 'inevitably emerge'. They also create a darkness where otherwise there would only have been a dispute. If *Capitalism, Socialism and Democracy* is not about the march from one economic system into another, then it is not clear what it *is* about.

Schumpeter in 1949 answered the critics who had called him defeatist by instructing them that he had merely been developing tendency laws in the frictionless vacuum of Malthus on the population ratios and Marx on the falling rate of profit. In 1946, in the preface to the second edition of *Capitalism*, he had issued a similar warning to over-serious readers who had assumed that 'my statements of tendencies amounted more definitely to prediction than they were intended to do' (Schumpeter, 1942a:413). The purpose of the book, he explained, had been to 'elaborate inferences from observed facts' (Schumpeter, 1942a:413) but not to provide a blueprint of an evolution that circumstances or even ideals might have it in their power to shunt on to an unexpected line. Schumpeter in 1946 did not say if the crew that rushes to the pumps will be a success in preventing the ship from going down or if romantic idealists will effectively be drowned with the rest by the *what has to be* of the deep. All he said was that he himself did not want to get involved in the campaign to corset a reasonable chance into a soothsayer's prophecy.

Schumpeter in 1949 and in 1946 clarified what he had intended to say in his 1942 book. He did not need to do so since his tendency law was clear enough from the start:

> Analysis, whether economic or other, never yields more than a statement about the tendencies present in an observable pattern. And these never tell us what *will* happen to the pattern but only what *would* happen if they continued to act as they have been acting in the time interval covered by our observation and if no other factors intruded. (Schumpeter, 1942a:61).

Schumpeter in 1942 had said that he was not speaking for or against collectivism but only 'extrapolating observable tendencies' (Schumpeter, 1942a:403) from the evidence that he had been able to assemble. Schumpeter in 1942 had pointed to a 'tendency toward socialism' (Schumpeter, 1942a:309) but had conceded that different variables could be the cause of different outcomes. Schumpeter in 1942 had stated that the historical progression was not yet far advanced, that in business life 'enterprise is still active' (Schumpeter, 1942a:163), that 'the leadership of the bourgeois group

[is] still the prime mover of the economic process' (Schumpeter, 1942a:163). In 1946 he said that the status quo is unlikely to change in 'a short run of fifty years or so' (Schumpeter, 1942a:382). In 1942 he had written that a century itself can be a short run in economic life (Schumpeter, 1942a:163). Many things can change in a short run that only becomes a long run in 2042. No one who read Schumpeter's book in 1942 could have been left in any doubt that Schumpeter was writing of let-us-assume likely-to-bes and not of a crumbling reality that would be on that very evening's six o'clock news.

Schumpeter in 1942 made clear that an extrapolation was not a fact. He had already said as much in *Business Cycles* in 1939: 'It is as unreasonable to expect the economist to forecast correctly what will actually happen as it would be to expect a doctor to prognosticate when his patient will be the victim of a railroad accident.' (Schumpeter, 1939:I, 13). The economist, unable to foretell next year's bad harvest and the high price of wheat, is even more in the dark when he seeks to anticipate institutional twists and turns extending far into history-to-come. The best he can do, as Schumpeter wrote in *Der Deutsche Volkswirt* in the year of the Great Crash, is to confess to his unknowledge and venture his estimate from the frequencies he has observed: 'He who attempts scientific predictions must speak of probabilities and tendencies which, as with a medical diagnosis, must be based on existing and anticipated facts and their *necessary* consequences.' (Schumpeter, 1929/30a:138). Predictions are 'probabilities and tendencies'. They are not certainties. What is being predicted might not happen at all: 'Theories in social science only refer to tendencies in the real world, never to the whole of reality itself.' (Schumpeter, 1915:560).

Schumpeter in 1908 had already sounded the same note of caution that he was later to repeat in the years of *Capitalism* and its exegesis. In the *Wesen* he had scolded the reader for assuming that tendency laws were anything more than the schoolboy truism that a stone if supported by a table is excused gravity's pull that would make it fall: 'What they mean is nothing other than that circumstances can intervene which produce results other than those foreseen by the law. That, however, is stating the obvious.' (Schumpeter, 1908:45).

Hypotheses are necessary. Otherwise the investigator would not know what to expect: 'They are not a part of our results ... but simply methodological tools, of which the value is defined by their success.' (Schumpeter, 1908:64). Even extreme empiricists need to depend on background normalcies in order to gain a purchase on behavioural regularities: 'Even the historical school cannot manage without hypotheses.' (Schumpeter, 1908:47). Hypotheses function to provide a stable framework for concept-recognition and the familiarity of association: 'Their only purpose is to supply a schema which provides a good picture of economic reality.' (Schumpeter, 1908:68). That, however, does not mean that they are incompatible with the *ab initio* new link. Rather the opposite – since it is the expectation itself that makes the unexpected stand out: 'The very fact that one experiences surprise proves that one is accustomed, with a high degree of certainty, to expect a specific sequence of actions.' (Schumpeter, 1908:40). We expect the sequence. We do not, however, necessarily find it. Matter is in motion. Entrepreneurship means the new. Thus does the eternity of revision forever drive a question-mark through the heart of the tendency law.

3.2 IDEOLOGY AND SCIENCE

A tendency law is not a projection of fact. Particularly where socialism is said to be the next stage on from the private corporation, where the bureaucrat is expected to plan initiatives once the owner-operator is gone, it is simply not possible to rely on evidence alone to quantify what the future will form and craft. The race having only just begun, the tendencies have not revealed enough of themselves 'to allow us to say with any confidence precisely how far they will go' (Schumpeter, 1942a:163). The evidence is not up to the job. Only the flash of insight will do. If Schumpeter had any real confidence in the finishes he predicted, the reason must have been that he knew he could count on ideology even where science could not prove he was right.

As with the future, so with the present: 'The problems of applied economics are seldom handled satisfactorily by the mere technician.' (Schumpeter, 1939:I, 6). Schumpeter, as much as he valued the precision of perfect knowledge, was fully aware that imagination must make of each of us an entrepreneur when he ventures into the shifting complexities of human interaction:

> There is no warrant for the view that what we cannot measure does, therefore, not exist.... Every economist who is at all worthy of this name acquires by lifelong familiarity with contemporaneous and historical fact a vision or an understanding of the intimate necessities in the life of the organism he deals with which carries him much further than the exact tools at his command. (Schumpeter, 1939:I, 6).

Understanding 'may count for more in remedial advice than provable theorems' (Schumpeter, 1939:I, 6). Vision may open doors which to the literal-minded and the unintuitive must always remain shut.

Vision is indispensable when actors and their observers set out to put the disparate into a pattern. Vision focuses the attention and unifies the unclassified. It is the 'preanalytic cognitive act that supplies the raw material for the analytic effort' (Schumpeter, 1954:41). Without vision the scientist would not know where to look or what data to collect. Because of vision he has a map to guide him when he calibrates what he can.

Vision is lag-stamped and history-ridden: 'In practice, of course, we hardly ever start from scratch so that the prescientific act of vision is not entirely our own. We start from the work of our predecessors or contemporaries or else from the ideas that float around us in the public mind.' (Schumpeter, 1949a:277). Vision is also shared and common, internalised socialisation that mass-produces the collectivised reflex: the 'analyzing observer himself is the product of a social environment – and of his precise location in this environment – that conditions him to see certain things rather than others, and to see them in a certain light' (Schumpeter, 1954:34). Handed-on values equip the economist with ideational capital even if the science of economics is itself to be strictly logico-experimental. Standard-size blinkers homogenise the economist into his fellow citizens' heuristics even if the price of the non-thinking is also the non-rational. Learned responses, in short, pre-date the impartial investigation and have an impact upon its course. Economics, Schumpeter asserted, was 'ideological almost by definition' (Schumpeter, 1954:42). His Presidential Address to the American Economic Association in 1948 was entitled 'Science and ideology'.

Schumpeter was prepared to acknowledge the functionality of belief systems and world views: 'Though we proceed slowly because of our ideologies, we might not proceed at all without them.' (Schumpeter, 1949a:286). Useful base points or distorting irrelevancies, however, his bedrock thesis was that the hidden lens is a fact of intellectual life: 'Ideologies are not simply lies. They are truthful statements about what a man thinks he sees.' (Schumpeter, 1949a:276). Some ideology, Schumpeter says, 'will always be with us' (Schumpeter, 1949a:286). That being the case, the social scientist has to enter into the mind of his subject in order to empathise with the prescientific vision that so greatly prefigures the books and the deeds.

Reading the work of an economic thinker, Schumpeter always began by searching out the narrow gate of vision that afforded the non-provable its open road into the hypothesis. In the case of Adam Smith, he believed the ideological gateway to have been the concepts of natural freedom, individual responsibility and political abstention that were the common property of the new middle classes: 'Adam Smith gave expression to the practical needs of his time, and his name is inseparably linked to the economic policy of the epoch.' (Schumpeter, 1952a:85). Adam Smith, 'remarkably superficial', 'not at all original' (Schumpeter, 1952a:85), contributed little or nothing that was not already 'in the air' in the Britain of his own times: 'The *Wealth of Nations* does not contain a single analytic idea, principle, or method that was entirely new in 1776. ... He disliked whatever went beyond plain common sense. He never moved above the head of even the dullest reader.' (Schumpeter, 1954:184, 185). Smith's economics would have sunk without trace had it not been for his vision, so precisely that of his time and place.

The classical economists and even the marginalists built their new models upon the same old foundations. The consequence was that the lessons of long-dead codifiers lived on, in a world that had changed, in the theories of Jevons and his free-enterprise successors. They 'visualized the economic process much as had J.S. Mill or even A. Smith .... They added nothing to the ideas of the preceding period.' (Schumpeter, 1954:892). They added nothing to the small-firm competitiveness that validates the invisible hand and ignores the joint-stock dynamic. They subtracted nothing from the first principles anti-statism that was at the root of 'the alliance of economic theory with the political liberalism of the nineteenth century' (Schumpeter, 1954:19). Schumpeter was always critical of economists who 'indulged their strong propensity to dabble in politics, to peddle political recipes' (Schumpeter, 1954:19). Most of all was he critical of economists who constructed their normative recommendations out of an outlook that was narrow, specific and resistant to the new.

The nineteenth-century free marketeers generalised from the Corn Laws and England to universals and absolutes: 'Most of them ... seem to have argued exclusively in terms of the English interests and problems of their time.' (Schumpeter, 1942a:75). Pretending to be an across-the-board conquest, their economic vision was no more than 'the typical views of the English bourgeois class': 'Bourgeois blinkers are in evidence on almost every page.' (Schumpeter, 1942a:75). Karl Marx, preaching individual fulfilment, consistently looking to science for salvation, was a new growth from the same old garden: 'Marxism is essentially a product of the bourgeois mind.' (Schumpeter, 1942a:6). Brought up to be bourgeois, Marx knew what to look for since people and past had so frequently pointed it out to him. His 'vision of the capitalist process had become set ... *before* his serious analytic work had begun' (Schumpeter, 1949a:281).

Alfred Marshall himself, author of the authoritative *Principles*, developed his supply and demand while trapped in 'his own schema of life's values', in 'the typical life of a Cambridge professor' (Schumpeter, 1954:129n). His prism was in harmony with his existence. It was also a manifesto for the knee-jerk frugality, the self-denying assiduity, the pleasure-less accumulation that Marshall saw around him in late Victorian England, regimented by asceticism and repressed into equilibrium. Marshall's vision was a partial vision and not a general vision. Like Adam Smith before him, he 'taught the gospel of his time without ever going beyond it or displaying a sense of its relativity' (Schumpeter, 1952a:207). Students of his mathematical functions drawn self-confidently as curves would do well to recall that Marshall lived a long time ago.

Keynes too was to pyramid a whole paradigm upon a myopia that he glimpsed while standing on the baggage of giants. The *General Theory*, misleadingly entitled, is not a *general* theory at all. More narrow, more specific, what it is is no more than an anxious Englishman's attempt to build a whole macroeconomics around 'his vision of England's ageing capitalism' (Schumpeter, 1954:1171): 'Keynes's advice was in the first instance always English advice, born of English problems even where addressed to other nations .... Like the old free traders, he always exalted what was at any moment truth and wisdom for England into truth and wisdom for all times and places.' (Schumpeter, 1952a:274).

Keynes's vision was England-specific and Depression-specific. Its viewpoints and creeds were those of the 'high intelligentsia of England' (Schumpeter, 1952:274), its theme of oversaving, stagnation, declining opportunities and involuntary idleness the reflection of life in an old country that had long been waiting for its stationary quietus. Keynes's personal failure to father a family is present on every page of his book: 'He was childless and his philosophy of life was essentially a short-run philosophy.' (Schumpeter, 1952a:275). So a fortiori is the state of his nation. That is why his tools, carefully selected to suit his purpose, cannot be expected to travel far: 'Practical Keynesianism is a seedling which cannot be transplanted into foreign soil: it dies there and becomes poisonous before it dies.' (Schumpeter, 1952a:275). Vision that leaps beyond the confines of the author's own time and place can evidently be a cause of instability and confusion. Most fundamentally, however, vision is indispensable because it concentrates the mind. Without vision there can, in economics, be no progress.

Keynes gives voice to 'the vision of decaying capitalism' (Schumpeter, 1949a:283), Marx to a world view of class conflict and iron-law have-nots, Smith to a middle-class idyll of thrift, money making and homeostasis. Each great economist does what he does because of the picture he has in his mind of the world as he imagines it to be. Schumpeter's own vision is no exception to the rule. Schumpeter's evolutionary economics is the story of how the entrepreneurial bourgeoisie and the leaderly aristocracy are being marginalised by a new elite of rational office-holders whose victory makes State socialism inevitable. Schumpeter's vision was not Schumpeter's ideal. It was, however, the window on the world of a social economist who believed that collectivism could be a workable proposition, who recognised that Golden Age Vienna was gone for good – and who, like Karl Marx, accepted that *what has to be* would always be recalcitrant to the tinkering of reform.

3.3 THE SOCIAL ECONOMY

Schumpeter was careful not to precommit economic science to the straitjacket circumscription of one-size-fits-all-forever:

> Science as a whole has never attained a logically consistent architecture; it is a tropical forest, not a building erected according to blueprint. One of the consequences of this is that ... the frontiers of the individual sciences or of most of them are incessantly shifting and that there is no point in trying to define them *either by subject or by method*. This applies particularly to economics, which is ... an agglomeration of ill-coordinated and overlapping fields. (Schumpeter, 1954:10).

Economics is an agglomeration and a mix. It is also a never-to-be-completed structure on which the concrete never sets.

The mix will vary. Not, however, the elements of which the discipline is compromised. The sub-fields that make up economic science tend to be relatively constant constants. They are four in number: economic theory, economic statistics, economic sociology and economic history.

3.3.1 Economic Theory

Economics is catallactics and the interpretation of price: 'The exchange relationship is the characteristic of our field. It separates the material we study from that which is not purely economic.' (Schumpeter, 1908:55). Economics does not presuppose powerless atomism in a *laissez-faire* market: 'The "laws of nature of economics" in no way demand free competition. They have no tendency to bring it into being.' (Schumpeter, 1908:193). Economics does not conclude that felt welfare will be maximised through self-seeking rational choice: 'The maximisation theorem is not essential .... It is possible to dispense with it without causing any harm.' (Schumpeter, 1908:197). Economics is the science that makes sense of exchange: 'The whole of pure economics ... consists in the relations of exchange.' (Schumpeter, 1908:187). That is all that economics is.

Economic theory is an *ex ante* body of plausible hypotheses that single out reasonable expectations about the workings of exchange. Its concepts are the artificial a prioris that enabled Austrians like Menger, Britons like Jevons, to pre-picture economic reality in advance of descending from the general to the specific in search of the facts. Economic theory is made up of the 'schemas', the 'models' and the 'theorems' (Schumpeter, 1939:I, 30) which concentrate attention on the most relevant aspects of the most relevant observations: 'A fact without analysis is silent. It is the result of many causes, many forces working against one another. It can be explained in a variety of ways .... We must analyse and we must isolate each distinguishable aspect of social phenomena.' (Schumpeter, 1915:558). Some core, some peripheral, some inconsequential, the 'raw facts are, as such, a meaningless jumble' (Schumpeter, 1939:I, 30). Perfect or imperfect, it is economic theory alone that can impose any logic on the non-ego discordance: 'We must put our trust in bold and unsafe mental experiments or else give up all hope.' (Schumpeter, 1939:I, 13).

Schumpeter's ideal is clearly a synthesis between deduction and induction, a division of labour such that theory provides the template and statistics fills in the blanks. The problem is that the theory, intendedly selective, may prove too thin to be capable of tracking the regularities. Schumpeter writes in the *Wesen* that responsible conjectures should not be regarded as the whole truth: 'The assumptions are not statements of fact ... but abstract constructs, of which the only sense and the actual service is to provide a schema for the price decision.' (Schumpeter, 1908:549). He also writes that economic theories are simplifications and therefore propositions which it will often be very difficult to falsify or confirm: 'It is certain that, in the real world, there are neither our "assumptions" nor our "laws".' (Schumpeter, 1908:527).

Schumpeter was aware that economic theory is a distillate and a caricature: 'Our picture itself, as far as it goes, is incomplete. It does not pick up a number of important phenomena.' (Schumpeter, 1908:572). Economic theory is a choice and a selection: 'We are observing the estimations of value of the *homo economicus* exclusively as a function of his economic situation.' (Schumpeter, 1906:533). Economic theory is not and cannot be a definitive photograph of all the detail that makes external reality so splendid and so full: 'No science is absolutely true to life. Only life itself is true to life.' (Schumpeter, 1932:601). Interpretation makes investigation possible but it does so at a price.

The opening line of *Economic Development* reveals Schumpeter's own reservations about the empirical status of the economist's sub-set: 'The social process is really one indivisible whole. Out of its great stream the classifying hand of the investigator artificially extracts economic facts.' (Schumpeter, 1912b:3). Indeed he does – if he knows what they are. Where, however, the purely economic is found only in combination with the resolutely non-catallactic, it will frequently be impossible to separate one tree from its forest, one chemical from its compound: 'A fact is never exclusively or purely economic; other – and often more important – aspects always exist.' (Schumpeter, 1912b:3).

Schumpeter knew that his pure economics was only one ingredient in a real, existing cake: 'The designation of a fact as economic already involves an abstraction.' (Schumpeter, 1912b:3). This is one of the reasons why he encouraged economists not to attach themselves to market liberalism or any other political *nostrum*. Methodologically speaking, it would be inappropriate for scientists to advocate or espouse since ethical notions like distributive justice have no place in *what is* investigation that ought to remain detached and dispassionate: 'Moralising judgements of value do not fit into the domain of a discipline intended exactly to describe reality.' (Schumpeter, 1908:245). No less important, however, there is the practical shortcoming that one-dimensional analysis might not be up to the task of accounting for the whole: 'Our theorems do not reflect the concrete circumstances of economic life.' (Schumpeter, 1908:583). People who believe what the economics textbooks teach them are likely to spend a great deal of their time making errors in the void.

The economics textbooks,

> like all pure theory ... cannot explain in full the true nature of economic phenomena. ... It is the same with the pure theory of any other science. Theory can only make a partial contribution to the understanding of economic life. No one today would suggest that economic life is solely dominated by purely economic influences .... All attempts should be rejected which seek, based on purely theoretical considerations, to justify or to attack existing conditions or to make recommendations for social policy. (Schumpeter, 1907:187).

Economic theory is not a complete theory of human action. It is 'nur ein Strahl der Erkenntnis, nicht mehr' (Schumpeter, 1907:188). *Ein Strahl* is better than *kein Strahl*. Its importance for all that should not be exaggerated by over-eager improvers determined to do good.

Schumpeter advises that economic theory can only be a first approximation: 'We cannot solve the great problems of the time from our own standpoint.' (Schumpeter, 1908:576). The Ricardians, less moderate in their aspirations, were more likely to assume a convenient bridge whenever they wanted to cross an inconvenient stream. Schumpeter, calling it the 'Ricardian Vice', was sharply critical of 'the habit of piling the heavy load of practical conclusions upon a tenuous groundwork, which was unequal to it, yet seemed in its simplicity not only attractive but also convincing' (Schumpeter, 1954:1171). He accused the Ricardians of deriving clear-cut policy recommendations from a misplaced concreteness, incomplete and biased. Ricardian theory is bad theory. Its failure does not prove, however, that no first approximation can ever be good.

Schumpeter, fully aware that there was much that theory could not do, nonetheless made tentative use of theory throughout his microeconomics of entrepreneurship and organisation, his macroeconomics of cycles and development. Shionoya is able to reconcile the agnosticism with the positivism by drawing a comparison between Schumpeter under the influence of Mach and Duhem and 'The methodology of positive economics' of Milton Friedman that appeared in 1953, 45 years after the *Wesen*. Writing of Schumpeter, Shionoya says: 'His standpoint can be best described as instrumentalism, that is, the view that theories are not descriptions but instruments for deriving useful results and are neither true or false.' (Shionoya, 1992:352). Schumpeter, Shionoya says, treated theories as instruments that systematised the facts. He accepted that the premisses might be arbitrary, the model a faltering first step. Assumptions did not matter. All that matters to the pragmatist is results.

Schumpeter as an evolutionary thinker came under the influence of Marx on the unstoppable momentum that would culminate in capitalism's collapse. Schumpeter as an economic theoretician lived in lifelong debt to Walras on the inherent stability of the auction price. Shionoya, recognising the disparity between the conflicting visions of Schumpeter's great spiritual fathers, suggests that Schumpeter was able to reconcile the evolution with the economising through his contention that the success of the market is also the failure of the system: 'The very success of the capitalist economy will produce the noneconomic factors that are inconsistent with it.' (Shionoya, 1992:355). Perhaps it is true that Schumpeter regarded the *tâtonnement* as the harbinger of the abyss. Even so, it is striking just how warmly the prophet of initiative was able to welcome the arid equilibration of the Walrasian cross. No evolutionary thinker before or since has shown so much enthusiasm for the neoclassical permafrost in which nothing grows and nothing dies.

Schumpeter as a theoretician reserved his highest praise for Walras: 'So far as pure theory is concerned, Walras is ... the greatest of all economists .... His system ... is the outstanding landmark on the road that economics travels toward the status of a rigorous or exact science.' (Schumpeter, 1954:827). Walras was the great pioneer, the great liberator 'whose system of equations, defining static equilibrium in a system of interdependent quantities, is the Magna Carta of economic theory' (Schumpeter, 1954:242). Walras saw that the general equilibrium of all prices and quantities had to be incorporated in a single system, a numerical matrix approximating the circular flow. It was an insight that Schumpeter believed to have opened his eyes: 'As an economist I owe more to it than to any other influence.' (Schumpeter, 1937:165).

The Walrasian pure logic is 'the only work by an economist that will stand comparison with the achievements of theoretical physics' (Schumpeter, 1954:827). The reason why it is so hardy is that Walras deliberately made it so focused. For Walras at least, 'the utility theory was nothing less than ultimate truth, the discovery of the key to all the secrets of pure economics' (Schumpeter, 1952a:127). No statistics, no sociology, no history interferes with the mathematics and the maximisation that grind out the price vector and ensure the efficient allocation of a fixed endowment: 'Nothing disturbs the unity of the whole picture. No other element is of importance in it.'

(Schumpeter, 1952a:74). Economic theory is about market valuation. Economic theory is about price.

Walras, Pareto, Edgeworth, Barone all saw that economic theory is about economising. So, importantly, did Menger and the Austrian theoreticians who shared his conviction that 'price formation is the specific economic characteristic of the economy – as distinct from all the other social, historical, and technical characteristics .... All specifically economic events can be comprehended within the framework of price formation. From a purely economic standpoint, the economic system is merely a system of dependent prices.' (Schumpeter, 1952a:84). Menger was an economist and he kept his eye on the ball: 'No economic sociology or sociology of economic development can be derived from Menger's work.' (Schumpeter, 1952a:86). Had Menger wanted to write about institutions, he would have chosen a different set of tools from those that mark out the economic theoretician as the theorist of price.

Schumpeter admired the equilibrium tidiness of comparative statics. He also recognised that the Walrasian *Gleichgewichtsmensch* was a world away from the hungry entrepreneur whom all but the economists knew to be the reason for real-world change without end: 'Our image of everyday reality, as we depict it, is in danger of being judged false. It misleadingly suggests a state of rest that never and nowhere exists.' (Schumpeter, 1908:567). The Walrasian matrix makes economic life a still photograph of an invariant commodity-set. It makes the price mechanism the unthinking adaptation to the external shock of war or flood rather than the social conduit for purposive transformation, internally generated. Walrasianism is a stationary vision of human powerlessness. It conceives of people as 'essentially passive' to an extent that Schumpeter, the action-minded evolutionist, was simply unable to accept: 'I felt very strongly that this was wrong, and that there was a source of energy within the economic system which would of itself disrupt any equilibrium that might be attained.' (Schumpeter, 1937:166). Comparative statics is a useful first step. Taken by itself, however, Walrasian conflict-resolution must leave economics stranded in the never-never-land of a science that will not grow up.

Schumpeter was attracted by the Walrasian balance of give and take. What he also found persuasive was the notion that the endstate in the capitalist economy can only be regarded as a general tendency on the road to something new: 'The thing that matters to us, is ... this tendency considered as an actual force, and not the mere existence of ideal equilibrium points of reference.' (Schumpeter, 1939:I, 70). A tendency is not a prediction where disequilibrium dynamics ensures that the status quo preceding a disturbance will never subsequently be restored: 'The waves of the sea return to the same level. Not so, however, the waves of economic life.' (Schumpeter, 1908:573). It is in the nature of innovative gain-seeking that it forever tries new techniques and satisfies new wants: 'The usual course of the economy is full of life and motion. It is in a state of continuous development.' (Schumpeter, 1908:567). It is not in the nature of enterprise, given capitalism, that it slumbers peacefully in perpetual rest. When we look at the economy at any point in time, what we see is not gravitation but 'constant activity' (Schumpeter, 1912a:465), not stock but flow, not *sub specie aeternitatis* but 'ein geschäftigtes Leben und Treiben' (Schumpeter, 1912a:465). What we see is the 'constant unfolding' (Schumpeter, 1912a:474), the unbroken chain of events. What we do not see is 'the balance of unchanging forces': 'Development and equilibrium ... are alternatives. The one excludes the other.' (Schumpeter, 1912a:474, 489).

Schumpeter believed that action and inaction were two different subject-clusters. They were not wings of a single building but separate structures on their own: 'Statics and dynamics are quite different areas. They deal not only with different problems but also must be studied with different methods.' (Schumpeter, 1908:182). Development 'is the most important of all the phenomena which we seek to explain' (Schumpeter, 1908:186). Yet development 'is not encompassed in our theory. The pure economic system allows for no development.' (Schumpeter, 1908:186). Economic theory as it stands, Schumpeter said, stops short at allocation and never moves on to model change: 'The methods of pure economics are at present only adequate for the former, and its main results only relate to the former.' (Schumpeter, 1908:xix). Theory will improve: 'Dynamics is just beginning to get started. It is a "land of the future".' (Schumpeter, 1908:183). Theory has not as yet changed very much.

Malthus and Ricardo constructed their law of diminishing marginal productivity on the assumption of constant agricultural technology. Their cost curves, like ours, were 'applicable only in quite short periods of time' (Schumpeter, 1908:568). The anti-interventionists opposed the maximum working day with the argument that legislation would reduce well-being when the opposite, long-run, was more nearly the truth: 'It may be a necessity for the development of the race. It can lead to technical progress. It can cause more output in a shorter time.' (Schumpeter, 1908:210). Some economists, recognising that static assumptions like these can do great harm, have already ventured out into the under-developed territory that is the 'land of the future'. They at least are prepared to admit that '"cetera" do not remain constant, should not remain constant' (Schumpeter, 1908:577). An example would be Böhm-Bawerk, whose 'third reason' for capital deepening clearly implies new production-functions in the course of uninterrupted time. Most economists have preferred to remain stunted in their textbook cocoon of perfect knowledge and perfect competition. Their decision to model 'more of the same' with 'more of the same' does not help economic science to move on. The Walrasian matrix is a useful first step. Taken by itself, it is simply not enough.

Walras, unlike Menger, used mathematics to make his market more precise. Schumpeter was full of praise for Walras but none the less never tried to saddle the Walrasian thoroughbreds for himself. As Mitchell writes: 'Despite his unabashed admiration of Walras' achievement .... Schumpeter never seems to have written an equation of his own. Like Mises and Hayek, he was indifferent to graphical analysis.' (Mitchell, 1984:149). Schumpeter felt that general equilibrium, interdependent causality, the pecuniary proxy for motivation all lent themselves naturally to the formal notation of 'number, weight and measure': 'Economics is the most quantitative, not only of "social" or "moral" sciences, but of *all* sciences, physics not excluded.' (Schumpeter, 1933:100). In spite of that he was content to leave it to others to write out the functions: '*Patron* of mathematical economics is perhaps the best way of describing his rôle.' (Samuelson, 1951:50).

Schumpeter was able to use mathematics. Largely self-taught, each day for 15 years while in America he sought to deepen his knowledge and seems to have enjoyed the challenge. At Harvard he taught a course on mathematical economics. (Leontief later took it over.) With Leonard Crum (who had a Ph.D. in mathematics and who had already done the bulk of the work for his *Quarterly Journal of Economics* supplement of 1938), he wrote a textbook, *Rudimentary Mathematics for Economists and Statisticians*, published in 1946. Schumpeter's first major article (in 1906) was on the use of mathematics in economic theory. His view, then as always, was that rubbish in means rubbish out, that 'mathematics provides no protection against error', but that a solid scaffolding does no harm to the builder who uses it to complement a full portfolio of skills: 'Mathematics is only a logical method which introduces nothing new, different, but also nothing incorrect.' (Schumpeter, 1906:530, 531). Whereas fellow 'Austrians' were suspicious of abstract symbols (their doubts were shared by the historicists who insisted upon factual evidence), it was Schumpeter's reply to both the theoreticians and the empiricists that there was no way for economics to advance without the exactness of Walrasian deduction.

Schumpeter could have used the mathematics. Given both the background and the commitment, it comes as something of a surprise to find that he did not. One reason is likely to have been the central theme of entrepreneurship itself: whereas rationality, rules and recurrence can be nailed into place with calculus, intuition, flair and insight do not fit easily into a mechanical expression. Another reason was the interdisciplinary dimension: culture, empathy, social systems, socialist democracy are by their nature qualitative, subjective and ambiguous. Like Menger, he knew that uncertainty makes fine-tuning into a guess: reflecting that 'dynamics takes away the clarity and the simplicity' (Schumpeter, 1907:201), he saw clearly that there is no equation for the clueless surprise. Like Marshall, he wanted to be read. Abstruse jargon drives the uninitiated to authors they can follow.

Overriding all was the nature of the beast. Schumpeter, Allen observes, was fond of 'oft-neglected facts, startling hypotheses, interesting paradoxes, intricate verbal analyses', of 'profound conclusions', of 'grand Schumpeterian flourishes': 'He had a historical, literary, and even romantic, outlook, not a mathematical turn of mind.' (Allen, 1991:II, 3). Schumpeter by temperament was a philosopher and a debater. The real surprise would have been if he had actually practised what he preached rather than abstaining so conspicuously from the mathematics that he had made his Mecca.

Schumpeter recognised his limitations. He thought that, at least in mathematics, he was not very good and that high theory would have to go on without him: 'I sometimes feel like Moses must have felt when he beheld the Promised Land and knew that he himself would not be allowed to enter it.' (cited in Swedberg, 1991:118). Leontief compares his impatience with his own suspected shortcomings to a 'true balletomane's attitude to the classical ballet' (Leontief, 1950:108), able to appreciate every nuance and yet unable to match the standard that he so much admires. Rostow says that his unrequited love for mathematics was a disappointment from which Schumpeter never really recovered: 'I believe Schumpeter's sense of failure derived, in part, from his inability to translate his powerful, correct understanding of the significance of innovations into either an elegant mathematical formulation in the style of Walras or a neat historical pattern.' (Rostow, 1991:xv). Schumpeter wanted to be something that he was not. He never forgave himself for being only Schumpeter, only the great visionary that he was.

The endorsement of mathematics was to prove a double-edged sword. Richard Swedberg is sensitive to the irony that more economists would today read *Capitalism, Socialism and Democracy* if thinkers like Schumpeter had not so willingly invested their influence in the formalists' cause: 'Schumpeter does not seem to have been aware at this time that by backing mathematical economics, he might also have helped to unleash forces that were hostile to his own project of *Sozialökonomik*.' (Swedberg, 1991:118). Schumpeter knew that context could all too easily be crowded out by logic:

> The ability to see things in their correct perspective may be, and often is, divorced from the ability to reason correctly and vice versa. That is why a man may be a very good theorist and yet talk absolute nonsense whenever confronted with the task of diagnosing a concrete historical pattern as a whole. (Schumpeter, 1942a:76n).

It is strange to think that Schumpeter himself in encouraging the mathematical economists may unintentionally have contributed to the counter-Schumpeterian revolution that values method even at the cost of content.

Schumpeter in Graz was complaining that his young charges were wasting their time: 'Of one hundred students, ninety-five gain nothing, nothing at all, from their university course in economics.' (Schumpeter, 1915:562). Schumpeter at Harvard was deploring the closing in upon itself that he had observed in his profession: 'Economics is getting better and better, but economists are getting worse and worse.' (cited in Allen, 1991:I, 173). Schumpeter believed that simplifying fictions were harmless in themselves if consumed in a mix. What he failed to recognise is that technical theory, universal and timeless, could in the long run represent a threat to the socio-cultural perspective. The eclipse has come to pass. Good Schumpeterians no longer study economics. The evolution of the discipline has crowded out the big questions that they might have asked.

3.3.2 Economic Statistics

Schumpeter believed that the economist had to have the facts if he was to do useful work: 'Economics will never either have or merit any prestige until it can figure out results.' (Schumpeter, 1952a:106). A founder of the Econometric Society, the author of the relatively empirical *Business Cycles*, Schumpeter clearly had one foot in the inductivists' camp even as he was campaigning for better mathematics as the deductivists had proposed.

Schumpeter, like Weber, contrived to side with both the pure theorists and the data-miners, first in the *Methodenstreit* of his student years and later in no-nonsense America where institutional economics was still an influential heterodoxy: 'In terms of their general assertions both in general are right ... . Each method has its own concrete area to which it is relevant. There is no point in arguing for general applicability.' (Schumpeter, 1908:6, 7). Different tasks require different tools: the historicists cannot explain price formation while the neoclassicals cannot describe organisational behaviour. That being the case, the real need is for collaboration and synthesis rather than the either/or and the team formation which Schumpeter associated with the pre-history of science: 'Within serious economic theory there are no such things as "schools" or differences of principle ... . The only fundamental cleavage in modern economics is between good work and bad.' (Schumpeter, 1928:49).

Schumpeter concluded that common sense was getting the better of the earlier divisiveness: 'Those economists who really count do not differ so much as most people believe.' (Schumpeter, 1927b:21). What he fails to say is why he thinks a new convergence will evolve. The omission is a serious one since he of all economists was especially aware that different visions must spotlight different scenarios: 'Like everything else, economic life may be looked at from a great, strictly speaking an infinite, number of standpoints. Only some of these belong to the realm of science, still fewer admit of, or require, the use of quantitative methods.' (Schumpeter, 1933:100).

Schumpeter's own practice gives no greater guidance on the division of labour which he himself believed to be the rational mix. He was an econometrician who never used econometrics. He did not employ simultaneous equations to estimate the cyclical interdependence of endogenous cause and effect. He failed to calculate the national income and the components of demand. He never established whether trend savings were in fact rising or going down. For a methodologist who returned so frequently to the feedback between expectation and outturn, he himself cannot be said to have taken a lead in throwing up 'best practice' in a convergent world where evidence is essential if conjectures are to be revealed as right or wrong.

3.3.3 Economic Sociology

Schumpeter saw economics as the study of the economy not as it *ought to be* but uncompromisingly as it *is*: 'Economics is only an observational and interpretative science.' (Schumpeter, 1942a:107). Cutting through the restrictive assumptions and the economic-man abstractions, what economics has to do is to open out its pure theory to the surrounding context in order to make sense of the real-world data that is seldom found save in an inter-disciplinary compound. Economic sociology is the branch of investigation which gives the facts-based economist the opportunity to trespass on to the common ground:

> There is nothing surprising in the habit of economists to invade the sociological field. A large part of their work – practically the whole of what they have to say on institutions and on the forces that shape economic behavior – inevitably overlaps the sociologist's preserves. In consequence, a no-man's land or everyman's land has developed that might conveniently be called economic sociology. (Schumpeter, 1952a:134).

Schumpeter did not favour a Comte-like merger of the separate social sciences: 'Cross-fertilization might easily result in cross-sterilization.' (Schumpeter, 1954:27). In the *Wesen* he argued that economics, respecting the academic division of labour, should filter out the extraneous impurities that divert pure catallactics from its unique and functional brief: 'There are many things that, while of decisive importance for economic life, nonetheless lie outside the area of economic science.' (Schumpeter, 1908:179). Time and place, race and leadership, climate and geography, all stamp their imprint on economic life. Not, however, on the thin lens of economic theory: 'We do not need these things .... The results of pure economics are independent of them.'

(Schumpeter, 1908:154). Studied on their own, their home is in the kingdom next door: 'The deeper reasons may be interesting but they do not affect our results. They belong to the field of sociology.' (Schumpeter, 1908:94). Economic sociology is the no-man's land – the everyman's land – that allows the variables to converse freely without having to state to which freestanding empire they are forced to belong.

Economics is the analysis and description of 'conduct ... directed towards the acquisition of goods through exchange or production' (Schumpeter, 1912b:3). Its concern is allocative efficiency and dynamic upgrading in a resource-constrained second-best where not all wants can be satisfied nor all needs met. Sociology is the science of 'social institutions and principles of social organization' (Schumpeter, 1914:104). Its subject matter is the meaningful interaction of interdependent decision makers embedded within a single network of community. Economics is about households that earn and spend, businesses that invest and sell. Sociology is about structured relationships and conventional procedures. The former is exchange based. The latter is institutional. They are not substitutes but complements: 'Sociology and economics pervade each other .... They are one.' (Schumpeter, 1942a:45). Economic sociology is the synthesis that captures the synergies between homeless negotiating and the rootedness of outward-reaching integration.

Schumpeter in his centenary appreciation of Marx's *Manifesto* defined economic sociology as 'the description and interpretation – or "interpretative description" – of economically relevant institutions, including habits and all forms of behavior in general, such as government, property, private enterprise, customary or "rational" behavior' (Schumpeter, 1949c:293). In an article on Wesley Clair Mitchell he made economic sociology 'the analysis of social institutions or of "prevalent social habits"' (Schumpeter, 1952a:246). In the *History of Economic Analysis*, returning once again to the non-ego consistencies of situated standardisation, vertical and horizontal, he said that by economic sociology he meant the 'analysis of economic institutions' (Schumpeter, 1954:819). Economic sociology, to Schumpeter, was institutional economics. It was the 'interpretative description' of the shared procedures and the sanctioned norms that circumscribe the economic exchanges of purchase and sale.

Veblen saw institutions as those 'habits of thought, points of view, mental attitudes and aptitudes' (Veblen, 1899:133) that are a conservative brake precisely because they are interpersonal and inter-temporal. Schumpeter took the same view of the collective and cultural baggage that buyers and sellers carry about with them when they negotiate their gains from trade. Institutions, he said, embrace 'all the patterns of behavior into which individuals must fit under penalty of encountering organized resistance', together with all the 'agencies for their production or enforcement' (Schumpeter, 1950a:438). Institutions are not a footnote *obiter dictum*. Rather, they are all around.

Sometimes the constraints will take the form of legal codes that impose an outsider's discipline upon 'contracts, property, inheritance, credit systems, taxation, labor relations, public or corporative regulation of economic activity' (Schumpeter, 1947:233–4). Sometimes the prescriptions will be as diffuse as a general valuation of the family, prudent parsimony, pecuniary self-interest, the minimal State, the leaderly State: ubiquitous ideology shoe-horns free will into choices so value-ridden that Schumpeter once exclaimed 'Don't ask me for rationality when I am speaking of human behavior' (Schumpeter, 1941:391). Always, however, the standards will be those of the group. Social actors who live in society live by a guiding light. Their behaviour is not fully theirs to control as they will.

Schumpeter throughout his life made it his practice to trespass into the no-man's land where he could combine his pure economics with its institutional counterparts. He attended the lectures of Edward Westermarck at the LSE in 1906–7. He taught the principles of stratification at Czernowitz, Graz and Columbia. He joined the German Sociological Association. He was an editor from 1916 to 1933, with Weber, Sombart and others, of the *Archiv für Sozialwissenschaft und Sozialpolitik*. In the United States, as President of the American Economic Association, he sought to organise joint sessions with the American Sociological Association. Schumpeter never saw himself as a sociologist per se. What he believed, however, was that the science of things had at all times to maintain a dialogue with the science of people.

Schumpeter's fascination with the *We* that situates the *I* is somewhat unexpected in the work of an 'Austrian' who was also an Austrian. Menger's *Principles* contains few collective nouns; while Austro-Hungary, polyglot and multinational, had no tribal consciousness, no median value-code. Mixed class as a child, an outsider-intellectual by temperament, a rootless cosmopolitan who belonged not much more to Dollfuss or Weimar than he did to the America of Mickey Rooney and Coca-Cola, Schumpeter could easily have become a stand-alone monad to whom the togetherness of *Gemeinschaft* was no more than the opiate of the chronically dependent. Instead he developed a sensitivity to the meaningful web and not just to the self-interested swap which anonymous strangers use to buy in what they need.

Schumpeter in developing a sociological awareness was no doubt influenced by the strength in his formative years of the Marxian and the historical schools: they had shown that an anthropocentric interpretation could be academically respectable. Catholic social economists like Heinrich Pesch had taught that even businessmen and their customers could not do as they pleased with their community's moral capital. Papal Encyclicals had blamed greed-is-good individualism for putting at risk the organic integration of fellow communicants, all parts one of another. Americans like Ely and Commons emphasized the importance even in the capitalist market of rules and heuristics. Labour in the inter-war years was the militant working class, not the disembodied first derivative. Intercourse and incorporation, in other words, were widely assumed to be a social fact.

A dialogue between the disciplines was not uncommon in an era when professionals were less sealed off by peer review and rigid departmentalism than they were later to become. Perhaps the Austro-German convention of studying more than one subject at university contributed to Schumpeter's belief that it was the *Fachidiot* who was the odd man out. So, arguably, did his own training in law, which gave him a conservative's appreciation of precedents and non-negotiables as the preferred alternative to the *Lord of the Flies*. Besides that, Schumpeter was writing at a time when distinguished contemporaries were, like him, exploring the common boundaries of economics and sociology. Max Weber, in *Economy and Society* and elsewhere, had anticipated Schumpeter's concerns with bureaucracy, charisma, the iron cage of non-chosen ideas, the continuing role of the hereditary aristocracy: Schumpeter's use of terms like 'economically relevant' and 'interpretative description', his reliance on ideal types and empathetic *Verstehen*, show how much he had absorbed from Weber. Wieser's *Social Economics* (1914) covered the whole of economics from the perspective of the group. Mannheim's *Ideology and Utopia* (1930) argued that perception could be the emanation of the economic base. Parsons's *Structure of Social Action* (1937) demonstrated that a (German-trained) economist could find normative binding even in the utilitarian positivism of pure theorists like Pareto and Marshall.

Influenced by the writers, Schumpeter was influenced even more by the theme. The greatest single factor that made Schumpeter a *sociological* economist was almost certainly his central concern with capitalist development itself. Bottomore is right to say that the assimilation of technical economics with institutional order has long had an appeal to social scientists who believe that catallactics is only a veil for more fundamental relationships: 'Studies of, and controversies about, capitalism and socialism have formed the central core of economic sociology, and even of whole sociological systems, since the middle of the nineteenth century.' (Bottomore, 1992:125). The principles of economics are also the principles of capitalism. The principles of catallactics are also the principles of integration. In putting flesh on the skeleton of exchange, Schumpeter was contributing to the grand tradition from Ferguson to Simmel that had seen the economic order as something more conclusive than indifference curves trading facelessly in a box.

Schumpeter was a *social* economist, unwilling to compromise on the imprimatur from without: 'Every individual is fashioned by the social influences in which he grows up. In this sense he is the produce of the social entity or class and therefore not a free agent.' (Schumpeter, 1931a:286). Yet Schumpeter was also a methodological reductionist, determined to freeze out collective choice in order to take the isolated individual as his factored-down unit of analysis: 'In the description of certain economic processes one had better begin with the actions of individuals.' (Schumpeter, 1908:91). The bottom-up approach, not a moral crusade but a practical point of departure, is known as methodological individualism. Schumpeter in the *Wesen* (he says so on page 94) was the first to use the term.

Methodological individualism must not be confused with normative individualism: 'The two have nothing whatsoever in common.' (Schumpeter, 1908:90). It does not preach the minimalist ethic that it is market rather than State that is the ultimate source of welfare and progress: 'The social policy-maker and the economist are often one and the same person.' (Schumpeter, 1908:92). Nor is it bound up with the libertarian assertion that society is no more than the adding up of its decentralised initiatives: 'A standpoint that we expressly reject' (Schumpeter, 1908:95), so radical an *ego* without the *alter* is, Schumpeter writes, 'untenable so far as it implies a theory of the social process' (Schumpeter, 1954:88–9). People do not live in a social vacuum. The first step cannot be the last word.

Methodological individualism is in no way a denial of the sociological imprimatur: 'We admit that social influences determine the conduct of the individual, and that the individual is an infinitesimally tiny factor.' (Schumpeter, 1908:93). Simply, the interdependence adds nothing to the modelling: 'It is ... of no consequence for the purposes of our discussion.' (Schumpeter, 1908:93). Methodological atomism 'asserts nothing and has no particular premisses' (Schumpeter, 1908:90). It is no more than a theoretician's attempt to interview the representative mind in private. Exchange is mental states like diminishing utility, not accounting balances like labour embodied: 'Value is a psychological phenomenon.' (Schumpeter, 1906:532). That is why the individualist approach is 'indispensable' (Schumpeter, 1908:596), why 'the starting point of our system must therefore be the economics of the individual' (Schumpeter, 1906:533). Only Crusoe can put a value on his felt pleasures and pains. Only Friday can quantify, subjectively, the intensity of his want.

Summed aggregates like 'labour' and 'capital' lack an inner dimension: 'Mere clotheslines on which to hang propositions', they are convenient fictions and not 'living and fighting entities' (Schumpeter, 1954:886) that have a private preference to reveal. Methodological individualism is a necessary first step. Even so, it is 'only' (Schumpeter, 1908:97) a first step. It should never be mistaken for a complete account: 'As soon as we cross the boundary from pure theory, the situation is different.' (Schumpeter, 1908:95). As soon as we cross the boundary from pure theory, the holistic perspective comes into its own: 'The individual is a *social* fact, the psychological an *objective* fact.' (Schumpeter, 1927a:274). Methodological individualism says how sensations are expressed. Economic sociology, however, is needed to explain how external conditioning made internalised representations a part of the self.

Writing of economic sociology, Schumpeter emphasised the time-dominated character of the blend. Economic sociology, he suggested, is 'a sort of generalized or typified or stylized economic history' (Schumpeter, 1954:20). Economic sociology is the realm of anchoring and standards, of overlapping memories and unchosen socialisation. A science of habits that are 'meaningful only with reference to the historical background from which they spring' (Schumpeter, 1954:4), of entrepreneurs who manufacture the future out of a past that they never designed, it is clear that the person to person nexus just as much as the shopper's attraction to the thing will only make sense when it is seen not as final endstate but as matter in motion: 'Economic analysis deals with the questions how people behave at any time and what the economic effects are they produce by so behaving; economic sociology deals with the question how they came to behave as they do.' (Schumpeter, 1954:21).

Genesis, origin, search, competition are core components of Schumpeter's sociological relativism. As Aréna and Dangel-Hagnauer write: 'Economic sociology, according to Schumpeter, can thus be defined as the science of the emergence, maintenance and decline of societal institutions and forms of organisation that influence economic behaviour.' (Aréna and Dangel-Hagnauer, 2002:3). Economic sociology, according to Schumpeter, is not merely interdependence but development as well: 'For Schumpeter, human motives are never strictly individual. Rather, they are always embedded in a social context and related to the historical circumstances under which they have emerged.' (Aréna and Dangel-Hagnauer, 2002:3). What this means is that economic sociology is the next stopping place on the historical journey even as it is nations that are more than 'amorphous agglomerations of individuals', classes that are more than 'mere labels affixed to economic functions' (Schumpeter, 1954:886). Peers influence choices: 'It is society that shapes the particular desires we observe .... The field of individual choice is always, though in very different ways and to very different degrees, fenced in by social habits or conventions and the like.' (Schumpeter, 1912b:91). So, however, does the cumulative pressure of 'the laws of social being and becoming' that are the cause and effect of 'the manner in which *concrete* conditions, and in particular organizational forms, grow and pass away.' (Schumpeter, 1918:101). People are on the horizontal axis. So, therefore, is time.

3.3.4 Economic History

Economic history is 'by far the most important' of the four 'fundamental fields' (Schumpeter, 1954:12) that sum up to economic science. Every event has a context. Each context is on the move. Schumpeter, sensitive to the evanescence of contingency, concluded that the 'subject matter of economics is essentially a unique process in historic time' (Schumpeter, 1954:12). He also expressed his regret that so few contemporary economists had any real feeling for the unbroken sweep of 'incessant and irreversible change' (Schumpeter, 1954:435): 'Nobody can hope to understand the economic phenomena of any, including the present, epoch who has not an adequate command of historical *facts*, and an adequate amount of historical *sense* or of what may be described as *historical experience*.' (Schumpeter, 1954:12–13). Nobody can hope to predict the future who has not also paid a visit to the past.

Schumpeter believed that evidence from the past was needed in order to complete some of the responsible economist's most pressing tasks: 'Only detailed historic knowledge can definitively answer most of the questions of individual causation and mechanism.' (Schumpeter, 1939:I, 200). Economic statistics draws together inductions relating to the recent past in order to identify shared origins and extrapolate probable landmarks. Economic history extends the series further backwards into the records to ensure that the information reveals the whole truth and not just the tip of the iceberg: 'Contemporaneous facts or even historic facts covering the last quarter or half of a century are perfectly inadequate. For no phenomenon of an essentially historic nature can be expected to reveal itself unless it is studied over a long interval.' (Schumpeter, 1939:I, 220). To be a student of the new it is necessary first to be a student of the old.

The past, for one thing, has not gone away. Handed on, remembered, non-chosen, non-rational, surviving, it is the conservative's contention that customs and habits, norms and rules, have an impact on present-day economising that begins the calculus before current supply and demand were even born: 'Economic action cannot be explained save with reference to economic action itself .... Among the influences which explain the asset-stock of observed individuals will be the asset-stock of an earlier time.' (Schumpeter, 1908:124).

Small businesses hang on despite the transition to corporate capitalism. The leaderly aristocracy basks in the long-gone glory of the feudal barons. Entrepreneurial departures extend established highways using inherited procedures. Social facts like these are illustrations of Schumpeter's belief that extinct functions can serve to reinforce or to retard the maximisations of the late capitalist age: 'Social structures, types and attitudes are coins that do not readily melt. Once they are formed they persist, possibly for centuries.' (Schumpeter, 1942a:12).

Embedded in structures or embodied in attitudes, it is in the nature of institutions that they have a life-force of their own. The investment, the schooling is a gradual process. Once in place, however, the deep-rooted reaction takes over and becomes an unthinking response. People 'cling as tightly as possible to habitual economic methods and only submit to the pressure of circumstances as it becomes necessary' (Schumpeter, 1912b:8–9). Even their perceptions of money have the character of a time-lagged second best:

> The marginal utility of money for each economic actor is the result of long experience and gradually becomes part of his 'flesh and blood'. ... It is the barometer and the regulator of his economic life. Thus he does not change quickly or easily. If his conditions were to change, he would still try to work with the same regulator, in which social and other non-economic considerations have a role. (Schumpeter, 1908:473).

Winter and summer come and go. The temperature, however, remains the enduringly fixated first Monday in May.

History is the memory of the past: 'The problems and methods that are in use at any given time embody the achievements and carry the scars of work that has been done in the past under entirely different conditions.' (Schumpeter, 1954:4). History is also the product of the present: 'The problem that is usually being visualized is how capitalism administers existing structures, whereas the relevant problem is how it creates and destroys them.' (Schumpeter, 1942a:84). As a historian of the future who recognised that dynamic capitalism was both the varying and the constant, Schumpeter refused to treat the economic process as spot allocation and nothing more. Capitalism is creative destruction. Without innovation the business interest would not be able to take home a profit: 'Stabilized capitalism is a contradiction in terms.' (Schumpeter, 1939:II, 1033).

Schumpeter in the preface to the Japanese edition of *Economic Development* made clear, more Marx than Walras, that he had been concerned with active initiative, not with spiritless conformity: 'I was trying to construct a theoretic model of the process of economic change in time, or perhaps more clearly, to answer the question of how the economic system generates the force which incessantly transforms it.' (Schumpeter, 1937:165). It is by no means common for an economist to study the way in which the economy 'transforms' the world around it – and does so 'incessantly', even when supply corresponds perfectly to demand. As Stolper says, referring to the Marshallian cross under assault from the Schumpeterian entrepreneur: 'Every equilibrium is different from every other one; it is always *an* rather than *the* equilibrium.' (Stolper, 1951:107). History is making itself. Final destinations are not on its route.

Schumpeter made it entrepreneurship that makes the market go round: 'Innovation is the outstanding fact in the economic history of capitalist society.' (Schumpeter, 1939:I, 86). It is novelty and renewal that turn simple replication into something more: 'The changes in the economic process brought about by innovation, together with all their effects, and the response to them by the economic system, we shall designate by the term Economic Evolution.' (Schumpeter, 1939:I, 86). Without discontentment there would be no progress; 'without entrepreneurial achievement, no capitalist returns and no capitalist propulsion' (Schumpeter, 1939:II, 1033). Economics in that sense is all but a pure theory of capitalism's history as the unfolding struggle to become more fully itself.

Yet it all happens gradually, not all at once but in a manageable flow: 'Things change slowly, especially in their core characteristics. To a large extent it is deceptive to speak of earth-shaking developments within a few years.' (Schumpeter, 1908:569). People speak of an industrial 'revolution'. They credit Pasteur with the antidote for anthrax. They date modern Protestantism from Luther's theses at Worms. In doing this they are taking the journalist's easy short cut of focusing on the spectacular culmination – 'It sums up rather than initiates' (Schumpeter, 1939:I, 227) – when a more complete account would be afforded by a reconstruction of a transition that 'would necessarily come about by slow degrees' (Schumpeter, 1939:II, 1034): 'The decisive step in bringing about a new thing or ultimate practical success is, in most cases, only the last straw and often relatively insignificant in itself.' (Schumpeter, 1939:I, 227). History is valuable because it situates the last step in the context of the many small steps that went before.

It is a fact that Schumpeter only in *Business Cycles* actually got down to the task of tracing out the sequence. Just as he was economical in his application of mathematics and statistics, so in *Economic Development*, in *Capitalism*, even in his late papers on the entrepreneur, does he show no more than a system builder's passing interest in naming names or citing instances. For all that, he had economic history in his blood. Schumpeter saw economic life as a river, not a lake. He believed that historical data are 'really the most important contributors to the understanding of present-day problems' (Schumpeter, 1939:I, 13). He also believed that logicians who flatten troublesome archives into stylised caricatures are likely to do great harm to the cause of economic investigation: 'Most of the fundamental errors currently committed in economic analysis are due to lack of historical experience more often than to any other shortcoming of the economist's equipment.' (Schumpeter, 1954:13). Remembering history or creating history, it was Schumpeter's conviction that mankind's history is the prediction of change and not just the closed-book record of the past.

4. The capitalist economy

The vision is clear: market capitalism which enhances the wealth of nations will evolve into economical socialism which will perform at least as well. Initially capitalism is competitive. Later it becomes 'trustified', 'regulated', 'organised', 'managed'. At the end of the day it will be controlled by the State.

This chapter is concerned with the transition from Adam Smith through Standard Oil to the National Board. It pays tribute to the old-style coordination of the butcher, the brewer and the baker who used to bargain and swap. It says that the giant corporation succeeded by the governmental bureau has nonetheless closed a door that can never again be re-opened.

The chapter is divided into three parts. The first, The definition of capitalism, examines what Schumpeter believed to be the unique characteristics of the historical transition that follows feudalism and gives way to Plan. The second, The entrepreneur, shows that Schumpeter looked to the high-powered explosive of the world-historical individual for the mould-breaking initiative that shakes up the circular flow. The third, Entrepreneurship – what it is not, nets out invention, risk-taking, error-correction and administration to demonstrate that Schumpeter's entrepreneurship is vigour, innovation and the implementation of the new.

4.1 THE DEFINITION OF CAPITALISM

Max Weber had emphasised the cultural binding in shared *ought-to-bes* like calculative rationality. Marx had concentrated on the labour–capital dialectic that divides the classes by surplus value. Schumpeter, in the *Economic Journal* in 1928, provided a slim, spare definition of his own. By capitalism, he wrote, 'we mean an economic system characterised by private property (private initiative), by production for a market and by the phenomenon of credit' (Schumpeter, 1928:48). Capitalism, he wrote, is the sum of three core features. Other characteristics, he believed, are twigs and leaves which must not be confused with the trunk.

Capitalism means private ownership of the physical (non-personal) means of production: contracting alone regulates access to the land, the mines, the plant. Capitalism also means welfare-seeking initiative mediated through supply and demand: it is a market-validated order built around private responsibility for losses and private appropriation of gains. Capitalism, most distinctively of all, means bank creation of the means of payment. It is the unique contribution of bank finance, essential to the smooth functioning of entrepreneurship, that marks out the capitalist system as a mode of pecuniary self-expression quite unlike any other.

4.1.1 Credit

Schumpeter terms the economic system 'commercial' (Schumpeter, 1942a:167) where it boasts the privateness and the catallactics but lacks the money multiplication that would make it properly capitalist. Credit is 'the *differentia specifica* distinguishing the "capitalist" system from other species, historical or possible, of the larger genus defined by the first two characteristics' (Schumpeter, 1928:48). Capitalism is the sum of three core features. Of the three it is the separation of funding from enterprise that constitutes the most salient breach.

Capitalism is a monetised and monetary order in which borrowing at interest allows the innovator the freedom to invest without personally having had to defer his gratification. As Schumpeter writes in *Business Cycles*: 'Capitalism is that form of private property economy in which innovations are carried out by means of borrowed money, which in general, though not by logical necessity, implies credit creation.' (Schumpeter, 1939:I, 223). Bank loans supply the venture capital. The bank and not the lender takes the risk. It is gain without pain, a positive-sum form of economic organisation in which the command over goods and services is made possible by 'the intervention of purchasing power created *ad hoc*' (Schumpeter, 1912b:116). There is no need for accumulation alienated through surplus value in the zero-sum sense of Marx or abstention induced through ascetic denial in the unintended-outcome sense of Weber.

Retained earnings are not an irrelevance. Writing late in life, and referring to the long-lived corporation rather than to the gifted new upstart, Schumpeter states that profits are a pool of resources and not merely a focus for ambition: 'The bulk of accumulation comes from profits and hence presupposes profits.' (Schumpeter, 1942a:16). Yet the intermediaries for all that play an active role. As brokers, it is they who allow the borrower to tap into another person's savings by means of 'the deposits which banks create for the use of the would-be entrepreneur' (Schumpeter, 1942a:16). As principals, it is they who allow investment to take place even where ploughing back is not enough: 'It is obviously possible to finance an investment by a bank loan in which case there is no point whatever in speaking of anyone's saving.' (Schumpeter, 1942a:396). Bank money is something new, something extra and something more: 'Capital is a concept of development to which nothing in the circular flow corresponds .... The entrepreneur does not save in order to obtain the means which he needs.' (Schumpeter, 1912b:122, 136).

Morishima and Catephores see what this implies: 'Schumpeter's contribution on the bankers' role of coordinating savings and investment was a decisive departure from the world of Say's Law; he almost completely prepared the way for the Keynesian revolution.' (Morishima and Catephores, 1988:26). In a sense he did. In contrast to theorists of economic development who make voluntary savings the bottleneck, Schumpeter treated innovativeness as the scarce productive factor but resourcing as a semi-free good that can without difficulty be found: 'The ownership of capital is not the precondition for the exercise of the entrepreneurial role.' (Schumpeter, 1929:236).

So long as investment is funded out of savings, the ability to add value imposes a ceiling on the capacity to create demand. The paper economy, liberating spending from earning, ends forever the tyranny of deferred gratification. The new entrant 'can only become an entrepreneur by previously becoming a debtor' (Schumpeter, 1912b:102). His opportunity to borrow and spend is unlikely to be blocked off by a shortage of loanable funds. Ready money from the banks will make new investment possible even where the supply of savings stubbornly refuses to play its part.

Yet paper credit without new goods and services tends to pull up the price level. Schumpeter had lived through the Austrian and German hyperinflations of the 1920s. Believing as he did that runaway price rises were among the greatest dangers to the capitalist system, it is striking how little he actually wrote about the anarchy that a compromise on sound money could bring in its wake. Nominal values always come under pressure where physical inputs, not infinitely elastic, have to be bid away from sunset combinations once the full employment maximum has been reached. Schumpeter seems not to want to acknowledge just how serious the resultant inflation can be.

An example of his one-sided approach to credit expansion is provided by his 1948 essay 'There is still time to stop inflation'. There he announces that 'the best remedy for inflation [is] an increase in production', but immediately adds that the antidote will only be effective if the monetary authorities simultaneously place a cap on fiduciary claims: 'If this increase in production is to have any positive effect, the volume of credit must not rise in the same proportion.' (Schumpeter, 1948:248). The volume of credit must not expand irresponsibly. It is a sound recommendation. The problem is that, condemning 'greenback' public finance in the American Civil War, he unreservedly expresses the opinion that where credit is concerned something is likely to go badly wrong.

Schumpeter in his 1948 essay says that the inflations of the 1920s were 'simple processes', the legacy of war finance, that could easily have been stopped in their tracks: 'But they were not stopped because the people who counted politically did not *want* to stop them.' (Schumpeter, 1948:241). The printing presses become attractive as the general election draws near while any attempt at a cure will mean 'readjustments in prices and production', 'losses and unemployment', that no rational vote-seeker can afford to risk: 'So inflation runs on by common consent.' (Schumpeter, 1948:242). The inference is that easy credit in the interests of political popularity can slip into destabilising hyperinflation brought on by democratic irresponsibility. It is possible that Schumpeter was too sanguine about the beneficial effects of money on demand in a liberal capitalism where the State is too frightened to turn off the tap.

Schumpeter was an anti-inflationist who never found the means to stop inflation in its tracks. One reason for his surprising tolerance of demand-led credit may have been the Thornton-like recognition, clearly expressed in a series of papers at the time of the First World War, that rising prices in certain circumstances can be a 'powerful cause of economic development' (Schumpeter, 1917/18:109). In 'Zinsfuss und Geldverfassung' (1913), in 'Eine "Dynamische" Theorie des Kapitalzinses' (1913) and especially in 'Das Sozialprodukt und die Rechenpfennige' (1917/18), he had argued that redistribution of incomes would be the consequence of uneven inflation; and that 'forced savings' in favour of profit recipients would then increase the pool of resources that investors could return to the economy as productive capital. Uneven inflation would transfer purchasing power from the consumers to the savers just as if the savings were the new abstinence of a single productive class.

Ricardo had said that the veil of money had no impact on the volume of capital. Distinguishing carefully between statics and dynamics, Schumpeter argues the opposite. At least in the disequilibrium period, he says, bank credit is 'the specifically capitalist way of bringing about economic progress' (Schumpeter, 1917/18:109). Not a passive broker but an active creator, the bank in creating money also creates inflation and expands the nation's wealth: 'The fact that bank money causes prices to rise is the cause of "forced savings". Even without the intention to save, a restriction of real incomes is brought about through the rise in prices. The consequence is that means of production are made free and the economic resources available for productive purposes increased.' (Schumpeter, 1917/18:108).

Schumpeter's point would seem to be a (guarded) defence of (moderate) inflation. It is a defence that is reassuringly belt-and-braces. Where intermediaries are in a position to create new means of payment, *ex post* redistribution from spenders to savers is not really needed in the way that it would be were withdrawals from a given national income to be the only source of capital for growth. Even so, that unintended redistribution has the same effect as the initial injection that pulls the prices up. In the one case as in the other, it is money that creates new capital and makes the economy grow.

4.1.2 Credit and Control

Only in 'Imperialisms' does Schumpeter make any sympathetic reference to the Austro-Leninist view of banks as the moving spirits in the foundation of cartels and trusts; or to interlocking board-memberships as the bond between high finance and manufacturing industry; or to shares permanently acquired by hands-on lenders in exchange for emergency overdrafts. In 'Imperialisms' he expresses the view that there is a 'close alliance between high finance and the cartel magnates, often going as far as personal identity': 'Monopoly capital has virtually fused the big banks and cartels into one.' (Schumpeter, 1918/19:200). In 'Imperialisms' he makes the assertion that small business foots the bills and big business pockets the profits: 'The policies of high finance are based on the control of a *large* proportion of the national capital, but they are in the actual interest of only a *small* proportion.' (Schumpeter, 1918/19:200). In 'Imperialisms', writing 'everywhere except, significantly, in England' (Schumpeter, 1918/19:200), he makes his only attempt to distinguish between the pro-active Continental institutions and the more cautious short-termism of the Anglo-Saxon deposit takers. 'Imperialisms' is the exception to the rule. Schumpeter's definition of capitalism and his description of credit are otherwise much more modest than those of the Austro-Marxian Rudolf Hilferding, whose *Finance Capital* in 1910 dealt with many of the issues in business policy to which Schumpeter a year later, in the *Theory of Economic Development*, was to turn his attention.

Schumpeter got to know Hilferding, together with Emil Lederer and Otto Bauer (Mises was also a participant), at a seminar led by Böhm-Bawerk in the University of Vienna in 1905–06 (Haberler, 1951:26). Böhm-Bawerk's doctrine of increasing 'roundaboutness', his prediction that the ratio of manufactured to non-manufactured inputs would rise over time, was well known to all. So was Marx's contention, in the third volume of *Capital*, that the banks would play an active role in bringing about the concentration and centralisation of asset ownership. Hilferding, like Schumpeter, threw himself into the ongoing debate. Hilferding, like Schumpeter, concluded that 'borrowed capital' and 'entrepreneurial profit' nowadays go hand in hand: 'Once the credit system has attained a certain degree of development, the utilization of credit by the capitalist enterprise becomes a necessity, imposed upon it by the competitive struggle.' (Hilferding, 1910:93).

Hilferding, like Schumpeter, maintained that finance through reinvestment was no longer the norm: 'The expansion of the corporation does not depend upon its own accumulation out of earnings.' (Hilferding, 1910:122). The sheer scale of activity puts corporate growth beyond the means of a single asset-holder: 'Present-day industry is carried on with an amount of capital far exceeding that which is owned by the industrial capitalist.' (Hilferding, 1910:224). Issuing more shares, borrowing money to buy new machines, it is the great achievement of the modern corporation that, 'independent of the size of individual amounts of capital', it 'can draw directly upon the combined capital of the capitalist class' (Hilferding, 1910:122, 123).

Hilferding, like Schumpeter, believed that the capital market had turned business expansion loose. In contrast to Schumpeter, however, he argued that the banks as a sector were doing more than merely putting credit at the disposal of enterprise: 'They become founders and eventually rulers of industry, whose profits they seize for themselves as finance capital.' (Hilferding, 1910:226). The banks have power and they want to make it into dominance: 'Finance capital signifies the unification of capital.' (Hilferding, 1910:301). The banks even now are the true but secret name for the commanding heights. Few people, Hilferding wrote, realise just how far the tentacles extend: 'Taking possession of six large Berlin banks would mean taking possession of the most important spheres of large-scale industry.' (Hilferding, 1910:368).

The banks skew credit towards large firms and away from small: productive economies aside, a loan to a corporation is easier to police. The banks hold similar blocs of shares and send their delegates to the same boards of directors: involved in common projects, they are in a strong position to promote cartels and encourage amalgamation. The banks themselves regard each other as legitimate takeover targets: 'In this way, the tendency of both bank capital and industrial capital to eliminate competition coincides.' (Hilferding, 1910:191). Adding together the underwriting, the co-ownership, the supervision, the personal connections, the promotion of concentration, what emerges is an image of the bank as a Machiavellian which is closer to Lenin's *Imperialism* (itself influenced by Hilferding's book) than it is to Schumpeter's more permissive, less manipulative interpretation of the flow of funds, alongside land, labour, capital and entrepreneurship, as 'the fifth constituent' (Morishima and Catephores, 1988:42) that makes the economy grow.

Schumpeter writes of credit where Hilferding writes of control. He makes little reference to centralised control monopolised by the intermediary interest. He shows little concern that the independence of industry might be swallowed up by the octopus of finance. Hilferding sees the banker as the supreme capitalist who manages the evolution into monopoly and predatory pricing. Schumpeter, more modestly, sees the banker as a credit-creator who passively accommodates his supply to the demand.

Yet credit remains integral to his definition; and Schumpeter for that reason had to acknowledge that paper was at or near the economic heart of production. Schumpeter in one place writes that the banker is 'the capitalist par excellence .... He is the ephor of the exchange economy' (Schumpeter, 1912b:74). Schumpeter in another place writes that 'the money market is always, as it were, the headquarters of the capitalist system' (Schumpeter, 1912b:126). The rhetoric is vintage Hilferding. The meaning, however, falls somewhat short of brokering a share-swap in order to corner a trade. The Schumpeterian money-merchant, more specifically, is the ephor of enterprise – 'the capitalist par excellence' (Schumpeter, 1912b:74) – to the extent that he fulfils two functions and two functions alone.

First, he is a source of funding for start-up entrants who by definition have little resourcing of their own. Credit is less important in the ongoing corporation where profits lead to investment and investment leads to profits: Schumpeter's evolutionary schema is less favourable to bankers than is that of Hilferding. Credit, on the other hand, is vital for the dynamic 'new combinations' of insightful new innovators: it is clearly Schumpeter's lenders as well as Schumpeter's entrepreneurs that make capitalist development a practical possibility.

Second, the banker is a screen, a filter and a judge. Borrowers in a fully-employed economy must compete with one another for funds. While the applicant who outbids will have a definite advantage, banks as profit seekers have to take a view on the long-term prospects of the projects. Their risk-taking cannot be compared to recreational gambling, let alone to dangerous sports. Banks are aware that not all investments can be financed nor all initiators given purchasing power. In their choice lies their function. As Morishima and Catephores put it: 'It is the bankers who constitute the selection committees for investment plans – they are the helmsmen of the capitalist economy.' (Morishima and Catephores, 1988:45).

The Schumpeterian bank creates money and assesses risk. Both of these functions are active ones, indicative of a financial climate in which it was deemed acceptable for the bankers to back winners and restructure markets. Banks in such a society can be the ultimate levellers, the source of equality of opportunity so radical that (in contrast to the pecuniary entry-barriers of Marxian stratification or the rigid bloodlines of aristocratic Vienna) any worker can found an enterprise if he can convince the money-men that he has the aptitude and the will to succeed. Nowadays, Schumpeter writes, 'it is leadership rather than ownership that matters': 'Risk bearing is no part of the entrepreneurial function. It is the capitalist who bears the risk.' (Schumpeter, 1939:I,103, 104). Thus do the money-men make possible an open road and an equal chance that welfare interventionists like Tawney would expect from comprehensive schooling and the National Health rather than from the narrow acquisitiveness of speculative talent-spotters who bankroll fresh potential.

Credit means the future. The innovator approaching the banker is making a statement about the history-to-come that he hopes to create: 'The most typical embodiment of future values is a new undertaking.' (Schumpeter, 1912a:170). Bankers in granting the loan are taking a view on embryonic expectations and unborn consequences. Perhaps they are signalling as well that, trust once established, they will continue to put money into the firm. Their action triggers off a sociological money-multiplier. The fact that one bank has lent serves as a reference that encourages other banks to lend. The echo effect is an important reason why the bank must assess each project prudently. No bank wants to lose its good name.

Credit also means the past. The banker must have a knowledge of the economic system, of the profits that can reasonably be achieved in a sector, even of the concrete borrower himself: 'He must also know the customer, his business, and even his private habits.' (Schumpeter, 1939:I, 116). Bankers in selecting projects are at the same time appraising individuals. In backing winners, they are making an evaluation which is not anonymous but personal. Their own profits as entrepreneurs are a reflection of their ability to tell the con-man from the visionary when they drink with the local talent-pool at the Chamber of Commerce do. Schumpeter does not say if this will change should banking as well as industry become a distant bureaucracy in which house procedures crowd out the personal touch.

The banker–borrower relationship is surprisingly rooted in an ongoing nexus. The institution of credit, more generally, it itself a hand from the past. In contrast to the barter swap, fiduciary paper is widely accepted for no better reason than the fact that it is widely accepted. It is a going concern. As with every contract made between strangers and their descendants, it has earned its legitimacy and has something to defend. Its grizzled looks convince the sceptical that it has stood the test of time. The past smoothes the way for the future. Without the institution of credit, the novelty of variation would never make its way upward from the word to the deed.

Schumpeter saw the money-man as the first rung on the ladder, the friend in need of the new entrant with an idea. Streissler, examining the evidence, said that even in pre-war Austria (let alone in more cautious Britain or the United States) the credit system was simply not as welcoming to the *ab initio* pacesetter as the rose-tinted Schumpeter believed it to be. Rather than the beardless whiz-kid, Streissler concluded, it was in fact the corporate bureaucracy with a track record and critical mass that was cornering the lion's share of the loans: 'Schumpeter misread the Austrian experience of the last two decades before World War One .... What was commonly called the "foundation of enterprises" thus basically was their drastic *reorganization*, not the starting of new enterprises but the act of giving old enterprises *a new start.*' (Streissler, 1982:74, 75).

Industrial restructuring, Streissler notes, is clearly an entrepreneurial activity in the sense of Schumpeter on 'new combinations'. Even so, he continues, the emphasis is different. Schumpeter expected the borrower to make the first move. In the Austrian experience, however, it was the lender that banged the heads together: 'In that case it was the *banks* that were the innovators not the reorganized industrial firms. For it was the banks that took the leading role; and they were by then old established firms, not newly created enterprises.' (Streissler, 1982:75). It was the established bank that came up with the idea. It was the established firm that got the cream. The result was giants lending to giants and a degree of cartellisation which is difficult to reconcile with Schumpeter's expectation of contestability through credit: 'Quite in contrast to Schumpeter the banks thus *impeded* competition and in consequence *decreased* the spread and adoption of new ideas in production.' (Streissler, 1982:76). Capitalism was Hilferding more than it was Schumpeter. Be that as it may, it was credit-dependent and thus Schumpeter's capitalism nonetheless.

4.2 THE ENTREPRENEUR

Schumpeter criticises Adam Smith for flattening the theory of economic growth into a single over-simplified cause: 'Nobody, either before or after A. Smith, ever thought of putting such a burden upon division of labor. With A. Smith it is practically the only factor in economic progress.' (Schumpeter, 1954:187). Schumpeter criticises Adam Smith for concentrating on a single variable when the truth is the bundle. Schumpeter himself may in turn be criticised for homing in not on land, labour, capital as a wonderland of possibilities but on the intuition and the determination that convert the promises into outcomes. One of Schumpeter's most lasting contributions was his insistence that entrepreneurship is at once a unique factor of production and the scarce social input that makes economic history unfold. From his *Theory of Economic Development* to his *Capitalism, Socialism and Democracy*, in his *Business Cycles* and in his three late papers – 'Comments on a plan for the study of entrepreneurship' ('The creative response in economic history') (1947), 'Theoretical problems of economic growth' (1947), 'Economic theory and entrepreneurial history' (1949) – that reflect his association with Arthur H. Cole's interdisciplinary Research Center in Entrepreneurial Studies at Harvard, Schumpeter returned again and again to the high Marshallian theme of 'the pioneering effort of constructive imagination' (Marshall, 1923:72). With J.A. Schumpeter it is practically the only factor in economic progress.

4.2.1 Creative Destruction

Capitalism, Schumpeter said, is a system that never sleeps: 'Capitalism ... is by nature a form or method of economic change and not only never is but never can be stationary.' (Schumpeter, 1942a:82). The capitalist system is not *stasis*, inertia or equilibrium. Rather, it is a vessel that never arrives at its port: 'In dealing with capitalism we are dealing with an evolutionary process.' (Schumpeter, 1942a:80). Capitalism is evolution. Evolution is change: 'In the wider sense it comprises all the phenomena that make an economic process non-stationary.' (Schumpeter, 1954:964).

One manifestation of capitalism's changefulness is its steady expansion, its linear growth. A more decisive indicator of its eternal restlessness, its permanent mutation, would be the novelty and the newness that shatter old moulds and give their successors no guarantee of long life: 'The fundamental impulse that sets and keeps the capitalist engine in motion comes from the new consumers' goods, the new methods of production or transportation, the new markets, the new forms of industrial organization that capitalist enterprise creates.' (Schumpeter, 1942a:83). Capitalism is the shifting frontier. It is more than passive adaptation and simple extrapolation from the past.

Capitalism is a system that incessantly reinvents itself because its home is the tempest that transforms all into disturbance: 'Every situation is being upset before it has time to work itself out. Economic progress, in capitalist society, means turmoil.' (Schumpeter, 1942a:32). Capitalism is a system that incessantly shifts its ground, that 'incessantly revolutionizes the economic structure *from within*, incessantly destroying the old one, incessantly creating a new one. This process of creative destruction is the essential fact about capitalism. It is what capitalism consists in and what every capitalist concern has got to live in.' (Schumpeter, 1942a:83). Capitalism, in short, is insight and obsolescence, disequilibrium and discontentment. It is the creation of a new experiment and the destruction of an old reality. It is not the quiet life.

Schumpeter says that creative destruction is 'the essence of capitalism' (Schumpeter, 1942a:104n). It is the economic logic of an unsentimental order that is driven by its inner dynamic forever to move on. A stationary economy, reactive, repetitive and routine, is a circular flow that admits of no surprises or shocks, 'an unchanging economic process which flows on at constant rates in time and merely reproduces itself' (Schumpeter, 1939:I, 35-6). Capitalism, bringing not peace but a sword, has little in common with the uninterrupted repetition, the unquestioning traditionalism, of the administered structure that, qualitatively as well as quantitatively, refuses to sample new dishes or try out new styles: 'Whereas a stationary feudal economy would still be a feudal economy, and a stationary socialist economy would still be a socialist economy, stationary capitalism is a contradiction in terms.' (Schumpeter,

1943:179). Schumpeter writes that 'capitalist reality is first and last a process of change' (Schumpeter, 1942a:77n). The change is the essence. Absent creative destruction, what remains would be perpetual imitation and thus not the essence of capitalism at all.

Marx and Engels in the *Manifesto* had brought out the unprecedented association between capitalism and creative destruction with a clarity that was not common in the early industrial society of 1848:

> The bourgeoisie cannot exist without constantly revolutionizing the instruments of production, and thereby the relations of production, and with them the whole relations of society. Conservation of the old modes of production in unaltered form, was, on the contrary, the first condition of existence for all earlier industrial classes. Constant revolutionizing of production, uninterrupted disturbance of all social conditions, everlasting uncertainty and agitation distinguish the bourgeois epoch from all earlier ones. (Marx and Engels, 1848:83).

Economic relations in the bourgeois epoch 'become antiquated before they can ossify' – and 'all that is solid melts into air.' (Marx and Engels, 1848:83).

It is a remarkable achievement. No class in history has ever shaped events and created facts to the extent that the bourgeoisie has done: 'It has been the first to show what man's activity can bring about.' (Marx and Engels, 1848:83). Schumpeter was convinced that Marx and Engels had been correct in their assessment of a historical watershed. What they, however, saw as the function of the bourgeoisie as a whole, Schumpeter believed to have been the contribution of a revolutionary sub-set within the class. The crucial difference, as Rothschild suggests, lies in the distinction between technology and competition on the one hand, the daring independence that seizes opportunities on the other: 'In a simplified way one could say that in the case of Marx it is capitalist development which creates the capitalist, while in the case of Schumpeter it is the entrepreneur who creates capitalist development.' (Rothschild, 1986:191). Rothschild is right. In the case of Marx things somehow happen and the bourgeoisie wakes up in charge. In the case of Schumpeter, however, it is the entrepreneur who creates the creative destruction that makes economic history stand up and cheer.

4.2.2 The Agent of Change

Schumpeter offers the following definition:

> The function of entrepreneurs is to reform or revolutionize the pattern of production by exploiting an invention or, more generally, an untried technological possibility for producing a new commodity or producing an old one in a new way, by opening up a new source of supply of materials or a new outlet for products, by reorganizing an industry and so on. (Schumpeter, 1942a:132).

Whether in the marketing of the product or the implementation of a breakthrough, the essence of the function consists in the economic adaptation of under-utilised newness. The entrepreneur is a person who can turn unrecognised novelty to economic advantage: 'The carrying out of new combinations we call "enterprise"; the individuals whose function it is to carry them out we call "entrepreneurs".' (Schumpeter, 1912b:74). It is the task of the entrepreneur not to *create from nothing* but to *put into practice*. In that way he translates inventions into innovations and makes microeconomics into free-wheeling search.

The entrepreneur is a pioneer who is able to 'act with confidence beyond the range of familiar beacons' (Schumpeter, 1942a:132). He is a leader who shakes up existing patterns and ventures into untried speculations that vacillating followers fear could end in failure. He is, in short, a pathbreaker who lays out a new road rather than a custom-controlled conservative proceeding unthinkingly down a logic-less track that time-out-of-mind has rendered sacred through spiritless repetition: 'His characteristic task – theoretically as well as historically – consists precisely in breaking up old, and creating new, tradition.' (Schumpeter, 1912b:92). The entrepreneur is the romantic poet's ego that eternally denies, the bold individualist's refusal to accept that the done thing is wise, the Weberian's charisma which accounts for disruption and redirection, the Hegelian's self-confident superhero who rewrites the rules of the game. He is not the contented conformist's socially-integrated businessman who ensures that his buying and selling never tests the limits of the shared way of life.

In aristocratic Vienna (where bankers were on the fringes of the upper class but merchants and manufacturers were tainted with new money that respected no roots), in sedate and stifling Vienna (where the challenge of bohemians like Klimt, Schönberg, Ernst Mach, had done little to alleviate the overarching consensus that there was little need for change), the entrepreneur will have been seen as a deviant and a misfit who regrettably disturbed an equilibrium that was not his to waste: 'Turn-of-the-century Vienna rejected most things different, including new ideas and innovations. Business and bureaucracy combined to stymie inventions and new products and processes and discouraged those who wanted to make improvements.' (Allen, 1991:I, 53). It was, in such a culture, a major departure from the canons of social respectability for Schumpeter, like Menger and Wieser, to glorify a dissident troublemaker who set at nought the tried-and-testeds of his fellow citizens. As Streissler writes: 'If it was already bad taste in Schumpeter's Vienna to speak highly of mere entrepreneurs, it was absolutely shocking in a conservative civil service state to praise anyone for creating disorder and worst of all to suggest that the creation of unrest could have a useful social function, could further material development.' (Streissler, 1982:67). Schumpeter first developed his theory of economics as entrepreneurship not in the go-ahead United States of the pro-business 1940s but in the complacent Vienna of 1906 and 1911. No one in the Harvard Business School or in Arthur C. Cole's interdisciplinary centre would have been especially shocked by the following dismissal of the 'man of equilibrium' as a man without fire: 'What a pathetic figure is the economic actor who is always searching anxiously for an equilibrium. He has no ambition and no entrepreneurial spirit. He is, in short, without force and life.' (Schumpeter, 1908:567). It was a far more shocking thing to say in the complacent Vienna of the Hofburg, Eisenstein and the Opera Ball.

Economic development is the work of mind more than it is the gift of matter: 'Economic progress is not *primarily* the result of an increase in factors of production, but the result of applying the quantities of them already existing to ever new ends and by ever changing methods.' (Schumpeter, 1927b:40). Economic development is not *primarily* the knee-jerk blending-in of more inputs with existing inputs, an 'unchanging repetition of the productive and consumptive process' (Schumpeter, 1935:139) that leaves the end products and the technologies comfortably unquestioned. Instead, economic development is *primarily* the radical infusion of new insights that open new doors, 'the unremitting efforts of people to improve according to their lights upon their productive and commercial methods, i.e., ... the changes in technique of production, the conquest of new markets, the insertion of new commodities, and so on.' (Schumpeter, 1935:138). Economic development, in sum, is not *primarily* the result of more labour and more savings but the result of irreverent alteration, endogenous and active: 'This historic and irreversible change in the way of doing things we call "innovation" and we define: innovations are changes in production functions which cannot be decomposed into infinitesimal steps. Add as many mail-coaches as you please, you will never get a railroad by so doing.' (Schumpeter, 1935:138).

Innovations are major departures which ride roughshod over the pusillanimous Prufrocks. Their actualisation is the task of the entrepreneur: 'The individuals who carry out [innovations] we call Entrepreneurs.' (Schumpeter, 1939:I, 102). The entrepreneur is 'the bearer of the mechanism of change' (Schumpeter, 1912b:61n), the creative destroyer who controls and directs: 'The defining characteristic is simply the doing of new things or the doing of things that are already being done in a new way.' (Schumpeter, 1946c:412). Entrepreneurship is a marketing strategy for a new consumable like toothpaste, the roll-out of an unimagined input like synthetic rubber, the adoption of a cheaper energy source like wind. It is the establishment or elimination of a cartel or a monopoly position. It is the opening up of a new trade route such as a canal at Suez which Leibniz had proposed but had had too little of the winner's determination himself to take beyond the drawing board. Entrepreneurship is innovation and the actualisation of innovation. It is no more nor less than that.

Entrepreneurship is at once the creation of the new and the destruction of the old. Successful entrepreneurship, more specifically, presupposes that the agent of change will be in a position to draw upon two core competencies: 'The entrepreneurial performance involves, on the one hand, the ability to perceive new opportunities that cannot be proved at the moment at which action has to be taken, and, on the other hand, willpower adequate to breaking down the resistance that the social environment offers to change.' (Schumpeter, 1946c:417). The first dimension is perceptual: the entrepreneur must be open and alert to spot his chance. The second dimension is volitional: the entrepreneur must move with determination to get things done. The successful entrepreneur, if his innovations are indeed to have an impact on the course of events, must be in a position to draw upon each of the two banks of skills.

Thus, at the level of perception, the entrepreneur must have the capacity to notice things that 'lie outside of the routine tasks which everybody understands' (Schumpeter, 1942a:132). Unblinkered and free, he must be quick enough to recognise an underutilised opportunity and confident enough to steer clear of the autopilot rut that condemns the imitating capitalist to the mediocrity of duplication: 'Most members of the class are handicapped in this respect. They can follow suit only when someone else has already demonstrated success in practice.' (Schumpeter, 1927a:244). The entrepreneur, above all else, must be a visionary who has a non-rational, non-calculative flair for sensing what history-to-come will want to buy and sell: 'Here the success of everything depends on intuition, the capacity of seeing things in a way which afterwards proves to be true ... even though one can give no account of the principles by which this is done.' (Schumpeter, 1912b:85). Information is a bind: it is hard to recognise what one does not know or take the high-value turning at the least visible landmark. Uncertainty is worse: it is many times harder to perceive what the future will bring since, as Shackle says, 'what does not yet exist cannot now be known' (Shackle, 1972:3). Unknowledge is the ultimate challenge to rational expectations. Yet every business is condemned by its implementation-lags to make its choices in the radical darkness that goes before the plan.

Menger in 1871 had made Austrian economics the study of never-ending disruption that crunches underfoot the number-cruncher's projections: 'A process of change involves a beginning and a becoming, and these are only conceivable as processes in time.' (Menger, 1871:67). Shackle a century later continued the tradition of guess and exploration by insisting that 'Austrian' economics could only be the story of 'conflict and cut-throat struggle', of 'break-away, of origination, of poetic creation or innovation': 'We cannot claim Knowledge, so long as we acknowledge Novelty.' (Shackle, 1972:23, 26). Schumpeter was a horse from the same venerable stable. He had to be. Creative destruction, spelled out as epistemics, is not the comfortable automaticity of computing and calculation but rather 'new situations, which also occur as soon as external factors unexpectedly intrude', 'new possibilities of business action which are as yet untried and about which the most complete command of routine teaches nothing' (Schumpeter, 1939:I, 98). Creative destruction means that the business changes its character, that the entrepreneur is not only reacting to uncertainty but forging unknowledge because that is what he does. This much can be said with complete certainty: 'The major elements in such an undertaking simply cannot be known.' (Schumpeter, 1939:I, 100). All the rest will only be revealed once history-to-come has drawn aside the veil.

Since 'new possibilities' are the means and the ends, the identification of appropriate information is itself an entrepreneurial act. A leader who creates new data is not a statistician who tabulates the 'right' magnitudes. The economics textbook gives a misleading impression of how business decisions are actually made when it makes choices such as the investment decision a matter of impartial cost–benefits and not of the images which flash through the imagination when the battle is hot and bloody:

> The social logic or objective situation does not unequivocally determine *how much* profit shall be invested, and *how* it shall be invested, *unless individual disposition is taken into account*. Yet when that is done, the logic is no longer inherent solely in the system as distinct from the individuality of the industrialist himself. (Schumpeter, 1927a:242–3).

Capital does not invest itself. Capital must *be invested*. Mathematics cannot model the unknowns: there are as many auctioneers as there are equations since different people see different things at different times precisely because they are different. Accountancy cannot photograph the trade-offs: the future exists nowhere save in one-off's inexplicable psyche until such a time as he changes his mind. Only the individual can say what he perceives. Only methodological individualism can show what feels right.

Creative destruction makes it difficult or impossible to forecast and estimate:

> While in the accustomed circular flow every individual can act promptly and rationally because he is sure of his ground and is supported by the conduct, as adjusted to the circular flow, of all other individuals, who in turn expect the accustomed activity from him, he simply cannot do this when he is confronted by a new task .... What was formerly a help becomes a hindrance. What was a familiar

datum becomes an unknown. (Schumpeter, 1912b:79).

Information is a bind: because time is limited but action cannot be put off, the skill of the entrepreneur lies in grasping the essential and disregarding the unnecessary rather than in doing the impossible, 'surveying exhaustively all the effects and counter-effects of the projected enterprise' (Schumpeter, 1912b:85). Uncertainty is worse: where creative destruction is at work, it is difficult to gain a purchase on 'those data which the individual strives to alter', all but impossible to secure a measure of 'those which he wants to create' (Schumpeter, 1912b:84). Only a limited number of people have the capacity to sense what is likely to dwell within the crystal ball. They are the ones best suited, at the level of perception, to make an entrepreneur's impact on the course of things to come.

Then, at the level of volition, the entrepreneur must have the strength of purpose to stand up to a business environment that 'resists in many ways': 'To overcome that resistance requires aptitudes that are present in only a small fraction of the population and that define the entrepreneurial type as well as the entrepreneurial function.' (Schumpeter, 1942a:132). The entrepreneur finds alternative sources of finance when existing bankers refuse. He develops a new sales pitch or even a new product when consumers are indifferent. He shrugs off the opprobrium of the fashion-victim conformist who ostracises him because he stands out from the herd. The entrepreneur is a fighter who treats impediments as enemies to be vanquished. He fights to win. Temporary setbacks only strengthen his resolve.

In the beginning was the word. The idea was not enough: 'Keen intelligence and active fantasy', valuable as they may be, are 'as meaningless as the canals on Mars' (Schumpeter, 1912a:163) for the challenge that is economic life. What is essential is not just the blueprint but its realisation: 'The indispensable and decisive element is the deed.' (Schumpeter, 1912a:163). To conjure up new combinations is not to force through a revolution. Needed as well is the grit and the resilience that never says die.

A will of iron is a major business asset: 'Successful innovation is ... a task *sui generis*. It is a feat not of intellect, but of will. It is a special case of the social phenomenon of leadership.' (Schumpeter, 1928:65). Schumpeter was a social elitist who confided to his diary that 'the enemy is the sub-standard', that 'equality of men is the most stupid of all credos', that democracy is no more than the 'govt. of fools for the fools by the fools' (cited in Allen, 1991:II, 189, 190). He consistently reached the conclusion that masterless men will stand in need of strong leadership if they are to make their way through the warren of their lives: 'The majority of people do not function promptly by themselves and require help from a minority.' (Schumpeter, 1912b:87). There is devolved decision making and factored-down initiative in Schumpeter's theory of the entrepreneur. There is also the 'Great Man' acceptance of the lead from above which makes the entrepreneur into a *Führer* whose captaincy is the reason why the craft ever reaches its port.

Schumpeter, referring as he does to the 'minority' that gives its 'help', to 'a small fraction of the population' that defies all adversity, to the 'sub-standard' that is the 'enemy', to 'most' businessmen who only 'follow suit', gives the impression that he believes skills and talents to be unequal and concentrated. Reviewing Hayek's *Serfdom*, he reinforces the impression by insisting that the aptitudes of the vanguard innovators are not matched by the imaginings of the median citizen who nowadays runs the show: 'The principles of independent initiative and self-reliance are the principles of a very limited class. They mean nothing to the mass of people .... It is this majority that the economic achievement and the liberal policy of the capitalist age have invested with dominant power.' (Schumpeter, 1946b:270). It is not a happy thought in a dynamic economy where it is not the median but the supernormal who gets things done.

Schumpeter gives the impression that he believes entrepreneurial potential to be a sharply-tapered pyramid, that he sees business acumen as a natural resource in threateningly limited supply: 'This mental freedom presupposes a great surplus force over the everyday demand and is something peculiar and by nature rare.' (Schumpeter, 1912b:86). The impression that the paired talents of perception and volition are inevitably 'peculiar' and 'rare' itself forms a part of Schumpeter's world-view: Schumpeter likes to suggest that the stock of creative destroyers cannot significantly be increased but that it can be depleted to virtual exhaustion through creeping bureaucratisation. The impression aside, what Schumpeter really believed about the distribution of excellence is likely to have been considerably less exaggerated.

The endowment is unusual. Not, however, quite as unusual as one might have supposed: 'The ability to decide in favor of untried possibilities or to choose not only between tried but also between tried and untried ones ... should not be thought of as confined to a few exceptional cases.' (Schumpeter, 1939:I, 99). Perhaps the best of the best are so scarce as to constitute a bottleneck. The same, however, need not be said of the second-rate and the third-rate innovators who power the cycle through 'swarming' into areas of snowballing growth. Entrepreneurship is not a yes/no but rather a normal distribution (Schumpeter, 1912b:81n; 1927b:28n). It is a spectrum of frequencies that moves in step with the population as a whole. In the words of Wolfgang Stolper: 'An entrepreneur is someone who sees that things could be done differently and who actually *does* something about it .... As Schumpeter pointed out, such a person is not all that uncommon.' (Stolper, 1994:59).

However limited, however modest, almost all of us have within our make-up an element of entrepreneurship that gives us the potential to do something new.

4.3 ENTREPRENEURSHIP – WHAT IT IS NOT

Innovation is the creative destruction that makes the economy evolve. The entrepreneur is the agent of change who makes the untried into a fact. Schumpeter is no doubt as to the significance of his result: 'Carrying out innovations is the only function which is fundamental in history.' (Schumpeter, 1939:I, 102). It is intelligence and alertness, energy and determination, that crumble the cake of custom. It is entrepreneurship that replaces today's Pareto optimum with tomorrow's different new thing.

The mould-shattering function is the distinctive one. It is also the *only* function that marks out entrepreneurship as quintessentially itself. Entrepreneurship is innovation and the actualisation of innovation. It must not be confused with the four complementary functions of invention, risk-taking, error-correction and administration which in Schumpeter's economics of evolution are separate, distinctive and non-entrepreneurial in nature.

4.3.1 Invention

Schumpeter makes clear that the thrust of entrepreneurship is not *ab ovo* discovery but rather facilitation and incorporation: 'This function does not essentially consist in either inventing anything or otherwise creating the conditions which the enterprise exploits. It consists in getting things done.' (Schumpeter, 1942a: 132). Research and development are conducted in-house in the large corporation. The frontiers of science and of organisational sociology are pushed back in the universities. A Faraday or a Bell will always be curious about why birds can fly and how an atom is split. Adam Smith wrote of 'Wonder' and Veblen of 'Idle Curiosity'. Schumpeter took on board the familiar. Beyond that, he showed little interest in tracing economic newness back to its source.

Schumpeter's concern was not the laboratories and the test-tubes that make the new discoveries: 'It is entirely immaterial whether an innovation implies scientific novelty or not.' (Schumpeter, 1939:I, 84). Rather, his concern was the process through which new developments like electrical power and the motor car become commercialised into a new production-function: 'Innovation is possible without anything we should identify as invention and invention does not necessarily induce innovation.' (Schumpeter, 1939:I, 84). Innovation is not another name for invention. It is, qualitatively speaking, an entirely different activity. Entrepreneurship refers exclusively to innovation. An entrepreneur who also invents must be regarded as holding two different jobs at once. He 'by accident unites two separate functions' (Schumpeter, 1912a:178). He is the exception. He is not the rule.

4.3.2 Risk-taking

There is a temptation to conceive of the entrepreneur as a hands-on capitalist who chances his own assets. Schumpeter categorically rejects the self-improver's idealisation of the businessman as an enthusiast who backs the bee in his bonnet with a re-mortgage on his home: 'Risk-taking is in no case an element of the entrepreneurial function. Even though he may risk his reputation, the direct economic responsibility of failure never falls on him.' (Schumpeter, 1912b:137). The word 'never' means what it says. The failure will have cost him his good name and the best years of his life but at least his money will be safe.

The entrepreneur will usually have more ideas than cash. That is precisely the point. Schumpeter, as was noted in the first section of this chapter, believed that fresh promise will normally be able to secure venture capital from financial intermediaries. The lenders in that way take over from the ideas-man the exposure to loss: 'The entrepreneur is never the risk-bearer .... The one who gives credit comes to grief if the undertaking fails.' (Schumpeter, 1912b:137). Fresh promise does not need past savings in order to exploit an opportunity. Besides that, even if fresh promise can indeed draw upon personal accumulation, still its role as an innovator will be entirely separate from its contribution as a capitalist: 'The entrepreneurial function is not, in principle, connected with the possession of wealth.' (Schumpeter, 1912b:101).

Economists, Schumpeter wrote, think far too much about the savings flow and not nearly enough about kaleidic exploration. Savings counts, he said, but is nonetheless 'completely overshadowed by the fact that development consists primarily in employing existing resources in a different way, in doing new things with them, irrespective of whether those resources increase or not' (Schumpeter, 1912b:68). Creative destruction is the element that adds the value: 'It is leadership rather than ownership that matters.' (Schumpeter, 1939:I, 103). Loanable funds and paper titles are important primarily because they serve as the permissive infrastructure for the relentless dynamic – and absorb all the risk of loss.

4.3.3 Error-correction

The Schumpeterian entrepreneur is a discordant destroyer who disturbs an existing equilibrium and disrupts a self-perpetuating flow: 'While each burst of entrepreneurial innovation leads eventually to a new equilibrium, the entrepreneur is presented as a disequilibrating force.' (Kirzner, 1979:111). The Schumpeterian entrepreneur is an initiator *ex machina* who thrusts 'spontaneous, disjointed change' (Kirzner, 1979:117) upon a placid status quo. He earns his living from the opportunities which timely and indomitable intervention can create. The Schumpeterian entrepreneur seizes upon self-satisfied complacency and transforms it into unanticipated development. The architect of new realities, he has little interest in some 'seething mass of unexploited maladjustments crying out for correction' (Kirzner, 1979:119). Unresolved chords remain unfinished business in a supply-and-demand disequilibrium that the textbook auctioneer has neglected to re-balance. Unresolved or unfinished, they are not likely to be a major concern in the baseline state of rest that the Schumpeterian creator makes it his study to destroy.

Schumpeter sees the entrepreneur as a cause of disequilibrium. Israel Kirzner objects that so one-sided an approach conceals the very real contribution of alertness and speculation to the correction of an existing inconsistency:

> It fails to throw into relief how the tension generated by the existing maladjustments draws the corrective entrepreneurial activity. It fails to reveal how it is the *market* that permits all this to occur. On the contrary, the entrepreneurship around which Schumpeter builds his system is in principle equally applicable to the centrally planned economy. (Kirzner, 1979:119).

What Schumpeter calls entrepreneurship, Kirzner is saying, is in reality an explanation of innovation and technical change. It is not an explanation of entrepreneurship as the mechanism through which the market without the auctioneer deals with both the perceptual and the volitional challenges that must be met if discordant forces are to be brought into mutual accord.

Creative destruction is Hamlet. Arbitrage is the Second Norwegian Officer. Kirzner is critical of Schumpeter for presenting an unbalanced account of how enterprise, evolution *and* error-correction actually work together in the real-world marketplace: 'Instead of seeing only changes the entrepreneur has wrought, we must focus on the opportunities that were *waiting* to be grasped by the entrepreneur.' (Kirzner, 1979:119). Introducing the missing sensitivity to current surplus or glut, emphasising the profit motive as the reason to react, Kirzner is able to argue that the impact of the entrepreneur is to smooth the economy into equilibrium and not merely to push it away:

> The existence of an as yet unexploited opportunity for entrepreneurial profit means that the existing state of affairs, no matter how evenly it seems to flow, is a disequilibrium situation .... This situation is bound to change, and the existence of

> profit opportunities is the leaven that gives rise to the fermentation of change. Thus in our discussion the entrepreneur is the equilibrating force. (Kirzner, 1979:111).

The big breakthrough is an entrepreneurial act. Economising through market adjustment is something that also happens. Schumpeter knew about price signalling and awareness even as he knew about market penetration and foresight. Somehow the intra-institutional response was crowded out by the novelty that makes economic history move. The result is that an innovator who is also an allocator may be said to be fulfilling two separate roles at once. Only the first of those roles is purely entrepreneurial in the strict sense of Schumpeter.

4.3.4 Administration

Entrepreneurship, finally, is not the obedient administration of habitual precedent: 'Entrepreneurship, as defined, essentially consists in doing things that are not generally done in the ordinary course of business routine.' (Schumpeter, 1949b:259). The natural superintendent is blocked and bounded by yesterday's practice: 'Where the boundaries of routine stop, many people can go no further.' (Schumpeter, 1912b:80). The natural entrepreneur, on the other hand, recognises no such limits since his *terra incognita* has never been mapped. Guided only by his 'flashes of insight' and his superhuman daring, it is his fate to deal exclusively with cases 'in which combinations that are *not* inherited from the past have to be set up anew' (Schumpeter, 1949b:258). Calculation and precedent enable the natural bureaucrat to add mailcoaches to mailcoaches without the need for critical reappraisal or self-doubting introspection. What no one can extrapolate, however, is the introduction of the train.

Entrepreneurship is not the comfortable certainty of managed adaptation to a stable environment. Instead it is the uncommon capacity, deriving inspiration from unknowledge, to be a leader in the 'creation that spells the obsolescence and consequent destruction of any industrial structure of production that exists at any moment' (Schumpeter, 1949c:302). Administration is the efficient stewardship of a continuing order. Entrepreneurship is a dream made economic. It is the unusual ability to turn shifting sands into a personal and appropriable rent: 'Outside routine most people find it difficult – and often are unable to act; those who can are rare and therefore not subject to competitive conditions, whence the phenomenon of profit.' (Schumpeter, 1927b:33).

4.3.5 Profit

Profit in the Schumpeterian system is the reward that accrues whenever a 'new combination' is successfully introduced: 'Profit as a special and independent value phenomenon is fundamentally connected with the rôle of leadership in the economic system.' (Schumpeter, 1912b:147). Profit exists because the entrepreneur exists: 'It is the premium which capitalism attaches to innovation.' (Schumpeter, 1918:113). Without the perception and the volition, without the *sui generis* of 'supernormal intelligence and energy' (Schumpeter, 1942a:16) that commands its residual, there would be interest on capital, windfalls for alertness, wages for management but there would be no profits.

Profit is always a monopoly reward. Whether in the short run (until new entrants follow up the lead) or in the long run (because unique aptitude cannot be mass-produced at will), it can never reach a competitive or a 'normal' rate. Factor price equalisation is evidently not to be expected in the case of entrepreneurship. Individuals and experiments being so heterogeneous, there is no reason to think that profit rates will ever converge.

Profit arises only in dynamic and exploratory situations. It would be zero in Walrasian general equilibrium, in the classical stationary state or in fully-planned socialism that has gone beyond the need to search. Zero profit to Schumpeter implies zero interest. No one would pay to borrow if the return on the investment did not cover the cost.

Schumpeter's zero interest presupposes perfect foresight: people must know not only that the present flow is static but that the future aggregate will be precisely the same. It presupposes a constant population and an invariant age-structure: the savings of the young must be exactly equal to the dissavings of the old. It assumes that replacement investment is funded out of depreciation allowances: at least in the equilibrium trap the incumbent business is fully self-reproducing. It assumes that there is no money illusion: the real rate and the nominal rate must be identical since an error in perception would be incompatible with the circularity of the continuing flow.

Zero interest abstracts from time preference: current and coming utility are equally weighted in the indifference fields of the borrowers and of the lenders alike. Zero interest abstracts from motivation: it is not clear (save, arguably, in the case of the owner-manager who at least pays himself a wage) why a firm just covering its paid-out costs would want to keep its capital stock intact. Zero interest abstracts from 'the loan made for consumption', 'for the purposes of my discussion quite irrelevant' despite the concession that 'I may have underestimated it' (Schumpeter, 1913:449): even if firms do not borrow to expand their inputs, households might choose credit in order to increase their final satisfactions. Zero interest abstracts from functionality: even in planned socialism a discounting rate would be essential if the social opportunity-cost were rationally to be estimated. Schumpeter's limiting case was first expounded in his *Economic Development* in 1911. Since then, authors like

Böhm-Bawerk in 1913, Robbins in 1930, Samuelson in 1943 have objected that Schumpeter's long-run equilibrium theory presupposes, assumes and abstracts to such an extent as to describe a fictitious republic that no traveller has ever seen. As Clemence and Doody say: 'The matter may appear to be of little practical importance, since everyone agrees that such a limit, if it exists, has never been approximated.' (Clemence and Doody, 1950:30).

Most problematic of all is the status of the entrepreneur. Kirzner writes that there is no room for uncertainty and judgement where automaticity and gravitation have brought into being a position of rest: 'In equilibrium there is no room for the entrepreneur.' (Kirzner, 1973:26). Schumpeter, reversing the proposition, would characteristically have said the opposite – that, given the entrepreneur, there is no room for an equilibrium. The entrepreneur launches the cycle when something new attracts his attention. Logically speaking, he will be especially assiduous in seeking out hidden opportunities where the return on his existing investments has become unacceptably low. Since Schumpeter postulates that inventions are abundant and opportunities inexhaustible, one would expect that the dynamism will be ongoing. A process without a break, small changes rather than a sudden once-for-all, evolution will be closer to the spirit of Schumpeter's economics than is the limiting case of the zero-surplus society. Profit is safe. Profit, after all, is the reward to the astute and imaginative who manufacture unknowable empires and sometimes win.

5. Corporate capitalism

Schumpeter by *Capitalism, Socialism and Democracy* had decided that history was on the side of the large corporation, long-lived and powerful. His vision of the iron cage of organisation, private sector or public sector, extended at once to the triumph of the giant bureaucracy and the decline of the individual entrepreneur. Schumpeter, like Marx, predicted the concentration of capital and the withering away of the petty bourgeoisie (Schumpeter, 1942a:140). The small firm in market economics has long been held up as the exemplar of all that is best in responsiveness and rivalry. Whatever it may have been in the past, the present has a need for a more substantial meal. The perfect competitor 'is in many cases inferior in internal, especially technological, efficiency. If it is, then it wastes opportunities.' (Schumpeter, 1942a:106). Obsolescent and uneconomical, no one in the circumstances will be very sorry to see it go.

Schumpeter from the early 1920s was saying that the future lay in the economies of size and the research and development that protected the large and weeded out the small. In *The Theory of Economic Development* he had tended to look to towering individuals for major new departures. By *Capitalism, Socialism and Democracy* he was writing as if newness had become the collective function of the group – if indeed there would still be room for significant newness at all. The contrast between the Schumpeter of 1911 and the Schumpeter of 1942 will be discussed in Individual and team, the first section of this chapter.

Section 2 is entitled Competition and monopoly. Theorists of competitiveness like Smith and Walras had relied on a multiplicity of near-substitute alternatives to keep down the level of prices and costs. Schumpeter, extending a warmer welcome to monopoly and the restrictive understanding, turned instead to product development and contestable markets for the compromise that would enable large organisations to perform large tasks but would prevent the depredation-minded from holding their fellow citizens for ransom.

Section 3, Monopoly and innovation, returns the discussion to newness. Even if the old-style entrepreneur has been assimilated into the job description that his hierarchy has imposed, still the economic function of entrepreneur*ship* might live on and prosper within the large organisation that wants to expand its market share. Corporate capitalism could be the vanguard. If it is, then no one should assume that bureaucracy is *ipso facto* a threat to creative destruction. If it is not, then the loss of the old-style family firm might also mean the loss of the elasticity that prevents the capitalist economy from stagnating into a never-changing nine-to-five.

5.1 INDIVIDUAL AND TEAM

The young Schumpeter tended to look to individuals for great things: 'New enterprises are mostly founded by new men and the old businesses sink into insignificance.' (Schumpeter, 1912b:136). The older Schumpeter tended to look to structures for the impetus that keeps innovation in play: 'The carrying out of new combinations must become in ever greater measure the internal concern of one and the same economic body.' (Schumpeter, 1912b:67). Both the new entrants and the continuing structures are in evidence in the *Theory*. What was to alter was the emphasis. In his early work one person still made a difference. In his later work it was the 'great combines' that were coming up with the big ideas. Schumpeter had changed: the First World War that wiped clean the slate, the death of his wife, mother and child just before his paper to the British Association on which 'The instability of capitalism' was based, may have darkened his world view into a new pessimism that reflected his troubled state of mind. So, however, had the underlying reality that formed the basis for his investigation: 'The difference so made is great enough to serve as the water-shed between two epochs in the social history of capitalism.' (Schumpeter, 1912b:67).

5.1.1 Competitive Capitalism: Entry

Capitalism is newness. Newness in competitive conditions typically means new blood: 'Innovation in competitive capitalism is typically embodied in the foundation of new firms.' (Schumpeter, 1928:70). The young Schumpeter in *The Theory of Economic Development* treats major discontinuities as the proof that new entrepreneurs have discovered new opportunities: 'New combinations are, as a rule, embedded in new firms which generally do not arise out of the old ones but start producing beside them.' (Schumpeter, 1912b:66). Fresh tasks presuppose fresh faces. In the wide-open market it is the interloper and not the incumbent who typically creates the destruction.

The interloper wins because he mounts a credible challenge. The incumbent loses because he no longer has the capacity to compete. Schumpeter, praising the new contender, is careful to make clear that innovation succeeds not least because the old defender does not make a determined effort to stay ahead: 'In general it is not the owner of stage-coaches who builds railways.' (Schumpeter, 1912b:66). Were the incumbent better prepared to move with the times, the opposition would not have found it so easy to force the existing players into an unanticipated retirement.

Adaptation is difficult where an established firm was once an ambitious moderniser that sank its bygones single-mindedly in a narrow and specific line: 'Most new firms are founded with an idea and for a definite purpose.' (Schumpeter, 1939:I, 94). Time and tradition make it difficult for an established firm to call into question the very essence of its *raison d'être*. Heuristics and organisational memory, reproducing date-stamped filters handed on from the past, circumscribe still further the mental freedom that summons up the unprejudiced response: 'All knowledge and habit ... sinks into the strata of subconsciousness.' (Schumpeter, 1912b:84). New firms create new procedures in such a way as to grasp history by the throat. Existing firms follow existing precedents and miss out on the insider's head start that might have been theirs.

The new firm is able to draw upon the capacity for lateral thinking and the sensitivity to epoch-making transformation of the founder-entrepreneur who gets things done. The established firm, repeating the same tired lecture, is singularly susceptible to the void at the top. The flair for business is the grave's greatest conquest: 'The function of the entrepreneur itself cannot be inherited.' (Schumpeter, 1912b:79). The initial mould-breaker once removed from the scene, there is no reason to expect that his blood descendants will possess his ability to swim against the stream. Rather than opting for qualitative breakthrough they will probably prefer the safe haven of knee-jerk marginalism and slow growth through more of the same. They add on further stage-coaches and laugh at the railways that are not pulled by a horse. They are managers and perhaps even capitalists. What they are not is entrepreneurs. That is why the new entrant will leave them far behind in the race.

The model is Marshall, who compared evolving businesses to the trees of the forest. On the way up the young trees must fight their way through 'the benumbing shade of their older rivals' – and 'a few only survive'. At the peak of their powers those best adapted to the environment will thrive and stand out: 'One tree will last longer in full vigour and attain a greater size than another.' Once past their prime, all that remains for yesterday's successes is the compost heap that nurtures the next hardy growth: 'Sooner or later age tells on them all.' (Marshall, 1890a:263). The trees of the forest rise and fall from dust to dust. The business firm lives out the same organic progression: 'A business firm grows and attains great strength, and afterwards perhaps stagnates and decays.' (Marshall, 1890a:269). The strength of the 'able and enterprising manufacturer ... cannot last for ever' (Marshall, 1890a:378–9). Hungry young firms come in and snatch the trophy that the founding father has become too feeble to defend. All things considered, 'the full life of a large firm seldom lasts very long' (Marshall, 1890a:239).

Marshall in 1890 predicted that, a generation or so gone by, 'the business almost invariably falls to pieces' (Marshall, 1890a:250). In 1919 he was conceding that the new twentieth century had brought with it a new business environment in which it would be increasingly common for the large corporation to enjoy a 'potentially permanent life' (Marshall, 1919:316). The watershed was 1910, when Marshall first qualified his life-cycle theory of the firm with the observation that recent years had witnessed the growth of 'vast joint-stock companies, which often stagnate, but do not readily die' (Marshall, 1890a:263). One year before Schumpeter's *Economic Development*, Marshall in the sixth edition of his *Principles* was already anticipating what Schumpeter in 1928 and 1942 was going to announce – that the new business vanguard is less frequently the new tree in the forest, more frequently the existing mountain that remains the tops.

Professional management, the older Marshall wrote, had meant that businesses were more and more being run not by founding visionaries but by salaried meritocrats, 'by a *succession* of able men' (Marshall, 1919:727, emphasis added). Besides that, there had been over time 'a tendency to an increase in the size of individual businesses' (Marshall, 1897a:307). Economies of size make it difficult for a new entrant to gain access to a level playing-field: vigorous or not, the dinosaur first mover has a formidable head start. The future is likely to build even higher the entry barriers to new initiative: 'No doubt some of the forces that are working against the small producer are growing cumulatively.' (Marshall, 1919:248). What is true of the trees in the forest need not any longer be true of the firms in the market. Professionalisation and scale, the older Marshall wrote, are putting paid to that.

5.1.2 Corporate Capitalism: Structure

The older Schumpeter, like the older Marshall, shifted the emphasis from the singleton to the collective, from the passing to the permanent, from the entrant to the structure: 'Innovation is ... not any more embodied *typically* in new firms, but goes on, within the big units now existing, largely independently of individual persons.' (Schumpeter, 1928:70). The perspective is an evolutionary one. Entrepreneurship in early capitalism was like visible leadership in a military campaign: 'Napoleon's presence was, and had to be, actually felt on his battlefields.' (Schumpeter, 1942a:133). Entrepreneurship in later capitalism has come to be vested not in the strengths and insights of the wild man with a mission but in the matrix of abstractions which welds the interchangeable parts into a decision-making machine: 'Economic progress tends to become depersonalized and automatized. Bureau and committee work tends to replace individual action.' (Schumpeter, 1942a:133). Once it was the new entrant of genius who struck while the iron was hot. Nowadays it is more likely to be the impersonal mechanism that gets things done.

Schumpeter by *Capitalism, Socialism and Democracy* had reached the conclusion that the future did not augur well for the idiosyncratic commander with a personal and private image of what could be achieved: 'Rationalized and specialized office work will eventually blot out personality .... The leading man no longer has the opportunity to fling himself into the fray. He is becoming just another office worker – and one who is not always difficult to replace.' (Schumpeter, 1942a:133). The leading man does not, 'any more', have the opportunity to depose old production functions or force through ground-breaking transformations. Large-scale enterprise has meant a gradual dethronement of chieftaincy through a steady 'mechanization of progress' (Schumpeter, 1942a:131). The result is that the nominal leader in corporate capitalism will often be little more than a figurehead puppet who merely takes the chair:

> The entrepreneurial function may be and often is filled co-operatively. With the development of the largest-scale corporations this has evidently become of major importance: aptitudes that no single individual combines can thus be built into a corporate personality .... In many cases, therefore, it is difficult or even impossible to name an individual that acts as 'the entrepreneur' in a concern. (Schumpeter, 1947:261).

It is difficult or even impossible to identify the moving spirit in large-scale enterprise. The reason is simple. There is no single corporate executive who is in overall control.

Early capitalism is the individual. Large-scale enterprise is the group. The evolution from Schumpeter's *Development* to Schumpeter's *Capitalism* is the evolution from the owner-operator to the role in a script. Schumpeter, like capitalism, had changed and moved on.

The distinction is a real one. So, however, is the continuity. Even in his *Development* Schumpeter predicted that, 'with time and progressive rationalisation', the scope for the forceful personality who intuits beyond calculation was likely to be limited by the imperatives of the structure: 'Therefore the importance of the entrepreneur type must diminish.' (Schumpeter, 1912b:86). Even in his *Cycles* and in his *Capitalism* Schumpeter acknowledged that, joint effort undeniably emerging as the new locus of initiative, the new entrant still retained a presence on the high road to Damascus: 'There is ... an obvious connection between innovation and the rise of new industries, although, of course, innovation may also rejuvenate old ones.' (Schumpeter, 1939:I, 95n). *Natura non facit saltum*. Just as the young Schumpeter anticipated the institutionalisation of charisma, so, it is clear, could the older Schumpeter return to the history-specific entrepreneur to account for the bracing cold shower of change.

The older Schumpeter, lengthening with Marshall the lifespan of the business perennial that need never die, was clearly not above a pragmatic appeal to the circulation of elites that had dominated his trees-in-the-forest youth. *Business Cycles* in 1939 was especially strong in its insistence that fresh faces still played an essential part in rescuing the macroeconomy from the trough: 'Innovations are always associated with the rise to leadership of New Men.' (Schumpeter, 1939:I, 96). Clogs-to-clogs and new contenders remain the ultimate guarantee that an ageing monopolist will not appropriate forever a power position that pays him a rent of abuse: 'Even in the world of giant firms, new ones rise and others fall into the background. Innovations still emerge primarily with the "young" ones, and the "old" ones display as a rule symptoms of what is euphemistically called conservatism.' (Schumpeter, 1939:I, 97). Schumpeter in 1939 was clearly not above a pragmatic appeal to the 'new' and the 'young' who had made capitalism work in his early *Development* of 1911.

There is continuity in Schumpeter's economics even as there is a marked shift of emphasis. The reason is the inherent gradualism of social mutation itself. Schumpeter was an evolutionary thinker interested at once in the present-day cross-section and in the history-to-come that developmental tendencies would breed and form. It is all too easy to forget that Schumpeter denied that the future apocalypse had already come to stay: 'The sector of concerns which are "big" ... is not as yet great enough to dominate the picture in any country.' (Schumpeter, 1939:I, 97). Schumpeter extrapolated the structure. What he saw, however, was still the entrant on his own.

5.1.3 Group and Growth

Entrepreneurship is a function. The entrepreneur is a pulse. Sometimes the service will be delivered by an individual. Sometimes, however, the mould-breaking will be done by a group. Either way, the position is clear: 'The entrepreneurial function need not be embedded in a physical person.' (Schumpeter, 1947:260).

The United States Department of Agriculture had altered the future of farming through new methods and techniques: 'In this case then it was the Department of Agriculture that acted as an entrepreneur.' (Schumpeter, 1947:260). Primitives and socialists had risen to new challenges despite the fact that they could not rely upon gain-seeking iconoclasts: 'The entrepreneurial function itself is not confined to capitalist society, since such economic leadership as it implies would be present, though in other forms, even in a primitive tribe or in a socialist community.' (Schumpeter, 1939:I, 223). As with the civil servants, the savages and the State, so with the modern corporation. The entrepreneurial function need not wither away merely because the collective personality has made itself joint master of the change: 'Technological progress is increasingly becoming the business of teams of trained specialists who turn out what is required and make it work in predictable ways.' (Schumpeter, 1942a:132).

The reference to 'teams' and 'trained', the quiet confidence of 'progress' and 'required', look forward to the internal division of labour of Galbraith's education-intensive 'technostructure'. Galbraith anticipates that committees of experts, 'more than the sum of isolated individual contributions' (Galbraith, 1965:88), will take over the decision-making function: 'Instead of genius, the large corporation makes use of the combined efforts of many men of specialized but not remarkable ability. It substitutes organization for exceptional individual qualifications.' (Galbraith, 1960:121). Galbraith is full of praise for the 'synthetic personality' (Galbraith, 1965:88) that, collaborating as a board, is successfully delivering the breakthroughs. The later Schumpeter, he writes, had seen what was happening. The later Schumpeter was a man 'in whose system the innovating role of large enterprises is strongly emphasized' (Galbraith, 1952:86n). Galbraith is understandably disparaging about *The Theory of Economic Development*. This he regards as a period-piece classic that has been overtaken by events: 'The book has receded in interest with the decline of the entrepreneur, the innovating hero whom it celebrates and whose displacement by the corporate bureaucracy – the technostructure – is a lesser theme of this book.' (Galbraith, 1977a:74). Galbraith clearly believes that, in its vision of modern business as a shared undertaking, *Capitalism, Socialism and Democracy* is by far the more lasting contribution.

Capitalism, Socialism and Democracy reaches the conclusion that the entrepreneurial function can be exercised even within a network of interdependencies. That post-Weberian acknowledgement of the team is its link to Galbraith's optimistic *New Industrial State*. The problem is that Schumpeter, in contrast to Galbraith, also reveals serious doubts about the strength of the dynamic. Schumpeter, associating newness with monopoly as he does, expresses the fear that 'innovation itself is being reduced to routine': 'Rationalized and specialized office work will eventually blot out personality, the calculable result, the "vision".' (Schumpeter, 1942a:132, 133). In its early stages the capitalist revolution squeezed out the habitual: 'It is much easier now than it has been in the past to do things that lie outside familiar routine.' (Schumpeter, 1942a:132). The danger is that in its later stages it will squeeze out the imaginative non-conformity that keeps creative destruction from the stationary state.

A new business in its take-off phase is dependent on the ambition and determination of a strong-willed subversive who gets things done. Once it is a going concern, however, the adult corporation can be administered even by a nonentity who falls far short of a Rockefeller: 'Though it does require genius of the first order to build up, e.g., the Standard Oil concern, it does not require genius to run it once it has been built up.' (Schumpeter, 1942a:402n). The model is Weber's routinisation, the older Marshall's trees of the forest that cease to develop but refuse to die. It is a curiously static approach to a contestable market where new oligopolists keep incumbent corporations on their toes and new combinations must forever be anticipated or matched. Be that as it may, Schumpeter seems to be assuming that brand loyalties and entrenched lifestyles will contain fickle changefulness within the limits of the middle manager who is in no way the equal of the founding entrepreneur: 'Progress becomes "automatised", increasingly impersonal and decreasingly a matter of leadership and individual initiative.' (Schumpeter, 1928:71). The supply of greatness contracts as the need for greatness becomes a thing of the past: 'Personality and will power must count for less.' (Schumpeter, 1942a:132). The organisation is rub-along. It has settled into a groove.

Radical entrepreneurship would be positively dysfunctional in so conservative a setting. The structure in place, the premium shifts from inspiration to quantification in order to make existing systems function well. Calculative rationality has little room for the gut reactions of the disequilibrium visionary who demands something new: 'The entrepreneurial function, owing to the steady expansion of the range of the calculable, is bound to become obsolescent.' (Schumpeter, 1942a:417n). Creative destruction is slowing from a run to walk. A good filing system is taking the place of the sudden unexplainable Eureka: 'The romance of earlier commercial adventure is rapidly wearing away, because so many more things can be strictly calculated that had of old to be visualized in a flash of genius.' (Schumpeter, 1942a:132).

What this presumably means is that people who can manipulate numbers on a computer screen will improve their static efficiency but will never dream up new resorts in mangrove swamps or recognise mass markets in the breakdown of caste. There used to be castles in the air. Now there are robots on expense accounts. If this is Schumpeter's point, then his deduction, as misleadingly Ricardian as the misplaced *ceteris paribus*, is not entirely fair. Measurement and flair are not substitutes but complements. Even genetic engineering or state-of-the-art inn-keeping can, after all, benefit from a rigorous use of information technology such as allows the decision maker the freedom to specialise on those acts of faith that cannot be left to mechanistic estimation alone.

As with quantification, so with administration. Capitalism pushes out the less efficient technologies and rationalises concentrated production in the Weber-like professional hierarchy: 'The largest scale unit of control is the consequence, and the largest scale unit of control tends to develop into something akin to a department of state, that is to say, it becomes bureaucratized and mechanized and the individual in that kind of a world counts for less than before.' (Schumpeter, 1941:359). Civil service or corporate service, it is function and not personality that processes the P33s and watches the clock. There is, Schumpeter writes, a 'difficulty, inherent in the bureaucratic machine, of reconciling individual initiative with the mechanics of its working': 'Often the machine gives little scope for initiative and much scope for vicious attempts at smothering it.' (Schumpeter, 1942a:207). Discouraged by 'blighting criticism of the efforts of others' (Schumpeter, 1942a:207), frustrated into repetitiveness by the bureaucrat's sense of futility, the non-conforming spirit gives up his attempt to become a Napoleon on horseback and reserves his best energies for his tea breaks and his stamp collection instead.

Schumpeter's conclusion is that narrowness has a soporific effect. People do not try new experiments since their performance assessment is based on a job description that the past has handed on. What this neglects, however, is that there is a difference between the quasi-Marxian estrangement of the desk-potato pen-pusher and the in-depth knowledge, the tried-and-tested rules of thumb, that empower the experienced office holder to think the unthinkable. A marketing manager may not be allowed to stray too far from the product assigned: that far is he trapped in the box. Yet his discovery of new outlets and appeals will nonetheless be a cause of congratulation and promotion: to that extent his formal status may have given him the chance to get ahead. Besides that, there can be discretion and devolution, quality circles and bonus schemes, within the parameters of the Weberian precommitment. Schumpeter himself writes as follows about the survival of enterprise *within* the large organisation: '"Giant" concerns ... often are but shells within which an ever-changing personnel may go from innovation to innovation.' (Schumpeter, 1939:I, 96). Large size can facilitate the process of innovation. Innovation need evidently not atrophy merely because wild men must hunt together in packs.

Evolution in any case is mere speculation in the absence of the facts. Schumpeter was too much of an empiricist to make a prediction without calling for the evidence. Convinced that entrepreneurship was in decline, he cautiously says: 'This is at present only an impression. It is for the historian to establish or to refute it.' (Schumpeter, 1946c:418). Business histories and even biographies of proven leaders are required, disaggregated by country and by branch of trade. Statistics must be collected on the change over time in the percentage of scientists, engineers and other graduates in the firm's labour force and on each firm's total expenditure on research and development. Data is needed on the number of patents registered, patents cited, patents (an *impact* indicator that is the *commercial* essence of newness) actually employed in the process of production. The facts are essential. Conjectures otherwise are no more than one person's opinion.

The proxies are a step in the right direction. Even so, they can never be more than an indication. Schumpeter did not recognise the near-impossibility of finding out the truth. Recorded inputs cannot unravel the secret of why it is that different firms score different outcomes even with the same know-how stock. Nor is it easy to make an estimate of the know-how stock itself. Not all innovations lend themselves to a patent. There is no good measure of tacit knowledge embedded in a house-own heuristic. There is no way to put a value on an internal reorganisation, a new source of supply, a new marketing strategy – all of them innovations in the sense of Schumpeter. Most of all is it difficult to assemble reliable information about the future reality to which Schumpeter's hypotheses explicitly refer. Present-day facts may suggest what is to come. What they cannot do is to confirm it.

Magic has been routinised. Rationality and bureaucracy stamp out initiative. Even allowing for the untestability of the evolutionary, Schumpeter in the end decided that restless search was vanishing into economic history, perpetuated by structure: 'This social function is already losing importance and is bound to lose it at an accelerating rate.' (Schumpeter, 1942a:132). Schumpeter was able to foresee a future in which creative destruction would disappear into the locked box of self-perpetuation: 'I hold that with increasing mechanization of industrial "progress" (teamwork in research departments and so on) this element and with it the most important pillar of the capitalist class's economic position is bound to crumble in time.' (Schumpeter, 1942a:411). A period of unprecedented novelty is drawing to a close. It is a development that Schumpeter regarded as retrograde and unhealthy. Evolution is evolution, however. Undesirable or not, we today must start from here.

5.2 COMPETITION AND MONOPOLY

Market liberals have been attracted by the ideal of the numerous and the passive. Neoclassical economists have tended to deny that concentrated power can be the source of allocative or productive efficiency. Schumpeter's position is different. Perfect competition, he maintains, is inferior to the large-firm alternative. The small price-taker 'has no title to being set up as a model of ideal efficiency': 'In the last resort, American agriculture, English coal mining, the English textile industry are costing consumers much more and are affecting *total* output much more injuriously than they would if controlled, each of them, by a dozen good brains.' (Schumpeter, 1942a:106). Competition among the few means freshness and improvement. Competition among the many leads to stagnation and waste.

Large-pool competition secured a more economical use of scarce resources than had the feudal traditionalism that went before it. Schumpeter's point is that big-business capitalism is more economical still: 'The actual efficiency of the capitalist engine of production in the era of the largest-scale units has been much greater than in the preceding era of small or medium-sized ones.' (Schumpeter, 1942a:189). Increasing size has made possible technological and organisational renewal that textbook competition could never have equalled: 'How modern capitalism would work under perfect competition is hence a meaningless question.' (Schumpeter, 1942a:189). It is a meaningless question for the simple reason that it has been big business and not small business that has delivered the unprecedented rise in wealth and living standards. As Galbraith has put it: 'Large tasks require large organizations. That is how it is.' (Galbraith, 1977b:277).

5.2.1 Improvement

Schumpeter is not alarmed by the undergraduate spectre of anaconda corporations that set prices in excess of marginal cost, restrict output despite the rise in the U-shaped average, squeeze out their windfall through pressing hard on the inelasticity of demand. Static inefficiency can undeniably be the consequence of bullying access to market power. Yet short-term price-setting is only a small part of what it means to be the market leader:

> As soon as we go into details and inquire into the individual items in which progress was most conspicuous, the trail leads not to the doors of those firms that work under conditions of comparatively free competition but precisely to the doors of the large concerns ... . Big business may have had more to do with creating that standard of life than with keeping it down. (Schumpeter, 1942a:82).

Big business is in the eye of the tornado. New methods of production (mechanisation, electrification), new goods and services (railways, cars), new titles and jurisdictions (mergers, joint-stock companies) – few of these disturbances that are also improvements would have come about had time-warped economists been believed when they insisted that once-was small business had to remain the signpost that points the way back to the Eden that was lost. Galbraith has expressed the condition well: 'In concentrating on the inefficiency of the steam engine – specifically the fact that it is not being worked at ideal capacity – [economists] have failed to notice that the owner was designing a gas turbine.' (Galbraith, 1952:92).

Like Schumpeter, Galbraith has welcomed the large-scale establishment precisely because it opens the frontier to new settlers and dispatches new ships on their voyage of exploration:

> A benign Providence ... has made the modern industry of a few large firms an excellent instrument for inducing technical change. ... There is no more pleasant fiction than that technical change is the product of the matchless ingenuity of the small man forced by competition to employ his wits to better his neighbor. Unhappily, it is a fiction. (Galbraith, 1952:86).

Scale spreads the overheads of product development. Diversification balances unforeseeable failures with high-profit success. Large organisations have the critical mass that gives them the freedom to try new experiments. Restricted production-runs do not. The result is that they have decisively been left behind by economic change: 'By all but the pathologically romantic, it is now recognized that this is not the age of the small man.' (Galbraith, 1967:42). Like Schumpeter, Galbraith is happy that history gave the small man the chance to make his mark. Like Schumpeter, Galbraith also believes that it is time for the economics of improvement to move onward with events: 'Technical development has long since become the preserve of the scientist and the engineer. Most of the cheap and simple innovations have ... been made.' (Galbraith, 1952:86). Smith started from Watt. We today, however, must start from Ford.

Large size can be in the public interest. Just as Galbraith writes that 'there must be some element of monopoly in an industry if it is to be progressive' (Galbraith, 1952:88), so Schumpeter concludes that there exist economies of innovativeness that are 'secured only on the monopoly level' (Schumpeter, 1942a:101). In such cases the theory of static misallocation and distortion of signals must give way to the improving dynamics of quality upgrades, falling costs and even of lower prices: 'Current economic theory is almost wholly a theory of the administration of a given industrial apparatus. But much more important than the manner in which capitalism administers given industrial structures is the manner in which it creates them ... . And into this process of creation the monopoly element enters necessarily.' (Schumpeter, 1942a:412).

Current economic theory, assuming *ceteris paribus* in the cost curves and holding constant all but quantity and price, is guilty of 'stressing a secondary element and obscuring the essential one' (Schumpeter, 1939:I, 97n). The essential element is change – and for that reason it is size. Large size is 'the most powerful engine ... of the long-run expansion of total output' (Schumpeter, 1942a:106). It would clearly be an error to speak with Brandeis of 'the curse of bigness' or to make irresponsible use of anti-trust legislation where a rule of reason would in practice deliver a higher standard of living. Large units 'largely create what they exploit' (Schumpeter, 1942a:101).

Rather than smashing the monopolies into competitors, it would make sense for governments to encourage the process of merger and takeover in order to put stagnant smallness to rout.

5.2.2 Rivalry

Large size makes improvement possible. By itself, however, it is a necessary but not a sufficient condition. Dominance could be the cause of the quiet life in preference to the hurly-burly of creative destruction. It could also mean the functionless deadweight of monopoly profit where the defenceless consumer has no alternative but to pay. Large size by itself is neither a guarantee nor a safeguard. The large size of the incumbent challenged by the large size of the entrant is more likely to ensure that the social interest is not absorbed into the company's paunch.

Alfred Marshall was able to be complacent about monopoly because he was confident that 'a very high price would bring rival producers into the field' (Marshall, 1890a:238): 'Nearly all the monopolies, that are of any practical importance in the present age, hold much of their power by an uncertain tenure; so that they would lose it ere long, if they ignored the possibilities of competition, direct and indirect.' (Marshall, 1919:397). Schumpeter shared with Marshall the moving picture of an evolving market in which 'one capitalist always kills many' (Marx, 1867:763) and is in his turn undercut into bankruptcy by the new predator in the forest: 'A monopoly position is in general no cushion to sleep on.' (Schumpeter, 1942a:102). Natural monopoly fenced in by high fixed cost is one exception. Tariff protection conferred by generous public authority is another. The rule, however, is competition, current and potential. Even the single seller in the market is held in check by unborn adversaries who have yet to target their guns.

Thus it is that a monopolist in an industry potentially contestable will be well advised to keep his prices close to the normal profits earned by the perfect competitor. His economic dominance will inevitably tempt him to maximise his surplus. What he also knows, however, is that lucrative windfalls leave him exposed to the new rival with a new product, a new brand or a new technique. Such entry 'disciplines before it attacks' (Schumpeter, 1942a:85). High profits are 'the baits that lure capital on to untried fields' (Schumpeter, 1942a:90): 'Outside the field of public utilities, the position of a single seller can in general be conquered – and retained for decades – only on the condition that he does not behave like a monopolist.' (Schumpeter, 1942a:99). Competition does not have to be actual to keep prices down. Sometimes the mere possibility will be enough.

Schumpeter was able to welcome the perennial gale of appropriable opportunity not least because of his conviction that no conquest confers the market stranglehold for all time. Competition, clearly, is 'temporarily suspended' (Schumpeter, 1942a:105) whenever something new becomes the sole property of the first settler to arrive. The threat of abuse is real. The privilege for all that is unlikely to be more than short-run and transitory. Time must pass for there to be 'structural changes requiring price adjustments' (Schumpeter, 1942a:94n). Sometimes a considerable period of time must elapse: 'To do justice to aluminum, rayon, or motorcar prices one must survey a period of about forty-five years.' (Schumpeter, 1942a:94n). Dynamic efficiency does not bestow its favours on the spot: 'We must judge its performance over time, as it unfolds through decades or centuries.' (Schumpeter, 1942a:83). In the medium term, however, competition will reassert itself as imitators invade a sector that has done particularly well; while in the very long run a fresh breed of innovations will push existing monopolies into the history books and create new licences and leases for themselves. Large firms defend. Large firms attack. At the end of the day, natural selection tells on them all.

5.2.3 Stability

Large size means change. It also means the lack of change: 'In the process of creative destruction, restrictive practices may do much to steady the ship and to alleviate temporary difficulties.' (Schumpeter, 1942a:87). The business environment is a roller-coaster in search of its tracks: 'Long-range investing under rapidly changing conditions ... is like shooting at a target that is not only indistinct but moving – and moving jerkily at that.' (Schumpeter, 1942a:88). Less than full competition has the function that it stabilises investment on the model of insurance or hedging.

The phenomenon is the familiar one, that 'motorcars are travelling faster than they otherwise would *because* they are provided with brakes' (Schumpeter, 1942a:88). Applied to the business, patent protection is one means of sealing in the returns to a costly new launch and the non-aggression cartel a signal that a beggar-my-neighbour struggle is not about to relegate paid-out overheads to the scrap-heap:

> The main value to a concern of a single seller position that is secured by patent or monopolistic strategy does not consist so much in the opportunity to behave temporarily according to the monopolist schema, as in the protection it affords against temporary disorganization of the market and the space it secures for long-range planning. (Schumpeter, 1942a:102-3).

An imitation barrier such as a secret is 'on balance a propelling and not an inhibiting factor' (Schumpeter, 1942a:88n). A long-term contract or repeat-purchase tying 'may in the end produce not only steadier but also greater expansion of total output than could be secured by an entirely uncontrolled onward rush that cannot fail to be studded with catastrophes' (Schumpeter, 1942a:91). Creative destruction, in short, may occur not in spite of restrictive practices but rather because of the safe harbour that they provide.

Large size is conducive to conspiracy in restraint of chaos. It is also conducive to short-term price management in preference to ephemeral signals that sway with the winds. Price rigidity damps down cyclical, seasonal and random oscillations that are not the product of fundamental changes in supply and demand: 'Total output and employment may well keep on a higher level with the restrictions incident to that policy than they would if depression were allowed to play havoc with the price structure.' (Schumpeter, 1942a:95). Prices must naturally be re-pegged where there is an underlying evolution in market conditions. Schumpeter's point is that the response should not be premature since flexibility carried to excess can easily upset capitalism's delicate mechanism. Constant prices limit the unemployment and the bankruptcies. They allow for a breathing space until it becomes clear that the market change is a permanent one. In such circumstances, 'what looks like rigidity may be no more than regulated adaptation' (Schumpeter, 1942a:95).

Galbraith sees the giant firm as a planning unit able to control its environment. Given the heavy capital commitment and the long gestation period, it has lost its Smithian, Walrasian freedom to trade at the unmanipulated market price. Success being the consequence of clout, large size is often desired not so much to secure technological economies or even to maximise short-term profits as to win and retain a position of power. Size is essential if business conditions are to be moulded and shaped. And there is more: 'For this planning – control of supply, control of demand, provision of capital, minimization of risk – there is no clear upper limit to the desirable size.' (Galbraith, 1967:85). Big is beautiful. The small ship doesn't stand a chance in the storm.

Schumpeter pioneered the idea of the capitalist corporation as a planning unit. As Galbraith was to do, he argued that size and stability are two sides of a single coin. In small-scale capitalism, fully nine out of every ten would-be entrepreneurs are driven on to the rocks by the ill-starred and the unforeseeable (Schumpeter, 1939:I, 117). In large-scale capitalism the multi-period firm is more likely to enjoy the ratchet effect of business success that cannot be undone. This is not to say that it is able to opt out of time-lags and non-rational expectations, or that it can push to one side the outside disturbances that can devastate an accommodation. Floods, earthquakes, wars, gold discoveries, new countries, bad harvests are unpredictable exogeneities that must forever threaten a going circular flow. The crucial point is that the larger the firm is, the better placed it will be to minimise the harm that cruel fate sends its way.

One reason relates to capital. The fact that Schumpeter writes of new entrants borrowing start-up credit should not obscure the fact that he also writes of incumbent enterprises financing themselves out of internally-generated profits. The existing firm can opt out of the scrutiny that goes with bank loans and can expand through ploughing back even when money is tight. The transcendence of the individual innovator may in that way emancipate corporate entrepreneurship from outside control.

Routine work within a patterned organisation itself makes bureaucratised business more predictable. Ancestral practices and learned impersonality are believed by Schumpeter to trap office-holders in handed-on structures that are stronger on repetition than on inventiveness. Even if they are, the rationalisation of production does confer on the existing firm the considerable benefit that technology plus size means power: 'The more accurately ... we learn to know the natural and social world, the more perfect our control of facts becomes.' (Schumpeter, 1912b:85). The control of facts makes possible the fact of control. Business is always a leap in the dark. Always, 'action must be taken without working out all the details of what is to be done' (Schumpeter, 1912b:85). Large size at least makes it easier to standardise the procedures.

Just as precedents stabilise, so too does collusion: 'Enlightened cooperation between manufacturers will be able to reduce the amplitude of business fluctuations a great deal.' (Schumpeter, 1941:401). Cycles are endemic and evolution is imbalance: 'Industrial change is never harmonious advance with all elements of the system actually moving, or tending to move, in step.' (Schumpeter, 1939:I, 101). It is the great contribution of oligopolistic joint action that it makes prices rigid and protects market share. Without the reassurance of coordination through mutual support it would be more difficult for the business organisation to plan ahead.

The status of the consumer completes the story of size. Schumpeter is convinced that the initial disturbance will generally be the supply-side breach. As much as want-satisfaction is the *sine qua non* for sale, still it is the producer and not the consumer who is responsible for new tastes that, left to the demand-side alone, would have remained boring, 'given', and forever the same: 'It is ... the producer who as a rule initiates economic change, and consumers are educated by him if necessary; they are, as it were, taught to want new things, or things which differ in some respect or other from those which they have been in the habit of using.' (Schumpeter, 1912b:65). It is the producer and not the consumer who interrupts the equilibrium. It is the seller and not the buyer who gets things done.

Habit is no longer the barrier to novelty that it was in the pre-capitalist era of self-reproduction. The incessant stream of new consumables and new techniques means that people whose custom is change will not resist innovation but rather accept it as a matter of course. Expectations are dynamic – but expectations are not sales. What is crucial is that business leaders must be in a financial position to 'educate' public opinion, to 'teach' potential consumers. Persuasion is expensive, while advertising and salesmanship require mass sales to recoup the spend. The firm that has size on its side can play the game and fight to win. The perfect competitor is more likely to be a fish out of water in the tough new world of supplier-led demand.

5.3 MONOPOLY AND INNOVATION

Capitalism and technology, historically speaking, have been 'essentially one and the same thing': 'The former was the propelling force of the latter.' (Schumpeter, 1942a:110). Adam Smith had situated his theory of economic causality in the context of large-pool competition. Schumpeter, reappraising the nexus, concluded that it was power and not passivity that lay behind the process of unending change. The task of this section is to establish whether Schumpeter believed imperfect competition to be the cause or the consequence of innovation. It also suggests that he was too quick to write off the continuing contribution made by the small firm to development and advance.

5.3.1 Monopoly as Cause

Schumpeter states clearly that monopoly makes innovation possible: 'There are superior methods available to the monopolist which either are not available at all to a crowd of competitors or are not available to them so readily.' (Schumpeter, 1942a:101). Nowadays, outside of agricultural mass production, 'perfect competition is the exception': 'There cannot be many instances of it.' (Schumpeter, 1942a:78, 79). This is just as well. Pushing back the boundaries is 'the outstanding feature of the typical large-scale unit of control' (Schumpeter, 1942a:101). It is not the outstanding feature of the invisible competitor that lacks the staff, the assets and the turnover to make a success of evolutionary economics.

Schumpeter in 1939 wrote that economic progress in the United States was 'largely the result of work done within a number of concerns at no time much greater than 300 or 400' (Schumpeter, 1939:II, 1044). The potential for mistreatment was tremendous. Secular upgrading, however, more than validated the trust: 'A system – any system, economic or other – that at *every* given point of time fully utilizes its possibilities to the best advantage may yet in the long run be inferior to a system that does so at *no* given point of time, because the latter's failure to do so may be a condition for the level or speed of long-run performance.' (Schumpeter, 1942a:83). By 'a condition' Schumpeter means 'a precondition'. Without the strategic dominance that a pure Smithian would regard as a restrictive threat to allocative efficiency, the capitalist system would hardly be able to report any dynamic efficiency at all.

Scherer, studying Schumpeter, concludes that Schumpeter did in fact believe that 'an *existing* monopoly position was an ideal platform for undertaking innovations': 'Schumpeter argued that large corporations possessing monopoly power were ideal vehicles for advancing industrial technology.' (Scherer, 1984:59, 222). Scherer, interpreting Schumpeter, is convinced that to Schumpeter 'market structure does make a difference': 'Despite the restrictive pricing behavior in which they indulge, he asserted, large, monopolistic firms are ideally suited for introducing technological innovations that benefit society .... Firms need protection from competition before they will bear the risks and costs of invention and innovation.' (Scherer, 1970:22, 408). Scherer, analysing Schumpeter, decides that the essence of 'the Schumpeterian hypothesis' is to be found in the contention 'that large corporations are uniquely powerful engines of technological advance' (Scherer, 1984:237). He then gives his own assessment of what the facts have to say about Schumpeter's investment in monopoly power already attained: 'On the whole, the hypothesis fares badly.' (Scherer, 1984:237).

Scherer has conducted a number of tests on the relationship between firm size (the proxy being sales) and productive R & D (the proxy being patents). His findings have not been able to 'rescue the Schumpeterian engine from disgrace': 'The evidence does not support the hypothesis that corporate bigness is especially favorable to high inventive output. If anything, the results show that firms below the half-billion dollar sales mark generate more inventions relative to their size than do giant firms.' (Scherer, 1965:191, 198). A reasonable threshold is necessary for the effective deployment of scientists and engineers. Expansion beyond that critical cut-off, however, 'does not in general contribute to a disproportionately greater output of patented inventions': 'By every measure used, the group of large corporations as a whole contributed fewer significant innovations, contest-winning technical advances, and invention patents per million dollars of R & D than smaller enterprises.' (Scherer, 1984:237).

Medium-sized is beautiful. Too big means diminishing returns or worse: 'Technological vigor appears to increase with concentration mainly at relatively low levels of concentration. When the four-firm concentration ratio exceeds 50 or 55 percent, additional market power is probably not conducive to more vigorous technological efforts and may be downright stultifying.' (Scherer, 1967:247). Intermediate is best. Kamien and Schwartz, surveying the evidence, see no reason to disagree with Scherer's assessment that it is moderate size rather than giant size that squeezes the maximum juice from the lemon of applied science: 'Empirical research reveals that an intermediate market structure, one that is neither perfectly competitive nor perfectly monopolistic, is usually most conducive to technical advance.' (Kamien and Schwartz, 1982:3).

Kamien and Schwartz are Schumpeterians in the same sense that Scherer is a Schumpeterian. They believe that disequilibrium is more prevalent than equilibrium and that technological advance makes a greater contribution to material well-being than does static optimisation. Nonetheless, they reach the broadly non-Schumpeterian conclusion that, 'beyond some magnitude, size does not appear especially conducive to either innovational effort or output': 'With the possible exception of the chemical industry, there is little support for the hypothesis that the intensity of innovational effort increases more than proportionately with firm size.' (Kamien and Schwartz, 1982:81, 84). Larger firms spend more on product and process development than smaller ones do. Sooner or later, however, the diseconomies of scale tell on them all.

5.3.2 Monopoly as Consequence

Schumpeter states clearly that monopoly power is the precondition for the quantum leap: 'The technological and organizational possibilities open to firms of the type which is compatible with approximately perfect competition could never have produced similar results.' (Schumpeter, 1942a:189). Schumpeter also states, and no less clearly, that monopoly power is not the cause but rather the consequence of 'new firms producing new commodities or old commodities by new methods' (Schumpeter, 1939:I, 67): 'Since the entrepreneur has no competitors when the new products first appear, the determination of their price proceeds wholly, or within certain limits, according to the principles of monopoly price. Thus there is a monopoly element in profit in a capitalist economy.' (Schumpeter, 1912b:152). In the one case the chicken precedes the egg: market power is needed if firms are to innovate. In the other case the egg precedes the chicken: new combinations are responsible for the conquest of the commanding heights. Schumpeter may be cited in support of both positions.

Scherer interprets Schumpeter as favouring the hypothesis that creative destruction is increasingly dependent on the attainment of critical mass. Anne Mayhew argues that such an interpretation in effect reverses the thrust of Schumpeter's message:

> Schumpeter actually argued that innovation *leads* to *temporary* monopoly, not that monopoly leads to innovation. Furthermore, Schumpeter's was not an analysis of which firms innovate or a defense of monopolies and oligopolies; rather it was an evolutionary analysis of *how technology in a specific institutional context* changes

> the structure of the economy and eventually changes the institutional context. (Mayhew, 1980:244).

Businesses want profits. Therefore they try new things. Size and power may be the consequence. Whatever they are, they are not the cause.

History in such a theory is inseparable from any prediction. Time-related words abound in Schumpeter's account of the quasi-rent as a short-term surplus. Consider the force of 'temporarily' in the following discussion of monopoly brought into being by progressiveness: 'Perfect competition is and always has been *temporarily* suspended whenever anything new is being introduced.' (Schumpeter, 1942a:105, emphasis added). Consider the restriction of 'from the start' in the following observation on the carrot of super-normal returns: 'The introduction of new methods of production and new commodities is hardly conceivable with perfect – and perfectly prompt – competition *from the start*. And this means that the bulk of what we call economic progress is incompatible with it.' (Schumpeter, 1942a:105, emphasis added). Consider the contribution of 'finally' in the following explanation of how it is that zero windfall, zero profit, zero interest reassert themselves through new entry, cumulative learning and just-adequate imitation: 'A tendency to reorganization in the industry will set in, which will *finally* restore the rule of the law of cost.' (Schumpeter, 1912b:135, emphasis added). What happens 'finally', permanently, at the end, is clearly not what happens 'temporarily' and 'from the start', before the 'fast seconds' and the 'slow thirds' have caught up with the initial innovators and mimicked their discoveries. In the words of Nelson and Winter: 'The returns to innovation stem from the transient monopoly of a new product or process provided by imitator lag.' (Nelson and Winter, 1982:279). In the short run we are all in control.

Mayhew is clearly right to interpret Schumpeter as asserting that a monopoly position can be the time-constrained consequence of entrepreneurial early adoption. Scherer, however, is equally right to interpret Schumpeter as contending that size and scale must inevitably be the platform and the precondition. Both interpretations of Schumpeter on monopoly are convincingly supported by the canonical texts. One way of reconciling what would otherwise have to be left as undigested inconsistencies would be to combine the two interpretations in a single macro-image and to treat them as two sides of the same coin.

Thus it could be said that innovation leads to monopoly; that monopoly profits lead to discretionary investment; that capital intensity leads to scale economies; that production runs spread R & D overheads; that product development means still more differentiation; that still more novelty means still more monopoly. Such a story combines both the cause and the consequence. It thus satisfies the condition of mutual determination that is stated by Nelson and Winter when they write: 'Market structure should be viewed as endogenous to an analysis of Schumpeterian competition, with the connections between innovation and market structure going both ways.' (Nelson and Winter, 1982:281).

The connections certainly go both ways. They do so in competitive capitalism when a short-run surplus is used as a fighting fund for imitation and new entry. They do so in corporate capitalism when, short-run or long-run, the rent of incumbency prolongs the lifespan and makes credible challenge more difficult. In the one case as in the other the 'transitory' scenario is fully compatible with the 'platform' precondition. Somehow, however, the proportions alter over time. The 'transitory' element is the business tautology that high returns are the motive and the incentive. It is always and everywhere a fact of business life. The 'platform' element comes into its own later on. The early monopolist could be 'transitory' even if he had no 'platform'. Nowadays it is more and more difficult to make good money out of luck and cleverness alone.

5.3.3 Business Size and Market Structure

Galbraith treats absolute size as a cast-iron indicator of relative strength: 'The larger the firm, the larger it will be in its industry.' (Galbraith, 1973:55). Schumpeter does the same. Speaking of absolute size he points to the lower average costs and the 'higher financial standing' (Schumpeter, 1942a:101) that are the cause and effect of research and development. Speaking of relative strength, he repeatedly refers to the price-shaping power that is conferred by perceived differentiation, supplier concentration and a catch-all agglomerate that he confusingly calls 'monopoly'. Schumpeter runs together the two separate constructs of *large* in relation to business transacted and *large* in relation to a clearly-defined sector. The result is a major ambiguity. Schumpeter's umbrella use of the construct of size makes it difficult to design a single test that would separate out the success that is due to innovation from the success that is due to muscle.

Schumpeter, like all economists in the 1930s, had been exposed to the *Monopolistic Competition* of E.H. Chamberlin (his Harvard contemporary) and the *Imperfect Competition* of Joan Robinson. He reviewed Joan Robinson's book in the *Journal of Political Economy* in 1934. Chamberlin and Robinson had in turn built on the historic insight of Alfred Marshall that each differentiated supplier, however limited its turnover, faces a 'particular demand curve' within the confines of its 'own special market' (Marshall, 1890a:379n). It is not clear how the consistent Schumpeterian would incorporate the fine heterogeneities of quality, atmosphere, service, access, freight, feel and image into his theory of absolute size and relative strength. Technological breakthroughs in the sense of Scherer cannot realistically be expected from a monopolist who hawks handsaws from a room above a pub. Yet it was the lesson of Chamberlin, Robinson and Marshall that the small-turnover monopolist is by no means an unrepresentative exception. Far from it – as Schumpeter himself explains: 'Every grocer, every filling station, every manufacturer of gloves or shaving cream or handsaws has a small and precarious market of his own.' (Schumpeter, 1942a:79). Each is one competitor among many. Each, however, faces a downward-sloping demand curve for his brand that is entirely separate from the demand curve that he shares with his genus: 'The possession of a special market ... gives scope for short-time strategy, for moves and counter moves which would not otherwise exist.' (Schumpeter, 1939:I, 66).

Differential fertility means that one acre of land is not precisely as valuable as the intra-marginal Ricardian plot. Differential productivity means that lumps of labour are in truth separate 'islands' (Schumpeter, 1908:353) rather than interchangeable parts. As with production, so with demand. A 'house', a 'beefsteak', an 'apple' is not a homogeneous category but a bundle of selling points: 'Goods of the same kind but different quality are, economically speaking, different goods.' (Schumpeter, 1908:344). In each case, the rule is this: 'The best piece also commands the best price.' (Schumpeter, 1908: 344). The law of the common price only applies where the peas in the pod have not a single distinguishing characteristic that makes the singleton stand out from the mass. Schumpeter as early as the *Wesen* was, however, stressing that not all black cats are equally black in the dark.

Schumpeter understood what it meant to be a little fish in a private pond: 'Differences in location and other factors which will induce customers to prefer, rationally or a-rationally, one firm to another, are of course unavoidable, irrespective of any intention to create them. And there is simply no such thing as a homogeneous commodity motorcar or liver pill.' (Schumpeter, 1939:I, 63). In the short run every successful innovator, however small, will be able to capture a supernormal profit for his lucky new process or method: 'Perfectly free entry into a *new* field may make it impossible to enter it at all.' (Schumpeter, 1942a:104–5). Some monopoly power is at once the incentive and the reward for the atomistic adventurer in the protected transition before entry and imitation eat away at the windfall that is conferred by distance or ignorance. Schumpeter believes that modern improvements in transportation and communications have a tendency to erode the local premium: 'Perfect competition has at no time been more of a reality than it is at present.' (Schumpeter, 1942a:81). His point is that improvements in the infrastructure will not be enough to end the economic power of the small-turnover monopolist with few close substitutes, a low price-elasticity of demand, an established name for excellence and a private clientele of its own: 'Where circumstances are favorable ... the consequences predicated ... may even in the long run prevail.' (Schumpeter, 1939:I, 66). Even the small firm can be very, very strong.

In the case of monopolistic competition the monopolist is small in absolute terms but large relative to its relevant market. Schumpeter does not say how such a firm should be integrated into the theory of creative destruction; or whether it should be lumped together with the perfect competitor, tiny in turnover and minuscule in influence. The giant oligopolist at least does not send out a mixed message on size. The economic implications of absolute size in a compound with relative size are, however, less clear. Sales in oligopoly, strategic and interdependent, are 'a function of the behavior both of the firm itself ... and of all the other firms in the field' (Schumpeter, 1939:I, 64). If the firms compete, undersell and innovate, the public interest is safe. If the cartel colludes to restrict its output, push up its price, de-escalate its product development, the expectation of progress is less certain. Confronted with the alternative scenarios, Schumpeter will say only that competition from newness is 'that kind of competition which counts': 'It becomes a matter of comparative indifference whether competition in the ordinary sense functions more or less promptly.' (Schumpeter, 1942a:84, 85). His declaration, that absolute size generates the benefits while the invisible hand is a vestigial myth, somehow fails to reassure the consumer that productivity gains will be translated into choices and prices in the shops.

Schumpeter, analysing well-being in the corporate age, says that Marshallian forward-falling average cost cannot possibly account for the steady rise in perceived value for money: what is 'more than anything else responsible for our impression of decreasing cost ... is innovation, the intrusion into the system of new production functions which incessantly shift existing cost curves' (Schumpeter, 1939:I, 91). The consumer secures a welfare gain since absolute size, through cost-cutting innovations, restores the output and the prices that relative size has already assaulted through monopolies and trusts. The result is that the large firm ends up 'doing the work ... of the competitive mechanism' (Schumpeter, 1942a:101) despite the fact that welfare-sharing was never a part of its intent.

It is all very tidy. Yet the action clause is not there. Absolute size cut loose from 'the competitive mechanism' cannot explain why the large firm should pass on its gains to the consumer rather than keeping prices constant and improving its profit position instead. Nor can absolute size convincingly account for the introduction of new technology: the large firm, logically speaking, could resist any change lest this threaten its sunk costs and its organisational memory. Schumpeter's answer is the threat of new entry and the contestability of high profits. It may not be enough. Without any reference to *early* competition and share-seeking behaviour it is simply not possible to see why the corporation should feel under immediate pressure to put the technological and engineering platform of absolute size at the disposal of a consuming public that wants productive advance but wants allocative efficiency as well.

Schumpeter was a market economist who showed little or no interest in what pricing can actually contribute to the market economy. The blind-spot is a curious one. Bureaucracy is not the only threat to creative destruction. Absolute size plus relative size minus same-side rivalry is just as great a threat. That is why economists who deny that corporate capitalism need become as unenterprising as the socialists' civil service will place emphasis on the optimality of good Paretianism. Anti-trust laws discourage oligopolists from putting accommodation in the place of struggle. Globalisation and liberalisation increase the breadth of the competitor pool. Privatisation and de-regulation reduce the scope for red tape and log-rolling, for quotas and subsidies. In ways such as these an active market bends even absolute and relative size to the service of the public interest.

5.3.4 Innovation without Monopoly

Schumpeter approximates the small and medium enterprise to the backwardness of peasant agriculture. A European accustomed to business concentration, he had little time for the American obsession with the acquisitive start-up who uses his acumen to fight his way into the Dream. Jewkes, Sawers and Stillerman, near contemporaries of Schumpeter, convey a different picture of the sources of innovation. Jet engines, televisions, insulin, silicon transistors, air-conditioning, masking tape, the Xerox copier, the safety razor, the Polaroid camera, the ballpoint pen, the radio, all are developments that originated in the small-firm sector. Of 61 major innovations that they documented in their classic study, Jewkes and his colleagues found that only 12 could be traced back to the laboratories of the large corporations. Formal research and development were concentrated in a small number of large companies: in 1964 in the United States only 300 firms accounted for 92 per cent of total expenditure (Jewkes et al., 1969:222). Success rates, however, were a different matter. The small firms were scoring more hits. They were doing so at a fraction of the cost.

Jewkes, Sawers and Stillerman, in contrast to Schumpeter, argue for an open mind. The small firm might be deficient in resources but might be desperate for a win. The nobody by definition has no laurels on which he can rest. The large firm might have funding in abundance but might be sluggish and risk-averse. Middle-aged complacency can mean a reluctance to branch out. Recognising that both kinds of firm have their advantages and their disadvantages, Jewkes and his colleagues decide that there is no infallible recipe – 'The forces which make for innovation are ... numerous and intricate' – and that an eclectic economy ought therefore to keep open a solid number of channels:

> Each and every route to innovation has its impediments .... The small firm may have the *will* to innovate; its birth, survival and growth may often depend upon the exploitation of a new idea, but it may lack the power to innovate because it cannot find sufficient capital. The big firm has large capital resources and thus possesses the *power* to innovate, but it may lack the corporate *will* to do so. (Jewkes et al., 1969:226, 228).

It is the attraction of the market economy that it allows the innovators freely to compete. The optimal size of the institution then emerges as the winning supplier of the winning idea.

Optimal size is often correlated with the life cycle of the firm. Even if long runs do have the edge in the reproduction phase, there is no guarantee that they will be of equal value at the exploration or the incubation stage. Where no one can predict which new growths will ultimately take, it would actually make sense for large firms to wait on the sidelines until they know what is likely to sell. They can in that way depend upon the small firm to conduct the trials but can copy it or take it over once it has established that its patents and its initiatives can be made to bear fruit.

Quick-wittedness is essential in the take-off even if mass capitalisation will later be better placed to exploit the promise of the new. Economic life being, moreover, a process and not a once-for-all, there is no reason to think that the sequence of gestations will ever end. The giant leaps are rightly celebrated by the bards and the bourses. The seamlessness of small increments is less frequently recognised by the OM or even the CBE. For all that, it is the small change and not the sudden bound that is the more usual cause of material advance. Schumpeter himself admits that continuity is a rock on which economics can build: 'Major innovations hardly ever emerge in their final form or cover in one throw the whole field that will ultimately be their own.' (Schumpeter, 1939:I, 167). What he does not see is that the small firm has the local knowledge and the hands-on experience that give it an insider's head start in the introduction of marginal know-how. Scherer supplies the missing connection: 'The sequential character of modern research and development ... makes it possible for small enterprises to play a creative role in major technological achievements.' (Scherer, 1970:416). The small firm can still play a significant part in the lottery of the new. The large firm, so much admired by Schumpeter, might actually have over-invested and not under-invested in in-house research that does not pay its way.

Small can be up-to-date. It can also be efficient. Schumpeter acknowledges the diseconomies that accrue in the large organisation, highly bureaucratised. Economists ought also to recognise the areas in which the entrepreneur-operator retains his historic comparative advantage. In manufacturing there are niche areas where a high-quality product requires specialist craftsmanship and sometimes also a network of personal contacts. In services there are trades like hairdressing, catering and medicine where it is a positive advantage to deal tailor-made and not mass-produced. New technology gives a new lease of life to the small firm: microelectronics allows functions to be performed at a distance which would once have had to be situated near the steam head. De-mergers and hived-off independents empower the company core to buy in consultancy or components from single-product outsiders. In that way is the omnibus conglomerate freed from the need to produce even peripheral excellence for itself.

Most big businesses were once small ones. Nowadays the small businesses can complement the large corporations. They therefore face no quasi-Schumpeterian imperative to grow themselves into obesity merely in order to survive. The large firm need not be the powerhouse of discovery. The small firm has economic advantages of its own. The implications of this line of reasoning can be unsettling indeed. If corporate capitalism is not a natural law, then neither is bureaucratised socialism the necessary next rung on the ladder of economic evolution.

6. The sociology of capitalism

Schumpeter was an interdisciplinary social scientist who wanted to understand the structures and conventions as well as the purchases and sales. Section 3.3 above explained that he made economic sociology one of the four pillars of his comprehensive economic science. Schumpeter recognised that the age of business and shopping had invested more heavily in impersonal rationality than it had in meaningful patterning: 'The building faces toward the economic side of life.' (Schumpeter, 1942a:73). Even so, he believed, the stable framework remains the precondition for the innovative break. The entrepreneur is dependent upon pre-existent values like rationality, social institutions like credit, social bequests like routine even as he constructs the new road along which future convoys will have to travel. Schumpeter was convinced that pattern maintenance and calculative catallactics pervade one another. He therefore proposed that capitalism be examined not just in terms of allocation and dynamism but also in terms of the classes and customs within which the economic processes were embedded. The market mechanism could not be understood on its own.

Schumpeter was an economist who believed that it would be unwise to wander too far from his home: 'The modern man has no choice but to specialize. We have got to do it.' (Schumpeter, 1931a:285). Yet he was also a *social* economist who knew that other people are as much his topic as are the things that they buy and sell. Schumpeter situates the entrepreneurial breach in the context of learned procedures and group understandings. He shows that intellectuals and bureaucrats subvert the decentralised order and pave the way to socialist rationality. He argues that planned statism is consistent with a variety of cultural configurations, that national character as well as production and trade shapes and forms the march of events, that corporatist consultation can rescue the individual from the dominance of elites. He maintains that historical research, cross-disciplinary by nature, confirms that the market-searching and the traditional fit together as a whole. There is, in fact, hardly a single topic in the whole of Schumpeter's economics which is so narrowly commodified that it is not related in some way to sociology. Schumpeter was the economic sociologist's economic sociologist. He was unable to focus on utility maximisation or individual choice without bringing in the relevance of social structures and social values as well.

This chapter, 'The sociology of capitalism', is concerned with three aspects of the market order which demonstrate that society has an impact upon its members even when the nature of their interaction is exchange. The first section deals with social stratification. Stating that 'economists have been strangely slow in recognizing the phenomenon of social classes' (Schumpeter, 1942a:13), Schumpeter filled in the societal space by arguing that individuals even as buyers and sellers are aware of their social location. The second section deals with forcible expansion through imperialism for which pre-capitalist militarism is entirely to blame. Peaceable free trade would dissolve the international tensions into international solidarity were it not for the 'psychological dispositions and social structures acquired in the dim past' (Schumpeter, 1918/19:187–8) that perpetuate the predatory mindset even when it has outlived its economic usefulness. The third section takes up the question of why people work. It argues that broad and far-reaching motivation, much more than mere money alone, is the reason why the business community aims forever at new and greater acquisitions. Status symbols, 'excess energy' (Schumpeter, 1918/19:191), the perpetuation of a family dynasty, 'the need for self-glorification and violent self-assertion' (Schumpeter, 1918/19:147) are a far cry from textbook hedonism and the self-governing decision maker whose life is his own. They are a reminder that Schumpeter was not able to think of supply and demand without thinking of the patterned matrix as well.

6.1 SOCIAL STRATIFICATION

The lasting contribution is the long essay of 1927 on 'Social classes in an ethnically homogeneous environment'. This essay, along with his study of 'Imperialisms' and his four major books, Schumpeter ranked among his 'most important works' (Sweezy, 1951:119). Schumpeter had already given lectures on social structure in Austro-Hungary and in the United States. In 1911 Chapter VII of his *Theory of Economic Development* had included an extensive discussion of class. By 1927 Schumpeter felt ready to put on record a major statement about layering and patterning in the era of achievement and change.

The hierarchy of recognised strata is a non-ego externality that is greater than its factored-down parts. Methodological individualism is fully compatible with the sociological perspective: only the discrete subjectivity can provide an insider's perspective on how it feels to live where he does. Substantive individualism, on the other hand, is a clear instance of the conviction reductionist falling victim to his own propaganda. The individual may be able to shop for his own preferred habitat. He is, however, powerless to insist on a different set of cultural reference-points: 'The class membership of an individual is a primary fact, originally quite independent of his will.' (Schumpeter, 1927a:236). Even in the age of Burke's 'sophisters', 'economists' and 'calculators', there is much that the individual must treat as a constant to which he must adapt.

Schumpeter was insistent that the basic building block in the analysis of stratification was the inter-generational clan and not the isolated one-off alone: 'The family, not the physical person, is the true unit of class and class theory.' (Schumpeter, 1927a:238). To that extent his theory of class is a theory of multiple unfreedoms as well. The individual as *homo economicus* does not make a rational choice of his class at birth. He develops his consciousness within a specific framework that shapes his attitudes before it maps out his fate. Even his marriage partner will tend to be a social near-neighbour in an overlapping location. Class is about family. It is the family that moves up or down. The individual stays or moves as a part of a group.

A class, Schumpeter wrote, is 'a special social organism, living, acting, and suffering' (Schumpeter, 1927a:232). It is an inter-temporal abode with 'its own peculiar life and characteristic "spirit"' (Schumpeter, 1927a:234). A class is a reality *sui generis* that the new member cannot mould and re-mould to suit his taste. A class is a stable set of coordinates that 'prevent the group from scattering like a heap of billiard balls' (Schumpeter, 1927a:233). It is not an *ad hoc* partnership that today's interest creates and tomorrow's interest dissolves.

Location is signalled through culture. Each class has a unifying code of conventions which ensure that its members will have a recognisable and a common way of life: 'A class is aware of its identity as a whole.' (Schumpeter, 1927a:234). The members of a class share habits which facilitate easy communication. They have background sympathies which enable them to interact easily with one another. They know at once when an interloper talks like an outsider, behaves like a stranger and obviously does not belong: 'They are in close association with one another; they understand one another better; they work more readily in concert; they close ranks and erect barriers against the outside.' (Schumpeter, 1927a:234). They do this for the same reason that two Englishmen abroad are bound together by fish 'n' chips and two *chevaliers* at a ball will talk of nothing but *la gloire*. Patriotism at the level of the nation has its counterpart in the allegiance that is inspired by shared dress and manners at the level of the class.

The members of a class situate themselves effortlessly with others of their kind. Enjoying 'ein gegenseitiges Sichverstehen und Miteinanderfühlen', they are birds of a feather who feel right in the company of their own: 'What is certain is that a group of economic actors will appear socially and especially politically to be a class where there is mutual comprehension and a feeling that they belong together. This will be simpler if they have a similar way of life. That in turn presupposes a similar economic level. Even there it is the feeling of belonging together and not directly the economic situation that is the decisive explanatory factor.' (Schumpeter, 1912a:528–9). The members of a class have a consciousness that makes them feel as one. It is the signs and signals that bring them together. It is not the economic basis but the social superstructure that conveys the message that they have come home.

A similar income band is the means to the end. The bank manager needs big money to join a golf club and the bricklayer needs moderate money to stand his round in the pub. Crucially, however, a similar ownership-position is not the difference that divides. The Ricardians and the Marxians had flattened the multifold complexities of the social pecking order into the one-dimensional determinism of land, labour and capital. Schumpeter found their emphasis on the ownership of the factors of production profoundly impoverished: 'Common interests ... do not lead to the constitution of a social class.' (Schumpeter, 1912a:528). A class first and foremost is a non-utilitarian thing. Arkwright and the Duke of Bridgewater, both entrepreneurs in the British Industrial Revolution, no more belonged to the same social stratum than do fellow passengers waiting for a single train: 'No barber becomes an aristocrat by virtue of the "Sir".' (Schumpeter, 1939:272). The Ricardians and the Marxians failed to see the invisible wall that separates the bank manager from the bricklayer despite the fact that both, materially speaking, are only paid hands bled dry in the service of absentee capital. Schumpeter was not prepared to follow the narrow economystics down the same dark track: 'The social pyramid does not consist of economic building-blocks. Economically, a successful doctor must be classified as a worker. Socially, however, he does not simply belong to the working class.' (Schumpeter, 1912a:528). There is more to class than distribution, re-distribution and *who gets what*.

The sociology of capitalism is a Pareto-like circulation of elites. Even if the social structure remains the same, the identity of the precise participants is subject to the entrances and the exits of the gain-seeking meritocracy: 'Each class resembles a hotel or an omnibus, always full, but always of different people.' (Schumpeter, 1927a:248). Capitalism is mobility at the same time that it is structure. There is mobility within a single class. There is mobility from one class to another. Intra-class or inter-class, here as elsewhere it is entrepreneurship that accounts for the turnover in the names and the faces.

People and their families rise up because of hard work and saving. Most of all, they rise up because someone has '*done something novel*', because someone has made a success of 'striking out along unconventional paths', 'getting out of the conventional rut', 'launching out into the unprecedented'

(Schumpeter, 1927a:263, 254). Transmigration is not the exception but the rule in a commercial society where enterprise enjoys an open road and lack of enterprise ensures an early fall: 'Class composition is forever changing, to the point where there may be a completely new set of families.' (Schumpeter, 1927a:248). Shifts in relative position reflect the 'different degree to which families are qualified to solve the problems with which their social environment confronts them' (Schumpeter, 1927a:273). One consequence is that the failures drop so quickly out of the bourgeoisie 'that the class itself always consists of families which are normally equal to their function' (Schumpeter, 1927a:269). Social stratification is a Darwinian struggle. The families at the top have the greatest aptitude for leadership and innovation – until, that is, they too lose their initiative and sink down in favour of the next new rival in the never-ending flow. Thus does the 'self-actuating logic of the competitive system' (Schumpeter, 1927a:243) stamp society with the microeconomist's die.

One consequence of the never-ending rise and fall is that class conflict becomes more muted and more damped. The capitalist class is no more than a selection of ambitious workers who made good. The working class is the ancestral home to which successful capitalists will one day return once they too have lost their bite. Given the opportunities to travel up and to travel down, class antipathies become less acute. Competition and attainment ensure that no one need feel trapped forever on the undecorated side of the barricades.

There is not in any case an unbridgeable gulf between the objectives of the wage earners and those of the profit recipients who give them jobs: 'The economic conflict of interest between the two is not very great. It exists. Yet it is only the conflict of interest one would expect between two participants in exchange. And the real community of interest is therefore not to be neglected.' (Schumpeter, 1912a:533). The buyer and the seller haggle over the price of sprouts without calling into question the legitimacy of the free-enterprise order. The same logic applies in the case of the employee and the employer when they negotiate fiercely for the mutually acceptable price.

The capitalists are the best customers of the proletarians. The two classes both draw an appropriable benefit from productivity and economic growth. The ritual insult while bargaining into being the market-clearing price should not be taken as proof that the labour–capital dialectic is home to an irreconcilable contradiction. When all is said and done, the gulf that separates the industrialist from the banker is at least as great: 'The entrepreneur is no less interested in low interest-rates than he is in low wages.' (Schumpeter, 1912a:534). No one would predict that the money-initiative dialectic will erupt into civil war. No more would it be legitimate to expect that the employers and the employees will challenge a complementarity from which each party has drawn such unprecedented well-being.

Schumpeter in the late 1920s was saying that innovation is 'the main lever, in fact, of the rise of industrial families' (Schumpeter, 1928:70). He had said the same thing in 1911 when he had explained that it was 'new combinations' introduced by new competitors that powered 'the process by which individuals and families rise and fall economically and socially' (Schumpeter, 1912b:67). Schumpeter in the *Theory of Economic Development* had contended that the a priori of overalls to overalls had been borne out 'well enough by the history of manufacturing families' (Schumpeter, 1912b:79). Manufacturing families gather no moss. That is why, he had insisted, entrepreneurship is typically the means to a class but that 'entrepreneurs as such do not form a social class' (Schumpeter, 1939:I, 104) *per se*: 'Because being an entrepreneur is not a profession and as a rule not a lasting condition, entrepreneurs do not form a social class in the technical sense, as, for example, landowners or capitalists or workmen do.' (Schumpeter, 1912b:78). Landowners talk about foxes, capitalists about City lunches, workmen about cloth caps. What could Arkwright and the Duke of Bridgewater possibly have in common apart from money making and the chance that the new technology will run out of steam?

The young Schumpeter associated the act of creation with the leasehold on class. So did the older Schumpeter who in *Capitalism, Socialism and Democracy* explained the 'incessant rise and fall of individual families into and out of the upper strata' in terms of the prizes and penalties of a system known to 'identify success with business success': 'Going up and going down means making and losing money.' (Schumpeter, 1942a:18, 73). The older Schumpeter in 1942 said that the able businessman, rising *into* the middle class and then rising *within* it, 'is likely to rise exactly as far as his ability goes' (Schumpeter, 1942a:74). Market commercialism, Schumpeter stated, 'tends to send up the able individual and, much more effectively, the able family' (Schumpeter, 1942a:188). It is in that way that modern capitalism, 'by the very law of its structure' (Schumpeter, 1942a:188), chooses for itself a bourgeoisie of faculty and not of birth. Its meritocrats have a proven track record. Its wealth creators know how to make the system work.

Schumpeter's assessment in 1942 is broadly the same as the sociology of his earlier writings: 'The bourgeois class, *ipso facto* also selects the individuals and families that are to rise into that class or to drop out of it.' (Schumpeter, 1942a:74). For once the continuity in his vision is a warning that there is a stranger in the house. The young Schumpeter was theorising for the one-leader firm. The older Schumpeter took the large corporation as his technological gold standard. The young Schumpeter attributed family status to company success. The older Schumpeter made rise a topic in occupational assessment and fall an indicator of professional under-performance. The owner-operated firm is not the long-lived bureaucratic hierarchy. The continuity in the sociology would seem to paper over the sharp break in the economics.

Exercising some imagination, one could seek to reconcile the two positions by saying that even in the age of the corporation the 'organisation man' still *achieves* his status through the exercise of the entrepreneurial *function*. One could defend the notion of the bureaucrat as an innovator by saying that theorists of the managerial revolution who predict passivity on the part of time-server salary-recipients underestimate the flair and intuition of MBA promotion-seekers imbued with the thrill of the chase. One could point out that, highly structured as they are, large firms in the older Schumpeter's economics are typically regarded as the major source of epoch-making new breakthroughs. Schumpeter writes that 'bureau and committee work tends to replace individual action' (Schumpeter, 1942a:133). Perhaps what this implies is that the bureau worker who contributes the most to the entrepreneurial function will be paid a merit bonus because he has delivered an entrepreneurial rent. Such a bonus is certainly an incentive to try.

Perhaps the life cycle construct sheds some light on the logic behind class. Schumpeter writes as follows about new businesses even in the modern age: 'Supernormal intelligence and energy account for industrial success and in particular for the *founding* of industrial positions in nine cases out of ten.' (Schumpeter, 1942a:16). Later on the corporations might move in to imitate and take over. In the beginning, however, it is supernormal shrewdness that catapaults a cook to the status of restaurateur and makes a trend-setting designer of a seamstress with panache. Especially is this possible in Schumpeter-type capitalism where saving out of income is not the precondition for start-up finance because of the almost unlimited availability of loanable credit: 'If it is otherwise in good condition, the family will find that in normal times credit is virtually thrust upon it.' (Schumpeter, 1927a:244). Advancement through profit-earning endeavour lives on in the new entrant who tries a new experiment and raises his family into a higher class as a result.

Schumpeter's 1927 paper is concerned with the unceasing exchange of position that is captured by the phenomenon of clogs to clogs in three generations: 'By and large, the families that led around the middle of the nineteenth century are not on top of the heap today.' (Schumpeter, 1927a:242). Just as it is concerned with evanescence, however, so it is concerned with stability: 'Classes, once they have come into being, harden in their mold and perpetuate themselves, even when the social conditions that created them have disappeared.' (Schumpeter, 1927a:237). Events evolve. Cloth cap and bowler hat go on and on. The emphasis on the past alongside the present, on the conservatism that complements the capitalism, significantly modifies the impression that it is entrepreneurship alone that permits a synthesis between economics and sociology. Entrepreneurship is certainly one bridge. Slow-moving tradition, however, is most definitely another.

Schumpeter writes as follows about the baggage of remembered time:

> Every social situation is the heritage of preceding situations and takes over from them not only their cultures, their dispositions, and their "spirit", but also elements of their social structure and concentrations of power .... This means that in explaining any historical course or situation, account must be taken of the fact that much in it can be explained only by the survival of elements that are actually alien to its own trends. (Schumpeter, 1927a:236).

The economic interpretation of class is marred by the flaw that it explains current stratification in terms of current cause. The truth, as it happens, is far more the envelope of haphazard accretions that refuse to go away: 'Human protagonists have always been shaped by past situations.' (Schumpeter, 1927a:237).

Schumpeter writes that different classes today 'stem from varying conditions' and 'bear the marks of different centuries on their brow' (Schumpeter, 1927a:237). The origins are forgotten, perhaps lost. The institutions for all that retain their legitimacy and their acceptability simply because they have become comfortably familiar and constitutionally entrenched. Embedded traditionalism ensures that the superstructure of law and custom 'always lags behind changes in the actual life situation' (Schumpeter, 1927a:262). It means that long-established hierarchies do not melt in passive response to an in-period reality that has moved on.

An illustration would be the Medieval nobility. In an earlier age it was a warrior caste that led from the front. By the time of Adam Smith the fourteenth earl was 'likely to don armor only when his portrait was to be painted' (Schumpeter, 1927a:266). Economic freedom meant that mercenary protection could be bought and sold. A whole class lost its primary function due to the dynamic of commerce. Interestingly, however, its secondary function lived on and transformed itself into a precondition for industry and trade: 'Their presence made for a most useful symbiosis.' (Schumpeter, 1941:344). The atavism of authority, Stolper says, is a public good which in Schumpeter's sociology is vital if market failure is to be kept at bay: 'In Schumpeter's view, the bourgeois stratum can survive only in symbiosis with something emotionally more uplifting than prices and products and production and economic well-being.' (Stolper, 1994:112). Not an anachronism but a part of the infrastructure, the aristocracy is a role-model which continues to symbolise the culture of obedience without calculation. Every factory owner dreams of a labour force which touches the forelock much as their long-forgotten ancestors did when they encountered the thirteenth earl on the road.

The social layers seem to have the character of a glacier that moves very slowly. Any theory of class must evidently 'include prior class structures among its data' (Schumpeter, 1927a:237). This stability is in sharp contrast to the perpetual rise and fall of specific families which lack any form of protected tenure. The bourgeoisie, Schumpeter says, is continually 'revitalizing itself' with high-powered fresh talent while at the same time encouraging tired incumbents who 'sever their active relation to "business"' to 'drop out ... after a generation or two' (Schumpeter, 1942a:134). The structure is a relatively constant constant. The lessees themselves are bound to come and go.

Relative positions are normally interchanged through unceasing mobility. Sometimes, however, they are not. Schumpeter is able in places to state or suggest that sitting tenants can resemble their building in the inter-temporal consistency of their *natura non facit saltum*. Even family success, he seems to be conceding, can sometimes be an inter-generational gift which prudent innovators can seal in and preserve.

This would be the case with the inter-generational transmission of portfolios and property. Even if the captain of industry cannot bequeath the nous, he can hand on the cash: 'A family position is created, which, for some time even if not for ever, is independent of entrepreneurial activity, or capacity for entrepreneurship.' (Schumpeter, 1929:236). Dividend recipients sunning themselves in Ibiza cannot be said to drop out of the middle classes merely because they have no continuing stake in the pursuit of novelty. Schumpeter writes of the 'driving force' that breathes life into the 'dead casing' of the firm that his 'social standing slips through the fingers of his successors, who may have inherited the booty but not the claws of the lion' (Schumpeter, 1912a:529). What is important to remember is that inherited money ensures that the class position will be perpetuated even if the offspring living off the usufruct do not have the skill to open up a new market or push through a new innovation. Armani opens doors. Prada commands respect.

As with the family trust fund, so with the in-breeding of Establishment fortunes. Pharmaceuticals inter-marries with land. Bourbon *fils* pairs off with Battenberg *fille*. The practice is a familiar one. It is a selective mechanism which serves to keep the blue blood blue: 'Coordinate families then merge into a social class, welded together by a bond .... This relationship assumes a life of its own and is then able to grant protection and confer prestige.' (Schumpeter, 1927a:279). On the one hand there are the entrepreneurs of the forest for whom the room at the top will forever be as insecure as any other revolving door on their return trip to the start. On the other hand there are the cognates of Windsor of whom the rock-like continuity closely resembles the time-out-of-mind antiquity of their much-visited house. Schumpeter wrote of class as personal achievement. He also recognised that unearned wealth for some will continue to accrue to a parental past. Entrepreneurs themselves do not stay together long enough to develop a common culture and cohesive set of dispositions. Their descendants who inherit the assets are more likely to know a good *langouste* and have a time-share in the sun.

The biological endowment reinforces the inherited wealth. Schumpeter, in an uncharacteristic tribute to physiology and anatomy, describes the bourgeoisie as 'a class which, by virtue of the selective process of which it is the result, harbors human material of supernormal quality' (Schumpeter, 1942a:204). The difference in capability at the start of life's race means marked variance in the performance that is observed: 'The modal individual in the bourgeois class is superior as to intellectual and volitional aptitudes to the modal individual in any other of the classes of industrial society.' (Schumpeter, 1942a:204n). This is not entrepreneurship even if it can be the mother and father of entrepreneurship. It is blood. Genes are not a business conquest. They are a handed-on head start.

Genes, wills and marriages all mean that class is perpetuation and not merely prize. Life chances and class-correlated attitudes can have no less conservative an impact on social location. Social impediments to vertical mobility are hardly mentioned at all in Schumpeter's theory of class. Brought up in the Austro-Hungary of lords, merchants and ploughmen, Schumpeter nonetheless opts for the characteristically American view that pecuniary accomplishment is the nub of social classification and that an able man will be able to live out his dream. There is nothing in his sociology about class solidarity, parental expectations, middle-class socialisation in the entrepreneurial values of ambition and exploration, working-class socialisation in the cannon-fodder canons of fitting in and plodding on. There is little about unequal opportunities in education or unequal access to network entry points. There is no discussion of racial differences and racial discrimination, conveniently netted out by the facile assumption of an 'ethnically homogeneous environment'. Schumpeter, in short, leads the reader to expect an attractive career open to the talents when there are equally persuasive reasons to expect a tendency for origins and destinations, in America as well as in Europe, stubbornly to move in step.

A vital reason why Schumpeter underestimated the length of the single family's tenure is that he concentrated on the entrepreneurial segment of the greater middle class while neglecting the more risk-averse segments that neither climb nor fall. He is aware of second-best 'industrialists, merchants, financiers and bankers' who do no more than let the business life tick over: 'They are in the intermediate stage between entrepreneurial venture and mere current administration of an inherited domain.' (Schumpeter, 1942a:134). He knows that knowledge-based professions like law, accountancy and medicine promise a middle-class status even to those who are not compulsively entrepreneurial: that is why the corporate executive or the public-sector bureaucrat is seldom sent to the tradesman's entrance despite the fact that he is not a kent face in hostile takeovers. Schumpeter is deliberately concentrating on a part only of the greater middle class. His analysis of social stratification in the circumstances tells only a part of the story.

Marx's association of class with capital is too single-minded a nexus. Schumpeter's explanation of social status in terms of commercial ingenuity is by the same token too narrow a focus. Schumpeter said that class is a complicated phenomenon which cannot be reduced to economic activity alone: 'When we speak of social structure in the capitalist economy, we do not mean that the economic organisation entirely explains the social.' (Schumpeter, 1912a:529). The problem is that, recognising the primacy of economics in the modern age, he built his economic sociology around the ladder and the precipice while neglecting or ignoring the other variables which impact upon the categories. Widening the perspective actually accentuates the conservatism. Flash Harry with his children goes up and down. The Jones family in Acacia Avenue goes on and on.

Schumpeter overestimated the significance of the entrepreneurial segment within the broader context of the greater bourgeoisie. Single-minded though he, like Marx, may have been, there is no mistaking the nature of his message: 'The entrepreneur must stand at the apex of the pyramid, social and not only economic.' (Schumpeter, 1912a:525). A future without the entrepreneur is a future without an apex. A future without an apex is a future without a bourgeoisie: 'Economically and sociologically, directly and indirectly, the bourgeoisie ... depends on the entrepreneur and, as a class, lives and will die with him.' (Schumpeter, 1942a:134). Since the bureaucratisation of decision making was already taking its course, the 'bourgeois stratum', Schumpeter solemnly announced, was inexorably writing itself out of the script.

Great crimes have been committed in the name of language. Schumpeter's use of the term 'bourgeois' is a precisely such a corruption of meaning. The 'bourgeois' in his sociology is not the Marxian proprietor of manufactured inputs who employs labour power and takes home surplus value. Nor, however, is the 'bourgeois' the Acacia Avenue accountant with two children in boarding-school education. The 'bourgeois' appears to be defined neither as the owner of a factor of production nor as the member of a closed-circle status group. Instead, the 'bourgeois' turns out to be a lion-clawed innovator on the look-out for something new. It is an idiosyncratic definition that not every reader will believe to be complete. It is for all that a definition that is perfectly in line with Schumpeter's assertion that the 'bourgeois stratum' will wither away once management ossifies into current administration and the booty sinks to zero because search atrophies in the stagnation of the assignment: 'The bourgeois strata that live on profits and interest would tend to disappear.' (Schumpeter, 1912b:131). Once the apex is gone, the pyramid will have no more life than a headless chicken that cannot understand why it *is*.

Schumpeter says that the entrepreneur is at the apex: 'So much and so many depend on him', 'his success impresses and fascinates', 'his voice makes itself heard in politics' (Schumpeter, 1912a:526). He dominates the economy. He captures the headlines. He lectures to the State. Every student of evolutionary economics knows that Schumpeter regarded 'the goods on hand, the buildings and machines in the factories' as but 'the shell of industry' (Schumpeter, 1912a:531): 'The means of production are replaceable, but not the leader.' (Schumpeter, 1912b:143). What must be added is that he believed the businessman at the apex to be a 'political and a social power' as well: 'His economic success, as with success in general, ensures his influence on other areas of life.' (Schumpeter, 1912a:526). Ordinary people walk in the shadow. The entrepreneur walks in the light.

The entrepreneur is the role model and the standard of excellence: 'Social life develops a bias in favour of his needs and orientation.' (Schumpeter, 1912a:526). People want what he wants because they idealise what he is: 'His conditions of life are taken to be generally valid. ... What the leaders value always becomes a value for the masses.' (Schumpeter, 1912a:526). His purchases become the benchmark that is copied and imitated: 'They lead to the unfolding of a demand for consumer goods of particular categories and types. Supply soon follows.' (Schumpeter, 1912a:527). His personal style marks him out as the front-runner in taste even as he is the front-runner in industry.

The necessary condition is the ability to spend: 'The possession of money becomes an index of his social position.' (Schumpeter, 1912a:526). Unlike Veblen, what Schumpeter would argue is that affluence by itself is not enough. To be situated at the apex, the high achiever must be seen to be performing great deeds: 'The entrepreneur relies upon his personal characteristics and nothing but his personal characteristics. His status as an entrepreneur is dependent on his accomplishments and does not survive his ability to perform.' (Schumpeter, 1912a:529). He is a leader not only because he has the accoutrements of Mammon but because he is the cutting edge.

It is a risky contention. Schumpeter admits that there are other rich people besides the entrepreneur. They too are in a position to command the spotlight even if they are mere survivals without a single new breakthrough to potluck into the public good: 'Nothing is so difficult to change as ideas and dispositions. Even a totally dispossessed feudal aristocracy will long retain its social prestige, even if not ... its leading role.' (Schumpeter, 1912a:528). A beached whale though he probably will be, the fourteenth earl is still protected on all sides by 'the blinding brilliance of old associations and the bulwark of customs rendered sacred through long usage' (Schumpeter, 1912a:535). Leaderliness to Schumpeter is the sufficient condition. Others, such as Tawney, say that the necessary condition alone is enough for a class to be perceived by the masses to be the apex at the top: '*Das Gentlemanideal* has them by the throat; they frisk politely into obsolescence on the playing-fields of Eton.' (Tawney, 1931:37).

Such 'docility', such a 'respect for their betters', such a 'habit of submission' (Tawney, 1931:74), ensures that entrepreneurship per se might not be the narrow gate. If standing is separate from innovation, then the Vice-President for Marketing or the senior civil servant need have no fear of being snubbed at the Reform Club or snipped out of the television news because he is making the old order work when he ought to be tearing it to shreds. Entrepreneurship can be a group thing and not the preserve of a single outstanding tiger hunting alone. Even if not leaderly, moreover, Sir Henry still has power and wealth, an attractive lifestyle and top-quality contacts. It is rather an exaggeration to say that the bourgeoisie 'lives and will die' with the rough diamond who ensures that all bets are off. The senior executive, the hospital consultant, the television producer are all at the apex as well. Even without the entrepreneur, there is every chance that social stratification will continue to assign a prominent place to the bourgeoisie that stands out from the crowd. The shared bourgeois culture will remain. Private property will remain. Nothing of significance will have changed at all.

6.2 IMPERIALISM AND EXCHANGE

Schumpeter's 'The sociology of imperialisms' was published in two parts in 1918 and 1919. Hobson (1902), Hilferding (1910), Rosa Luxemburg (1913), Lenin (1917) and Bukharin (1917) had already written on the same theme of national aggrandisement and market economics. It had been their conclusion as Marxists that capitalism is the cause of aggression and militarism, that conquest is the cost-effective seizure of wealth. The earlier authors had taken for granted that when money talks the society listens. Schumpeter's sociology of imperialisms in sharp contrast takes nothing on trust. Even the subject matter is given in the plural. Each imperialism has its own special features. Each imperialism must be treated as a sub-case that is distinctive and unique.

Schumpeter's definition puts bourgeois profit-seeking firmly in its place: 'Imperialism is the objectless disposition on the part of a state to unlimited forcible expansion.' (Schumpeter, 1918/19:183). Imperialism is discrete political intervention. It is not the automaticity of supply and demand. Imperialism is advantage-seizing by force. It is not the mutual-gain expectation of consensual exchange. Imperialism above all else is 'objectless'. It is not goal-directed and purposive but rather the expression of an instinctual compulsion that acknowledges no utilitarian limit. Imperialism is entirely non-rational and non-calculative. In that way it is more nearly the economics of the miser or the workaholic than it is the prudent cost–benefiting of the bourgeois profit-seeker which to the Marxists drives the political elite into territorialism as the best-paying choice.

Schumpeter uses language like 'hegemony', 'dominion', 'victory for the sake of winning', 'war for the sake of fighting', to underline his conviction that imperialism, 'an aggressiveness for its own sake', is only tangentially a matter of goal attainment and the pursuit of interest: 'It values conquest not so much on account of the immediate advantages ... as because it *is* conquest, success, action.' (Schumpeter, 1918/19:343). Primary are 'the instinctive urge to domination', 'the dark powers of the subconscious', 'the need to hate', 'the need for self-glorification and violent self-assertion' (Schumpeter, 1918/19:147, 148). Secondary only are the justifications and the rationalisations that veil the 'objectless' in a web of fictions that owe little or nothing to the bedrock will to win. The imputed logic arrives with the philosopher *post festum*. The latent wish is a psychological predisposition that is active from the start.

Corfu in 1863 is a case in point. The island was of no real strategic or commercial importance to Britain. The mother country had nonetheless to pretend to itself that it was. To surrender Corfu would have been seen as a humiliating loss of face. It would have been the trigger for a level of 'public indignation' comparable to that later aroused by the Boer War – when 'there was not a beggar in London who did not speak of "our" rebellious subjects' (Schumpeter, 1918/19:148, 149). Imperialism both in the Mediterranean and in Africa gave the British people the chance to translate its hostility to foreigners and outsiders into a game that could be won, 'much as a card player vicariously satisfies his primitive aggressive instincts' (Schumpeter, 1918/19:148), much as hunting and sport provide some relief for a thirst that can never be slaked.

Resonances abound in Schumpeter's account of 'an aggressiveness that is only kindled anew by each success' (Schumpeter, 1918/19:143). There is Hegel on the ever-questing *Weltgeist* and Nietzsche on the irreducible *Wille zur Macht*. There is Freud on the repression of Eros and Thanatos, and Pareto on the hard-core 'residues' that underlie the superficial verbalisations of the 'derivations'. There is Veblen on conspicuous consumption as conspicuous prowess. There is Original Sin as the Hobbesian's witness of last resort. What there is not is Marx. Colonialism, older than capitalism, was not a way of safeguarding lucrative investments. Bellicosity, different from accumulation, was not a device for protecting market share. Coercion was not invented to squeeze surplus value from poor countries abroad. Rather, force is a natural growth that has its roots in the blood-lust of the body and the fantasy-life of the mind.

Conquering instead of conquest becomes the motive. In poorer societies hunger made struggle the precondition for survival. In more affluent societies the zero-sum urges may at last be said to have 'outlived their usefulness' (Schumpeter, 1918/19:164). The urges have turned functionless and vestigial. The urges for all that still drive and impel. Imperialism in modern times 'calls into play instincts that carry over from the life habits of the dim past. Driven out everywhere else, the irrational seeks refuge in nationalism.' (Schumpeter, 1918/19:147).

Imperialism is living proof that pre-capitalist reflexes influence and shape a social reality that no longer depends on warfare for food. Body and mind, trapped in their squirrel wheel, are conspicuously reluctant to move on: 'Inherited dispositions', once firmly established, 'tend to maintain themselves and to continue in effect long after they have lost their meaning and their life-preserving function.' (Schumpeter, 1918/19:188). Body and mind are rut-bound entities. An important reason is that economic biology does not act alone but rather in alliance with political sociology. It is not just in-bred instincts but also dominant elites that Schumpeter has in mind when he states so unequivocally about the stranglehold of time gone by that 'the dead always rule the living' (Schumpeter, 1918/19:214). History refuses to be buried in the archives. Imperialism is living proof that past militarists lead present cohorts into limitless expansion explicitly because the 'traditional habit of war' (Schumpeter, 1918/19:185) is all that they know.

Thus, in ancient Egypt and Persia, a defence structure once put in place had a tendency to press for national policies that made sense to a social group that took its self-image from the show of violence: '*Created by wars that required it, the machine now created the wars it required.*' (Schumpeter, 1918/19:157). It had to do so. A social group had come into being that viewed warfare as its main profession and not simply as a means–ends response to need: 'Life and vocation are fully realized *only* in war.' (Schumpeter, 1918/19:158). The social group was 'motivated by warlike instincts and interests' (Schumpeter, 1918/19:157). It should surprise no one that it did not lobby for peaceful coexistence and the conversion of swords into ploughshares that would effectively have marginalised its standing.

As had the ancient Egyptians and the Persians, so too the Arabs in the eighth century had come under the control of soldier-rulers whose world view was walled in by narrow occupationalism: 'War was the normal function of this military theocracy.' (Schumpeter, 1918/19:167). Jihad may have been the consequence, but it was the office-holders and not the Prophet who were the immediate cause: 'Their social organization needed war; without successful wars it would have collapsed.' (Schumpeter, 1918/19:167). The soldier-rulers, behaviourally and politically, had blinkered themselves into a one-way street. No endogenous force existed that could pull them back: 'Had an Arab been asked why he fought, he might as a born warrior, on proper reflection have countered with the question as to why one lived.' (Schumpeter, 1918/19:170). The reaction would have been non-rational. The consequence was the spread of the religion because of the animal spirits and the vested interests that gave to the expansionism a momentum of its own.

Even an absolute monarch like Louis XIV had been driven into foreign wars because earlier feudalism had burdened him with a full-time estate of knights and warriors. Even a political autocrat who could say 'I am the State' knew that his nobles had 'martial ideas', a 'warlike past' and 'bellicose instincts' (Schumpeter, 1918/19:183). Such seasoned warriors were accustomed to conflating action with *military* action. They might have revolted against his rule had Louis XIV denied them a practical outlet for their warlike proclivities. Writing just after Germany's defeat in the First World War, it is possible that Schumpeter was thinking of the Kaiser and the Junkers when he was writing of the way in which the aristocracy had forced Louis XIV to act out the rituals of the past.

Sociological functionalists like the economic determinists believe that present-day activities generate the conventions and hierarchies that they require in order to fulfil their tasks. A theorist of lagged articulation such as Schumpeter is far more sensitive to the heritage of memories and practices that fulfil the promise of social conditions thrown up by an age that is not our own: 'Because of the persistence of such habits, they will always, to a considerable degree, be dominated by the production context of past ages.' (Schumpeter, 1918/19:144). Once in place, the past is reluctant, as is shown by the case study of expansionism, to commit voluntary euthanasia in the interests of an up-to-date code:

> Imperialism is thus atavistic in character. It falls into that large group of surviving features from earlier ages that play such an important part in every concrete social situation. In other words, it is an element that stems from the living conditions, not of the present, but of the past – or, put in terms of the economic interpretation of history, from past rather than present relations of production. (Schumpeter, 1918/19:188).

Traditions have continuity. Past classes have not gone away.

Imperialism is a survival from the pre-capitalist stage of economic evolution. The Marxists had argued that aggression is the superstructure of private property. Herbert Spencer, on the other hand, had maintained that market contracting, inherently peaceable, is the very stuff of which the 'industrial' and not the 'militant' society is made. Schumpeter, convinced that imperialism is no more than a remnant left over from the tribal economy, opted for Spencer over Marx and thus for the prediction that conflicts would wither away since wars are 'troublesome distractions' in a shopkeeper culture where money and not power is the overriding concern: 'In a purely capitalist world, what was once energy for war becomes simply energy for labor of every kind.' (Schumpeter, 1918/19:191). Capitalism is not the cause of imperialism. Rather, it is the antidote to the militarism and the nationalism that inevitably arise whenever a warlike class is obliged to live off the exertions of others.

Schumpeter was unambiguous in his conclusion that the exchange economy is not fertile soil for the obsession with conquest: 'Capitalism is by nature anti-imperialist.' (Schumpeter, 1918/19:194). Autocrats seize territory because a pugilist loves a fight. Their spiritual descendants force through the me-first mercantilism of monopolistic guilds and protective tariffs because an enemy is always a problem to be solved. Plutocrats in contrast rank freedom of trade above the scramble for colonies. They see no need for gunboat diplomacy when the division of labour can secure a mutually acceptable consensus. Schumpeter in only four words captures the essence of the big step upwards from guns to butter: 'The bourgeois is unwarlike.' (Schumpeter, 1918/19:212). The Hohenzollerns, the Hapsburgs and the Romanoffs were being swept away at the very time that Schumpeter was writing his pure theory of struggle. It is possible that he was receptive to the new businesslike order not least because the children of Herbert Spencer would be more likely to keep the peace.

The commercial classes know that beggar-my-neighbour policies are unlikely to maximise their profits. Tariff walls protect domestic industry but they invite retaliation from foreign rivals. Legalised cartels provoke competitive dumping that can undercut at home even as it bankrupts abroad. Colonial preference excludes unexpected gatecrashers but also reduces the purchasing power that could have been the source of new jobs and incomes for all: 'Even cartels cannot do without the custom of their foreign economic kin.' (Schumpeter, 1918/19:203). In the limit the international conflict of interest could rescue the militaristic classes from their steady decline: 'War may call them back into life.' (Schumpeter, 1918/19:155). Imperialism may then reassert itself even though it is not the best-paying solution for a nation that has the alternative of the gains from trade. If the generals do crowd out the shopkeepers, then at least it would be true to say that the shopkeepers have only themselves to blame. Knowing that beggar-my-neighbour politics must fail where the nationless anonymity of complementary self-interest was more likely to succeed, still they rejected the automaticity of the worldwide invisible hand. They called for government intervention when the slippery slope, as Hayek has consistently said, must lead back to guns and away from the butter that would have been the more constructive advance.

Economics is anti-imperialist. Political economy is more ambiguous. Probably, however, it is anti-imperialist as well.

State intervention can involve a tension between the minority stake and the collective interest. Protective tariffs illustrate well the trade-off of welfares that can exist where one redistributive lobby secures a concession for which all other producers and consumers will have to pay the price: 'Protective tariffs do not automatically grow from the competitive system. They are the fruit of political action – *a type of action that by no means reflects the objective interests of all those concerned*.' (Schumpeter, 1918/19:206). *One* can benefit. *All* cannot. That is why publicity and democracy, revealing the mutually-negating impact of special-gains legislation, will build up an unstoppable coalition at home in favour of the freedom of trade. Economic aggression, clearly, 'becomes impossible as soon as the majority of those whose consent is necessary realize their true interests' (Schumpeter, 1918/19:206). Subsidies and quotas, boycotts and bombs are not, as the Marxians had contended, a necessary part of capitalism. Rather, they are only practical politics if the majority are unaware of their rational self-interest, economically defined.

Economic self-interest, pre-dating capitalism, is not the product of the modern market order: Schumpeter cites the case of early tribes which enter into conflict over salt deposits or access to the sea (Schumpeter, 1918/19:141). Non-economic self-interest, accompanying capitalism, is, on the other hand, a reason for saying that even in a commercial society cost-conscious calculativeness will not be as powerful as the Spencerians would expect. Schumpeter observes that American public opinion has been in favour of tariffs not out of admiration for big business but because the American people 'wish to build and keep a world of their own' (Schumpeter, 1942a:55). Monopolists exaggerate their own persuasiveness: 'No tariff was ever wholly or even mainly due to this particular cause.' (Schumpeter, 1942a:54). Just as interest predates capitalism, so, it would appear, does culture dilute economics. Schumpeter tends to argue that a nationalistic economic psychology is a consequence of a lagged social structure. Should 'a world of their own' be a cultural motivator in itself, his theory of the transcendence of conflict may be criticised for its underestimation of a collective consciousness that does want beefsteaks but wants other things as well.

The Marxians would object that Schumpeter on imperialism is a theory of the gains from trade that fails to probe into the inner logic of the system. It could be that sustained underconsumption at home will force the developed countries into zero-sum battles over such markets as can still be found. It could be that multinationals with a stake in foreign oil will take over from the feudal residue the unthinking insistence on the big stick that speaks for law and order. It could be that a nation experiencing a secular decline in its domestic rate of profit will have a collective incentive to place its investments in virgin territory abroad: 'If capital is sent abroad', Karl Marx says, 'this is not done because it absolutely could not be applied at home, but because it can be employed at a higher rate of profit in a foreign country.' (Marx, 1884:256). It is the export of capital and not the export of commodities that in Marx's own estimation accounts for monopoly-capital territorialism and the protectiveness of the colonial system: 'Capitals invested in colonies, etc. ... may yield higher rates of profit for the simple reason that the rate of profit is higher there due to backward development, and likewise the exploitation of labour, because of the use of slaves, coolies, etc.' (Marx, 1884:238). Profits are high, but only so long as the windfalls are defended. Thus does the flag follow not trade but investment for the simple reason that the saving countries no longer generate the most lucrative openings.

Schumpeter was aware that metropolitan capital was moving to the Empire. Referring explicitly to his own 'third Kondratieff', he cites British investment in rubber, oil, sugar, in Egyptian cotton, in South African gold and diamonds, as 'examples for the way in which England, more than through domestic development, took part in the industrial process which carried that Kondratieff prosperity' (Schumpeter, 1939:I, 430). Schumpeter did not deny that investment matters. What he did deny was that a war such as the First World War would be the likely result of the competition to find projects. Britain had invested successfully in American railways and Argentinian meat without the need to send in the dragoons or build a tariff wall. Entrepreneurs were introducing new innovations and creating new booms without the need to look abroad for the coolies and the chances. All things considered, Schumpeter decided, the Marxians were employing a theory of profit and loss which erroneously built war and not peace into their political economy. Opting for Spencer and not for Marx, Schumpeter endorsed the view that the failure of the United States to annex either Canada or Mexico was not the exception but the rule. It showed that imperialism had had its day.

6.3 MOTIVATION

The entrepreneur is money-motivated. Pecuniary success in capitalist conditions will be 'very difficult to replace ... as a motor of industrial development' (Schumpeter, 1912b:94).

The businessman wants money. What should not be forgotten is how much else he wants as well. Living on the upward-sloping supply curve, it is not just cash that makes the entrepreneur a driven man but also the prospect of supplementary prizes, the mix of 'other stimuli' (Schumpeter, 1939:I, 130). Alfred Marshall writes that 'the love of money is only one among many'

(Marshall, 1890b:281). Schumpeter was a multidimensional social economist who was keenly aware with Marshall that the fruits of labour are normally more than material hedonism alone.

It is a commonplace that rich industrialists live in the lap of luxury because they have the means to pay. What is no less true is that they 'do not seek the means with the objective of living surrounded by luxury' (Schumpeter, 1912a:137). The living standards are an unintended outcome. They are not the reward that drives the natural creator to bring something new into being. Schumpeter says that 'economic ends do not have to be hedonic' (Schumpeter, 1912a:151). The men who have made modern industry are in fact remarkably uninterested in the consumption that their exertions make possible: 'They have not devoted much thought to the hedonic fruits of their labours.' (Schumpeter, 1912a:137). One implication is that production will not cease once pressing consumer needs have been met.

Marshall writes that money is often desired not as an end but as a measure: 'Those business men, on whose work the progress of industry most depends, care for wealth more as an indicator of successful achievement than for its own sake.' (Marshall, 1907:331). His recognition that business can be a game and winning an end in itself is closely paralleled by Schumpeter's assessment that profit is made the object not least because it is an 'index', 'a very accurate expression of success' (Schumpeter, 1912b:93, 94). Schumpeter says that the entrepreneur is imbued with 'the will to conquer; the impulse to fight, to prove oneself superior to others, to succeed for the sake, not of the fruits of success, but of success itself' (Schumpeter, 1912b:93). Money making is a function of energy and ability, not merely the accident of chance: 'The game is not like roulette, it is more like poker.' (Schumpeter, 1942a:73). Invidious comparison is all about. It helps to explain what business leaders want when they go to work.

The entrepreneur competes fiercely because he is fiercely competitive. His action may even be called 'unmotivated' in the sense that it is not the emanation of a properly costed audit so much as the affirmation of a fundamental need to advertise himself and prove that he is good: 'Great property means a powerful position in society and economy, not merely the possibility of extensively satisfying one's wants as a consumer.' (Schumpeter, 1912a:138, 139). Veblen wrote as follows about the conspicuous consumption of the *nouveaux riches* who had had the good fortune to score the goals: 'So far as regards those members and classes of the community who are chiefly concerned in the accumulation of wealth, the incentive of subsistence or of physical comfort never plays a considerable part .... The dominant motive was from the outset the invidious distinction attaching to wealth.' (Veblen, 1899:36). Ostentation was the passport to standing. Schumpeter like Veblen was absolutely convinced that the men who have made modern industry value the Newport yachts and the Picasso originals very little for their own sake, almost exclusively because of the pecuniary prowess which they symbolise and put on display. The expensive consumables are not demanded for their intrinsic merits. They are the tangible proof that their owner was the victor in the struggle and in that way the better man.

Profit-seeking in business may be likened to trophy-seeking in sport. In each case there is the will to better an opponent. In each case there is Spencerian peace and a respect for the rules of the game. Yet sheer malevolence is also a part of man's motivational make-up; and Schumpeter was too much of a realist to assume away this most familiar of man's non-rational instincts. As he interjected in an era that had witnessed the Nuremberg rallies and known the blind hatred that led to Auschwitz: 'Why should we refuse to recognize the truth which life teaches us every day – that there is such a thing as pugnacity in the abstract that neither needs nor heeds any argument and cares for nothing except for victory as such?' (Schumpeter, 1942a:340). Schumpeter in the *Theory of Economic Development* had written that business success can sublimate the drive for supremacy and in 'Imperialisms' that the exchange of equivalents can be the cause of organic solidarity. In *Capitalism, Socialism and Democracy*, however fleetingly, he showed that even the free trader can have days of despair when he puts back his Locke and reaches instead for his Hobbes which better captures the instinctual pugnacity of wild animals only partially tamed.

Thinkers can trick the naked ape into their own favourite cause: 'Any intellectual can fill the void behind that brute violence in the way that suits his taste.' (Schumpeter, 1942a:340). Unionists and revolutionaries – 'the syndicalist anti-intellectualism of the fist' (Schumpeter, 1942a:340) – can dispense altogether with reason and appeal directly to the viscera for results. Most disturbing of all is the Hitler-like figure who wants to squeeze his opponents until the pips squeak or worse: 'He may even glory in the slaughter – some neurasthenic degenerates do, and others, the communists from failure and resentment, experience satisfaction at the sufferings of a certain class of victims.' (Schumpeter, 1942a:362). Economic sociology is concerned with man as he is and not man as he ought to be. In *Capitalism, Socialism and Democracy*, however fleetingly, Schumpeter took the economics of invidious comparison as far as is humanly possible along the sociological knife-edge that extends from winning in a product launch to winning through ethnic cleansing, the terrorist atrocity and the drive-by shooting.

Reassuringly, the passages in which Schumpeter refers to the *bellum* that is just beneath the veneer are so few as to be seen as exceptions. Invidious comparison in Schumpeter's economic sociology almost always stops short of the destructiveness of malice. The Schumpeter of 'Imperialisms' would say that it had been contractual interdependence itself that had schooled out the theft and made dysfunctional the exercise of quasi-feudal violence. That in itself would be a strong argument for an exchange economy and for the capitalist order.

There is invidious comparison in Schumpeter's spectrum of motives. There is also the inbred need for meaningful productiveness that Veblen called the instinct of workmanship – 'a taste for effective work, and a distaste for futile effort' (Veblen, 1899:29) – and Marshall characterised as 'a delight in doing noble and difficult things because they are noble and difficult' (Marshall, 1907:330). In Schumpeter's economics this vision of a master builder who takes his self-image from imagination made material through accomplishment becomes 'the joy of creating, of getting things done, or simply of exercising one's energy and ingenuity' (Schumpeter, 1912b:93). Irrespective of the conspicuous success and even of the cash, what such a born self-starter most urgently requires is stimulus, excitement and the challenge of the hurdle: 'Our type seeks out difficulties, changes in order to change, delights in ventures.' (Schumpeter, 1912b:93–4). People enjoy the opportunity independently to shape their circumstances. Most of all the entrepreneurial type glories in risk and uncertainty because they give him the job satisfaction that is fostered by decisions that make a difference and is stifled by constraints to which he must adapt.

The non-entrepreneurial type, treating action as the cost of a benefit, will conceivably balance the pleasure of acquisition against the pain of exertion until he reaches the utilitarian equilibrium that is the *stasis* anticipated by Gossen's Law. The entrepreneurial type, however, is forever on the move: 'The strong man wants to change things and, for the sake of daring and changing, continually carries out new plans.' (Schumpeter, 1912a:145). Hungry for 'the pleasure of creating something new' (Schumpeter, 1912a:142), determined to 'stamp his spirit on economic conditions' (Schumpeter, 1912a:143), 'activity for him is an end in itself' (Schumpeter, 1912a:145): 'Such men create because creation is in their nature.' (Schumpeter, 1912a:138). Like the painter, like the poet, it is only when he is creating a future that is not the same as the past that the business leader feels fulfilled and truly himself: 'What such individuals want is more and more deeds, more and more victories. Arrival at the destination is never grounds for lethargy or rest.' (Schumpeter, 1912a:146).

The hedonic personality can settle into an equilibrium state. Not so the energetic type, for whom one victory is only the invitation to a new campaign. He is always on the look-out for the chance to produce change, for new ways to 'interrupt the continuity of economic transformation': 'The carrying out of new combinations is the form and content of development. The driving force is the intervention of a leader.' (Schumpeter, 1912a:162n). He notices the opportunities and breaks down the barriers not because he craves the end-product goods and services but rather because he is the plaything of inner impulses that draw him to 'activities' in the sense of Marshall and only secondarily to Marshall's 'wants' (Marshall, 1890a:75–6): 'The entrepreneur is a person who carries out new combinations. Non-hedonic activity is always necessary to do that.' (Schumpeter, 1912a:172). The age of rational action is made an economic reality by a non-rational agent whose passions and emotions make him eternally unsettled: 'The call of entrepreneurial adventure is too deep-seated to cease dramatically *of itself*.' (Schumpeter, 1939:II, 1036).

The entrepreneur is a driven man because that is what he *is*. The man of action cannot stop and cannot rest because of 'the urge to keep busy' (Schumpeter, 1912a:145) that has him in its thrall. To say that he struggles to a peak and then rests on his laurels is to misunderstand the psychology of a being forced on by a '*Drang*', by a '*Notwendigkeit*' (Schumpeter, 1912a:141, 145) which even a *Mann der Tat* is unable to control: 'Neither consideration of the effort nor satiation of his hedonic needs lames his lust for action.' (Schumpeter, 1912a:145). Addicted like the gambler to the game, he has to keep going even when he has won his match. Surmounting obstacles is the only life he knows: 'To suppose otherwise of our type is to rob him of his true being.' (Schumpeter, 1912a:150).

The only time that he withdraws from the field of battle is when, *anno domini* having worn him out, 'the shadows of evening fall across his days and he no longer feels himself to be the match for younger opponents' (Schumpeter, 1912a:147). Sooner or later even a Great Man runs out of puff. As is illustrated by the novelist who writes himself out or the painter who rehashes his single inspired canvas, the peak may be reached sooner than the physiologist or the gerontologist might have predicted:

> He lives only for a fraction of his physical life. The artist, the scholar, the politician, the captain of industry as well – they all have a relatively short space of time for really creative activity. Afterwards they become exhausted. The man is no longer 'himself'. He no longer conceptualises new things but only carries out what he has already prepared. (Schumpeter, 1912a:147).

The Muse is fickle and old age can set in young. As long as he is in his prime, however, it is the energetic type and not the hedonic type that makes history happen and the future take note: 'He is the agency of economic development.' (Schumpeter, 1912a:147). His striving and struggling is first and foremost the proof that making the world different is firmly within his grasp. If his motivation were narrowly means–ends, mankind might still be in the caves. Because, however, he is forever on the edge, no equilibrium can last for long: 'Pleasure from action itself, without any other motive, is definitely a psychological reality.' (Schumpeter, 1912a:145)

The instinct of workmanship is a positive-sum drive. The same is true of the parental bent. Historically speaking, 'the most glamorous' of the aims of the bourgeoisie has been 'the foundation of an industrial dynasty' (Schumpeter, 1942a:156). The bourgeois tends 'to work and to save primarily for wife *and children*' (Schumpeter, 1942a:160). It is the 'family motive' (Schumpeter, 1942a:160), so unjustly neglected by the utilitarian individualists, that lies at the root of 'the dream and the will to found a private kingdom' (Schumpeter, 1942a:93). Time horizons are short where *homo economicus* has no progeny to whom he can pass on his realm. Savings are greater and profits are higher where the captain of industry is labouring for his lineage and for unborn generations yet to come.

Private kingdoms were part and parcel of early capitalism. In the family firm, 'the success of the enterprise and the success of the enterpriser were one and the same' (Schumpeter, 1929:240). The early enterpriser was motivated by 'duty' and 'love' not least because his success was shared altruistically with others for whom he cared: 'His labour was dictated by his sense of duty, which was directed to the extension of his business – a concrete, determinate, individual business, which he loved non-rationally down to its very walls – and the natural desire to retain and improve his social position, which had its centre in the family home.' (Schumpeter, 1929:230). In early capitalism the success of the competitor was the success of his house. In corporate capitalism the textbook individual is more likely to be on his own.

The continuity is not just the bloodline but the place of residence as well. The bourgeoisie is wont to invest in a home – a town house, perhaps also a place in the country – in order to secure a stable locational setting for multi-period interaction. The furniture and the pictures, durable and accumulated, are the consumers' capital against which 'the rich life of a numerous family can unfold' (Schumpeter, 1942a:159). They are the props and the settings which show that a change of cast need not mean a change of script. They are the insignia and the symbols which the descendants display in order to prove that today is but a part of the Burkean great chain.

Schumpeter, writing of motivation in the purest capitalist case, assigns pride of place to the family and the family home. He does not deny that there are other influences – consider Puritanism in the sense of Weber and competitiveness in the sense of Marx – that promote exertion and encourage frugality. What he says, however, shows that he has read Marshall, who opted for 'chiefly' when Schumpeter used 'primarily' instead: 'Men labour and save chiefly for the sake of their families .... Family affection is the main motive of saving.' (Marshall, 1890a:189). It was Schumpeter's view that there is a 'capitalist ethic that enjoins working for the future irrespective of whether or not one is going to harvest the crop oneself' (Schumpeter, 1942a:160). No account of motivation in the sociology of capitalism will ever be complete which does not assign the highest importance to future kindred who point proudly to the past.

7. The socialist economy

The future is unknowable. Probability is less uncooperative. Schumpeter as an institutional economist identified a 'tendency toward socialism' (Schumpeter, 1942a:309) which suggested to him that the age of the capitalist might be nearing its end: 'Things and souls shape themselves for socialism automatically, i.e. independently of anyone's volition.' (Schumpeter, 1942a:220). Tomorrow or the next day we are all likely to be making our living under socialism. This chapter explores the nature of the economic reality that never-chosen evolution is imposing upon us and is making our own.

Socialism builds on capitalism. Section 1, State socialism, returns to Chapter 5 to show that the business corporation is at once the harbinger and the exemplar of the bureaucratic State that will take over the reins. Section 2, From corporation to state, explains that socialism enjoys a high income-elasticity not because under-performing capitalism spells misery and Marxian impoverishment but rather because welfare-enhancing capitalism must paradoxically 'break to pieces under the pressure of its own success' (Schumpeter, 1942a:134). Section 3, Countervailing forces, ends the chapter on a hesitant note. The track record of the corporate sector, the healthy contribution of small business, principled resistance from people who do not want the change, all will work against the inevitable. Perhaps it is they that will have the last word.

7.1 STATE SOCIALISM

The essence of socialism is that it 'turns on an exclusively economic point' (Schumpeter, 1942a:169). The attraction of socialism is that it is the better tool: 'There is a strong case for believing in its superior economic efficiency.' (Schumpeter, 1942a:188). That is the crux. Schumpeter's socialism 'has nothing to do with the presence or absence of social classes' (Schumpeter, 1942a:19), with social justice and social solidarity, with the expropriation of the expropriators, with the negation of alienating toil. Socialism is not about upward equalisation and not about the inclusion of the downtrodden. Rather, Schumpeter's socialism is about performance. The selling point of socialism is that it delivers the goods: 'Socialist management may conceivably prove as superior to big-business capitalism as big-business capitalism has proved to be to the kind of competitive capitalism of which the English industry of a hundred years ago was the prototype.' (Schumpeter, 1942a:196).

Schumpeter in *Capitalism, Socialism and Democracy* was saying that socialist control would prove the more efficient means. In his earlier essays he was not so certain. In 1920/21, in 'Sozialistische Möglichkeiten', he had stated frankly that directive socialism in his opinion 'inevitably leads to a reduction in production and a worsening of the situation of all groups in society' (Schumpeter, 1920/21:458). In 1928, in 'The instability of capitalism', he had conceded that the new, socialist state of affairs would necessarily bring with it 'some sacrifice of economic welfare' (Schumpeter, 1928:72). In 1927, in 'Unternehmerfunktion und Arbeiterinteresse', he had warned that the inevitable was bound to mean a lower level of material prosperity: 'Ideals cannot be defeated through economic arguments. Yet the truth is that socialism ... cannot be economically justified .... It is impossible to avoid the conclusion that socialism would mean an economic loss for *all* classes.' (Schumpeter, 1927c:167). By 1942 he had decided that socialism would not be an economic catastrophe. In the 1920s he had expressed serious doubts about the capacity of the economic system to survive the loss of the entrepreneur who made the economy spring into life.

7.1.1 The Definition of Socialism

The word socialism, Anthony Crosland warned, will suggest different things to different thinkers: 'There is therefore no point in searching the encyclopaedias for a definitive meaning; it has none, and never could.' (Crosland, 1956:64). There are many definitions of socialism, each of them with its costs and its benefits. Predicting but not proposing, Schumpeter's search was easier than would have been that of a moral philosopher or a political activist. Like Marx, he was obliged by his determinism only to describe in advance 'the kind of socialism that may be looming in the future' (Schumpeter, 1942a:162). He was not obliged to argue the toss, only to anticipate the outcome.

Approaching socialism as a scientist and not as an arbiter, Schumpeter decided that its hard core would have to be control. The centrepiece of socialism, Schumpeter concluded, would be 'the migration of people's economic affairs from the private into the public sphere': 'I define (centralist) socialism as that organization of society in which the means of production are controlled, and the decisions on how and what to produce and on who is to get what, are made by public authority instead of by privately-owned and privately-managed firms.' (Schumpeter, 1950b:421). Centralised decision making is at the very heart of the definition: 'By socialism we shall mean an institutional arrangement that vests the management of the productive process with some public authority.' (Schumpeter, 1943:175). By socialism we shall mean a Ministry of Economic Affairs: 'It is hardly possible to visualize a socialist society in this sense without a huge bureaucratic apparatus that manages the productive and distributive process.' (Schumpeter, 1950b:421).

The leaderly State is central to the definition. Writing in Vienna just after the Russian revolution, Schumpeter insisted that it would be top-down and not friendly cooperation that would ultimately carry the day: 'The meaning of socialisation – this cannot be repeated too often – lies in the need for a conscious economic plan for the whole economy .... For the economy of private property and free competition is nothing less than anarchic.' (Schumpeter, 1920/21:460). Socialisation is the concentration of the decision-making function. It is 'the transformation of an economy which depends on private property and private initiative into a socialist economy ... in which a central organ controls all means of production, works out an economic plan, and regulates the distribution of final goods as between the individual citizens.' (Schumpeter, 1920/21:458). Socialism means that the politician and the civil servant will have to take over from the fumbles of factoring down if the negation of drift is effectively to be negated by science.

Socialism is control. For that reason, experiments in devolution such as guild socialism, syndicalism, anarchism, Fourier's *phalanstères* and Owen's New Lanark do not really count as socialism at all. Socialism, Schumpeter emphasises, is not leaderless withering away but rather its opposite – the 'conquest of private industry and trade by the state' (Schumpeter, 1950b:421). Like Marx, Schumpeter's posture was that of a dispassionate futurologist who took little interest in utopian dreams that could never be implemented. That was just the point. Centralist socialism 'seems to me to hold the field so clearly that it would be a waste of space to consider other forms' (Schumpeter, 1942a:168).

Schumpeter knew that his definition was narrow and biased. In an uncharacteristic late passage he seems even to be expressing some doubts: 'I speak of centralist socialism only because it holds a place of honor in the discussion. But other possibilities should not be neglected.' (Schumpeter, 1950b:422). Schumpeter in places could be uncharacteristically open: 'Some form of guild socialism is not entirely off the cards.' (Schumpeter, 1950b:422). The exceptions aside, what is clear is that he remained faithful to the State: 'By socialist society we shall designate an institutional pattern in which the control over means of production and over production itself is vested with a central authority.' (Schumpeter, 1942a:167). Central authority is the hard core of his socialism on which Schumpeter was not willing to compromise. Writing the history of the future, Schumpeter was convinced that it was the bureaucratic State and not the devolved anachronism that would be the beneficiary of corporate capitalism's decline and fall.

Schumpeter says that control under socialism will be nationalised into a political choice: 'The economic affairs of society belong to the public and not the private sector.' (Schumpeter, 1942a:167). He is considerably less forthcoming on the question of public ownership. It is almost certainly implicit in his collectivisation that property rights and not just power will be transferred from the periphery to the centre. Implicit or not, Warren Samuels is right to criticise Schumpeter for leaving the details of post-capitalist asset-holding to be read between the lines: 'Having defined capitalism in terms of private ownership, he may be chided for finessing the question of state or public ownership .... If "public" does not mean "state", then what does it mean?' (Samuels, 1985:88).

Most people have decided, Samuels reports, that the titles to the assets were to be vested in the State: 'Most people have equated public with state and both with socialism in interpreting Schumpeter's central argument.' (Samuels, 1985:88). A reasonable guess would probably be that Schumpeter wanted the shares to be bought over for fixed-interest bonds; but that the State as the residual profit-taker should grant operational autonomy in order to protect profit-seeking public corporations from day-to-day interference. The arm's-length principle had been endorsed by the German Socialisation Commission in Berlin. The Commission had also advised that nationalised coal should not be given a public subsidy and that worker ownership would be a major threat to efficiency. Schumpeter had been a member of the Commission. Association is no proof of commitment. Schumpeter himself having written relatively little about ownership, the Commission at least throws one small ray of light on what he may have continued to believe.

7.1.2 The Middle Way

There is only one name on the ballot. Or is there? Schumpeter, notably in the post-*Capitalism* years that had witnessed the success of Labour in Britain and of social democracy abroad, was prepared to hint that there might after all be more than a single road leading on to a single end. In 'The march into socialism', written in 1949, the paragraph that begins 'I do not advocate socialism' concludes with the admission that observable tendencies 'may be compatible with more than one outcome': 'Existing tendencies, battling with resistances, may fail to work themselves out completely and may eventually "stick" at some halfway house.' (Schumpeter, 1950b:422). Centralist socialism is likely. It is not certain. People still have free will.

Schumpeter was aware that reformers believed social welfare in alliance with pragmatic interventionism to represent a viable 'third way'. The Attlee Government in Britain, coming after his major publications, had shown that there could be a future of compromise in *selective* nationalisation, poverty relief, fiscal redistribution in the sense of Tawney, perceived equality in the sense of Titmuss, citizenship rights in the sense of T.H. Marshall. Schumpeter seems to have found it difficult to reconcile the reality of the mixed economy with his all-or-nothing expectation that full statism alone would be history's choice. In one place he describes the ideological moderates' 'gratis services' paid for through 'the vast productive possibilities of the capitalist engine' not as middle-ground socialism but merely as '*laborist capitalism*' (Schumpeter, 1950b:425). Elsewhere, writing that public regulation of enterprise 'differs but little from genuinely socialist planning' (Schumpeter, 1950b:424–5), he reflects that Labour's managed interference is not a bulwark against further disintegration but rather the 'proof that the ethos of capitalism is gone' (Schumpeter, 1942a:416). Aware that Britain and other European countries had opted for the middle way, Schumpeter seems to have found it difficult to decide if the halfway house he had seen was halfway capitalist, halfway socialist or halfway a mixture of the two.

Hayek, whose *Road to Serfdom* appeared only two years after Schumpeter's *Capitalism*, had no confidence in anything less than the Manichean either/or:

> Mere common sense proves a treacherous guide in this field .... Both competition and central direction become poor and inefficient tools if they are incomplete; they are alternative principles used to solve the same problem, and a mixture of the two means that neither will really work and that the result will be worse than if either system had been consistently relied upon. (Hayek, 1944:31).

Hayek stated clearly that there was and could be no such thing as a 'third way'. The Schumpeter of 1949, conceding the possibility of a 'movable halfway house' (Schumpeter, 1950b:425), was more tentative and more open-minded.

It may, of course, have been the case that he saw the middle ground not as a long-run equilibrium but simply as a short-run stopping place in a Hayekian evolution that had yet to make its way from classical *laissez-faire* to its centralist antithesis. Speaking of European Fascism, Schumpeter decides that it is only a temporary shelter on 'the road that leads from capitalism to orthodox socialism' (Schumpeter, 1939:I, 105). Speaking of the United States, he suggests that Roosevelt's halfway house will not long outlive its architect. Regulations and transfers, he said, would indeed prolong the life of American capitalism – 'but only for the next half century or so. The long-run diagnosis elaborated in this book will not be affected.' (Schumpeter, 1942a:398). In the short run the development 'may eventually "stick"'. In the long run we will nonetheless all of us be red.

A half century on from 1942, close enough to 1984, is 1992. Marking the year when the Berlin Wall was to have reached San Francisco, Bottomore wrote that Schumpeter spoke too soon. Living only 30 years later, Bottomore said, Schumpeter 'would doubtless have paid greater attention to the possibility of his halfway house becoming rather more like a permanent residence than a mere transit camp' (Bottomore, 1992:130). It is impossible to say what Schumpeter's permanent residence would have been in the United States of nationalised rail or the Thatcherite Britain in which the Health Service remained ring-fenced. What is clear is that even Schumpeter could see that the socialism that he predicted might not in the end be the only game in town.

7.2 FROM CORPORATION TO STATE

Schumpeter shows a surprising lack of interest in real-world statism. There is little attempt in his work to model the dynamics of *dirigisme*, despotism, Stalinism, totalitarianism despite the fact that his Harvard years were also the age of the dictators. Schumpeter was expounding his future at a time when Hitler, Mussolini, Franco and Salazar were so prominently his present. He seems nonetheless to have had little real curiosity about the relationship between the centralist socialism that he predicted and the repression of individual freedom that was already the order of the day in most of continental Europe.

The omission is especially striking in view of his recognition that even in the liberal democracies the coming socialism could in the event be stifling and tyrannical: 'There is little reason to believe that this socialism will mean the advent of the civilization of which orthodox socialists dream. It is much more likely to present fascist features.' (Schumpeter, 1942a:375). Socialism can be profoundly ugly. The Gulag by 1992 might have made its way to Leicester Square. In spite of that Schumpeter shows a surprising lack of interest in real-world statism. The capitalist bureaucracy must evolve into the socialist bureaucracy. There is nothing more to say.

7.2.1 The Organisational Economy

Socialism means bureaucracy: 'I for one cannot visualize, in the conditions of modern society, a socialist organization in any form other than that of a huge and all-embracing bureaucracy. Every other possibility I can conceive would spell failure and breakdown.' (Schumpeter, 1942a:206). Yet capitalism means bureaucracy as well: 'Surely this should not horrify anyone who realizes how far the bureaucratization of economic life – of life in general even – has gone already.' (Schumpeter, 1942a:206). Bureaucracy is absolutely up to the challenge: 'There is no reason to believe that it will break down under the task.' (Schumpeter, 1942a:185). The business corporation is performing well despite the fact that it is being operated by its salaried executives. There is no reason to believe that the sensitivity to surplus and cost will be any greater or any less if the salaried executives were to be re-named civil servants instead.

Executives in corporate capitalism do not hazard their own money or bear financial liability for their own mistakes. In that sense there has already occurred what Karl Marx called an 'abolition of the capitalist mode of production within the capitalist mode of production itself, and hence a self-dissolving contradiction which *prima facie* represents a mere phase of transition to a new form of production' (Marx, 1884:438). Marx anticipated that, in late capitalism, the sheer concentration of productive assets would bring about a 'transformation of the actually functioning capitalist into a mere manager, administrator of other people's capital' (Marx, 1884:436). Schumpeter, building on Marx, agreed that big business has a socialist dimension to the extent that the joint-stock administration 'ousts the entrepreneur and expropriates the bourgeoisie as a class' (Schumpeter, 1942a:134). Private or public, we are almost all working for someone else.

Bureaucracy is here to stay: 'It is an inevitable complement to modern economic development and it will be more than ever essential in a socialist commonwealth.' (Schumpeter, 1942a:206). The separation of ownership from control in the capitalist private sector has shown that ruin need not result if it is the employees who decide. The State when it socialises will only perpetuate the tradition of the labour-managed firm: 'The kind of responsibility that exists in the large-scale corporation could no doubt be reproduced in a socialist society.' (Schumpeter, 1942a:206). Selection and promotion will be as meritocratic and as rational as they were when Moneybags ran the show. Inertia will be no more prevalent and initiative no more discouraged. The tea breaks will be no longer and the dental package no more generous. Big business or big socialism, the organisation man is unlikely to notice the difference when he sits down at his desk.

Galbraith, like Schumpeter, is a theorist of managerial capitalism, capable of describing the shareholder as a 'purely passive recipient of income', prone to regard the management as a 'self-governing, self-perpetuating bureaucracy' (Galbraith, 1973:81). Even Galbraith, however, has said that Schumpeter had a tendency to over-simplify the divide: 'I would argue, in contrast, that there was far more vigour and also more innovating power in managerial capitalism than Schumpeter foresaw and also more administrative difficulty in the socialist alternative than the rest of us realised.' (Galbraith, 1977a:74). Even Galbraith would say that Schumpeter failed to grasp that business bureaucracies and State bureaucracies can be subject to significantly different pressures. Large organisations are a mixed bag. They are not all the same.

Especially telling is the status of profit. The Ministry has no charter to maximise its surplus for the State. The executives of a company know that they are playing toward a different goal. The ends being different, the debate then turns on the extent to which the salaried will reliably serve the interests of the absent despite the fact that the servants of the company, like the servants of the Ministry, do not have a personal stake in the gains.

Schumpeter is dismissive of the contribution that private ownership can make to efficiency. Within the large firm, he writes, 'the figure of the proprietor and with it the specifically proprietary interest have vanished from the picture' (Schumpeter, 1942a:141). Schumpeter, sounding remarkably like Tawney – 'Payment without service is waste' (Tawney, 1921:80) – has nothing positive to say about distant coupon-clippers whom he describes as 'dematerialized' and 'functionless' (Schumpeter, 1942a:142). A less pessimistic assessment would, however, be that capital still has teeth even where the corporation is large.

In some cases the founder and his relatives retain an active involvement: Schumpeter himself speaks of 'family ownership of controlling parcels of stock' (Schumpeter, 1942a:163). In all cases, moreover, the shareholders have an interest in competitive dividends and good capital gains. The larger the stake, the greater the care. Not anonymous and passive but active and watchful, institutional investors and individual players with significant blocs put pressure on managements to improve. They sell out, pushing down the asset value and inviting a hostile takeover, when their agents and representatives consistently under-perform. The vigilance of the oligarchs and grandees provides an umbrella even for the small, the dispersed and the ill-informed. Capitalism without capitalists is not on the horizon.

The survival of profit seeking is further ensured through productivity payments, promotions and share options. Denying strongly that *les affaires, c'est l'argent des autres*, Hilferding makes much of incentive schemes such as these to explain why even professionals on salary have become imbued with the 'lust for booty, which slumbers in every capitalist soul': 'The managers who are at the top of the industrial bureaucracy have a stake in the enterprise, not only because of the bonuses they earn, but still more important, because of their generally substantial shareholdings.' (Hilferding, 1910:121–2, 126). The office holder will be proxied by his section's track record when he applies for a senior position elsewhere. The team leader will be at risk from retrenchment should his company, under-achieving, have to merge with a competitor. The career businessperson, most important of all perhaps, sees himself as a free enterpriser and not a latent socialist who was born to be a cog in the Weberian wheel. The business schools produce few young executives who are indifferent to very high pay in exchange for a major contribution to their chosen corporation's profit-and-loss. Efficiency and innovation are likely to be safe in their hands. Good Samaritanism through the Welfare State is a different matter.

Schumpeter ignores or underestimates the significance of profit-seeking in the economics even of *corporate* capitalism. Since no analogous pressures exist in the public sector, he is wrong to treat the two incentive structures as if they are the same. In doing so, however, he was standing on the shoulders of giants. Berle and Means in 1932 had already declared that Adam Smithian self-interest had ceased to be the guarantee of economical good husbandry: 'The explosion of the atom of property destroys the basis of the old assumption that the quest for profits will spur the owner of industrial property to its most effective use.' (Berle and Means, 1932:9). Berle and Means believed that 'the position of ownership has changed from that of an active to that of a passive agent' (Berle and Means, 1932:66) and that, nowadays, 'the interests of ownership and control are in large measure opposed' (Berle and Means, 1932:123). Once upon a time private vices had meant public virtues. The separation of ownership from control put an end to that: 'This dissolution of the atom of property destroys the very foundation on which the economic order of the past three centuries has rested.' (Berle and Means, 1932:8). Nowadays, 'it is no longer the individual himself who uses his wealth' (Berle and Means, 1932:8). Nowadays it is the kitchen staff who plan the menus and the plutocrats upstairs who eat what they are given.

Mass production and mass distribution have rendered indispensable the multi-unit organisation. Internalised allocation and managerial structure, Chandler writes, were thus 'the institutional response to the rapid pace of technological innovation and increasing consumer demand' (Chandler, 1977:12). Capitalism has grown on a large scale. The consequence has been coordination through hierarchies in place of exchanges negotiated and priced: 'The visible hand of management replaced the invisible hand of market forces where and when new technology and expanded markets permitted a historically unprecedented high volume and speed of materials.' (Chandler, 1977:12). Ownership has surrendered to management. Bureaucrats transact but they do not necessarily sell. Adam Smithian economics relates to an articulation through bargains and swaps that is less and less our own. What is needed today, if Berle and Means and Chandler are correct, is an organisational economics which helps to predict precisely what it is that office holders on a salary will want to demand and supply. Here Schumpeter may be criticised for leaving his corporate capitalism without anything that can be called a behavioural theory of the firm.

Schumpeter treats the business as a black box. Galbraith anticipates that his planning technostructure will pursue beyond-profit objectives like job satisfaction, growth and security (Galbraith, 1967:118–19, 138–45). Chandler is confident that career managers have consistently 'preferred policies that favored the long-term stability and growth of their enterprises to those that maximized current profits' (Chandler, 1977:10). Schumpeter, agreeing on the administration, is remarkably silent on the maximand. It is a major omission. Particularly is it a loss for a methodological individualist, committed as he must be to an explanation of the organisation that builds upwards from each component part.

A Herbert Simon would find it improbable that the office holder 'turns off the switch of his own desires from nine to five' (Simon, 1957:167). A Max Weber, on the other hand, sees the bureaucrat as an automaton who subordinates his interests to the charter of the group: 'Entrance into an office, including one in the private economy, is considered an acceptance of a specific obligation of faithful management.' (Weber, 1948:199). Schumpeter, writing of convergence, is closer to the single-valued *Wertrationalität* of Weber than he is to the open-ended imaginativeness of Simon. It is arguably because he is European enough to believe that no decent servant would cut corners on his duty that he says little about behavioural goals such as sales maximisation, conspicuous publicity, defensive reinvestment, prestige purchased at the cost of dividends. His image of the organisation is different from that of a Galbraith, a Chandler or a Simon. History-hallowed and consensually-accepted, the success indicator of profit might be safe in the hands of his paid executives for the myopic and narrow reason that it might be the only success indicator that they know.

7.2.2 The Evolution of Socialism

Schumpeter like Marx is attracted by the economic explanation of social causality, by 'the theory that the economic pattern is the really operative element in the sum total of the phenomena that we call society' (Schumpeter, 1942a:169). As Marx had done, he conceived of the transition to socialism not as the outcome of principles and ideals but as the institutional consequence of unfolding capitalism itself. Conscious choice arrives after the event. It is 'economic process' – the 'prime mover' (Schumpeter, 1942a:162) – that is chiefly responsible for the change.

Schumpeter like Marx anticipates 'socialization in a state of maturity' (Schumpeter, 1942a:221): capitalism then having run its course, evolutionary tendencies will 'strongly point to socialism as the heir apparent' (Schumpeter, 1942a:61). He shows little interest in 'socialization in a state of immaturity' (Schumpeter, 1942a:223): since the transition will only take place in the fully developed or 'fettered' stage, he sees no reason to 'waste space' (Schumpeter,

1942a:219) on doomed experiments such as that of Lenin's Bolsheviks where violent revolution and 'millions of victims' (Schumpeter, 1942a:362n) were unable to make a success of something that, given time, would have happened in any case. Given time, the 'economic process tends to socialize *itself*' (Schumpeter, 1942a:219). Given time, 'Marx's *vision* was right' (Schumpeter, 1942a:162).

Schumpeter like Marx was prepared to wait until competitive capitalism had completed its historical mission. Marx defined the end of prehistory in terms of the class consciousness of the revolutionary proletariat. Schumpeter did so in terms of the giant corporation, able to 'automatize progress' and to make individual initiative 'superfluous' (Schumpeter, 1942a:134). An economic base of small and medium-sized firms, of go-ahead entrepreneurs and weak bureaucracies, does not lend itself to socialisation from within: 'Attempts to establish socialism now would, for most of the great nations and many small ones, undoubtedly amount to courting failure.' (Schumpeter, 1942a:228). The position will be very different once 'the requisite stage of industrial development has been reached' (Schumpeter, 1942a:167). Devolved alertness once trapped within an administrative routine, big business will at that stage have produced a planned economy of its own. It is a corporate socialism which without any significant change in the nature of the function can and will come under the sway of the wise commander who gets things done: 'We can assume that here the State itself takes over the entrepreneurial activity.' (Schumpeter, 1912a:173).

History is on the horizontal axis. Capitalism fails because it succeeds. The invisible hand ends up by devouring its own favourite sons: 'The true pacemakers of socialism were not the intellectuals or agitators who preached it but the Vanderbilts, Carnegies and Rockefellers.' (Schumpeter, 1942a:134). Big business swallowed up little business. At some stage there will be no one left to call himself a capitalist: 'The perfectly bureaucratized giant industrial unit not only ousts the small or medium-sized firm and "expropriates" its owners, but in the end it also ousts the entrepreneur and expropriates the bourgeoisie as a class.' (Schumpeter, 1942a:134). Living standards have risen to unprecedented heights. The progress, however, has come at a Faustian cost.

Destiny is on the horizontal axis. At some critical threshold the system effectively changes its name. Well and good – but Peter Wiles is only one among many to have dismissed as an 'absurdity' the notion that such a critical point exists: 'There is of course no such requisite stage, however primitive, and this proves Schumpeter's unconscious Marxism. For an Austrian he was very German. CSD is a late-19th-century *Stufenlehre* and its author must be denominated a *Kathederkapitalist*.' (Wiles, 1981:156, 157). What Wiles is saying is that Schumpeter had injudiciously fallen under the spell of the

German Historicists and their Marxian counterparts. Their naive over-confidence had led him to expect a single path with a single destination when in fact the historical trajectory could only be a spectrum of tendencies. Austrians like Hayek and 'Austrians' like Shackle were so sensitive to unknowledge that they proclaimed themselves unable to guess the contours and shapes of a history-to-come that no one had seen. Wiles, who was not a full-blooded intellectual agnostic, would say that Schumpeter could usefully have leavened his stages of growth with a reasonable openness to the Austrians' uncertainties of discovery, pluralism, deviation and surprise.

Across-the-board affluence is itself a strong reason not to chance the next stage. Schumpeter, defending prosperity, was able to argue against the Marxians that even matter decisively in motion would pale into insignificance when compared with the high living standards that free-enterprise capitalism had been able to deliver: 'A sensible workman ... might well come to the conclusion that, everything considered, he is not doing so badly.' (Schumpeter, 1942a:144). People like to live well. They will oppose any development that they believe to be a threat. The 'colossal industrial success' of the United States and other advanced countries, Schumpeter himself concedes, might actually 'annihilate the whole case for socialism so far as it is of a purely economic nature' (Schumpeter, 1942a:382). The fruit is ripe for the plucking. No one, however, has any wish to kill the golden goose. The logic is that of the determinist. The prediction, however, is defiantly the status quo.

Evolution might 'stick' at the corporate stage because that is what the voters want. Warren Samuels says that he sees no reason to expect State socialism at all where the concentrations and the conglomerates have proven themselves to be a viable third choice: 'What I am suggesting ... is that *by Schumpeter's own account*, individualist entrepreneurial capitalism and public-sector control of production and distribution are not the only alternatives. By his own account, the corporate system seems to be a third alternative, the capitalist successor to individualist entrepreneurial capitalism.' (Samuels, 1985:91). Early capitalism is small-scale and Smithian. Late capitalism is 'private socialism' (Samuels, 1985:61), centralised and planned. Samuels points out how illogical it is to treat petty capitalism as the essence of capitalism, to regard technocratic and coordinated capitalism as but the anteroom to the State. What would make more sense, Samuels writes, would be to say that capitalism in the corporate stage has merely evolved into itself. Having done so successfully, there will be no need for it to evolve into anything else.

Capitalism can 'stick' at the corporate stage without moving on to the State. Socialism by the same token can come into being before big business has become its own to inherit. Schumpeter expresses his tendency laws with such passion that the reader all too easily forgets that they are not intended to be confident predictions. Other things can alter. Evolution can take a different path.

Thus Third World governments are seen to introduce centralist planning and to nationalise their productive base. They do so because they believe that pre-industrial socialism will produce more immediate and substantial development than would a reliance on patient bureaucratisation that one day will usher in control. Richer democracies, again, are known to vote for left-leaning tribalism because of an extra-economic commitment to cohesion and compassion. Their generous welfareism is one that transcends the baubles and trinkets of satiated affluence: 'Much of the propelling force of socialism comes, even today, from those irrational longings of the hungry *soul* – not belly.' (Schumpeter, 1942a:308). Their free choice of intervention is one that is difficult to situate in the uncompromising framework of the momentum inherent in matter.

Exogeneities abound. War is a historical accident that is a world away from economic predestination: 'It was a war and the consequent military and administrative breakdown which produced the bolshevist regime ... . No amount of unscientific determinism avails against this fact.' (Schumpeter, 1942a:422). The war and not the proletariat was at the root of the Russian revolution. So was the unforeseeable 'fluke' (Schumpeter, 1942a:359) that the Germans allowed Lenin to cross their territory en route home to the Finland Station. National character played its part in helping the Bolsheviks to harvest the fruits of chance: 'The trouble with Russia is not that she is socialist but that she is Russia.' (Schumpeter, 1942a:404). National character is an exogeneity and not the passive rubber stamp for dialectical inevitability. Its explanatory power, as Schumpeter stated in his Lowell Lectures in 1941, is very great indeed: 'Hitlerism is typically German; Fascism is typically, nationally Italian; bolshevism is Russian, but not American. Whatever comes will be a growth wearing the color and the flavor of the soil.' (Schumpeter, 1941:397). Of the soil – and not of the economy that Schumpeter more commonly made the essence of the dynamic against which there could be little defence.

The visible hand can shape the pattern of evolution. A contemporary of Hitler and Stalin, a student of Hegel on masterful Caesars who do not wait to be asked, Schumpeter must have seen the extent to which determined politicians could take a lead. The Red Army is a convincing illustration of history's reluctance to let unguided events fall where they may. In the words of Peter Wiles: 'Socialism has spread by force of Soviet arms .... There are very few exceptions to this simple military rule, which is much more important than all talk of convergence (a concept Schumpeter did not use), or of automatic peaceful socialization (which he did) .... We need conquest theories, not convergence theories.' (Wiles, 1981:155). Schumpeter, admittedly, did add a short section on 'Russian Imperialism and Communism'

(Schumpeter, 1942a:398–406) in the 1946 edition of his *Capitalism*. This acknowledgement of political expansionism that does not wait for the fruit to be ripe is very much in line with his early essay on 'Imperialisms' as the highest stage of domination-seeking egoism. It is a recognition of non-rational aggressiveness which, in Wiles's view, not only reveals Schumpeter to have been 'a cold warrior before the Cold War' but also 'destroys his whole thesis': 'If that is what socialism is like, capitalism will not peacefully grow into it.' (Wiles, 1981:155).

Capitalism grows into socialism. Socialism does not return the compliment. As far as Schumpeter was concerned, the transition is a ratchet and the transformation irreversible: 'Steps so responsibly taken will not have to be retraced.' (Schumpeter, 1942a:378). Socialism is the end of history. A final destination has no need to evolve.

History, however, plays strange tricks. Mrs Thatcher denationalised the public utilities. President Reagan marginalised the Keynesian macro-economics. Russia broke up the Soviet Union. China re-positioned itself from plan to market. Nationalism and fundamentalism, feminism and environmentalism, distance political economy from the cost–benefit trade-off of Left versus Right. Schumpeter believed that scrambled eggs, once scrambled, would never be unscrambled again. History has shown that the unexpected loves to happen. Capitalism and socialism are wilder beasts than even a careful scholar like Schumpeter seems to have been able to imagine.

7.3 COUNTERVAILING FORCES

Big business gives way to big government because that's the way it has to be: 'The inference as to the transition to a socialist regime in such fullness of time is obvious.' (Schumpeter, 1942a:219). The inference was obvious to Schumpeter. It cannot be said to have been obvious to his readers. Especially problematic are three core areas where Schumpeter, providing multiple answers to one and the same question, seems to have wishy-washed away his very real uncertainties.

First, there is efficiency. Corporate capitalism is at the coalface of technological and managerial innovation. It is the engine of progress. Corporate capitalism is also a matrix of interchangeable bureaucrats making decisions in teams. It is susceptible to inertia. Suggesting both that the large firm is the mould-breaker and that it is asleep on the job, Schumpeter was at once a Weberian who expected duty and a Schumpeterian who expected change. The mix is a problem – but it is not an equal mix. Schumpeter seems to have concluded that the corporate personality on balance is keeping alive the tradition of creative destruction. That being the case, there is unlikely to be any strong desire to move on to something new.

The situation is different where private enterprise becomes a backwater of inactivity. The real disillusionment sets in not when business is proactive and entrepreneurial but when it is exhausted and unimaginative, not 'when capitalist evolution is in full swing' but later on, 'as soon as it *permanently* slackens down' (Schumpeter, 1942a:194). The exhausted stage is the saturated equilibrium, the Smith-like, Mill-like end of the road. It is something that Schumpeter both anticipates and fears once dynamic capitalism 'has sown its wild oats, done its work and is approaching a stationary state' (Schumpeter, 1942a:178).

Speaking of the stationary state, Schumpeter describes it as mind-numbing changelessness. There the past-perpetuating make the choices, the adventurous are frozen out and the *coup de grâce* is not the Leninist bang but an inaudible whimper: 'Socialism of a very somber type would almost automatically come into being.' (Schumpeter, 1942a:131). So stationary a state is undeniably a microeconomic spectre. A *single* tree in the Marshallian forest can undeniably secure its tenure and thereafter develop no further. What is far less likely is that *every* tree in *every* forest will *simultaneously* exhaust the limits of its potential. New prospects are constantly coming on stream. New entrants are continually breaking in to compete. What one cannot do, all businesses together can. What they can do is to nip sombre socialism in the bud.

Second, there is the small-firm sector. Schumpeter believed that late capitalism is the epoch when the large corporation comes into its own. Socialism, he wrote, 'will inherit a "monopolistic" and not a competitive capitalism' (Schumpeter, 1942a:189). The theorists of powerless and perfect competition would evidently do well to recognise that their models are not for all seasons: 'We need not trouble about the competitive case except incidentally.' (Schumpeter, 1942a:189).

Schumpeter, in emphasising the role of what Galbraith calls the 'planning system', seems to be writing off the contribution of what Galbraith calls the 'market system'. His perception of the small firm as the pinprick impact of a self-liquidating sector is not borne out by the evidence. Galbraith himself estimates that his two 'systems' are approximately equal in size, each accounting for approximately one half of total non-State value-added in the economy (Galbraith, 1973:59). In neglecting one half, Schumpeter is neglecting the appreciable share in economic performance that is represented by small businesses which have not evolved into the corporate hierarchies that evolve into the State.

Schumpeter does not say that the late capitalist future has already become his present. He in fact denies that the Adam Smithian small operator can only now be visited in the history books: 'Competition, actual and potential, is still a major factor .... Enterprise is still active .... The bourgeois family has not yet died.' (Schumpeter, 1942a:163). Nor does Schumpeter say that the small business will inexorably be driven to the wall by Marx on concentration in collaboration with Weber on the organisational chart. Even under socialism, he observes, the movement towards the monolith need not 'work itself out completely' nor the independent farmer or tradesman be squeezed forever out of a decent living in the shadow of the great: 'A large fringe may therefore be covered indefinitely by compromise arrangements.' (Schumpeter, 1950b:423). To say that Schumpeter knew nothing of the small or medium enterprise, either in his own time or in the future, would clearly be an exaggeration. The fact remains that he did not integrate its survival into his theory of large size and socialism. Had he done so, he would have found that what Marx calls the 'petty bourgeoisie' was simply not prepared to lie down and die.

Third, there is principled resistance. Max Weber had said that norms have legitimacy and ideas have consequences: 'Very frequently the "world images" that have been created by "ideas" have, like switchmen, determined the tracks along which action has been pushed by the dynamic of interest.' (Weber, 1922/23:280). It was a lesson that Schumpeter was reluctant to take to heart. It is not men's ideals but unstoppable capitalism itself, he wrote, that 'shapes things and souls for socialism' (Schumpeter, 1942a:220). In the market for apples and pears the consumer is king. In the market for economic systems, 'the logic of the situation will carry the day' (Schumpeter, 1932:603). The 'repulsive rationality of the coming times' is not going to be much fun: 'I share the rejection of my own times of the rationalisation of life and thought.' (Schumpeter, 1932:602). Acceptance or rejection, there is no escape: 'Unfortunately, however, the process has acquired its own momentum .... The romantic reactionaries and their work do not stand a chance.' (Schumpeter, 1932:602).

Value judgements are 'of little interest' (Schumpeter, 1942a:129) in the strict evolutionary order. Even so, ideals and preferences do exist and must be taken into account in any responsible assessment of the dialogue between the *ought-to-be*s and the outturns. The Marxian proletariat, pushed or pulled, at least had a desire for the classless society that lay beyond the revolution. No one but a technocrat or a politician could get much satisfaction from the well-ordered dystopia that Schumpeter draws aside the curtain to reveal. Yet no one speaks out against the statism, 'prognosis' but not 'desirability' (Schumpeter, 1942a:61), which is steadily crushing valued plurality underfoot.

Schumpeter in 1942 expressed the view that the inescapable was not expecting much opposition: 'Resistance will be weak .... Cooperation will be forthcoming from the greater part of *all* classes.' (Schumpeter, 1942a:221). In 1946, aware that even his strongest supporters were calling him defeatist, he modulated his fatalism to extend the option of resistance even to the sailors trapped in a sinking ship: 'The crew can sit down and drink. But it can also rush to the pumps .... What normal man will refuse to defend his life merely because he is quite convinced that sooner or later he will have to die anyhow?' (Schumpeter, 1942a:413). It is difficult to imagine a less enthusiastic defence of free will than that. Even so, it is not a passive pass-through that allows all-conquering statism to nationalise the tendency laws and do what it wants.

Resistance is possible. Nor will the countervailing values necessarily fall on stony ground. Schumpeter in 1941 conceded in his Lowell Lectures that even ideas still had a chance: 'Fighting for capitalist civilization is not a hopeless task .... The flu need not develop into pneumonia.' (Schumpeter, 1941:398). It was a dangerous admission for a determinist to make. Some people will say that they prefer oligopoly to allocative efficiency and believe that Coca Cola, Microsoft and British Telecom, although private, are involved in a satisfactory amount of product development. Other people will say that they oppose the merger of the civil service with the industrial bureaucracy lest the monopoly hierarchy that results, in Swedberg's words, 'strengthen the power of the state by doing away with its most important competitor under capitalism' (Swedberg, 1998:79). Such people are not putting pipe dreams in place of reality. Rather, they are defending a going concern against an alternative which they regard as ethically inferior. Schumpeter in 1942 said that centralist socialism was on its way, 'independently of anyone's volition' (Schumpeter, 1942a:220). Schumpeter in 1941 accepted, however, that socialists who counted their chickens might be underestimating the strength of the popular vote.

8. Market and plan

Socialism is the superior tool: 'Solution of the problems confronting the socialist management would be not only just as possible as is the practical solution of the problems confronting commercial managements: it would be easier.' (Schumpeter, 1942a:186). Seldom has a case for socialism been argued so strongly by an anti-socialist who had no liking for it. The inference to be drawn from Schumpeter on systems is in the circumstances a reassuring one. Not only is socialism inevitable, it is good economics as well.

The subject of this chapter is the comparative performance of the institutional alternatives. The ingredients are always and everywhere the same: local scarcity, unit cost, next-best foregone, calculation, coordination, signalling. It is the combinations and permutations that differ so radically. Hayek and Mises favoured decentralised decision-making: they attacked the disciplined goose-step of distorting command. The Stalinist Plan had no room for supply and demand: unfocused search could only dissipate the people's niggardly endowment. Barone and Lange modelled the 'best of both worlds' of the systemic cross-breed: in market socialism the lion of flexible pricing would lie down with the lamb of the sheltering State. Schumpeter, predicting the tendencies and assessing the implications, knew that market and plan was a mansion with many wings and many hidden doors. No one knew better than Schumpeter that the institutional alternatives were not a simple either/or.

This chapter is concerned with the kaleidoscope functioning of market and plan. Section 1, Productive efficiency, explains why Schumpeter believed that centralist socialism would keep down the waste: information, public finance and social discipline are three of the reasons that he provides. Section 2, Market socialism, explains that Barone and Lange were able to marry up the best features of Ministry and auction while Hayek and Mises insisted that, especially in economics, hybrids are known to be sterile. Section 3, Allocative efficiency, continues the discussion of politicised quantities, free-market prices. The section shows that Schumpeter endorsed the compromise model of Barone and Lange but that there was as much authority as exchange in the socialism that he believed to be on the way.

8.1 PRODUCTIVE EFFICIENCY

Dynamic efficiency is about innovation and change. It seems to be system-neutral. Schumpeter did not say that a government bureaucracy would be in a position to rescue creative destruction from the limbo to which it had been relegated by the sluggishness of dinosaur corporations. What he did say is that socialism had a comparative advantage in the area of productive efficiency. The superiority of socialism lies not in the ability to stimulate exciting new departures but in the second-best economics of maximum output from a real, existing endowment. It is *Hamlet* without the prince but better than no *Hamlet* at all.

Static efficiency to Schumpeter means minimum slippage in the conversion of physical resources: 'Economic efficiency of a system we will reduce to productive efficiency.' (Schumpeter, 1942a:189). Inputs being scarce, ceiling output must be secured from the limited potential: 'We shall call that system relatively more efficient which ... would *in the long run* produce the larger stream of consumers' goods per equal unit of time.' (Schumpeter, 1942a:190). Like Veblen, Schumpeter is measuring his success rate in the technological metric of physical heat into physical light. Revealed preferences and final-degree exchange play no part in the condition he proposes.

Schumpeter, concentrating on engineers' efficiency, is curiously reluctant to extend the discussion to wants and utilities. Happiness or contentment, he seems to be saying, is not really economics at all but rather psychic satisfaction, invisible and unmeasured. Ideological socialists will enjoy socialism for its own sake whereas conviction capitalists will prefer a different package: value-free economics, proceeding *de gustibus*, cannot rank the two sets of tastes. Inter-temporal comparisons are impeded by the fact that different times mean different products: especially will this be a problem where the capitalist market and the socialist plan do not, because of a world-view divide, target an identical mix of goods. Inter-personal comparisons are difficult to make since scientific economics has no way of quantifying the discrete individual's cardinal state of mind: 'Most modern theorists would discard this argument.' (Schumpeter, 1942a:191). Levellers often legitimise a more equal distribution of purchasing power with the conjecture that a reassignment of claims from the over-fed to the deprived will produce a rise in the nation's felt welfare stock: satisfaction, methodologically speaking, could just as easily remain constant or even fall. What all of this means is that Schumpeter found it so difficult to conceptualise meaningful proxies for consumers' perceptions that he made the decision to concentrate, like the physicist, on objective magnitudes instead. Socialism maximises the productive efficiency. There is no other test that the economist can apply.

8.1.1 Socialism as an Information Pool

Socialisation captures for the nation the productivity gains from maximum-attainable size. Horizontally, the public corporation exploits its forward-falling supply curve and keeps down its average cost. Vertically, the social monopoly rationalises its channels from the production-line to the shops and eliminates the middleman who wants his cut. Both in the horizontal and in the vertical sense, the socialist single concentrate is able to achieve a degree of productive efficiency that multiple-firm profit-seeking cannot equal. An important reason is the economy of information. In capitalism scarce resources must be squandered on perishable business intelligence. In socialism the Ministry of Production makes its knowledge of the economy, comprehensive, encompassing and reliable, into a free-on-demand public good.

Perfect competition is at risk from the anarchy of the common-trigger stampede: rationality for the member must spell irrationality for the club. Oligopoly is exposed to radical uncertainty and the indeterminacy of price: gaming interdependence means transaction costs, duplicated effort and excess capacity. Monopoly is not the safe harbour that it seems: moves and counter-moves are the blocking strategy that keeps out the new entry that will lead to the cartel that will splinter into the price war. No firm in the private sector is in a strong position to make a well-informed business choice. Capitalists will clearly be envious of socialists. Socialists at least know where they stand.

Socialism, in Schumpeter's interpretation, is the communism of precision: 'In a socialist economy everything ... is uniquely determined.' (Schumpeter, 1942a:194). Energy and other resources are in that way saved through the supersession of capitalist confusion. In a socialist economy the central planning body serves as a clearing house for information. This ensures that there will be neither shortfalls nor gluts. Suppliers, fellow travellers and no longer rivals, are encouraged to cooperate and share: 'The managements of socialized industries and plants would be in a position to know exactly what the other fellows propose to do and nothing would prevent them from getting together for concerted action.' (Schumpeter, 1942a:186). Such disclosure, such collusion mean that managements will be freed to focus their attention on genuine imponderables that central planning plus concerted action cannot neutralise in advance. It is economic to opt for so information-efficient a procedure. It is rational to opt for 'anything that shortens, smoothens or safeguards the road' (Schumpeter, 1942a:194).

The planners can see the wider picture. The benefits that accrue in the macro-economic areas of stabilisation and growth argue strongly for the visible hand.

Top-down guidance moderates the amplitude of the cycle. A socialist plan, assuring 'systematic coordination and orderly distribution in time of new ventures in all lines' (Schumpeter, 1942a:195), tends to minimise the loss and disturbance that can so easily be the multiplier effect of novelty and obsolescence. Microeconomic preventives, stemming booms, slumps and 'temporary paralysis' (Schumpeter, 1942a:195) before they occur, are economically less destabilising than is stop–go *ex post* macroeconomics that fights the fire when the damage is done. In the short run there is less idle capacity and less unemployment. In the long run redundant plant and labour will be redirected more rapidly to other outlets – 'which, if the planning lives up to its possibilities at all, might in each case be waiting for them' (Schumpeter, 1942a:196). In the short run and the long run both, forward-looking omniscience strikes at the causes of the ups and downs with a degree of success that must in itself be a strong endorsement of the State and its precision targeting: 'The planning of progress ... would be incomparably more effective ... than any automatic or manipulative variations of the rate of interest or the supply of credit can be.' (Schumpeter, 1942a:195).

The socialist State ensures in addition that sub-standard practice is modernised and outdated technology made state-of-the-art. So effective is its leadership that pejoratively to use 'bureaucracy' and 'interference' as synonyms for slippage and sloth is to substitute prejudiced libertarianism for an impartial appraisal of the costs and the benefits. Inefficient is the small or medium-sized competitor, so often 'indifferently managed in some respect or other' (Schumpeter, 1942a:197). Inefficient is the litigation that is the deadweight of contract, an economic loss symbolised both by lawyers' fees and by the 'unproductive employment of many of the best brains' (Schumpeter, 1942a:198). Efficient is the large corporation with its rational hierarchy of economical office-holders. Efficient is the modern State where skilled Weberians give constructive support to wise politicians who know what to do. Socialism, Schumpeter believed, is the superior tool. The invisible hand lacks the knowledge that would allow it to compete.

8.1.2 Socialism and Public Finance

Under capitalism the tax system is oppressive and minus-sum. Under socialism it is a well-oiled machine that functions with minimum loss. Public finance is a further argument in support of the centralised order.

In all the stages that lead up to socialism the governors and their administrators live on a value-added that is produced in the private sector. The relationship between the rulers and the taxpayers is not a happy one: 'Nothing else brings out so well the wastes that result from the conflict of structural principles in a social body. Modern capitalism relies on the profit principle for its daily bread yet refuses to allow it to prevail.' (Schumpeter, 1942a:198). The fiscal transfer weakens business through its draining away of much-needed investment capital. The 'hyperprogressive methods of taxation' (Schumpeter, 1950b:428) employed by soak-the-rich interventionists have a disincentive effect on the commitment to labour and to parsimony. Inland Revenue tax collectors absorb resources and put nothing back. All things considered, taxes under capitalism are 'a major factor in the explanation of unsatisfactory economic performance' (Schumpeter, 1942a:198).

Under socialism, fortunately, the tax take will no longer be a threat to productive efficiency: 'No such conflict, consequently no such wastes, would exist in socialist society.' (Schumpeter, 1942a:198). Schumpeter's reasoning is that the State under socialism will alone be the residual claimant: the only capitalist, it will have no need to tax away profits that it already receives. Personal income tax will wither and die: gross incomes become net incomes since the State as property-owner deducts its own share at source. The new method of collection, Schumpeter wrote, will be a major advantage of the coming collectivisation of capital: 'Here we have got hold of one of the most significant titles to superiority that can be advanced in favor of the socialist plan.' (Schumpeter, 1942a:199). Socialism makes public finance a paying proposition. Capitalism makes it a wet blanket that damps down the flames.

8.1.3 Socialism and Social Discipline

Socialism is more efficient than capitalism for the final reason that it better bonds the parts into a whole. Capitalism is individualistic (thereby eroding the mutual support of community networks). Capitalism is egalitarian (thereby making it more difficult for the leadership to assert its rightful authority). Capitalism is calculative (thereby undermining the habituated loyalties of convention and tradition). Capitalism is hedonistic (thereby causing impatient citizens to put present convenience before long-term involvement). Capitalism is not, in sum, an economic system that produces the cultural capital it requires to fulfil its own potential. Socialism, on the other hand, is well placed to get things done.

Socialism, through its single-class economics and through the interdependence of its organicism, boosts morale because it makes employees aware that they belong to a team that is larger than the self. The 'class-war complex', 'drab routine', a general state of bewilderment as to the 'economic significance of measures and processes' give way to 'enthusiasm', professional pride and 'a healthier attitude toward his duties' than the worker could possibly have had in 'a system he has come to disapprove' (Schumpeter, 1942a:211, 212, 213). Self-discipline and group discipline become more rigorous. It is the lesson of socialism that sacrifice and attachment are somehow the citizen's sacred trust.

The socialist order apparently convinces the *I* that he or she is a valued participant in the *Us*. Productivity goes up. Restiveness goes down. The reason is clear: disruptions at work would be 'nothing else but anti-social attacks upon the nation's welfare' (Schumpeter, 1942a:212). Workers who strike come to 'do so with a bad conscience' and 'meet public disapproval' (Schumpeter, 1942a:212) when their betrayal becomes known. No one in a socialist society wants that. The socialist economy operates in 'a society that once more believes in its own standards' (Schumpeter, 1942a:215). The consensus in place, social discipline becomes self-enforcing and the need for an authoritarian government becomes less and less.

Yet some control will always be needed since there will always be some disagreement. Sectional interests, geographical and industrial, will continue to clash. Trouble makers, even in socialism, will stir up unrest as a means of furthering their career. Above all, there will be the 25 per cent of the population that are 'subnormal': suffering from 'moral or volitional defects', their insensitivity to informal pressures is so marked as to make them 'the great enemy of humanity' (Schumpeter, 1942a:213). Even if the culture is indeed consensual, there will always be a residuum of hooligans and free riders. Coercion will be indispensable in order that potential deviants be kept in line. Here too it is the socialist system that is the more effective in containing the disease.

The socialist leadership has at its disposal more 'tools of authoritarian discipline' (Schumpeter, 1942a:215) than does any capitalist counterpart. Capitalist firms can dismiss, but alternative employers abound: socialism has more nearly a monopoly corner in the access to sustenance. Schooling under socialism can be used to 'create an atmosphere favorable to factory discipline' (Schumpeter, 1942a:217): the State through its indoctrination of the young can mould a public opinion in its own desired image. Trades unions under socialism are less likely to oppose than to propagate the State-imposed public interest: in the Soviet Union the union representatives, reluctant to criticise the 'ruling set', have let themselves 'become organs of authoritarian discipline' (Schumpeter, 1942a:217). Managements in socialism are less likely to be constrained by worker-friendly legislation. Intellectuals in socialism are less likely to be allowed to grow into a hostile cabal. A walk-out is more likely to be prohibited by law. A strike is more likely to be called a 'mutiny' (Schumpeter, 1942a:215). Socialist autocracy, like socialist consensus, has, in other words, an unquestioned superiority over even corporate capitalism in the preservation of social discipline. Productive efficiency is the result. Under Stalin the trains ran on time.

It is not very appealing. The unions will lose their independence. Propaganda will manipulate the consensus. Critical thought will be thought subversive.

Perhaps there will be spying to ensure that teachers do not deviate from the party line. Perhaps there will be genetic engineering to re-programme the bottom 25 per cent. The culture will favour integration and disparage independence. Schumpeter says that culture under socialism is indeterminate. He also says that culture under socialism is organicist. The contradiction proves that even Schumpeter could make mistakes. The prediction is less tolerant of human error. Productive efficiency will be maximised through regimentation. Entrepreneurship will be treated as a threat to the plan.

The State, meanwhile, will be able to dispense with taxation since under socialism it will become the supreme profit-recipient. Schumpeter argues that the suppression of the tax return is a significant saving. What he is forgetting is that the planners cannot pocket a surplus that unambitious bureaucrats have failed to create. Privatisation and competition could conceivably produce a greater taxable capacity for the State. This is a dynamic advantage which the statics of productive efficiency is unable to incorporate. Economics also teaches that profits without productivity-rises can be as much of a disincentive as tax: consider Stalin's 'scissors' redistribution, where a higher share for investment meant lower wages and even starvation for labour. Schumpeter says that profits are superior to taxes when static efficiency is being assessed. His focus itself is of little interest. The real claim to superiority, go-ahead and not stationary, relates to the ability to expand fiscal potential through the growth of the economy. It is not the focus of Schumpeter's socialism to use public finance in order to make progress happen.

Information in Schumpeter's socialism is no less short-horizoned. The regularities will be extrapolated and the hog cycle straightened out. Reliable statistics on all demand and supply functions will be collected and exogenous shocks like bad weather modelled into solid probabilities. Even in a static world, Schumpeter's reality will not be 'uniquely determined' unless and until the planners are in full command of infinite millions of facts, all perfectly understood. Schumpeter seems not to grasp the magnitude of the task. Change will exacerbate the data problem. Where evolution upsets the equations and the information required does not exist, the planners will have little choice but to own up to their ignorance and leave it to creative destruction to experiment itself into success or failure. Schumpeter was reluctant to admit that socialism could be the cause and not merely the consequence of stagnation. His analysis of productive efficiency provides no justification for his unfounded belief that *what had to be* had also to be *good*.

8.2 MARKET SOCIALISM

Hayek and Mises had been students of marginalism and markets at the

University of Vienna – and so, virtually at the same time, had Joseph Schumpeter. He, like Hayek and Mises, had learned his economics from Philippovich, Wieser and Böhm-Bawerk who had learned about utility-seeking and want-satisfaction in the long shadow of Carl Menger himself. Schumpeter throughout his life could write as the Austrian proceduralist that by conviction he always was. As late as 1948, for example, he was speaking out as if a Hayek or a Mises on behalf of 'those of us who believe that return to the principles of private enterprise will most speedily repair the ravages of the war' (Schumpeter, 1948:247). Yet there was a difference. Schumpeter's fellow Austrians put their faith in unintended consequences and not in the wise leadership of central authority. Schumpeter, on the other hand, tended toward the view that he was the witness to an irreversible evolution. The age of economic freedom was drawing to a close.

The individual entrepreneur was in decline: organisations and bureaucracies were pushing the small competitor out. Powerful monopolies fixed administered prices: perfect price-takers would soon be a thing of the past. The Soviet experience had not discredited the momentum: Gosplan had never become a 'full-weight realization' of the collectivist's 'mental image' (Schumpeter, 1942a:187). All things considered, Schumpeter said, it was inappropriate for Smithians like Hayek and Mises to throw out socialism in the dogmatic belief that the market must always be the superior tool. The market is not what it was. We today start from here and not from 1776. Socialism, moreover, is not Stalin's Moscow but rather 1908. We today start from Barone and not from the Communist Party that never understood how to make the thing work.

8.2.1 Barone and Lange

Enrico Barone's paper, 'The Ministry of Production in the collectivist State', was first published (in Italian) in the *Giornale degli Economisti* in 1908. It was reprinted (in an English translation) in Hayek's *Collectivist Economic Planning* in 1935. The Marxists had said little about how socialism would work in practice. Barone, who was not a Marxist, used mathematics to show that even after the means of production had ceased to be private property rational calculation could still be productive of a Pareto-optimal welfare peak.

Pareto in his *Cours d'Economie Politique* had demonstrated in 1897 that the free market could bring into being a comparative statics equilibrium in which no one could be made better off unless someone else were to be made worse off. Exchange is essential if slack is to disappear: without the proportioning of costs to benefits there will always be unexploited gains. Capitalism, however, is not: Pareto in the second volume of his *Cours* said that even socialism – *market* socialism – would be able to slim itself into the no-wastage nirvana. It was upon that insight from Pareto's *Cours* that Barone constructed his Ministry and his theory of guidance as a *tâtonnement*, second best.

Barone writes that economics remains economics even when the régime goes red: 'If the Ministry of Production proposes to obtain the collective maximum – which it obviously must, whatever law of distribution may be adopted – all the economic categories of the old régime must reappear, though maybe with other names: prices, salaries, interest, rent, profit, saving, etc.' (Barone, 1908:289). So must 'the same two fundamental conditions which characterize free competition': 'We refer, of course, to the conditions of minimum cost of production and the equalization of price to cost of production.' (Barone, 1908:289). Private property is not the precondition for a Pareto optimum. Perfect competition is, however, the ideal-type *sine qua non*. Without that basepoint and that filter, there is no theoretical reason why the best product mix should ever emerge.

Walras used the fiction of an auctioneer in order to demonstrate the manner in which the market puts a value on output. In the real world, competitive capitalism is more likely to grope its way to equilibrium by means of trial and error. Market socialism, Barone said, has no choice but to emulate the *prix crié au hasard* of the darkness that has lost its auctioneer if its Ministry is successfully to map out the input combinations that will maximise well-being and wealth: 'The determination of the coefficients economically most advantageous can only be done in an *experimental* way .... The Ministry of Production could not do without these experiments for the determination of the *economically* most advantageous technical coefficients if it would realize the condition of the minimum cost of production which is *essential* for the attainment of the maximum collective welfare.' (Barone, 1908:288).

Barone, in a section of his paper entitled 'The equations of the equilibrium insoluble a priori', advised his Ministry that it could not plan without the subjective preferences that consumers alone were in a position to reveal. Determined to be Paretian, it 'must *of necessity* resort to experiments on a large scale in order to decide *afterwards*' (Barone, 1908:289). General equilibrium is determinate – but only if the market is enlisted to help the planners learn the facts.

A planning board could generate Paretian outcomes equivalent to those of profit-seeking perfect competition. Barone's compromise message was refined in the 30 years following the publication of his paper by distinguished economists like F.M. Taylor (1929), H.D. Dickinson (1933), Abba Lerner (1934 and 1937) and R.L. Hall (1937). Of particular sophistication were the two articles by Oscar Lange which appeared in the *Review of Economic Studies* in 1936 and 1937. They were republished (with Taylor's Presidential

Address to the American Economic Association on 'The guidance of production in a socialist state') as *On the Economic Theory of Socialism* in 1938. Lange, a young Polish economist with Marxist sympathies, was a Rockefeller Fellow at Harvard at the time. At Harvard he and Schumpeter had discussed his theory of supply and demand once private property had been abolished.

The technical conditions were those of the competitive market. The managers reporting to the Central Planning Board were to select the method of production that minimises average cost; to equalise the marginal product of each factor of production per unit of money; to produce as much of each good or service as will equate the marginal cost and the price of the product. These rules 'perform the same function that in a competitive system is carried out by the private producer's aiming to maximise his profit' (Lange, 1936/37:76). The profit motive drops out under socialism. The output of each plant and industry and the total demand for the factors of production is nonetheless fully determinate and precisely the same.

Quantities, of course, must clear. That Marshallian balance, neither an excess nor a shortfall, must be the core objective of any responsible Board: 'The Central Planning Board performs the functions of the market ... It fixes the prices so as to balance the quantity supplied and demanded of each commodity. It follows that a substitution of planning for the functions of the market is quite possible and workable.' (Lange, 1936/37:82–3). The Board has no need to solve a priori equations or to estimate *ex ante* probabilities. All that it has to do is to pull a random number out of the air and then to monitor inventory surplus or inventory deficit as the planners adjust their provisional values through successive rounds of sequential experimentation: 'Thus the accounting prices in a socialist economy can be determined by the same process of trial and error by which prices on a competitive market are determined.' (Lange, 1936/37:87).

Socialism allocates by the market's own rules. Socialism if anything is actually the more successful player. The Board, for one thing, can take advantage of its unequalled overview to reduce the number of trials needed to reach a stable equilibrium: 'The Central Planning Board has a much wider knowledge of what is going on in the whole economic system than any private entrepreneur can ever have.' (Lange, 1936/37:89). The Board, again, can internalise the externalities and put *all* of the costs into the total cost function: 'Only a socialist economy can fully satisfy the claim made by many economists with regard to the achievements of free competition.' (Lange, 1936/37:107). Nor would it be correct to assume that all of competition is necessarily free: 'The most important part of modern economic life is just as far removed from free competition as it is from socialism.' (Lange, 1936/37:120). Monopoly capital means price inflexibility. The sensitivity of the Board is made that much more attractive by the failure of the post-Smithian mammoths to keep their data stock up-to-date.

Socialism is fully able to cope with resource allocation. It is, however, at risk nonetheless: 'It seems to us ... that *the real danger of socialism is that of a bureaucratization of economic life*.' (Lange, 1936/37:109). The real danger is not the price vector but the suppression from above. Yet, being realistic, there is no way that 'the same, or even greater, danger can be averted under monopolistic capitalism' (Lange, 1936/37:109–10). Organisations are a fact of life. State-sector bureaucracies at least are accountable to the wider public – and private-sector corporations are not. Socialism in a second-best world is likely for that reason to be the more responsive choice: 'Officials subject to democratic control seem preferable to private corporation executives who practically are responsible to nobody.' (Lange, 1936/37:110). Lange does not say what happens when the control is less than democratic. There is no Stalin and no Communist Party in his model of utility and price.

8.2.2 Hayek and Mises

Hayek, like Mises, was a strong advocate of 'the pricing system in market exchange' (Hayek, 1988:14). This he regarded, as had Adam Smith, as a set of beacons for 'ordering human economic cooperation that exceed the limits of our knowledge and perception' (Hayek, 1988:14). The reality of *what is* is dispersed through a multiplicity of minds. Past experience is a poor guide to a hidden future that has yet to be fashioned. Central planning cannot reconcile the choices since the central planners can never know the relevant facts: 'We are not intellectually equipped to improve the working of our economic system by "planning" or to solve the problem of socialist production in any other way without very considerably impairing productivity.' (Hayek, 1935b:241). Market exchange alone can select and position since undirected individuals alone can carry out an unrestricted search.

The social process is a 'voyage of exploration into the unknown' (Hayek, 1949:101). The destinations cannot be established until the discoveries have been made. It is in precisely that realm of radical uncertainty that lies behind the unknowledge veil that factoring down and devolved decision-making come into their own: 'Nobody can know *who* knows best .... The only way by which we can find out is through a social process in which everybody is allowed to try and see what he can do.' (Hayek, 1949:15).

Central planning goes with grandiose conceits like historicism, scientism, Marxism, determinism, the stages of economic growth, the labour theory of objective value. Intellectual approaches like these appeal strongly to natural architects who are confident about the data and convinced that social engineers can build to last. Yet the economic problem is subjectivity and not just technique. Information on personal preferences and best-ranked initiatives is held by each independent actor and coordinated through competitive pricing. The planners don't stand a chance. Lacking knowledge, their would-be rationality 'is not a practical solution', 'humanly impracticable and impossible' (Hayek, 1935b:207, 208). Barone and Lange wanted market socialism. They should, Hayek believed, have gone for the free market instead.

Mises, like Hayek, was a strong supporter of market search as rational valuation. Exchange is the essence of economic activity. It is only through the revelation of preference that subjective trade-offs can be quantified and compared: 'Where there is no market there is no price system, and where there is no price system there can be no economic calculation.' (Mises, 1922:131). The sphere of economic activity is the sphere of the monetary swap. Without the freedom to price there can be no logic in allocation or accounts: 'All economic change, therefore, would involve operations the value of which could neither be predicted beforehand nor ascertained after they had taken place. Everything would be a leap in the dark.' (Mises, 1922:122).

Mises was an epistemological sceptic who insisted that no *whole* can ever *know*: 'The specific goals that people aim at in action are very different and constantly change.' (Mises, 1949:77). Because they are very different, the one-off alone can measure the need that he wishes to satisfy: 'The spheres of rational action and economic action are ... co-incident. All rational action is economic. All economic activity is rational action. All rational action is in the first place individual action. Only the individual thinks. Only the individual reasons. Only the individual acts.' (Mises, 1922:113). Because they constantly change, lasting values must give way to temporary ports of call since it is in the nature of entrepreneur-driven history that it always moves on: 'The great mass of people are incapable of realizing that in economic life nothing is permanent except change.' (Mises, 1922:213). Market pricing deals at once with the heterogeneity and the evanescence. It does so because it is free, spontaneous and uncoerced.

Market capitalism is the economic order that makes the most of scarce information: 'Capitalism is the only conceivable form of social economy which is appropriate to the fulfilment of the demands which society makes of any economic organization.' (Mises, 1922:220). Centralised socialism, on the other hand, is nothing less than 'the renunciation of rational economy': 'Without calculation, economic activity is impossible. Since under socialism economic calculation is impossible, there can be no economic activity in our sense of the word.' (Mises, 1922:119, 122). Socialism means 'the centralized control of the whole of production by one social or, more accurately, state organ': where 'everything depends on the orders of the supreme authority'

(Mises, 1922:15, 185), purposive search must atrophy since regimentation makes even entrepreneurs into pawns. Socialism means that 'the socialistic State owns all material factors of production' (Mises, 1922:36) and bends them to its own narrow objectives. Where the authoritarians receive all the profits, the business community has little incentive to take gambles that could sour into loss.

Market socialism, self-evidently, must always be a contradiction in terms. State control by definition makes outcomes different from what they otherwise would have been: 'Where private property exists, only market prices can determine the formation of income .... Any deviation from market prices destroys the equilibrium of economic life.' (Mises, 1922:254). State ownership by definition cuts administration loose from personal exposure: 'The attributes of the business man cannot be divorced from the position of the entrepreneur in the capitalist order.' (Mises, 1922:216). Market socialism must fail for the same reason that centralised socialism must fail – because it is unwilling to leave it to ordinary men and women to make the most of their own scarce initiative. State planners lack the knowledge to mimic perfectly the perfect market. Exchange is one polar option. Dominance is the other. There is no third way.

Mises denied that market socialism could be either rational or responsive: 'It is hardly possible to construe the market process in a more erroneous way.' (Mises, 1949:354). Schumpeter, predicting socialism but prescribing prices, took a different view: 'The economist who settled the question in a manner that left little to do ... was Enrico Barone.' (Schumpeter, 1942a:193). An Austrian and an enterpriser like Hayek and Mises, it was nonetheless to the mixed model of Barone and Lange that he turned for the reassurance that market socialism could generate allocative efficiency in the sense of the Pareto optimum while at the same time stimulating productive efficiency in the technologist's metric of fully exhausted physical endowments.

8.3 ALLOCATIVE EFFICIENCY

Schumpeter believed that there was a 'family likeness' between capitalism and socialism. The reason was that both economic systems were alike dependent on 'the perfectly general logic of choice', 'the molding influence of mere rationality' (Schumpeter, 1942a:182). Where resources are scarce and the economy is in need, there is no prudent alternative but to rely on supply and demand that has shown itself to be the most efficient means.

Schumpeter, in his review of Joan Robinson's *Imperfect Competition*, defends priced socialism as the obvious mixture of market with plan: 'The theory of free competition is the only avenue to a rational theory of planning and of centralistic socialism.' (Schumpeter, 1934:125). Capitalism has demonstrated that pricing makes decentralised decisions both determinate and consistent. Market socialism moves without hesitation into the house that capitalism has built: 'Socialism could after all only use capitalist mechanisms and categories.' (Schumpeter, 1942a:182). Only means only. Economics is universal. So is supply and demand.

Schumpeter states that the coming socialism can be made to make sense: 'There is nothing wrong with the pure logic of socialism.' (Schumpeter, 1942a:172). His compliment is a tribute not just to the Ministry of Production but to the souk and the bazaar where it went to school: 'The socialist miracle does not create a logic of its own.' (Schumpeter, 1942a:182). Commercial or collectivist, we today all believe that the norm is efficiency. We also believe that the means to the end is the self-interested swap.

Robert Heilbroner greeted Schumpeter's logic with a strong sensation of *déjà vu*: 'In crucial respects Schumpeter's socialism is surprisingly like capitalism. It is governed by the same principles of "efficiency" – better achieved than under capitalism, Schumpeter expects – and it retains the all-important division between managers and workers. Socialism is, in a word, a more *rational* form of capitalism.' (Heilbroner, 1984:259). As far as Heilbroner was concerned, Schumpeter's socialism is only *Übercapitalism* without the capitalists. The owners had already become vestigial organs like the appendix in the antecedent era of the huge corporations. All that socialism had to do was to tidy up the survivals and to trust to the salaried to keep up their good work.

Schumpeter and Heilbroner agree that there is a 'family likeness' that links up the future with the present. What must not be forgotten is that there are significant differences as well. Market socialism is a volatile synthesis. Schumpeter on *market* suggests that socialism will be more of the same. Schumpeter on *socialism* shows that market may become the poor relation as the State assumes control.

8.3.1 Market

Pricing under market socialism will remain the responsibility of unguided exploration. Values gravitating automatically to the market-clearing level, the Ministry will have to adopt *those* prices and *no other* prices or be faced with inventories that it does not want. Schumpeter, a lifelong admirer of Walras, was clearly pleased that the socialist equilibrium would have a subjective dimension. The Ministry would not promulgate prices in keeping with some historic standard such as average cost or labour embodied. Instead they would leave it to the consumer to reveal the precise magnitude of his willingness to pay.

Inputs as well as outputs are to be made subject to the same market valuation of 'whatever the traffic will bear'. Rent must be assigned, as 'an index of economic significance', in order that plots of differing fertility might be costed and compared: 'If this were not done the commonwealth would be behaving irrationally.' (Schumpeter, 1942a:181). Capital must be discounted against a reference-point rate of interest in order to allow for the proportioning of profit to the opportunity cost outside. Labour power must be waged and sold in order to facilitate the transparent substitutability of one marginal product for another. The perceived contribution of the factors of production is evidently not to be *imputed* by the planners from the market value of the final consumables. Both sets of prices, instead, are to be ground out through the market mechanism, as if guided by an invisible hand.

8.3.2 Socialism

Schumpeter's demand is in-period and utility-maximising. Schumpeter's supply, however, is an exogeneity from the Ministry, decided upon by the planners before the auction sale is even announced. The demand curve is price-sensitive and purpose-seeking. The quantity supplied, however, is a mystery and a black box. Schumpeter's market socialism makes its home in the Marshallian market period where supply means *supplied* and demand makes the price. In that sense it should be called half-a-market socialism. One blade of the scissors is ordered and paid for. The other blade of the scissors just arrives.

The quantity supplied in Marshall's market period is the material embodiment of the price that was expected when, yesterday, the fishermen set off to fish. The quantity supplied in Schumpeter's market socialism is less easy to interpret. Schumpeter does not say if the output was targeted by his planners because of the likely effect on price. Nor does he say if the relationship between the forecast price and the historic cost was intended to produce a specified quantity of surplus. All that he reveals is that the planners decide. The *what* could be selected to meet a want or to satisfy a need. The *how much* could be a reflection of an opportunity cost or a physical bottleneck. Schumpeter never says where manna comes from or takes the reader on a trip behind the *fiat*. Fewer cigarettes today, more tea trolleys tomorrow – all that he reveals is that the suppliers will be told the numbers when the politicians decide that they have a genuine need to know.

Schumpeter could have brought his quantity supplied within the rubric of market socialism by means of making the supply curve as well as the demand curve a function of price. He did not do so. Planning, he seems to have believed, would lose its *raison d'être* if the planners had to give up so much control. The consequence of his choice is an asymmetry which sharply differentiates his socialist market from the earlier capitalist market upon which he believed that it would have to be modelled. Demand prices the stock. Supply is *quantity supplied*. It is half-a-market socialism in which the economy relies on the *ex machina* because even freedom is in need of control.

In the absence of a supply schedule the *what* and the *how much* will come to be determined by the politicians and the civil servants who stamp their choices upon the plan. It is only possible to say that socialism will be welfare-maximising if it is known that the ordinals and the cardinals of the decision makers will closely resemble the preference functions of their fellow citizens. Schumpeter nowhere recognises the need for market socialism to be able to model a prediction of consumer sovereignty. Without that prediction, the danger is real that an indicative socialism committed to Paretian optimality in the eyes of the individual will tip over into an imperative socialism, run by paternalists and totally out of sympathy with the Paretian's precondition of demand-led supply.

Consumers want Marx's *Capital*: the planners supply them with Hayek's *Serfdom* instead. Consumers want ten cheap coffees: the planners provide five unpriced coffees and leave it to the market to determine if the coffees will be sold at a low or high price. In cases such as these the planners are fixing quantities in line with their own values rather than trusting to consumer sovereignty to serve as their populist guide. While an elitist might say that the sheep in the end will come to thank the wise shepherds who washed their brains, a libertarian economist will state that the shopper needs no nanny to tell him what he wants to buy. Schumpeter's *market* socialism is modelled on market economics. Schumpeter's market *socialism* ought in the circumstances to come with a guarantee that the individual will not be swallowed up by the plan. It is reasonably clear that it does not.

The problem is a real one for a model of allocative efficiency. Schumpeter acknowledged the need for a behavioural interpretation of the planners' ambitions (Schumpeter, 1942a:Ch.22). What he did not do is to integrate his political with his market theory or to recognise just how much there is that could go wrong. Party politicians might set the quantity supplied with one eye on marginal constituencies and the other eye on the median voter: the risk is that passionate minorities will be denied their preference and that market variety will be squeezed into a single public choice. Salaried officials might slip into the organisational self-perpetuators of inertia, precedent, stereotyping, empire building – all of them frustrations of purpose on a par with the date-stamped inflexibilities of corporate capitalism that Schumpeter described so evocatively as 'obstructions opposed to the will of the people by outworn institutions controlled by groups interested in their preservation' (Schumpeter, 1942a:236). Schumpeter's quantity supplied, determined in the dark by leaders who are themselves under-explained, is a shoe hanging from a bootstrap that no one seems to hold.

The suppression of competition further alters the incentive-structure. Market socialism, made to mean same-side rivalry for demand, could have the effect of forcing socialised enterprises to match the product to the preference and to keep their charges down. Competition would in that way make public corporations cost-aware, obliged to satisfy their customers or to face a ruinous loss of revenue.

Schumpeter frequently states that the four walls of bureaucracy have 'a depressing influence on the most active minds' (Schumpeter, 1942a:207). Economics on a salary is unlikely to score well in either productive or dynamic efficiency. Corporate capitalism is susceptible to ossification because the post-entrepreneurial organisation faces no pressure to be go-ahead or even cost-effective. Centralist socialism in the Soviet Union (the only planned economy when Schumpeter was developing his theory of economic systems) had had no greater success in subordinating the nine-to-fives to the will of the absentee. Schumpeter in the circumstances could have accepted that there was much in both economic orders that could go wrong – and that there was a real need for an economic 'third way' if the wheels of trade were properly to go round.

Competition between socialised corporations could have been just such a compromise between private gain-seeking and the monopoly of command. Schumpeter, however, was simply unprepared to countenance any *market* socialism that would make active use of same-side undercutting. His reason is a strange one for an economist with a stake in efficiency. Socialism, he says, is committed to cohesion. Exchange, quite different, is the Hobbesian *bellum* through and through. The market in the socialist economy would 'go far toward reproducing the antagonisms of capitalist society' (Schumpeter, 1942a:168). Assuming that 'antagonisms' are socially inferior to sociability, it will then be 'essential' to exclude 'sectional interests' (Schumpeter, 1942a:168) lest social harmony give way to selfishness and self-advancement.

Market socialism means coexistence whereas market competition means private advantage. It is an explicit selling point of the coming centralism that it will prevent aggressive rivalries from destabilising the community. Centralism by its very charter is 'intended to exclude the existence of a plurality of units of control such that each of them would on principle stand for a distinct interest of its own' (Schumpeter, 1942a:168). Distinct interests breed disharmony. Disharmony to a socialist is morally wrong.

Socialism, Schumpeter says, need not be monolithic. As in private business, operational autonomy will very often be granted to line managers and divisional heads. The 'rational amount of freedom' will, of course, be 'experimentally found' (Schumpeter, 1942a:168). The sole objective being performance, trial and error alone, not invariant dogma, will throw up the maximising structure.

Devolution to facilitate productive efficiency is fully compatible with the moral value of socialism as cohesion. Competition between fraternal cost centres is not. Since Schumpeter also says that socialism, about economics, is culturally indeterminate, it is not easy to reconcile his fraternalism with the ethical agnosticism that he simultaneously propounds. Perhaps they cannot be reconciled at all. Schumpeter's socialism would arguably have had a greater appeal to economists if he had dropped the cohesion but retained the efficiency. Competition could then have become the mechanism that makes the public corporations in the end the servants of the public interest.

Technologically, multiple competitions might fail to achieve their vitally Schumpeterian economies of size. Politically, only the anarchists and the syndicalists, never the planners like Barone and Lange, were prepared to contemplate the potential loss of control. Few economists in 1942 believed that socialism could cut corners on scale and leadership. Schumpeter made common cause with the consensus view. In so doing, however, he left a gap at the heart of his socialism which made it unlikely that his market, Pareto-optimal, would successfully cut away all wastage and slack. If corporate capitalism is doomed because of its internal contradictions, then so is centralist socialism equally doomed because it too cannot make its office holders fully subordinate to its asset owners. Competition in the sense of Hayek and Mises might at least ensure that bureaucrats, public sector or private, remain accountable and alert.

Market socialism is supply and demand. Market *socialism* is the wild card that sets the interventionists loose. Quantity is imposed. Preference functions are nannied. Competition is suppressed. Distribution, finally, is taken out of economics. In capitalism the factors, the classes and the individuals are paid what they are worth to the boss. In socialism the allocation of purchasing power will be a response not just to productivity but to poverty, inequality and investment as well.

Sometimes the socialists will passively follow the market differentials: 'Socialism need not be egalitarian.' (Schumpeter, 1942a:179). Sometimes, however, the State will press on principle for the redistribution of income. It is in cases like these that the rate of economic growth might be retarded by the negative effect on effort and accumulation.

Schumpeter, who writes with such concern about disincentives under capitalism, does not directly address the economics of a market socialism that levels down. Possibly he was reasoning that planning itself would be in a position to alleviate any shortage. Capital is a case in point. Whereas the minimal State cannot force spendthrifts to be economical, the socialist State can correct a market failure through the commitment of its own tax revenues to plant. Also, under socialism, there could and should be 'something analogous to credit creation' (Schumpeter, 1942a:180). Borrowing had fuelled private capitalism even where there was little explicit ploughing back. Market socialism could continue the practice. Irrespective of the distribution of incomes, public corporations could always turn to the banks.

Barone and Lange, taking their blueprint from Pareto, believed that market socialism could produce a zero-waste general equilibrium as if guided by a Walrasian auctioneer, costless, quick, fully informed, never wrong. Their standard of excellence was minimum average cost of production and across-the-board proportionality of price to marginal cost. Their market benchmark was the passivity of perfect competition.

Schumpeter knew the benchmark but he also knew the corporation. Convinced that modern capitalism was an era of powerful monopolies and rigid prices, he was unable to share the view of the market socialists that trial and error would lead the real-world economy into the equilibrium utopia of Paretian efficiency. Perhaps it might have done so in early Smithian free competition before capitalism went corporate and authority succeeded to search and catallactics. We today, however, are obliged to compare second best with second best, not pure textbook with pure command. If socialism is imperfect, so too is the market.

Schumpeter, moreover, recognised that the Pareto optimum is a static standard whereas entrepreneurship, innovation, speculation and experiment tend forever to shake things up. Freezing recorded signals into the rational calculus of the Planning Board might make sense if the prices genuinely cleared the markets – and if economic reality did not rapidly move on. Only in a motionless environment, Hayek writes, can the information set be called complete: 'We should not expect equilibrium to exist unless all external change has ceased.' (Hayek, 1935b:212). Yet economic reality does move on. With that evolution comes the likelihood that the Ministry's multi-period prices will become out-of-date, haphazard and confused. Where the auction sale is once-for-all, trial and error might contribute something to the plan. Where the shake-up lasts an infinity, there will be a stronger temptation to close the Ministry and rely on the spot in-period instead.

Schumpeter, attracted by allocative efficiency, was aware that both imperfect competition and unceasing dynamics stood between his market socialism and the more optimistic Paretianism with which the economics of Barone and Lange is imbued. Schumpeter was attracted by the motherhood-and-Chelsea-Flower-Show ideal of a position of rest in which there can be no transfer of resources without there being an equivalent or a greater destruction of social values. Unlike Barone and Lange, however, he makes no prediction that his market socialism will bring about the position of bliss. The most that can be expected is that more bliss will be the consequence of his compromise than was dreamt of in the Kremlin's regimentation of supply.

Yet there is regimentation of supply even in Schumpeter's market socialism. The planners can take the lead and need not obediently follow. Market socialism, *socialism* as well as market, can evidently have other objectives besides the Paretian's maximand of allocative efficiency.

The planners, for one thing, have the deciding vote upon the *what*. They might opt to shadow the consumer's preferences, self-perceived, but they might also seek to impose superior preferences of their own. There is no guarantee of freedom of choice in Schumpeter's socialism, no assurance that the individual will be permitted to spend his money in the way he sees fit. Alone in possession of his subjective data, the shopper may well feel that he is being denied the gains from trade that would enable him to maximise his utility.

The planners, again, fix the *how much*, the quantity supplied. The price is demand-determined. The stock, however, is restricted by decree. The possibility is real in so asymmetrical a case that there will be not a normal profit but instead a windfall or a loss. Such a surplus or a deficit, not in proportion to cost, is a non-functional quasi-rent. It is a non-Paretian failing that will be a feature of the long run and not just the market period. There is in Schumpeter's socialism no new entry, no competition, no profit-seeking ambition that would attract in the innovative and bid away an excess.

The planners, finally, take a view on distribution. They do this through taxes and subsidies but also, and more subtly, through their influence on final output. Schumpeter makes no prediction about the *what* or the *how much* of labour supplied: his socialism is compatible both with compulsion on the military model and with the free choice of occupation. In planning output, however, his planners will inevitably have a knock-on effect on labour and its reward. In fixing the number of buses the State is fixing the number of drivers. Limiting the buses it may even be causing the drivers to earn a super-normal income. That super-competitive overhang would vanish at a stroke if prices and quantities, both of inputs and of outputs, were allowed to reach their free-market levels. Quantity fixing is income fixing by the back door. It is not in the spirit of allocative efficiency. In a second-best world, however, semi-market socialism might be less inefficient than corporate capitalism or repressive command that are the more familiar ways in which post-Smithian economics tries to match the demand to supply.

9. The sociology of socialism

The capitalists pushed the aristocrats to the brink of extinction. The next step will be for the capitalists to dig their own grave: 'The very success of the business class in developing the productive powers of [the] country ... has paradoxically undermined the social and political position of the same business class.' (Schumpeter, 1950b:423). Soon it too will be no more.

The bourgeoisie will flourish only so long as the entrepreneurs hold sway (Schumpeter, 1942a:134). The legitimacy of the property-owning class is not in doubt so long as its leading members are known to be the iconoclasts who usher in the new. Things change radically when it is the bureaucrat on a wage who, working in a team and seldom pictured in the press, makes the decisions that shape people's lives. Corporate capitalism is an epoch in which labour and not capital is put in control. Centralist socialism, creating nothing new, merely perpetuates the tradition of post-entrepreneurial choice when it concentrates command in the hands of salaried politicians who take no share in the profits of the firm.

The sociology of capitalism gives way to the sociology of socialism once an obsolete and functionless social grouping has without disruption been tidied out of the way. This chapter is concerned in three sections with three aspects of the society that is to come: cultural values, national character and the potential for Catholic corporatism. It is not concerned with class location and class consciousness. Schumpeter, like Marx, has little or nothing to say about social stratification in the one-class society where the sole surplus is controlled by the State.

It is an unsatisfying interpretation of a multi-faceted phenomenon. Schumpeter underestimates the significance of full compensation paid in bonds. Where the wealth holders lose their profits but hold on to their interest, and at least until death duties make a major dent in their holdings, propertied Knightsbridge will be able to sustain its accustomed lifestyle despite Schumpeter's insistence that the fall of the entrepreneur will also mark the end of the non-working classes. Schumpeter never explains why he thinks that a shareholding bourgeoisie transformed into an interest-earning bourgeoisie will necessarily enjoy less esteem than will a hands-on bourgeoisie merely because the high-minded moralist will deny that an absentee investor can have a function.

Schumpeter is weak on perception and self-perception as the reinforcers of the social order. As with the *rentiers*, so with the *apparat*. Schumpeter neglects the social distance that opens up when the new class of office holders (many of them existing managers already in post) refuses to see itself as the better-educated brethren of the unwashed production-line. There is little or nothing in his sociology about the reactions of the manual proletariat to the new locus of control. Nor is there any recognition that power itself, and not just wealth, can become a focus for cloth-cap resentment if not for social-class conflict.

The workers play no part in the transition. Marx believed that the reserve army would rise up in revolt. Schumpeter, less dramatically, expected that it would be big business itself that would sound the knell. What the blue collar will make of the white collar implosion the reader is not told. There is no real need for the shop floor's perceptions to be unpacked. Schumpeter's socialism is a single-peaked society in which salaried professionals are firmly in control. Little account of labour is needed to complete a sociology that begins and ends so single-mindedly at the top.

9.1 CULTURE AND SOCIALISM

Socialism, historically, has assumed that economic change is the operative cause: 'Every socialist wishes to revolutionize society from the economic angle and all the blessings he expects are to come through a change in economic institutions.' (Schumpeter, 1942a:169). Socialism has taken it for granted that material consumption would rise once the fetters and contradictions had been transcended by an economic order that could unlock full productive potential. Yet socialism, historically, has also insisted that the economic dimension, of all the aspects of man's Good Life, is not 'the only or even the most important one' (Schumpeter, 1942a:169–70). Socialism does not say that 'nothing is worth struggling for except beefsteaks and radios' (Schumpeter, 1942a:170). What socialism says is precisely the opposite: 'Socialism aims at higher goals than full bellies .... First and foremost, socialism means a new cultural world.' (Schumpeter, 1942a:170).

Socialism, first and foremost, is a creed and a vision that speaks to the heart even before it engages the mind: 'The popular appeal of socialism is due *not* to what can be rationally established about it.' (Schumpeter, 1942a:308n). Socialists, first and foremost, are mystics and idealists who hunger for absolute values that provide a focus for their quest: 'Marxism *is* a religion ... a system of ultimate ends that embody the meaning of life and are absolute standards by which to judge events and actions ... a guide to those ends which implies a plan of salvation.' (Schumpeter, 1942a:5). Socialism only exceptionally will make its earthly paradise the economist's fuller trough:

'Only outright beefsteak socialism can be content with a goal such as this.' (Schumpeter, 1942a:184). Socialism more commonly will build on the mundane, taking it as the prerequisite for the next step up but then 'dreaming of new cultural forms for the human clay, perhaps of a new clay withal': 'The real promise of socialism, if any, lies that way.' (Schumpeter, 1942a:184). Socialists have moral values and they want non-commercial things. Their 'new cultural world' is more than maximum consumption alone.

The attraction to the visionaries and the mystics is the 'new cultural world'. The problem is that there is not a single median code but rather a spectrum of values and value systems. Schumpeter's *socialism* is Schumpeter's *socialisms*. There seems not to be a consensus on the cultural standards that socialists uniquely recognise and call their own.

Socialism, Schumpeter says, can be aristocratic or democratic, atheistic or theocratic, individualistic or regimented, consultative or paternalistic, warlike or pacifist. Some socialists assign a high priority to economic efficiency while others are more attracted by belonging and community. Some are openly meritocratic and achievement-orientated while others preach the convergence of approximation and overlap. Some build their future on the working-class ideal of neighbourhood support while others want a radical break through the white heat of technocracy. The variants are infinite – and each and every one is, culturally speaking, socialist. People are attracted to socialism because of its 'new cultural world'. Its new cultural *world* is, however, its new cultural *worlds*. They are multiple and varied. Marx posited a unique ideational superstructure growing out of a unique productive base. Schumpeter posited the 'Cultural Indeterminateness of Socialism' (Schumpeter, 1942a:170). All values are welcome and all will find a home.

That said, there are three values which, historically, have emerged as salient in the literature of socialism. These may be called liberty, equality and fraternity. Each, interestingly, can undermine as well as reinforce Schumpeter's univalued prediction of socialist economics as plan with price. Schumpeter's sociology of culture does not establish that socialist values will make socialist economics a viable proposition and not a wilderness of dysfunctionalities. Schumpeter, as will become clear from the examples of liberty, equality and fraternity, may be criticised for leaving the socialist edifice uncompleted and without a roof.

Thus liberty could mean self-actualising creativity in place of production-line squeeze-out: this would be a threat to the economies of size without which nothing would remain of Schumpeter on the corporation and beyond. Post-capitalism could lead to power sharing, workplace democracy and worker-directors instead of the autocracy that values nothing but the throughput: Schumpeter rejected self-management as an investment in self-image that would slow down the process of advance. A socialist commitment to self-rule could even undermine the legitimacy of the planners themselves. Not everyone regards himself as a valued participant when it is the generals and not the privates who pluck the *what* and the *how much* out of the air. Their initiative allows the citizen to have an impact upon the price but denies him the opportunity to stamp his imprint upon the quantity. There is a culture of socialism that would find such exclusion morally as unacceptable as the marginalisation of a colonial territory that is ruled from without.

Equality is a second salient value that real-world socialists have tended to endorse. Schumpeter, aware that the median socialist is hostile to excessive social distance, acknowledges the prominence of the *desideratum*. Thus, speaking of market-determined pay differentials, he says that there are limits beyond which supply and demand will not be allowed to go: 'The principles of socialist society would not admit of making them the criterion of distribution.' (Schumpeter, 1942a:173). What Schumpeter does not see is the way in which such principles cut across the fundamental notion in his price socialism, that a stock is paid what its purchasers believe it to be worth. *Ex ante* a prices and income board would distort the information encoded in the signals. *Ex post* a progressive tax would be a disincentive to labour supply. *Ex ante* there is an inconsistency between Schumpeter's market socialism which cannot economise on price and the egalitarian culture which wants to cream off even a functional surplus because it is morally wrong. *Ex post* there is an inconsistency between reallocating the *for whom* and keeping up the quantity of output. *Ex ante* or *ex post*, there is likely to be a fundamental conflict between equality in the culture and efficiency in the economy which remains Schumpeter's proof of success.

Fraternity is a third value that has had a prominent place in the socialist credo. Mutual aid and social solidarity are long-established socialist objectives. It is not only the socialists who have recognised the value of harmony and peace. Schumpeter himself was not in favour of competition between State-owned firms because, setting the comrades against each other, it could introduce conflict into the consensus of plan. It was almost certainly that same mistrust of particularism within holism that made him so critical of trade unions that negotiated for their members even at the expense of their nation: 'The real problem is labor. Unless socialization is to spell economic breakdown, a socializing government cannot possibly tolerate present trade-union practice.' (Schumpeter, 1942a:379). Harmony is a social value that, in Schumpeter's perspective, was incompatible with the shop stewards, the sentimental proletarianism, the syndicalists, the communes – with all the intermediate loyalties, in short, which could put the fraternity of some on a collision course with the organicism of all. The advocates of working-class self-help would take quite a different view of what it means to be integrated and at one. Even social thinkers who agree on fraternity can disagree on the institutional structures that best translate their value into practice.

Not, of course, that different thinkers will necessarily agree on the same cultural values. Liberty, equality and fraternity dwell with a myriad of other absolute ends in the black box of cultural indeterminateness. Even a Schumpeter cannot know which of the many socialisms will be the next to be taken out.

Some socialists will reject the market mentality on the grounds that a culture of supply and demand must inevitably 'distort and degrade their creed' (Schumpeter, 1942a:170). Most, probably, will apply the pragmatic test of performance. Private vices were the genesis of public virtues in the heyday of entrepreneurial capitalism. Self-interest can remain the guiding light even in a socialist economy that has suppressed the profit motive and gone over to plan.

Socialism does not require 'a wholesale reformation of souls or of behavior' (Schumpeter, 1942a:185) in order to deliver efficiency and a good rate of growth. Its success does not presuppose an 'exclusive reliance on a purely altruistic sense of duty' (Schumpeter, 1942a:207). It does not depend on the wisdom of 'demigods' or of 'archangels', human beings on an 'ethical level that men as they are cannot be expected to reach' (Schumpeter, 1942a:202). The unfolding of socialism is not subject to a delay while the restructured socialist man develops some latent 'Rousseauism' that has been stunted and repressed by greed. On the contrary: 'No such fundamental reform of the human soul would now be necessary in order to make socialism work.' (Schumpeter, 1942a:203). Socialism can work even with human nature as it is and with habits which only in the long run (if at all) are malleable and open to reconditioning. Self-interest is enough. Self-seeking is good.

Self-seeking is the constant. The proximate rewards are more mutable. Sometimes people require a payment in money. Sometimes, however, they accept their differential in the form of social standing and social recognition. Man is an embedded animal, hungry for respect. Money itself is the purchase of social deference even as it is the purchase of goods and services. Wealth is an advertisement that the wealth holder has satisfied his examiners. So is the CBE, the military medal, the privilege of 'being allowed to stick a penny stamp on their trousers': 'Why not? Trotsky himself accepted the Order of the Red Flag.' (Schumpeter, 1942a:208). Self-seeking can extend to prestige-symbols and need not stop short at cash. That is why a socialist society is under no obligation to purge the culture of self-interest. All that socialism has to do is to pluralise the prizes and re-focus the scope. Politicised and centralised, 'a socialist community is in a particularly favorable position to do this' (Schumpeter, 1942a:208).

In the capitalist system 'pecuniary gain is the typical index of success'

(Schumpeter, 1942a:208). In socialism there are supplementary validators that can induce productive effort and also acknowledge it. Economic development even within advanced capitalism is already eroding the primacy of Veblen's conspicuous consumption: 'Capitalist evolution itself tends to weaken that motive for desiring wealth.' (Schumpeter, 1942a:208). Schumpeter does not explain why the captains of industry were becoming so modest: perhaps it is because corporate bureaucrats are on a salary scale whereas old-style entrepreneurs had to display their profits as Versace and Dior. Whatever the reason, the inference is clear. As pecuniary gain becomes relatively less pressing, so even within corporate capitalism does the door open to a broad range of sources of distinction. Socialism would have been more difficult in the nineteenth century. It was capitalism even before the advent of socialism that made self-seeking sensitive to approbation that cannot be reduced to money-seeking alone.

9.2 NATIONAL CHARACTER

Schumpeter in writing about socialism makes allowance for the fact that different countries have different cultures. The differences relate to the transition, dependent as it is on 'traits ... congenial to the individual national soils' (Schumpeter, 1942a:363). The differences relate to the endstate, a reflection of 'the social and racial environment of which not only the labor men but also the intellectuals are the products': 'Every country has its own socialism.' (Schumpeter, 1942a:325). The rule is general and the destination is the same: 'The capitalist process slowly socializes economic life.' (Schumpeter, 1942a:310). Still, however, different countries have different cultures. They will have different experiences as they advance into their future carrying with them the shared memories of their past.

Sweden illustrates the point. Swedish social institutions must be traced back to 'the stuff the Swedish nation is made of and to its exceptionally well-balanced social structure. That is why it is so absurd for other nations to try to copy Swedish examples; the only effective way of doing so would be to import the Swedes and to put them in charge.' (Schumpeter, 1942a:325). In Sweden the socialist party expanded gradually until ultimately it acceded to power. Its road was not encumbered with obstacles because it had on its side the sociology and the mentality of a nation that was relatively sympathetic to collective action and to the State.

France was different. Typically 'the country of the peasant, the artisan, the clerk and the small *rentier*' (Schumpeter, 1942a:336), it had a tradition of individualism and conservatism which made it resistant to large-scale industrial bureaucracies and leaderly regulation by the State. The sheer diversity within French society – the multiplicity of unstable affiliations, the anarchist tradition, the regionalist tendencies, the State-within-the-State of the Catholic Church – prevented the development of a unified political coalition capable of matching what Labour in Britain had done: 'The social pattern ... precluded the emergence of great and disciplined parties of the English type.' (Schumpeter, 1942a:337). Where the government had been up-and-doing, moreover, it had discredited itself through 'political inefficiency, incompetence and frivolity' to such an extent that the electorate 'placed no trust in the state, the political world, the scribblers': it 'had no respect for any of them' (Schumpeter, 1942a:339). Socialism in France would have stood a better chance if the nation had been less heterogeneous and the interventionists less slovenly – if the French, in other words, had been more like the Swedes.

The United States, in common with France, had a culture as a nation that made it difficult for socialism to sink deep roots and take hold. America was virgin territory, a sky's-the-limit continent characterised on the one hand by 'capitalist evolution rushed on at such a vertiginous pace' (Schumpeter, 1942a:331), on the other by the geographical safety valve of unbounded manifest destiny. Both the new industrial frontiers of classless creative destruction and the juicy carrot of a new start in the West defused the tensions that lead in dead-end societies to the storming of Bastilles because storming is the only way to seize bread. No one in the United States had any reason to feel underemployed or frustrated – least of all the worker whose proletarian status was only a temporary stop on his open road to plutocracy through accomplishment: 'The average, competent and respectable workman was, and felt himself to be, a businessman. He successfully applied himself to exploiting his own individual opportunities .... He understood and largely shared his employer's way of thinking.' (Schumpeter, 1942a:331). Money-making and acquisitive social mobility were in the air: 'The scheme of values that arose from the national task of developing the economic possibilities of the country drew nearly all the brains into business and impressed the businessman's attitudes upon the soul of the nation.' (Schumpeter, 1942a:331). America's business was business, not the welfare of the under-achieving and not the filial perpetuation of the time-out-of-mind *done thing*. Dissident intellectuals, always a small minority, 'accepted this scheme of values': 'If they did not, Main Street refused to listen.' (Schumpeter, 1942a: 331).

France was resistant to socialism because it was a going concern, a long-established network of interests, loyalties and affiliations. The United States was resistant to socialism because its culture was new and not old, its social classes fluid and not fixed. The contrast is a telling one. The French feared a revolution because it would interrupt the flow. The Americans welcomed deal-making because it would make them prosperous. Naturally ambitious, they concluded that 'socialism and socialists were un-American' (Schumpeter, 1942a:336). Naturally pragmatic, of course, they were quick to compromise on principle when in the 1930s macroeconomic failure convinced them that the New Deal was the best way to keep free enterprise afloat.

Britain provides a final illustration of the way in which national experience can mould national character and national character impact upon the march into socialism. The Labour Party under Clement Attlee had been returned to power in 1945. Schumpeter regarded that 'official adoption' of parliamentary socialism, 'in a peaceful way without a break in legal continuity' (Schumpeter, 1942a:220, 221), as an important demonstration of his thesis that, the appropriate stage of economic evolution reached, democratic elections could bring about epoch-making change without credible opposition and without the violence of a revolution: 'There is not much danger of this.' (Schumpeter, 1942a:221). Britain had voted in its socialists. It was unlikely ever to change its mind. Writing in the preface to the 1949 edition of his *Capitalism*, Schumpeter expressed the view that even British Conservatives could see that natural irreversibilities had made them into yesterday's men: 'Socialism has ceased to be resisted with moral passion .... And *this* is the writing on the wall – proof that the ethos of capitalism is gone.' (Schumpeter, 1942a:416).

British socialism has built on British institutions. Schumpeter is in no doubt that it was the British base that made the socialism viable: 'Fabian socialism requires English political society.' (Schumpeter, 1942a:336). The State could be trusted because of pre-socialist morality socialised into the 'unrivalled integrity of the English politician' (Schumpeter, 1942a:229). The State would be efficient because even before 1945 it could draw upon 'an experienced bureaucracy of irreproachable culture and moral standards' (Schumpeter, 1942a:229). The politicians incorruptible, the civil servants public-spirited, British socialism built with top-quality materials. Without those unexplained exogeneities the socialist project would never have advanced so far.

A further exogeneity was the British ruling class, 'uniquely able and civilized' (Schumpeter, 1942a:229) but nonetheless aristocratic enough to command obedience and respect. The British ruling class had long been prepared to recruit the best brains from all social groups and to absorb new ideas into its ongoing conventions: it was a class that combined 'adherence to formal tradition with extreme adaptability to new principles, situations and persons' (Schumpeter, 1942a:229). Even a Trotsky could have been incorporated into a leaderly elite that wanted to rule but was willing to evolve. Schumpeter's suggestion that Trotsky in Britain might have ended his career as the 'Earl of Prinkipo' is not so far-fetched in the light of the numerous trade unionists and left-wingers who have acquired a platform in the House of Lords. It has been of great benefit to British socialism to have inherited a ruling class that was so open-ended and open-minded. Russian socialists, less fortunate in their externalities, had no choice but to make their own luck.

Yet another exogeneity in the British case was the historical accident of war. Writing in the Second World War, Schumpeter was able to predict the nature of the political victories that would be the lasting spillover of the battles: 'There cannot be any doubt that the present conflagration will ... mean another great stride toward the socialist *order*.' (Schumpeter, 1942a:374). The First World War had already shown, Europe-wide, the extent to which mobilisation and common cause could bring the socialists into office. The Second World War would prove once again that not evolution and not revolution but the enemy from abroad would make Attlee succeed where Marx had failed: 'Socialism is a practical proposition that may become *immediately* practical in consequence of the present war.' (Schumpeter, 1942a:410). The British socialist Richard Titmuss, looking back on the National Health and the nationalisation of steel with the historian's knowledge of what was to come, would not have wished to disagree: 'War, as a total experience, has done more to shape the evolution of social policy in Britain – and to greatly extend the role of Government – than any other major historical set of causal agents.' (Titmuss, 1970).

War creates an intervention ratchet: investment controls and regulatory restrictions once in place, 'they will be put to other uses' (Schumpeter, 1942a:375) but never liquidated or relaxed. War inculcates a habit of command-following and passivity: 'People properly conditioned to accept governmental "directions", do not mind them greatly.' (Schumpeter, 1942a:418). War in Britain gave Labour high-profile experience in the cross-party coalition: its leaders in that way acquired general credibility as a possible future government. War gave rise to strong ministries which had fine-tuned the capacity to plan: 'Huge bureaucracies have developed that by now are powerful enough to hold their ground and to implement policies of fundamental reconstruction.' (Schumpeter, 1942a:374). War was an accident. It was, however, an accident which had made socialism more attractive and the hands-off market less acceptable: 'English people on the whole have become state-broken by now.' (Schumpeter, 1942a:229). *Dirigisme* was here to stay.

British socialism had been the product of historical exogeneities but it had also been the consequence of economic inevitability. The process is a universal one, the evolution the property of all industrial countries. In the specific case of Britain, there were a number of areas where the ineluctable even before Attlee already cast its shadow before.

There were, for example, concentrated, bureaucratised concerns in areas such as road and rail transport, mining (especially coal mining), building and building materials, the production and distribution of electricity. In areas such as these 'the gain from rationalizing coordination of services might be substantial' while the loss from any 'perceptible slackening of entrepreneurial effort', as may be instanced by the status of iron and steel, would be minimal or non-existent: 'There is hardly much danger of losing the fruits of any entrepreneurial impulses.' (Schumpeter, 1942a:229, 230, 231). State intervention in important areas like electricity, Schumpeter wrote in the Second World War, is nowadays 'not only approved but demanded by *all* parties' (Schumpeter, 1942a:229). The reason was not just market failure. The reason was the beginning of the end.

Also about to tumble over from private to public were those areas of capitalist activity which were already State in all but name. The Bank of England was one of these. The Labour Government in 1946 made up its mind to nationalise the Bank. The decision was highly symbolic – 'but its practical importance may well be equated to zero: the bank has been practically a department of the Treasury ever since 1914 and under modern conditions no central bank can be anything else.' (Schumpeter, 1942a:377–8). Nationalisation in such a case is no more than the conversion of the parastatal into the State. It is therefore logical that the British in 1946 were able to back up their Government with 'all but universal consent' (Schumpeter, 1942a:378). Schumpeter may have believed that private insurance would be the next of the capitalist redundancies to tumble over the line into the State. Wasteful of selling costs, duplicating social insurance in a range of fields, private insurance is like a private Bank, *de facto* a collective facility that must be rescued from commercial under-performance by the sensible heirs to Barone and Lange.

The British people held strong views on electricity and on the Bank. Their stage of economic evolution meant that they were increasingly prepared to accept nationalisation in cases where small units were not up to the task and where large organisations, their managements intact, could easily be grafted on to the State. The British people by the same token were not prepared to endorse encroachment into the entrepreneurial sector. It was 'not ripe for successful one-stroke socialization' since there the 'concentration of corporate control has not gone far enough' (Schumpeter, 1942a:229). Corporate capitalism had not *yet* gone far enough. The English were the passengers of their times. As their economy changed, so would their national culture and their attitude to the State.

9.3 POWER AND PARTICIPATION

Alfred Marshall, writing of the trade unions that they were 'a greater glory to England than her wealth' (Marshall, 1897b:400), welcomed intermediate associations because 'his little republic' gives the ordinary British worker the valuable opportunity to get involved: 'His connection with it on the one hand diminishes his freedom and his responsibility with regard to the conduct of his own life, and on the other hand gives him a responsibility in the ordering of the affairs of others. It educates him in the virtues and vices of patriotism.' (Marshall, 1875:364). Marshall was attracted by the ideal of the citizen as a team player even as that same individual was a self-serving economic man.

Schumpeter's view of the nation as a matrix of its groups was more ambiguous. In the core books the vision was stark: bureaucratic capitalism lets the boss make all the choices while bureaucratic socialism is the same without a breach. In the fringe articles the position is more equivocal: works councils offer the soul an microsocial affiliation, Papal Encyclicals show that the corporate body can inculcate a culture of harmony and bonds. Journeying from the Jesuits' Theresianum through Kautsky and Bauer to American Protestantism and then back to the Popes, Schumpeter's reservations are at least as interesting as the mainstream position of control from above which makes his sociology of social evolution so uncompromising an account of autonomy dispossessed by authority and elite.

9.3.1. Industrial Democracy

Even in *Capitalism, Socialism and Democracy* Schumpeter said that people were rational enough to lead their own lives: 'In the ordinary run of often repeated decisions the individual is subject to the salutary and rationalizing influence of favorable and unfavorable experience.' (Schumpeter, 1942a:258). The market itself is an education in buying shoes and pricing melons: 'It is simply not true that housewives are easily fooled.' (Schumpeter, 1942a:258). Daily life teaches each social actor 'the things that directly concern himself, his family, his business dealings, his hobbies, his friends and enemies, his township or ward, his class, church, trade union or any other social group of which he is an active member' (Schumpeter, 1942a:258). At the national level people may be ill-informed, personal experience limited. At the micro-level, however, the position is different. The shopper has learned where to go for grapes. The voter in the village knows who would make a good mayor.

As with the grapes and the mayors, so perhaps with the nuts and the bolts. The worker operating the machine, close to his craft, has the personal experience that is grease to the wheels of entrepreneurial adaptation. Industrial democracy and hands-on participation might be an asset in the microcosm of local knowledge where units are small, iterations familiar and actors in a position to recognise the logic of their interactions. The shopper for grapes and the voter in the village are living proof. Some of the time at least, Sir does not necessarily know best.

Schumpeter could, clearly, have left open the door to workplace democracy and to a socialism of bottom-up. Tawney argued that it was economically efficient as well as morally just that power should be shared with the rank-and-file who have the feel of the trade in their fingers: 'It is idle to expect that men will give their best to any system which they do not trust, or that they will trust any system in the control of which they do not share.' (Tawney, 1921:149). The fact is that *Capitalism, Socialism and Democracy* preached a very different gospel: 'Effective management of the socialist economy means dictatorship not *of* but *over* the proletariat in the factory .... As a matter of practical necessity, socialist democracy may eventually turn out to be more of a sham than capitalist democracy ever was.' (Schumpeter, 1942a:302). Because the socialist economy is fully compatible both with democracy and with exclusion, there is no ideological reason why bottom-up involvement should not coexist with post-capitalist control: 'Between socialism as we defined it and democracy as we defined it there is no necessary relation.' (Schumpeter, 1942a:284). The obstacle is purely economic. Tawney believed that shop-floor participation was needed to make the modern factory hum. Schumpeter believed that 'democratic meetingism' (Schumpeter, 1942a:216) was a waste of time. It was 'the nightmare of every responsible socialist' (Schumpeter, 1942a:226n). Inevitably, it would have to go: 'Much of this economic democracy will vanish into thin air in a socialist regime.' (Schumpeter, 1942a:300n).

In late capitalism the works councils, the shop stewards, the worker managers, the union directors had democratised that which does not lend itself to representation, participation, decentralisation or the competition of elites. The outcome had been a babel of confusions. Managers had had to resist unwonted interference from 'fussing citizens' committees or by their workmen' (Schumpeter, 1942a:299). The comrades themselves had come to recognise 'the true significance of restiveness at work and especially of strikes' (Schumpeter, 1942a:212). The wider community had begun to resent the 'anti-social attacks upon the nation's welfare' (Schumpeter, 1942a:212) that were being mounted by the special-interest coalitions. In the end the multiple involvements will have to be abandoned. Socialist planning, authoritarian and single-minded, will prove '*the only means of restoring social discipline*' (Schumpeter, 1942a:215). Consultation will talk itself into oblivion. Under the new feudalism the economy will jump through all the required hoops.

Schumpeter in *Capitalism, Socialism and Democracy* said that he knew of 'no responsible person' (Schumpeter, 1942a:299) who could see a constructive role for workplace democracy. In the firm as in the nation, he insisted, leadership is the business of the governors and not of the mob. In

'Sozialistische Möglichkeiten von Heute' he had been more open to the possibility that factory-level involvement would introduce active democracy into industry and trade. It was the message of 'Socialist possibilities of today', published in 1920/21, that participation at work was the harbinger of the socialism that was to come:

> In the factory there has been a development analogous to that in the State. Just as in the State Parliament represents particular interest groups, ... so the workers in the firm come to have an influence over the issues that directly affect them .... This tendency will become stronger and, as things are now proceeding, will lead to a 'constitutional' factory and later to the rule of labour alone. (Schumpeter, 1920/21:487).

The workers have a felt desire to register their opinion. That wish will lead to the dictatorship of the proletariat, as if driven by a political determinism that sees no need to wait for the economy to mature.

The works council movement was strong in Europe (especially in Germany, Austria and Russia) in the aftermath of the First World War: the term 'soviet' refers explicitly to collaborative decision-making. The cooperative movement in Britain, long a force in Northern working-class life, was expanding its interest from consumption to production: the early 1920s was the period in which guild socialists like G.D.H. Cole and Arthur Penty were at their most active and most influential. In Austria Otto Bauer, arguing that the bourgeois State would never attack the bastions of capitalist production or property, was announcing that social reconstruction via the democratisation of management would have to be the necessary first step.

Bauer believed that socialism at the national level would have to grow out of self-government at the base. It would be the product not of politicians and bureaucrats but of education through participation in the plant. Schumpeter, as Medearis writes, entered into the spirit of his times and took the socialists' line on the potential for change: 'Schumpeter shared the Austro-Marxists' view that the council movement represented a democratization of industry – a process that was analogous to political democratization .... Schumpeter, like Bauer, doubted the viability of any attempt to usher in socialism before the spread of the council system had done its work.' (Medearis, 2001:58). Schumpeter did not much like the council movement: 'There is not even a hint that the archconservative Schumpeter approved of the process – on the contrary, he regarded it with unconcealed aversion.' (Medearis, 2001:61). Aversion or not, he knew what was in the wind and seemed to regard the option as a reasonably viable choice.

Schumpeter in his essay on 'Socialist possibilities' made clear that democracy at work develops simultaneously with systemic transition in the nation as a whole: 'Workers councils and socialisation go together. They tend to reinforce each other and to develop at approximately the same time.' (Schumpeter, 1920/21:474). Educating, influencing, transforming, they tend to lead the workers in the direction of the rule of labour. Important as they are, however, still the Marxian emphasis on capital ownership has a complementary role to play: 'Socialisation will cause a fundamental change in our political institutions.' (Schumpeter, 1920/21:473). Property is closely correlated with power. That is why a move towards socialism automatically makes the government more open to more socialism still: 'Parliament by its very nature is a union of class-based organisations. These classes today are defined with reference to control of the means of production.' (Schumpeter, 1920/21:476). Parliament will come to mean something quite different once the socialisation of capital has restructured the economic base.

Socialism was possible. Syndicalism, on the other hand, was 'unacceptable' (Schumpeter, 1920/21:487). Worker ownership would make no economic sense: 'That would be group capitalism in place of individual capitalism.' (Schumpeter, 1920/21:487). Socialism is statist, large-scale and planned. It is not the competition of small-scale agglomerations for relative sway. Worker ownership is not an option that could be entertained. Democratic participation is a different matter. Schumpeter in his 1920/21 essay saw a future for a new distribution of power at work. It was a future which he almost immediately put out of his mind. *Capitalism, Socialism and Democracy* in 1942 condemned in no uncertain terms any questioning of the long-established division of labour between the body and the brain. In 1945, however, an opportunity to lecture in Montreal was to demonstrate that the fringe had not entirely been crowded out by the mainstream. Schumpeter in 1945 was still capable of saying that participation as well as remuneration can satisfy man's most fundamental economic needs.

9.3.2 Catholics and Corporatism

Schumpeter was baptised and brought up a Roman Catholic. Never a devout church-goer, he converted to Lutheranism in 1925 in order to facilitate his divorce from Gladys and early re-marriage to Annie. In the last five years of his life, however, he showed an unexpected interest in the solidaristic cooperativeness of the Catholics' corporatism that had been endorsed so strongly by Pope Pius XI in *Quadragesimo Anno* (1931) and before that by Pope Leo XIII in *Rerum Novarum* (1891).

Leo XIII had warned that egotistical utilitarianism could mean the callous ill-treatment of isolated and defenceless workers. It was an unappealing alternative to grabby Marxism that was seeking inequitably to rob recognised owners of their natural rights and to divide the Father's children who ought instead to be 'united in the bonds of friendship, but also those of brotherly love' (Leo XIII, 1891:12). Both concord and prosperity waited on a 'third way', neither covetous capitalism nor avaricious revolution. That 'third way' would assign a particular importance to social duties alongside individual entitlements: 'It is one thing to have a right to the possession of money, and another to have a right to use money as one pleases.' (Leo XIII, 1891:11). Participation at work, contributing much to a society committed to harmony and mutuality, not just to materialism and greed, would be a valuable part of that common ground that brought together the liberals and the labourites. It would show that hostility between the classes was an error of judgement, that capital and labour were symbiotically interdependent, that mutual respect would prove the *via media* that would lead to 'piety and morality': 'Workmen's Associations should be so organized and governed as to furnish the best and most suitable means ... for helping each individual member to better his condition to the utmost, in body, mind and property.' (Leo XIII, 1891:27).

Leo XIII had emphasised that rights come with duties attached. So, 40 years later, did Pius XI: 'The right of property must be distinguished from its use.' (Pius XI, 1931:137). The economy exists in order to foster the common good: 'The good of the whole community must be safeguarded.' (Pius XI,1931:141). It will be better safeguarded through the cooperative endeavour of labour and capital than it will through the selfish acquisitiveness of narrow-minded conflict: 'A bond of union is provided ... by the common effort of employers and employees of one and the same group joining forces to produce goods or give service.' (Pius XI, 1931:148). What this means in practice is that industrial groups should join together to form a corporate association that would transcend their restrictive sectionalism: 'We deem it advisable that the wage contract should, when possible, be modified somewhat by a contract of partnership .... In this way wage-earners are made sharers of some sort in the ownership, or the management, or the profits.' (Pius XI, 1931:144). Pius XI, a clergyman and not an economist, wanted to protect the faith and speak for God. Even so, his underdeveloped notion of a nation of groups did seem to him to promise social and productive benefits as well.

Schumpeter, who grew up in Catholic Austro-Hungary where the Church had played an important role, was fully aware of what the Popes were saying. Politically, he had joined the Christian Social Party in Vienna in 1919: mistrustful of democracy, capitalism, the Jews, the disintegration of authority, it was also in favour of the corporatist ideal as a step in the direction of moral reform. Sociologically, his basic building block was always the family: dynastic, responsible, non-rational, it was itself a corporation that situated self-interest in the context of a group. Economically, his vision was the reflection of Austro-German (and later American) big business, not of the perfect competitiveness of the British 1840s: the corporate principle would only continue the tradition of collusion and collectivism that free enterprisers were misguidedly making the target of the Sherman Act. Intellectually, his long-standing belief in the aristocracy (like the family in decline) meant that he was looking for a new source of legitimation and authority in the void. His instinctive romanticism inevitably attracted him to the pre-capitalist chivalry of tradesmen's self-regulation in the Medieval guilds.

Schumpeter did his greatest work in America: a country which had never shown much interest in corporatism, it was at war with the Fascists who had used intermediate associations not as a vehicle for democracy but as a means for the suppression of dissent. His economic vision was orientated towards bureaucracy and efficiency: self-government fits uneasily into the work of an author who believed that consulting the poorly-informed was more likely to diminish productivity than to augment it. Even Vienna in the age of Schumpeter was arguably a secular and a sceptical place: his friends probably thought of him as an unsentimental scientist with little interest in the Church. It is easy enough to think of reasons why Schumpeter should have been profoundly indifferent to corporatism. Even so, politically, sociologically, economically, intellectually, it is no less easy to understand the long-standing sources of attraction to an author who had grown up not just on Menger and Marshall but on Othmar Spann and Ignaz Seipel as well.

Schumpeter had always had a religious side to his make-up. His personal cult of '*Die Hasen*' (hidden even from his closest friends), the way in which that communion sustained him throughout a quarter-century of mental distress, his frequent descriptions of Marxism as a religion, all show that belief went deep in his psyche. In the 1940s, Allen says, he seems to have been moving in the direction of a more traditional God. He began to say his prayers regularly and to mark holy days like Good Friday. Reading his unpublished diary, Allen comments: 'Although he never mentioned Christ or Christian theological propositions, on those holy days he seemed more at peace with himself and expressed fewer complaints and less cynicism.' (Allen, 1991:II, 199). It was in that refreshed frame of mind, Allen writes, that he came to find his way to the guarded corporatism of his 1945 lecture:

> Although Schumpeter had created his own personal religion, and never expressed much interest in any formal, church-related, religion, he still maintained high respect for the Roman Catholic Church. Regarding the church as a part of society's cement and an institution commanding near-universal esteem, he believed it could influence the economic order. True, he looked upon the church as a remnant of feudalism, and, as such, prerational; but even though feudalistic, it had played an equally important role in the success of capitalism. In 1945, Schumpeter began to think the church could play an important role as capitalism fades. (Allen, 1991:II, 163–4).

The catalyst for his renewed openness to Catholic social thought appears to have been the invitation he received from Emile Bouvier, a Jesuit teaching at the University of Montreal and his former student at Harvard, to give an address at a gathering of Canadian businessmen in 1945 on some aspect of capitalism in the post-war world. The theme of the conference as a whole was a challenging one: 'Comment sauvegarder l'entreprise privée?' Schumpeter in *Capitalism, Socialism and Democracy* had already said that the chances were slim.

The title of the paper – 'The future of private enterprise in the face of modern socialistic tendencies' – seemed to indicate that Schumpeter would effectively be repeating his prediction that the big-business bureaucracy would inevitably be succeeded by a centralising statism, autocratic and authoritarian. His audience must have been somewhat surprised when he declared instead that the Pope, through the doctrine of 'voluntary associations', had in fact found the useful 'third way' that would allow private property and spontaneity to co-exist with social harmony and autonomy without force: 'The corporate principle organizes but it does not regiment.' (Schumpeter, 1946a:404). The Pope had had in mind a moral ideal. Crucially, the Pope had been preaching sound social economics as well: 'He was showing us a practical method to solve practical problems of immediate urgency.' (Schumpeter, 1946a:404).

Schumpeter in his 1945 lecture, distancing himself from the economic exploitation of classical Marxism, returned to the more urgent threat identified by the Vatican and the Encyclicals that market individualism and utilitarian rationality could be the cause of 'social decomposition' and 'social disintegration' (Schumpeter, 1946a:403). Even now, Schumpeter wrote, our 'common culture and faith' have been put at risk by Enlightenment egotism, to such an extent that 'our society is in the process of falling apart' (Schumpeter, 1946a:403). Shared values are weak, the political elite lacks a sense of purpose, and the threat is real that decision-making will become immobilised in the moral vacuum that leaves each atom a stranger to every other: 'Families, workshops, societies do not function if nobody accepts his duties, if no one knows how to make himself accepted as *leader*, and if each applies himself to constantly drawing up a balance sheet of his personal and immediate benefits and costs at any given time.' (Schumpeter, 1946a:403). *Laissez-faire* freedoms *do not function* if social responsibility is repeatedly sacrificed to disembedded expediency. Private enterprise itself becomes an impossibility. The warring factions refuse to acknowledge any entitlement but their own.

One solution is the totalitarian State in the sense of the Hobbesian Leviathan. A very different solution is the thicket of professional associations that had been endorsed by secularists like Durkheim, theologians like the Popes. Compulsion, they said, might produce acceptable outcomes but it did not train the moral sentiments. Without such an education, social order without divisive *anomie* could never be an *ethical* choice. Schumpeter in 1945 came down on the side of supply-based corporations able to enlist the loyalty of employee and employer alike, able to coordinate production plans without the market instabilities of gaming oligopolists. Private enterprise is preserved even if decentralisation ceases to mean active competition. Collaborative interdependence is ensured even if planning is performed without the socialist State. Schumpeter in 1945 knew that corporatism had been discredited in the public mind because of its association with Mussolini's Fascism. This seemed not to worry him. He, after all, knew that the Vatican and the Encyclicals lent their authority to his cause.

Schumpeter after Montreal returned only twice to the idea of corporate action such as would prevent the producers from spoiling the common market and would leave little room for the class struggle of capital and labour. In 'The march into socialism', dating from 1949, he said that social reorganisation in line with Catholic teaching, 'though presumably possible only in Catholic societies', could well provide 'an alternative to socialism that would avoid the "omnipotent state"' (Schumpeter, 1950b:422). In the *History of Economic Analysis*, uncompleted at his death, he conceded the possibility of 'a society – and a state – operating by means of self-governing vocational associations within a framework of ethical precepts' but then abandoned the discussion on the grounds that corporatism is policy and policy options would have to wait: 'Since it is a normative program and not a piece of analysis no more will be said about it in this book.' (Schumpeter, 1954:765). Some other book would have to take on the Catholicism and the corporatism, the moral reform that led to the social reform that led to the economic reform. Some other book would have to describe in detail how innovation would be protected and new entry assured in a conservative new world where faith would be the cause and the consequence of social solidarity expressed through work.

Schumpeter never wrote the missing book on the religious economics of post-capitalist associationalism. He never proved that something nearer to guild socialism than to centralist socialism could raise living standards without the need for a Ministry that dictates. His halfway house was built in the same darkness that conceals his evolving religious convictions in the last years of his life. Even so, it is the black swan that calls into question the generality of his prediction. If the Popes can solve the economic problem, the Stalins and the planners need not apply.

10. Continuity and change

Marx was up-to-date. His economic interpretation took for granted that current attitudes and structures were a reflection of current economic conditions and dominant productive imperatives. History explained the evolution of the present. Inherited patterns, however, no longer played a significant part in moulding and shaping the patterns of the future.

Marx, treating bygones as bygones, was content to start from here. Schumpeter, more anchored, was a theorist of lagged adaptation who looked backward in order to look forward. He did this because, empirically speaking, the past had not gone away: 'Social structures, types and attitudes are coins that do not readily melt. Once they are formed they persist, possibly for centuries.' (Schumpeter, 1942a:12). Free people freely choose their best-judged course of action. They make their free choices within the framework of vestiges and survivals that define for them the continuing path.

Schumpeter as an empiricist concluded that handed-on institutions were all around. Schumpeter as a functionalist also believed that the conservatism had an active role to play: 'No social system can work which is based exclusively upon a network of free contracts between (legally) equal contracting parties and in which everyone is supposed to be guided by nothing except his own (short-run) utilitarian ends.' (Schumpeter, 1950b:423–4). Capitalism thrives because the past fulfils its function. Capitalism would decline if the remembered and the pre-filtered lost their hold. Orderly change presupposes cultural continuity. There is no other way.

The remembered and the pre-filtered keep the pace of transmutation within the manageable tramlines of *natura non facit saltum*: 'Just as the existence of an efficient opposition is a requirement for the orderly functioning of democratic government, so the existence of economic forces that resist institutional change may be necessary in order to keep the speed of this change within the limits of safety.' (Schumpeter, 1950b:427). The checks of conservatism are needed to balance the dynamism of progress. The problem is that capitalism itself is eroding the very foundations upon which it depends for its own sustainable success: 'The capitalist order not only rests on props made of extra-capitalist material but also derives its energy from extra-capitalist patterns of behavior which at the same time it is bound to destroy.' (Schumpeter, 1942a:162). Capitalism is doomed not because of the malintegrated working class but because of the manner in which capitalism itself 'undermines the social institutions which protect it': 'Capitalist evolution tends to wear away its socio-psychological bases.' (Schumpeter, 1942a:61, 214). A system that 'attacks its own institutional framework' (Schumpeter, 1942a:141) cannot be expected to last forever. Feudalism was destroyed by its enemies because the rising middle classes could not advance within its rules. Capitalism takes its own life because it incorrectly assumes that the cultural underpinning is at variance with utilitarian advance.

The institutions in a state of decay, 'the bourgeois fortress thus becomes politically defenceless' precisely because the bourgeoisie itself comes to share in the 'atmosphere of almost universal hostility to its own social order' (Schumpeter, 1942a:143). It is clearly not just the post-feudal conventions but also the class that owes its dominion to the post-feudal rules that sinks into a decline: 'The scheme of values of capitalist society, though causally related to its economic success, is losing its hold not only upon the public mind but also upon the "capitalist" stratum itself.' (Schumpeter, 1950b:424). In the end the cultural decay and the class-based self-loathing will sound the knell of an economic system that was fated to collapse: 'Entrepreneurs and capitalists – in fact the whole stratum that accepts the bourgeois scheme of life – will eventually cease to function.' (Schumpeter, 1942a:156). It will cease to function. It will cease to exist. Schumpeter writes that 'capitalism is being killed by its achievements' (Schumpeter, 1942a:410). He also believes that it is now too late to put back the clock.

Capitalism, committed to economic change but dependent on cultural continuity, is always and everywhere a vulnerable growth. It is with the unstable mix of learned embeddedness and gain-seeking opportunism that the present chapter is concerned. Section 1, Society, deals with the aristocracy, the intelligentsia and the family to show how changing conditions are poisoning the environment for a delicate plant. Section 2, Economy, examines the core building blocks of property and rationality to establish in what way the values of capitalism may also be called the system's fatal flaw. Section 3, Polity, looks at taxation and regulation to show how, in two ways, the State is challenging the legitimacy of market homeostasis and is setting itself up as a rival for social esteem.

10.1 SOCIETY

Capitalism is a rich mix of social affiliations. That mix is not a friction but 'the essence of the social process': 'A purely capitalist society – consisting of nothing but entrepreneurs, capitalists, and proletarian workmen – would work in ways completely different from those we observe historically, *if indeed it could exist at all*.' (Schumpeter, 1943:177). The Marxian dialectic flattens the multiplicity into a spiritless duality that recognises no complexity and acknowledges no past. A more realistic approach to the social organism would be to emphasise the symbiosis between modern and pre-modern elements in a social matrix that is more than the sum of its workshops: 'In the capitalist epoch, the classes that are the products of the capitalist process are hardly ever found alone.' (Schumpeter, 1943:177). The aristocracy, the intelligentsia and the family are three loci of belonging which, non-capitalist in origin, have an especial impact on the functioning and the future of the present-day economic system.

10.1.1 The Aristocracy

Capitalism was born into a late-feudal world. The landed classes ruled by birth and blue blood. They expected obedience because their status was ascribed. The merchants and manufacturers when they arrived on the scene were able to travel free on the cultural habits that had been gifted and passed on by a pre-business elite that had little or no respect for the Industrial Revolution:

> The workman's readiness to obey orders was never due to a rational conviction of the virtues of capitalist society or to a rational perception of any advantages accruing to him personally. It was due to discipline inculcated by the feudal predecessor of his bourgeois master. To this master the proletariat transferred part of that respect – by no means all of it – that their ancestors in all normal cases bore to their feudal lords. (Schumpeter, 1942a:214).

Unthinking loyalty, 'unquestioning subordination within the individual firm' (Schumpeter, 1942a:214), are not top-up luxuries but rather normative necessities, 'essential for the efficient working of the institutionalized leadership of the producing plant' (Schumpeter, 1950b:423). Order-following, Schumpeter says, is 'essential' – and gain-seeking commercialism is not strong enough to teach the masses to respect the leadership that commands them. That is why the Earl of Tewkesbury and the Dowager Marchioness of Bath may be said to play so important a role in the correction of market failure. The labourer obeys the boss because Gradgrind shares in the aura of the Lord of the Manor. The present produces the future because the past provides the *noblesse oblige*. Irrational elements make rationality possible. The aristocracy is not a functionless relic but an indispensable exemplar. Without the Queen to admire there would be unreliable interest at best, Marxian force at worst, but not the enthusiastic acceptance of hierarchy upon which economic and social order so much rely.

The aristocracy legitimates. It also gets involved. The bourgeoisie is and was a selling class, able to take a lead in matters of business but too uninspiring, too 'unheroic', too deficient in the 'mystic glamour' that is needed for 'the ruling of men', to bend a whole nation to its will: 'The stock exchange is a poor substitute for the Holy Grail .... The ledger and the cost calculation absorb and confine.' (Schumpeter, 1942a:137). Strong in rationality but weak in charisma, the businessman does not look like a statesman. He might also lack the strength of purpose that is needed for hard decisions: 'Knowing this he wants to be left alone and to leave politics alone.' (Schumpeter, 1942a:138). Economic leadership is a world away from political leadership. Historically speaking, the bourgeoisie 'did not make a conspicuous success of ruling' (Schumpeter, 1942a:137) when it had the chance.

The capitalist process generates the revenues that pay for the court, the army, the parliament and the bureaucracy. What it cannot do is to command emotive allegiance or produce captains able to decide where the ship of state ought to sail: 'The bourgeois class is ill equipped to face the problems, both domestic and international.' (Schumpeter, 1942a:138). That is why the bourgeois society is dependent upon 'a protecting framework not made of bourgeois material': 'Without protection by some non-bourgeois group, the bourgeoisie is politically helpless and unable not only to lead its nation but even to take care of its particular class interest. Which amounts to saying that it needs a master.' (Schumpeter, 1942a:138). The bourgeoisie is a class which, reasonably successful at making money, lacks the self-confidence that would empower it to say boo to the proverbial goose: 'The bourgeois can't rule, he can't lead.' (Schumpeter, 1941:360). The landowning class, conveniently enough, fills the potential void. The collapse of the Weimar Republic testifies to the *bellum* that is just around the corner when there ceases to be a mutually-beneficial division of labour between the classes from the past and the classes that make the cash registers ring.

The aristocracy, Schumpeter writes, 'made things a lot easier for the bourgeoisie by staying in political power for the greater part of capitalist history' (Schumpeter, 1942a:214). In Britain, for example, 'the aristocratic element continued to rule the roost *right to the end of the period of intact and vital capitalism'* (Schumpeter, 1942a:135). The descendants of Hastings and Agincourt, the Conservative Party and the House of Lords possess precisely those attributes in which the shopkeepers and the factory owners are most deficient. Those qualities are 'the lordly attitude', the 'ability and habit to command and to be obeyed', that 'cast a halo' and make the beneficiary 'a ruler of men' (Schumpeter, 1942a:137). The comparative advantage lies in presentation, prestige and decisiveness, not in throughput, productivity and product development. The selling point is evidently enough to win popular support. Thus does the bloodline of the Medieval knights transform itself into the politicians, ambassadors, military officers and senior civil servants – the 'school tie', the old boy network, the Pall Mall Club – despite the fact that the job description has been subject to significant modification since the time of Bosworth Field.

Capitalism succeeded to feudalism because it could rely for good governance on an establishment class which had 'outlived the social and technological conditions which had given rise to it' (Schumpeter, 1942a:137). The landed interest by the Victorian period had lost its economic supremacy. Unexpectedly, however, it had acquired a new functionality as the mainstay of the post-agricultural order: 'The steel frame of that structure still consisted of the human material of feudal society.' (Schumpeter, 1942a:136).

A steel frame being tough and resilient, it is a surprise that law-givers with a constituency in atavism did not do their best to favour land and to block the progress of capital. Counter-intuitive or not, the historical record leaves no room for doubt. The ruling aristocracy consistently did what it had to do to foster the expansion of industry and trade: 'Domestic and foreign policies and institutional changes were shaped to suit and propel that development.' (Schumpeter, 1942a:136). The reason was public finance. As landowners the aristocrats had a private stake in rent. As politicians, however, they had to steward well the new-found El Dorado that paid for the public services. A Marxian would contest the logic but the facts speak for themselves. The ruling aristocracy put its political identity above its economic identity. It served as a steel frame within which the post-agricultural order could grow into its realm.

Where the middle classes are in a position to do the job well, they may be expected to be given their head. This is the case with municipal government. Roads, sewers and water supply lend themselves easily to 'treatment by the methods and in the spirit of the business office' (Schumpeter, 1942a:138). Administrative functions such as these are, by their very nature, 'akin to business management' (Schumpeter, 1942a:138). They can safely be delegated to the business interest. Where the middle classes are, however, unable to make a success of a task, there the upper classes must be ready and able to take over the reins. An example would be the Netherlands, commercial in time of peace but accustomed in time of war to call in 'a warlord of feudal complexion' (Schumpeter, 1942a:138). A latent reserve when negotiation was enough, a mailed fist when an aggressor had to be stopped, it was the experience of the Netherlands that the descendants of the fourteenth earl reliably corrected the market failure and just as reliably handed back the mandate as soon as the crisis was past. In bad times as in good times, Schumpeter concluded, the aristocracy in the era of the bourgeoisie is not just a Marxian fetter but a social support as well.

The upper classes look after the middle classes. The middle classes, historically speaking, have been far less generous to the upper classes that have cushioned capitalism and kept it alive. The king no longer rules by the grace of God. The barons were marginalised by the Magna Carta. Free trade did nothing for the inherited head start that paid Eton fees through the Corn Laws. Capitalism in the Marxian schema has to smash the surviving feudalism that is a lion in the path of its sustained expansion. Capitalism in Schumpeter's economics shares in the impetus to create through the destruction of the class before.

To Marx, co-existence being unthinkable, the elimination of the aristocracy is only an inevitable step in the passage towards the two-class and then the one-class society. Schumpeter accepts that the aristocracy is losing its role but takes the view that the evolution has a negative aspect. The Marxians and the liberals alike had failed to recognise what it means to shatter a double-edged sword. In breaking with the past, Schumpeter said, capitalism not only routs a date-stamped factor-income but also puts its own future prosperity at risk: 'In breaking down the pre-capitalist framework of society, capitalism thus broke not only barriers that impeded its progress but also flying buttresses that prevented its collapse.' (Schumpeter, 1942a:139). The bourgeoisie needs the aristocracy. Inadvertently, it also destroys the collaborator upon which it depends.

Schumpeter is insistent that the mix is indispensable: 'An industrial and commercial bourgeoisie will in general not be able to exist except in symbiosis with a non-bourgeois stratum.' (Schumpeter, 1942a:167). His words 'not be able' are a source of concern in the light of his conviction that capitalism, while 'removing institutional deadwood', has counter-productively been 'removing partners of the capitalist stratum' (Schumpeter, 1942a:139) as well. The weakening of the aristocracy has meant both a decline in the mentality that self-enforces discipline and a leadership hiatus that has left the bourgeoisie 'politically helpless', unable to 'take care of its particular class interest' (Schumpeter, 1942a:138). In destroying feudalism, capitalism also undermines itself. Schumpeter takes 'that symbiosis of classes which owe their existence to different epochs and processes as the rule rather than as an exception' (Schumpeter, 1942a:139). He also believes that the classes from the past are being driven back into the history books by the self-aggrandisement of market capitalism itself.

10.1.2 The Intelligentsia

The bourgeoisie 'produces the rope which is going to hang it' (Schumpeter, 1941:260). Schumpeter is referring not to the classical proletariat. He is referring to the new intellectual estate, negative, rootless, always a threat. The Smiths and the Humes in the early days had argued strongly for the emancipation of initiative. *The Edinburgh Review* and *The Economist* had disseminated the message that acquisition is good. That, however, was *then*. Schumpeter's anxiety relates to *now*.

Schumpeter sees the intellectuals as a distinctive group. Their status is bounded and self-aware even if they do not form an economic class in the Ricardian–Marxian sense of factor ownership: 'They develop group attitudes and group interests sufficiently strong to make large numbers of them behave in the way that is usually associated with the concept of social classes.' (Schumpeter, 1942a:146). They are a thinking estate, most of them with higher education, many of them employed as writers and journalists. Intellectuals are 'people who wield the power of the spoken and the written word' and who do so, in contrast to politicians, without 'direct responsibility for practical affairs' (Schumpeter, 1942a:147). Intellectuals are opinion-formers and consensus shapers. That is why they are a problem. The Smiths and the Humes wanted capitalism to become the dominant mode. Intellectuals today would much prefer to see socialism instead.

The model is the Marxian endogeneity of the bourgeoisie which creates the proletariat, the negating class which brings down the curtain on a moribund order. The intelligentsia, although a classless class, closely resembles the proletariat in its Janus-faced nature. It is at once the product of capitalism and a danger from within: 'Capitalism inevitably and by virtue of the very logic of its civilization creates, educates and subsidizes a vested interest in social unrest.' (Schumpeter, 1942a:146). As in the Marxian case, capitalism is beset with an internal contradiction. Capitalism is the social fact that brought the intelligentsia into being. Capitalism is also the detested focus for its implacable hostility.

Once there were only the scribes in the monasteries. The capitalist revolution magnified the influence and popularised the media. The printing press and economies of scale made possible a mass market for books and newspapers. Rising living standards and increasing leisure boosted the demand for information and entertainment. The *laissez-faire* ideology in which private enterprise held so significant an interest freed social critics from the discipline of stifling censorship. The capitalist era, in short, gave potential heretics an unprecedented opportunity to peddle their wares.

The *Zeitgeist* was on the side of thought and expression. Calculative rationality provided a framework for fresh evaluation. Product differentiation supplied the model for ideational pluralism. Individualism and tolerance were in the air. So was the habit of shopping and shopping around which made the consumers and not the State the 'collective patron' (Schumpeter, 1942a:149) of the freelance opinion formers. Nor should it be forgotten that the capitalist system, skills-based and knowledge-intensive, has led to a sizeable expansion in across-the-board education. Mass literacy is the precondition for mass reading even if not for mass radio and mass television. The era of the bourgeoisie is also the era of the intelligentsia. The scribes would never have advanced beyond the monasteries if it had not been for the economic transformation in industry and trade.

The intelligentsia has never enjoyed so much power and so much prestige as in the era of the bourgeoisie. In spite of that the intellectuals, critical and angry, have consistently expressed their 'moral disapproval of the capitalist order' (Schumpeter, 1942a:153). In biting the hand that feeds them, their seditious disloyalty would seem to be at variance with the social conditions under which their own standing is likely to be the most secure. Schumpeter believes that he is able to account not only for the antagonism of the articulate but also for the fact that 'this hostility increases, instead of diminishing, with every achievement of capitalist evolution' (Schumpeter, 1942a:153). At the heart of his theory is education. Strictly speaking, it is excessive education, unneeded education, education turned malign through over-supply and over-consumption. A nation that practises sound manpower planning will be less at risk from its thinkers. Yet we start from here; and modern societies have a tendency to provide too much.

Schumpeter writes that the escalation in the educational sector is 'fostered by public opinion and public authority so as to go much further than it would have done under its own steam' (Schumpeter, 1942a:152). Business rationality would have led to the activity being discontinued at a lower level of output. Popular attitudes and State intervention lead instead to an overhang of trained graduates relative to the number of white-collar vacancies. Many would-be professionals will have in consequence to scale down their aspirations. Swelling the ranks of the 'unemployed or unsatisfactorily employed or unemployable', they enter into the specifically Schumpeterian 'host of intellectuals' – and 'they enter it in a thoroughly discontented frame of mind' (Schumpeter, 1942a:153).

Over-expansion of education is especially hard on the irredeemably second-rate. Credentialled and certified, they find it psychically unacceptable to take up a manual occupation. Over-expansion, however, means that students without natural ability are taught by instructors without natural ability. More means worse, inferior plots produce inferior harvests, and the end result is an unwanted surplus of mediocrity. Instances abound where, 'among a dozen applicants for a job, all formally qualified, there is not one who can fill it satisfactorily' (Schumpeter, 1942a:152). Those who can, do. Those who can't become intellectuals. Frustrated and excluded, 'discontent breeds resentment' (Schumpeter, 1942a:153). A hostility to capitalism is in that way born which owes much to personal disappointment and very little to socialist philosophy's rights and wrongs.

Education in the capitalist age is by virtue of its economic mission pragmatic, rational and questioning. That in itself undermines the respect for tradition that once built a cocoon around the business system. Here once again it proves to be the case that capitalism 'creates a critical frame of mind which, after having destroyed the moral authority of so many other institutions, in the end turns against its own' (Schumpeter, 1942a:143). Education drills the intellectuals in identifying shortcomings and spotlighting faults. Their taught skills become their stock in trade since it is only through nibbling away at the capitalist status quo that the outsider class can acquire any real sense of self-worth and social purpose: 'The intellectual group cannot help nibbling, because it lives on criticism and its whole position depends on criticism that stings.' (Schumpeter, 1942a:151). Its whole position depends on fault-finding and point-scoring. The salaried executive too afraid of 'obloquy' (Schumpeter, 1942a:214) to answer back, the bourgeoisie as a class too meek to mount a defence, the likelihood is high that the gravediggers will win the debate. They will succeed not least because the capitalists will have lost the will to argue persuasively for their cause.

Schumpeter believed he was living in an 'atmosphere of hostility to capitalism': 'The public mind has by now so thoroughly grown out of humor with it as to make condemnation of capitalism and all its works a foregone conclusion – almost a requirement of the etiquette of discussion.' (Schumpeter, 1942a:63). For that virtual eclipse the chattering and the scribbling classes must bear a considerable part of the responsibility. Sometimes the 'coffeehouse conspirator' (Schumpeter, 1942a:8) will fail to convince: consider the rift between the Marxian theorisers and the shop-floor activists, identified by Schumpeter in his centenary essay on the *Communist Manifesto*, that had opened up 'because the masses felt that the Marxist ideology was not their own but *that it was imposed upon them by intellectuals*' (Schumpeter, 1949a:290). More typically it will be the theories and slogans of the left-wing 'tutors of the mass mind' (Schumpeter, 1942a:26) that will eventually win out. They may be expected in the end to impart 'a revolutionary bias to the most bourgeois trade-union practices' (Schumpeter, 1942a:154).

Intellectuals trade in ideas. Teachers and propagandists, they strive to create an ideational superstructure that the economic basis might not otherwise have brought into being: 'The masses have not always felt themselves to be frustrated and exploited. But the intellectuals that formulated their views for them have always told them that they were.' (Schumpeter, 1942a:26). Intellectuals also take a political lead: 'Socialism ... would be nowhere without the intellectual leader of bourgeois extraction.' (Schumpeter, 1942a:311n). Whether the focus is the Fabians within British Labour or

Lenin's Social Democratic Party of 1898, the rule is that the masses are not in the vanguard but must be 'talked and bullied into consent': 'The spearhead will be formed by intellectuals assisted by the semi-criminal rabble.' (Schumpeter, 1942a:310).

Marx and Engels predicted that intolerable suffering and the labour–capital divide would radicalise the exploited and give an impetus to class war. In fact the proletariat seldom became resentful or antagonistic, let alone disciplined or revolutionary. Pathological cheating undermines trust and cyclical unemployment obscures the memory of a secular rise in living standards: for the myopic masses 'it is the short-run that counts' (Schumpeter, 1942a:145). In normal circumstances, however, the relationship between the classes is peaceful and constructive, 'primarily one of cooperation' (Schumpeter, 1942a:19). At least it would be, in the absence of 'typical bourgeois intellectuals' (Schumpeter, 1942a:312) like Marx and Engels. Typical bourgeois intellectuals take control of the labour movement. They make it into 'something that differs substantially from what it would be without them' (Schumpeter, 1942a:154).

The labour movement can mean trade unions seeking to restructure relative shares. A vote against free markets in the obvious sense that the bargaining is collective, still this cannot be called a popular demand for the overthrow of the system: 'The labor movement is not essentially socialist, just as socialism is not essentially laborite or proletarian.' (Schumpeter, 1942a:310). What converts the labour movement from a negotiating to a fighting force is not the bottom-up dynamic but rather the Leninist deus ex machina of 'a band of intellectuals officering the rabble' (Schumpeter, 1942a:330). In Russia the Marxian ideology was introduced by 'an intelligentsia whose ideas were as foreign to the soil as were the Paris dresses of Russian society women' (Schumpeter, 1942a: 326). The ideology was foreign, the labour movement captured by the 'imported radicalism and the group interest' (Schumpeter, 1942a:326) of educated misfits who had never seen a lathe or plough. If the 'rabble' had a failing, it must have been 'the utmost docility' (Schumpeter, 1942a:328) with which they accepted that the self-selected had a natural right to lead.

The intellectuals got their way – and not just in Russia: 'The public mind has renounced allegiance to the capitalist scheme of values. Private wealth is under a moral ban.' (Schumpeter, 1943:183). Socialism is coming. Public opinion has been shaped. Intellectuals who trade in 'theories and slogans' (Schumpeter, 1942a:154) have a grip of steel which their students and their readers will underestimate at their peril.

10.1.3 The Family

Looking back to the golden age of capitalist aspiration, 'the family and the family home used to be the mainspring of the typically bourgeois kind of profit motive' (Schumpeter, 1942a:160). That is how things used to be in the high-Victorian entrepreneurialism of Buddenbrooks and Soames Forsyte that Schumpeter had seen in his youth. Less and less were kinship and base the irreducible building blocks of the corporate capitalism, 'unromantic and unheroic' (Schumpeter, 1942a:160), that had become the successor to the old-style intergenerationalism of sentiment and blood. In this way as in others, economic evolution had been chipping away at the buttresses that, analogous to those of the great gothic cathedrals, were serving as *outside* supports that protected strong structures from collapse.

The founding of a family and the perpetuation of a dynasty have lost much of their imperative force. Marriages end in divorce. Children put rebellion above filial loyalty. Couples frequently have one child or no children at all. Children satisfy needs that contraception cannot touch: 'Having children means having one of the strongest desires of the human heart. A childless family is not a healthy family; it is psychologically warped.' (Schumpeter, 1941:379). The family, moreover, is a guarantee that men will add value and accumulate: 'One of the strongest incentives to save is the wife and children, and if there is no wife and children there would be a reduced tendency to save.' (Schumpeter, 1941:376). The self unfolds. The economy expands. The family has a purpose and function. In spite of that it is in decline and the decay is not difficult to explain: 'It is wholly attributable to the rationalization of everything in life.' (Schumpeter, 1942a:157). The cost–benefit mentality spreads from Scrooge's counting-house into Cratchit's private home. This is 'one of the effects of capitalist evolution' (Schumpeter, 1942a:157).

Men and women, because of capitalist evolution, 'acquire the habit of weighing the individual advantages and disadvantages of any prospective course of action' (Schumpeter, 1942a:157). Initially in the commercial classes, later on in the aristocracy and the proletariat as well, they act as if guided by 'a sort of inarticulate system of cost accounting' (Schumpeter, 1942a:157) that assigns little importance to morals and affects. In a post-peasant society, 'children cease to be economic assets' (Schumpeter, 1942a:157). They do not even repay the debt of dependency by caring for their aged parents when in need: 'The modern child doesn't give a damn what happens to his parents. They think it is just as well to leave them to public charity.' (Schumpeter, 1941:379). The modern parent must clearly decide if the joys of parenthood are really worth the sacrifice of money, comfort, freedom from care, alternative opportunity-sets that are the full cost of family ties. Modern parents have been doing their sums. Falling birth rates have been their rational reply.

Schumpeter feels that their narrow balance sheet gives them an incomplete picture. The psychic and spiritual benefits of parenthood tend to escape 'the rational searchlight of modern individuals who, in private as in public life, tend to focus attention on ascertainable details of immediate utilitarian relevance' (Schumpeter, 1942a:158). Consumers of children ignore or undervalue 'the contribution made by parenthood to physical and moral health' (Schumpeter, 1942a:158). They do not take into account the hidden imperatives of human nature that make most women and many men desperate to pass on what they *are*. They put to one side the structural needs of the 'social organism' for which Schumpeter's model may have been the fall in European population in the run-up to 1939. The balance sheet is misleading. But that is what people want.

Gain-seeking capitalism does not mean the same once effective birth control makes it possible to ensure that there will not be any heirs: 'With the decline of the driving power supplied by the family motive, the businessman's time-horizon shrinks, roughly, to his life expectation.' (Schumpeter, 1942a:161). He might therefore not see the need for assiduity and abstinence to the same extent that he would have done had he believed he had a commitment to his progeny. Horizons become shorter. Self-denial becomes less.

The founding-father who passes on his business to a lineage without end has an incentive to fight the trade unions and keep out the State. The childless capitalist will be more passive, more complaisant, more willing to make compromises or to give in. In corporate America, for example, 'there was no real resistance anywhere against the imposition of crushing financial burdens during the last decade or against labor legislation incompatible with the effective management of industry' (Schumpeter, 1942a:161). The capitalist with an infinite life-span makes a stand. The childless capitalist 'does not really care' (Schumpeter, 1942a:161). You can't take it with you. Neither can he.

Investment is threatened. Efficiency is threatened. Even the genetic pool is at risk. In one of his few references to eugenics (a subject much debated in the 1930s) Schumpeter warns that it is the good stock that is most likely to eliminate itself: 'The men and women who want to do something in this life don't want children in the next room. They will be the ones to restrict families first.' (Schumpeter, 1941:377). Intelligence weeds itself out. Entrepreneurship becomes a one-match game. Capitalism is not the capitalism that it was when the capitalist laboured in order that known others might perpetuate his tournament.

As for the family home itself, it too becomes a burden and a drain. Higher taxes make it too expensive. Smaller households mean that a small flat will be just as convenient. Consumer durables take the place of staff. Friends are entertained in the restaurant or club. The seigniorial lifestyle withers away. It withers away because capitalism more and more means that the isolate should live for himself and live for today.

Capitalism, Schumpeter writes, is more than the housewife's choice between peas and beans or the worker's freedom to change his job: 'It means a scheme of values, an attitude toward life, a civilization – the civilization of inequality and of the family fortune. This civilization is rapidly passing away, however.' (Schumpeter, 1950b:425). Intergenerationalism is rapidly passing away. Capitalism will not long survive the altruism that gave to the profit-seeking its charter and its sense of purpose.

10.2 ECONOMY

Capitalism is the cause and effect of economic institutions that make the post-feudal order function well. It is also the reason why those very institutions mutate into an enemy and turn against the system. Early capitalism made good use of private property and calculative rationality to maximise the gains and minimise the leaks. Later capitalism discovered to its cost that it had set loose a code of conventions which even its maker was no longer in a position to control.

The previous section, emphasizing the ubiquity of the invariant and of the lagged, showed in what way Schumpeter believed that the framework of early capitalism 'had nonbourgeois girders in it which voluntarily and involuntarily the business class progressively removed' (Schumpeter, 1941:344). The present section, concentrating on the core values that made capitalism rich, returns the even more surprising verdict that capitalism itself has no good defence against the worm within. Schumpeter writes that free enterprise cannot last: 'There is inherent in the capitalist system a tendency toward self-destruction.' (Schumpeter, 1942a:162). Having destroyed the pre-capitalist authority of the kings and the popes, the aristocracy and the family, the pure economic mindset 'goes on to attack private property and the whole scheme of bourgeois values' (Schumpeter, 1942a:143). Early capitalism had just enough of the property and the calculativeness upon which it was functionally dependent. Later capitalism has too much. It cannot survive.

10.2.1 Property

In early capitalism the business was owned by the family and run by the *paterfamilias*. The public company breaks the link: 'The capitalist process, by substituting a mere parcel of shares for the walls of and the machines in a factory, takes the life out of the idea of property.' (Schumpeter, 1942a:142). The small or medium enterprise is a focus for affection and self-definition, much as the householder loves his home and the peasant loves his land. The giant corporation is only an earning asset, a prudent investment and not a way of life: 'Dematerialized, defunctionalized and absentee ownership does not impress and call forth moral allegiance as the vital form of property did. Eventually there will be *nobody* left who really cares to stand for it.' (Schumpeter, 1942a:142).

The owner-operated business is the natural home of the capitalistic values. Economic determinism, however, leaves self-enterprise behind: 'The capitalist process unavoidably attacks the economic standing ground of the small producer and trader.' (Schumpeter, 1942a:140). As capital becomes concentrated and ownership becomes joint-stock, so the independent proprietors sink into the ranks of passive employees and scarce talents fade because they no longer have an outlet. Even allowing for the economies of scale and the technological superiority in research and development, the debasement in the nation's character-capital represents a considerable cost indeed: 'The very foundation of private property and free contracting wears away in a nation in which its most vital, most concrete, most meaningful types disappear from the moral horizon of the people.' (Schumpeter, 1942a:140–41).

Capitalism requires capitalists who know how to make the system work. Capitalism also eradicates the conditions in which the relevant people with the relevant aptitudes will thrive and dominate. Thence the conclusion, that what Schumpeter terms the 'Evaporation of the Substance of Property' (Schumpeter, 1942a:156) is at one and the same time an evaporation of functional alertness and the moral allegiance that makes good performance a mission and not just a quid pro quo. Schumpeter is in no doubt as to what it all means: 'The capitalist process ... attacks its own institutional framework.' (Schumpeter, 1942a:141). As if using up its irreplaceable reserves of coal and oil, capitalism is depleting the scarce personal aptitudes that alone can save it from regimentation without vision.

The separation of management from ownership in the modern large organisation means that business decisions are increasingly made by salaried bureaucrats who are administering a property that is not their own. The executive in such circumstances is bound to wonder why he should exert himself for the sake of other people whom he has never even met: 'His will to fight and to hold on is not and cannot be what it was with the man who knew ownership and its responsibilities in the fullblooded sense of those words.' (Schumpeter, 1942a:156). Decisions in corporate capitalism are made by employees on a payroll, a group which 'rarely if ever identifies itself with the stockholding interest' (Schumpeter, 1942a:141). In corporate capitalism, in fact, 'mere stockholders ... have ceased to count at all' (Schumpeter, 1942a:156). Private property has not been abolished. Still, however, it has acquired a new meaning in an era when behavioural objectives are at least as important to the executive as the profits in which he has no share.

Likely to move on to another job, the executive has little of the multi-period devotion one would have found in the courageous determination of the founding father. His meekness, his caution, is matched by that of the anonymous shareholders, dispersed and weak, who eschew confrontation and sell out instead. Moral allegiance evokes no real resonance: 'The holder of the title loses the will to fight, economically, physically, politically, for "his" factory and his control over it.' (Schumpeter, 1942a:142). Absentee ownership takes the life out of the assets. Small shareholders invest little time or attention in something that is after all only a minor part of their income-stream. The consequence is private property without the private proprietors whose supervision is essential if the agents and representatives are truly to keep organised capitalism on its toes.

10.2.2 Rationality

Scarcity was the mother of invention. Because resources were limited and efficiency was the precondition for survival, the norm of rationality came into its own as the selective standard most likely to keep the tribe alive: 'The rational attitude presumably forced itself on the human mind primarily from economic necessity; it is the everyday economic task to which we as a race owe our elementary training in rational thought and behavior.' (Schumpeter, 1942a:122). Matter came first: 'All logic is derived from the pattern of the economic decision.' (Schumpeter, 1942a:122–3). Mind arrived *post festum*: 'The economic pattern is the matrix of logic.' (Schumpeter, 1942a:123).

Rationality, like profit-seeking and self-interest, pre-dates the capitalist system. Even primitive man could not rely on magic, intuition or knee-jerk traditionalism for the more urgent of his physical needs. Yet it was under modern capitalism that problem-solving reason was able most rapidly to conquer high ground: 'Capitalism develops rationality.' (Schumpeter, 1942a:123). Money came to be generally used as a medium of exchange. Double-entry bookkeeping facilitated cost–profit calculation. The competitive market put a premium on logical inference from real-world evidence. Earned status in place of feudal ascription freed the mind to explore new avenues. The world was changing. Modern capitalism was increasingly dependent on numerical quantification and unemotive definiteness, detached precision and an empiricist bias. Without the optimising mindset it would not be able to maximise its returns.

Scarcity at first, market capitalism later on – Schumpeter was in no doubt as to the more powerful cause: 'Capitalism – and not merely economic activity in general – has ... been the propelling force of the rationalization of human behavior.' (Schumpeter, 1942a:125). It was capitalism that produced the new secularism and the scientific revolution: 'The rugged individualism of Gallileo was the individualism of the rising capitalist class.' (Schumpeter, 1942a:124).

It was capitalism that produced the new *Geist* – 'the spirit of rationalist individualism, the spirit generated by rising capitalism' (Schumpeter, 1942a:124) – that legitimated the mathematico-experimental transition. The 'propelling force' that 'generated' the reasoning was, in short, property-owning commerce, unsentimental and practical: 'Rising capitalism produced ... the mental attitude of modern science.' (Schumpeter, 1942a:124).

Much of scientific advance has been a direct response to the new business environment: 'Airplanes, refrigerators, television and that sort of thing are immediately recognizable as results of the profit economy.' (Schumpeter, 1942a:125). Even where technology is not directly exploited for profit, still 'capitalist rationality supplied the habits of mind that evolved the methods' (Schumpeter, 1942a:125–6). In that sense modern medicine and hygiene are 'by-products of the capitalist process' despite the fact that the hospitals and clinics do not consciously work 'in a business spirit' (Schumpeter, 1942a:126). The cures for cancer and other diseases will be 'as much capitalist achievements as motorcars or pipe lines' (Schumpeter, 1942a:126) despite the fact that the entrepreneurial investigators have no personal interest in gain.

The vision is one-dimensional and simplistic, conjectural history and not a full factual account. Schumpeter like Marx stresses the power of the economic base where a Weberian would point to non-economic elements such as Protestantism or Confucianism to show that the ideational superstructure can exert an independent pull. Theorising but not demonstrating, Schumpeter cites no evidence that would not be equally consistent with the hypothesis that rationality was the cause, capitalism the effect of the ethos. What he says is that capitalism needs logic. What he does not show is that capitalism successfully *produces* the orientation that it *requires*. His account of the origins of rationality is an assertion and not a proof. Perhaps the same must be said of the internal contradictions that make the norm a reason for implosion and end.

As early as his 1928 paper on 'The instability of capitalism' Schumpeter had expressed his concern that problem-solving calculativeness was outgrowing its own social role: 'Capitalism, whilst economically stable, and even gaining in stability, creates, by rationalising the human mind, a mentality and a style of life incompatible with its own fundamental conditions, motives and social institutions.' (Schumpeter, 1928:71–2). Rationality is making itself *the* axial principle rather than one pillar of society among many. In doing so, it is threatening to bring down the profit-maximising edifice as a whole.

Tradition is the first victim of change. Schumpeter as a conservative believed that the participants in a going concern spend much of their time in the past: 'Nothing is so retentive as a nation's memory.' (Schumpeter, 1942a:100). He welcomed the reinforcement of the established not least because it complemented well the current: 'Utilitarian reason is ... weak as a prime mover of group action. In no case is it a match for the extra-rational determinants of conduct.' (Schumpeter, 1942a:144). The extra-rational props are indispensable if group activity is to proceed without a hitch. The problem is that rationality is an imperialistic norm, quick to conquer new ground even if in the process it kicks away capitalism's most vital supports: 'Capitalist civilization is a rationalist civilization. It tends to eliminate extra- or hyperrational sanctions and habits of mind without which no society can exist.' (Schumpeter, 1943:141).

The quantity and quality of labour supplied is an illustration of the way in which belonging evokes the commitment that money alone cannot buy: 'The average workman would not believe you if you told him that his true reward was a satisfaction of employment, loyalty to the firm, and so on. Yet these are the things that keep society together.' (Schumpeter, 1941:359). Purposive work and attachment to sub-groups, not just the cash nexus and the matrix of exchange, are indispensable if the society is to be unwavering and consensual. The business mentality and its means–ends mindset are a threat to the settled affiliations and the ongoing hierarchies without which citizens will become consumers and take nothing on trust: 'Capitalistic activity, being essentially "rational", tends to spread rational habits of mind and to destroy those habits of super- and subordination that are nevertheless essential.' (Schumpeter, 1950b:423). Efficiency blunts efficiency. It is an outcome that no capitalist could predict.

Capitalism teaches a questioning and a doubting attitude. Like other revolutionary ideologies that have their roots in the scepticism of the Age of Reason, it 'spurns allegiance to extra-rational values' (Schumpeter, 1942a:144) and inspires no emotional attachment. Such a commitment to absolutes is 'the very thing capitalism is constitutionally unable to produce' (Schumpeter, 1942a:145). Determined to make bygones forever bygone, capitalism wields Occam's razor to pare away all but hedonistic self-interest and the doctrine that the shopper is the sovereign judge: 'Our inherited sense of duty, deprived of its traditional basis, becomes focused in utilitarian ideas about the betterment of mankind.' (Schumpeter, 1942a:127). It is not enough. The 'rationalisation of the soul' has meant, for many people, a 'feeling of the meaninglessness of capitalist values', a 'feeling that the civilization ... has played itself out' (Schumpeter, 1941:393). Rationality moderately mixed with ethics can be a force for affluence and order. Capitalism makes even ethics a matter of choice. In that way the system thinks itself to death: 'Capitalism creates a critical frame of mind which, after having destroyed the moral authority of so many other institutions, in the end turns against its own.' (Schumpeter, 1942a:143).

Capitalism is dull and unexciting: 'The capitalist process rationalizes behavior and ideas and by so doing chases from our minds, along with metaphysical belief, mystic and romantic ideas of all sorts.' (Schumpeter, 1942a:127). The magnetism of the natural leader is more than his cost-effectiveness. The flair of the born entrepreneur is not a time-series from his computer. People take risks because adventure is an adrenaline-rush. People break moulds because they hazard in order to trump. The poetry of business makes the economy a mirage of surprises and a maze of accidents. Calculative rationality, on the other hand, crowds in the uninspiring vision of the Economic Man, of Marshall's textbook endstate that, Victorian, middle class, life-denying, 'knows no glamour and no passion' (Schumpeter, 1942a:104). Such a calculus will feed the stomach and clothe the body. It will not, however, inspire the love and the dedication that will put men on the barricades. It is much more likely to put men to sleep.

10.3 POLITY

Schumpeter, not an anarchist, looked to the State to provide the infrastructure of law and order, national defence and essential public goods that corrected a market failure and complemented narrow capitalism's unprecedented success. He saw no contradiction but rather common sense in the fact that his political economy was intendedly a mix of public planning and market inventiveness: 'No social system is ever pure.' (Schumpeter, 1943:176). Even Lenin's Russia found room for the New Economic Policy. Even classical England was regulated by the State: 'People were at no time allowed to do with their own quite as they pleased, and society at all times limited the range within which they might freely contract.' (Schumpeter, 1943:176).

Schumpeter was insistent that what is called the capitalist economy was in truth a mix. What he feared was not State intervention per se but rather dysfunctional interference that could 'hamper and paralyze the private engine of production' (Schumpeter, 1942a:197). Nowadays, Schumpeter wrote, 'public policy grows more and more hostile to capitalist interests'. Soon public policy will be 'a serious impediment to its functioning' (Schumpeter, 1942a:154). Capitalism tends to destroy itself. One reason is that it asks its government to go too far.

10.3.1 Taxation

Capitalism in its earliest stages was a levelling-up ideology, in favour of occupational and geographical mobility, opposed to the feudal barriers that sealed off the peasant from the lord: 'Capitalism provides ... the ladders for talent to climb.' (Schumpeter, 1942a:188). Early capitalism shared its moment in time with equality before the law (that no class should enjoy special privileges or exemptions) and equality of opportunity (that every citizen, irrespective of birth, should be guaranteed the *carrière ouverte aux talents*). Later capitalism was to expand into a third equality – the equality of outcomes, levelling down and politicised redistribution. That third equality was to be its nemesis. Reallocation of endowments through the progressive income tax is 'an expression of an anti-capitalist attitude' (Schumpeter, 1942a:192). It is 'possibly the forerunner of complete elimination of the typically capitalist income brackets' (Schumpeter, 1942a:192). It is the socialist revolution without the need to storm the Winter Palace, the expropriation of the bourgeoisie 'without *formally* destroying the legal framework of the capitalist order' (Schumpeter, 1942a:378). Creeping socialisation is insidious and under-appreciated. It is also far advanced already.

Looking at the world in the wake of the Second War, Schumpeter wrote that taxes had been forced up and that the burden had become intolerable: 'In no country will war taxation of business and of the business class be reduced in the proportion in which it was reduced after 1919. This may in itself suffice to paralyze the motors of capitalism for good.' (Schumpeter, 1942a:374). In Britain alone, taxation 'need only be left as it is in order to make full and genuine socialism practically inevitable before long' (Schumpeter, 1949d:311). Throughout Europe, the election of social democrats had meant 'large and rapidly increasing public expenditure ... financed by methods ... which drained the sources of accumulation' (Schumpeter, 1942a:372). It is never sensible to 'paralyze the motors' and 'drain the sources' if the State retains its commitment to the rapid rise in living standards that ordinary people have come to expect: 'No society can long survive that doesn't deliver the promises it holds out. This being so, this taxation is a serious spoke in the wheel.' (Schumpeter, 1941:366).

Not all taxation, in Schumpeter's opinion, was condemned to be an obstacle and an impediment. The sales tax, for example, puts no damper on economic progress when it raises money for public projects: 'At moderate rates and in a country as rich as the United States it is an excellent and perfectly harmless tool of public finance.' (Schumpeter, 1942a:389n). Schumpeter, an economist and not an apologist for the rich, goes so far as to say that the defence of functionality and incentive does not mean that whatever is, is good: 'This does not mean that ... nominal incomes would have to go to anything like their present heights.' (Schumpeter, 1942a:209). There is in any case a substitution effect as well as an income effect which might induce people to work harder and save more: 'Moderate taxation ... may even act as a stimulus.' (Schumpeter, 1939:II, 713n). Some taxation does no visible harm.

The danger is not from all tax but from ill-advised tax. This means that the tax system must be carefully reappraised. To protect economic growth reinvested earnings should be tax-exempt. To protect adventurous speculation there should be full deduction of business losses. To lock in the intergenerational gift, death duties should be significantly reduced: striking at the family fortune, they strike at 'one of the essential elements of the capitalist scheme of things' (Schumpeter, 1942a:389n). Most important of all, the income tax should not seek to get blood from a stone: 'Only a low level of income tax has the moral sense of the taxpayer on its side.' (Schumpeter, 1929/30b:130). Without that moral commitment, the income tax will become 'a cause of disturbance of the economic process, a reason for general disorganisation' (Schumpeter, 1929/30b:130). Convinced that he is being robbed in the street, the taxpayer's psychology 'becomes that of a wild beast' (Schumpeter, 1929/30b:130). No society can function smoothly where the rank and file feel that they are being mugged by their lieutenants and generals. Carefully reappraised, however, there is no reason to think that the tax system will necessarily undermine the capitalist order. The State exists and it must be paid for. That is a fact of economic life.

Prudent public finance need not bring about the collapse of the system. Fiscal sociology, however, is playing for the opposite side. Citizens expect the State incessantly to increase its spending. Voters demand that high incomes should bear a disproportionate burden. Intellectuals disseminate moral disapprobation of wealth, inequality and profits. The government cannot afford to be indifferent to underlying currents of opinion such as these: 'Social atmosphere or code of values affects ... the spirit of legislation.' (Schumpeter, 1942a:155). Indeed it does. Socialism is on its way.

Fiscal sociology is the interdisciplinary subject-area that examines the socio-political ramifications of taxing and spending. The need for the new field of *Finanzsoziologie* had been identified by Rudolf Goldscheid in 1917 in his book *Staatssozialismus oder Staatskapitalismus*. Without sociology, Goldscheid had argued, there was no way to make sense of the social tensions that always accompany the imposts and the transfers: 'The most serious deficiency of our whole body of social science is that we lack a theory of financial sociology and that the problems of public finance remain without sociological foundation. Only sociology can show how social conditions determine public needs and the manner of their satisfaction by more direct or more indirect means, and how ultimately the patterns and evolution of society determine the shaping of the interrelations between public expenditure and public revenue.' (Goldscheid, 1925:202).

By sociology, Goldscheid clearly means stratification: 'Tax struggles were the oldest form of class struggle.' (Goldscheid, 1925:202). In the Middle Ages the masses came inevitably to cover their monarch's needs since demesne property supplemented by reckless borrowing was simply not enough to cover the princes' extravagance: 'Thus exploitation by the State ended up in exploitation of the tax State.' (Goldscheid, 1925:205). In modern capitalism it is the new princes of industry and trade who have learned so expeditiously how to spread the public butter most thickly on their own private cake: 'Always the capitalists have needed the State to establish profits on a really grand scale, never have they been able to consolidate their economically, socially and politically predominant position without the backing of the public finances.' (Goldscheid, 1925:211). The capitalists demand more and more from their State. Tax revenues, however, are not infinitely elastic. Spending and taxing are 'class-bound at every level' (Goldscheid, 1925:209). The consequence of the class State could only be a fiscal crisis, disastrous but inevitable.

Schumpeter, much impressed by Goldscheid's economic sociology even if less in sympathy with Goldscheid's Marxist gloss, built upon Goldscheid's insights in the public lecture on 'The crisis of the tax state' that he gave in Vienna in 1918. Like Goldscheid he sought to show that the public sector could not be understood through narrow economics alone. Like Goldscheid he predicted that the contradictions would take their toll and that the fiscal crisis was only a matter of time. Living in debt-ridden Austria at the end of a ruinous war, perhaps Schumpeter thought that the much-feared beast was already loose on the Ring.

Historically speaking, Schumpeter said, the evolution of the nation is encoded in its budget: 'The spirit of a people, its cultural level, its social structure, the deeds its policy may prepare – all this and more is written in its fiscal history. ... He who knows how to listen to its message here discerns the thunder of world history more clearly than anywhere else.' (Schumpeter, 1918:101). The fiscal record unravels all the mysteries: 'The budget is the skeleton of the state stripped of all misleading ideologies.' (Schumpeter, 1918:100). The budget is the *who gets what*, the *who pays*. Nothing could be more pregnant with useful information than that.

The budget is the key that opens all the doors. Nothing is so valuable for an understanding of political processes as an ability to decode the *how much*, the *what kind*, the *for whom* of public-sector earnings and disbursements. Almost a quarter of a century after 'The crisis of the tax state', Schumpeter was reiterating his contention that money is a language which even politics has learned to speak: 'The budget connects everything that a nation is, does, and intends. Every national volition reflects itself in the budget, the national character and the national past.' (Schumpeter, 1941:363). Some see the State as a sword in the land of the *bellum*. Schumpeter sees it as a balance sheet in a world of contributors and beneficiaries.

The modern State is the creature of its fiscal requirements: 'Without financial need the immediate cause for the creation of the modern state would have been absent.' (Schumpeter, 1918:108). The luxury of the court was a costly burden. It was, however, a *private* responsibility which the consensus believed that the crown alone should bear. War was different. A 'common exigency' perceived, a 'common purpose' (Schumpeter, 1918:106, 110) served, war was deemed a *public* concern to which all the citizen-beneficiaries had a user's obligation to pay their share.

Defence was the original public good. Complex capitalism subsequently multiplied the demands. It did so at such a rate that ultimately the capacity of the tax base was left behind: 'No need for more funds can push it further out.' (Schumpeter, 1918:113). High taxes retard industrial development through striking at energy, ambition, innovation and capital formation: there is a limit beyond which taxes cannot go 'without first damaging and then destroying the tax object' (Schumpeter, 1918:114). High taxes beyond some threshold (the argument recalls the much later Laffer Curve) cause the take not to go up but to go down: 'There exists a level beyond which further tax increases mean not an increase but a decrease of yield.' (Schumpeter, 1918:112). Public finance presupposes a healthy private sector – otherwise there would be nothing left to tax: 'In this world the state lives as an economic parasite.' (Schumpeter, 1918:112). Public finance also disrupts the workings of private self-interest upon which its own future depends. There is no solution.

The contradiction is precisely as O'Connor says it is in his book on the in-built fiscal crisis: 'Every economic and social class and group wants government to spend more and more money on more and more things ... but no one wants to pay new taxes.' (O'Connor, 1973:1). People expect more services. They resist more taxes. The gap between the desired and the realised, Schumpeter said, is a legitimacy vacuum which once again shows that capitalism cannot last: 'The hour will come. *That* too is certain.' (Schumpeter, 1918:131). The collapse is not imminent: 'This hour has not yet struck.' (Schumpeter, 1918:131). In the long-run, however, the fiscal crisis is condemned to live out its fate.

Taxation is de facto confiscation on a par with Lenin's enforced sequestration. Intolerable marginal rates – rates in excess of 20 per cent (Schumpeter, 1929/30b:130), let alone 25 per cent (Schumpeter, 1939:II, 712) – engender a 'loss of much-needed efficiency' (Schumpeter, 1942a:382). They induce scarce professionals like doctors and engineers to put less of themselves into their work. In the long run the economy will turn socialist. Levelling-down taxation will have been a cause: 'The income tax can only function properly if its rate is seen to be moderate.' (Schumpeter, 1929/30b: 130). Crucially, however, the cause of the cause will have been the citizen's demand to feast well at the buffet: 'State spending must also be moderate. This points to the Night Watchman State of the liberal epoch.' (Schumpeter, 1929/30b:130). That in essence is the fiscal contradiction. No one wants to do without the free lunch. No one, accordingly, can escape the socialism which is its price.

10.3.2 Expenditure

The State in corporate capitalism is under pressure to do more and more. It is expected to use macroeconomic policies to stabilise total demand and to even out the cycle. Its involvement in the attainment of full employment without inflation and of sustained economic growth (discussed in detail in Chapter 12) extends not just to monetary and fiscal management but also to the direct controls it must exercise over the commodity and the labour markets. It is expected to intervene in the microeconomy to protect reasonable competitiveness while not endangering the social gains from size; to supply public services like the Post Office and public goods like the law courts on a tax-subsidised basis; to take the lead in social welfare and social legislation because the poor cannot be neglected nor the unprotected abused. As Schumpeter puts it, referring to the real-world compromise and not to the textbook ideal type: 'We have traveled far indeed from the principles of laissez-faire capitalism.' (Schumpeter, 1950b:424).

We have travelled far indeed. We are destined to travel further still. Managed capitalism is a tightrope act, forever at risk 'if the private-enterprise system is *permanently* burdened and "regulated" beyond its powers of endurance. In this case, an outright socialist solution may impose itself even on the enemies of socialism as the lesser evil.' (Schumpeter, 1950b:425). The early Factory Acts and the State-sector schools did no real damage to the smooth functioning of market capitalism. The New Deal and Attlee's Labour, on the other hand, overstepped the bounds and went too far: 'Policies of that type are in the long run incompatible with the effective working of the system of private enterprise.' (Schumpeter, 1942a:64).

The system cannot function well where its operations are hobbled by the State. As its performance becomes worse, however, public opinion demands not less interference but rather more. It is then that the nation falls back on a Central Board or a Ministry of Production (Schumpeter, 1942a:168), on a 'huge and all-embracing bureaucratic apparatus' (Schumpeter, 1942a:206) because the Plan at least will make things work. The slippery slope of moderate interventionism may evidently be seen as a memento mori of 'the extent to which capitalist interests can in fact be expropriated without bringing the economic engine to a standstill' (Schumpeter, 1950b:425). Fettered capitalism gives way to centralist socialism. Economic performance is rescued but private enterprise ceases to be the *primum mobile* of growth.

Inexorable interventionism is the product of the past as well as the response to the present. Self-reinforcing and driven on by momentum, it is a snowball tendency that has endogenised the dynamic of experience.

Controls introduced in a crisis become a part of a settled way of life: 'There is no reason to believe that governments will ever relax the hold they have gained on the capital market and the investment process.' (Schumpeter, 1942a:375). Taxes increased in a war are unlikely to be repealed in the peace. Emergencies suppress markets and demonstrate that planning can succeed. The deus ex machina is not the sine qua non. Historically speaking, however, the record confirms that the adventitious has on balance accelerated the unstoppable: 'Such events and the situations created thereby may remove obstacles from the path of the more fundamental tendencies .... Evolution toward socialism would be slower in their absence.' (Schumpeter, 1950b:427). Old obstacles removed, new irreversibilities then take their place. De-control, it would appear, is not an option. As Schumpeter puts it, writing of Labour Party policies even in the inter-war years: 'Steps so responsibly taken will not have to be retraced.' (Schumpeter, 1942a:378). Permanent means permanent. Socialism does not change its mind: 'The postwar world will hardly be a place for privately controlled trade and industrial venture.' (Schumpeter, 1943:186).

As with yesterday's rules, so with yesterday's office holders. The drift into socialism is facilitated by the fact that State bureaucrats are not in sympathy with the profit-seeking class. At least in Europe, Schumpeter writes, civil servants have come from a culture that is of 'pre- and extra-capitalist origin': 'They never identified themselves wholly with the bourgeoisie, its interests or its scheme of values.' (Schumpeter, 1942a:155). Their reservations made them receptive to the *dirigisme* of the intellectuals, some of whom indeed secured positions in public service. The Depression correctives rapidly followed by the centralisation of war augmented their numbers and consolidated their influence: 'Huge bureaucracies have developed that by now are powerful enough to hold their ground and to implement policies of fundamental reconstruction.' (Schumpeter, 1942a:374). It is a great deal of power to leave in the hands of people who, mistrustful of commerce by virtue of non-capitalist socialisation and definitely not Weberian cogs with no active interest of their own, have an ideological attraction to a government that is up and doing. Some theorists have postulated that the bureaucrat's self-interest is linked to the expansion of his bureau. Schumpeter says that what the bureaucrat really wants is to show private capitalists how things should be done. Either way, the expansion of the State is assured.

The past makes a contribution to the socialism of today. So does the present. Some projects, quite simply, are better suited to public administration than they are to private enterprise. These are, moreover, projects which enjoy a high income elasticity of demand: 'With increasing wealth certain lines of expenditure are likely to gain ground which do not naturally enter into any cost–profit calculation, such as expenditure on the beautification of cities, on public health and so on.' (Schumpeter, 1942a:120). At the margin, and over time, the public good property becomes more conspicuous and more pressing.

The private sector is seen to fail. Equally important, the economical State is trusted to succeed: 'An ever-widening sector of industrial activity tends to enter the sphere of public management, such as means of communication, docks, power production, insurance and so on, simply because these industries become increasingly amenable to the methods of public administration.' (Schumpeter, 1942a:120). What this means is clear enough. Absolutely and relatively, the share of the State is induced by rising income levels to expand.

In richer countries the nation grows into the socialism that it cannot avoid. Yet in poorer countries too it can be the government and not the market that will occupy the commanding heights. Germany in the Middle Ages is a Third World case that demonstrates how the leadership can initiate change in what would otherwise have been a self-reproducing circular flow: 'In Germany, in particular, the prince and his bureaucracy became for centuries the dominant factor in economic life .... Was it not – again, in Germany – the state rather than the entrepreneur which initiated modern industry? The answer ... is in the affirmative.' (Schumpeter, 1939:I, 234, 235). It is entrepreneurial for the State to identify human capital bottlenecks and correct them through liberalised immigration; to encourage technology transfers through tax exemptions for multinational investment; to ensure start-up capital and a stable wage and price environment; to insist on the cold shower of global free trade in order to shake domestic businesspeople out of their over-protected lassitude. Schumpeter says little about forms of creative destruction such as these in his *Theory of Economic Development*. Elsewhere, however, he is more forthcoming about the State as a catalyst that makes history happen. 'Statecraft', he writes in *Business Cycles*, is productive and challenging. It is not a burden on the economy but 'a particular kind of entrepreneurship' (Schumpeter, 1939:I, 235).

In embryonic capitalism private initiative is under-developed and the State makes up for the deficiency. In advanced capitalism the public-goods primacy and the efficiency of administration give the State the comparative advantage. Logically, therefore, it must be only in the intermediate stage, neither Medieval Germany nor contemporary America, that profit-seeking capitalism has any chance of outperforming a political economics that does not take private gain to be its *summum bonum*. The State sector primes the pump. The capitalist sector takes up the torch. At the end there is socialism, and the State once again becomes the master of the craft.

The State can be productive. It can also be generous. Not a remembered adaptation but a fresh response, the welfare State shows that capitalism is a system that cares. There has never been 'so much active sympathy with real and faked sufferings, never so much readiness to accept burdens, as there is in modern capitalist society' (Schumpeter, 1942a:126). Capitalism produces the means. Capitalism produces the will. Capitalism is welfarist through and through.

The necessary condition is the means. Schumpeter writes that economic growth is itself an anti-poverty policy. It has been instrumental in raising the living standards of all but the residual poor: 'If capitalism repeated its past performance for another half century ... this would do away with anything that according to present standards could be called poverty, even in the lowest strata of the population, pathological cases alone excepted.' (Schumpeter, 1942a:66). Economic growth, given enough time, will 'eliminate anything that could possibly be described as suffering or want' (Schumpeter, 1942a:384). Schumpeter, disagreeing strongly with Marx, denies that social welfare 'has been forced upon capitalist society by an ineluctable necessity to alleviate the ever-deepening misery of the poor' (Schumpeter, 1942a:127). What he argues is the opposite, that capitalism means not accelerating immiseration but rather a steady reduction in the pool of the absolutely deprived.

The mainstream in capitalism will earn life for themselves and earn it very well. The 'pathological cases', unable to secure a toehold on the escalator of economics, will be in a less attractive position. In respect of care for the unemployed, for 'the aged and sick, for education and hygiene and so on' (Schumpeter, 1942a:71), the capitalist system leaves a market failure which none but the State is able to correct. It is able to do so because the capitalist market sector has generated the resources that are needed for relief. The British socialist Anthony Crosland was insistent that material advance alone could free up the social dividend: 'Rapid growth is an essential condition of any significant re-allocation of resources.' (Crosland, 1971:75). In stating that economic growth alone can produce the surplus for reform, he was echoing his much-respected Schumpeter whom he had first read at the Front. Schumpeter said that social welfare 'presupposes previous capitalist success' (Schumpeter, 1942a:69). It was the necessary condition. A polity cannot spend resources that its economy has not first been able to create.

The first condition is the means. The second condition is the will. Here again Schumpeter believed that economic growth had been on the side of sharing and aid. In the nineteenth century there was no social guarantee that the 'private life of the unemployed' should not be 'seriously affected by their unemployment' (Schumpeter, 1942a:70). We today, acknowledging 'the duty in question' (Schumpeter, 1942a:71), unreservedly validate the 'political volition' (Schumpeter, 1942a:69) which in richer countries has meant that the State provides adequately for those that market failure forgets.

Welfare and affluence go hand in hand. The reasons, never ranked in Schumpeter's disparate writings, would seem to be a mixed bag of opinions and interests. Intellectuals, hostile to supply and demand, use their books, newspapers and party-political speeches to champion the inclusion of the less-advantaged. The decline of the dynastic family reduces the resistance of the wealthy to redistributive tax. Equality, cultural and political, is a popular expectation: the needy are not seen as a race apart. The cyclical downturn is a threat to social stability: 'Secular improvement that is taken for granted and coupled with individual insecurity ... is of course the best recipe for breeding social unrest.' (Schumpeter, 1942a:145). There is a matrix of 'genuine group-wise volitions', a 'will of other groups to help' (Schumpeter, 1942a:270), a caring externality which is an island of sentiment in a sea of bottom lines. There is a growing acceptance that altruism by mutual coercion is indispensable effectively because the gift relationship is so necessary for the good health of the whole: 'We had better recognize from the start that exclusive reliance on a purely altruistic sense of duty is as unrealistic as would be a wholesale denial of its importance and its possibilities.' (Schumpeter, 1942a:207). The reasons are a mixed bag. They add up to the conclusion that the wish for welfare, like the means for welfare, has in the past gone hand in hand with capitalism's supportive advance.

The future, however, is more of a problem. Schumpeter is committed to the proposition that capitalist civilisation, self-destroying and self-transcending, is at variance with 'its own law of life' (Schumpeter, 1943:181). It is, and has been 'for some time' already, 'in a state of decay': 'The capitalist process undermines the structure of capitalist society.' (Schumpeter, 1943:178). Welfarism is not an exception to the rule that the middle-ground compromise must become full socialism given time.

The resource base, for one thing, is not ring-fenced against over-use. Schumpeter is confident that wise and sensible politicians will be able to tap into the surplus from growth 'without violating the organic conditions of a capitalist economy, including high premia on industrial success and all the other inequalities of income that may be required in order to make the capitalist engine work according to design' (Schumpeter, 1942a:384). What he also knows is that not all politicians will abstain from the temptation to proceed 'without undue strain on the system' (Schumpeter, 1942a:70). Short-horizoned levellers whose taxes cut the national dividend down to size and whose obsessive egalitarianism is a '*significant interference with the capitalist process*' (Schumpeter, 1942a:69) must evidently be seen not just as the enemies of the plutocrats but of the needy poor as well: 'The real tragedy is not unemployment *per se,* but unemployment plus the impossibility of providing adequately for the unemployed *without impairing the conditions of further economic development*.' (Schumpeter, 1942a:70). The real danger is not benefits per se but the 'economically irrational methods of financing relief' (Schumpeter, 1942a:71) that strike at once at the social dividend and at underlying development itself.

Revenues are one threat. Outgoings are another. Schumpeter refers with some concern to 'rates that are high relatively to wages' and to the 'loose administration of unemployment benefits' (Schumpeter, 1942a:386). So open-handed an approach to income maintenance, he believes, can paralyse the will of the recipients to contribute to economic growth. He also expresses serious reservations about 'that spirit of waste that delights in spending a billion where 100 million would do' (Schumpeter, 1942a:385). Duplicate bureaucracies, lax administration, public sector mismanagement in general, mean that welfare will be uneconomical because the welfare providers feel no sense of responsibility to the nation that must pay the bills.

It is the very nationalism of welfare, interestingly enough, that was a third and final reason why Schumpeter believed that welfare within capitalism would lead to the adoption of defiantly statist aims. Social democrats, British and German, have praised social welfare as a force for collective solidarity and cohesion. Schumpeter had spent too long in the society of the free-market liberals to have other than mixed feelings about thinkers who made the fate of their country more than the sum of its parts: 'To exalt national unity into a moral precept spells acceptance of one of the most important principles of fascism.' (Schumpeter, 1942a:352n). No doubt it does. It also means that the citizens come to see their State as an expression of themselves. Socialism for them will feel not like a radical breach but merely like more of the same.

11. Continuity, change and socialism

Schumpeter said it was very likely that capitalism would self-destruct. He also said it was very likely that socialism would take its place. His evolutionary schema was therefore the dual prediction that the success of capitalism would be the failure of capitalism and that the antithesis of capitalism would in the end be its phoenix and its rising star: 'Its very success undermines the social institutions which protect it, and "inevitably" creates conditions in which it will not be able to live and which strongly point to socialism as the heir apparent.' (Schumpeter, 1942a:61). The blue tendency is sunset capitalism, bleeding from a thousand wounds, 'decaying, shading off into something else, or tottering toward a violent death' (Schumpeter, 1939:II, 908). The red tendency is sunrise socialism which knows that yesterday's decline and fall is also today's viable new start: 'Things and souls are transformed in such a way as to become increasingly amenable to the socialist form of life.' (Schumpeter, 1942a:162). The blue tendency and the red tendency are not separate developments, two things apart. Instead they are a continuing skein, as closely intertwined as today and tomorrow, as much a single whole as creative destruction: 'The capitalist process not only destroys its own institutional framework but it also creates the conditions for another.' (Schumpeter, 1942a:162). Because capitalism *is*, therefore socialism *will be*.

Schumpeter, looking to the future, anticipated that red would win and blue would lose. It was not a forecast that inspired in him any real enthusiasm: 'I come to the diagnosis that the system will not survive ... although I am not a Marxist and although I have no tendency for socialist systems at all.' (Schumpeter, 1936a:306). It cannot have been easy for Schumpeter to have lived throughout his life with the conviction that something in which he believed was unlikely to last very long. For a lifetime anxiety it undoubtedly was. Schumpeter in 1942 said of his *Capitalism, Socialism and Democracy* that the book reflected 'the bulk of almost forty years' thought, observation and research' (Schumpeter, 1942a:409). His recollection was sound. Schumpeter's pessimism was not simply a reaction to the Great Depression of the 1930s when many feared that capitalism was on the point of collapse. His idea of system failure antedates the Wall Street Crash by at least a decade.

Thus, in his essay on 'Imperialisms', written while the Austro-Hungarian empire was dissolving around him, he had said it was 'certain' that successful capitalism would convert its own victory into defeat: 'Capitalism is its own undoing but in a sense different from that implied by Marx. Society is bound to grow beyond capitalism, but this will be because the achievements of capitalism are likely to make it superfluous.' (Schumpeter, 1918/19:218n). At the same time, in 'The crisis of the tax state', he had announced that a Marx-like barrier would one day block the further expansion of the system: 'The hour will come. By and by private enterprise will lose its social meaning through the development of the economy and the consequent expansion of the sphere of social sympathy .... Society is growing beyond private enterprise and tax state.' (Schumpeter, 1918:131).

In 1920/21, in 'Sozialistische Möglichkeiten von Heute', Schumpeter returned to the theme of entrepreneurial individualism in decline, bureaucracy and the State already looming up on the horizon: 'We have to distance ourselves from all judgements of value and simply ask ourselves if there is a tendency towards socialism in the economic and social facts of our time .... The question can only be answered with an unequivocal "yes".' (Schumpeter, 1920/21:462). Desires and wishes are no more than 'blosses intellektuelles Moussieren' (Schumpeter, 1920/21:456). Given time, economic evolution would prove far stronger than 'the longing of the human heart for paradise' (Schumpeter, 1920/21:459). Given time, the last word would be encoded in the simple truism that the rain clouds must first have gathered for there to be rain: 'Always the economic revolution must first have occurred for a political revolution to be a success.' (Schumpeter, 1920/21:455).

Schumpeter in his 1920/21 essay was able to say what would bring about the end. The reasons are the same as those he gives in *Capitalism, Socialism and Democracy*, published more than 20 years later. The first is the acknowledged superiority of the large organisation that Marx had correctly made 'the high road to socialism': 'There is a tendency for the more progressive firm to push out the older one. The more progressive firm is almost always the larger.' (Schumpeter, 1920/21:462–3). The second is calculative purposiveness that eats away at tradition and habit: 'The competitive economy ... has developed another tendency from its own necessities which clearly points to socialism: it has introduced rationality into economic life.' (Schumpeter, 1920/21:464). Concentration and centralisation mean that joint-stock administrators on a salary come to run what once would have been genuinely devolved means of production like the peasant farm or the family business: 'The competitive economy has the tendency to gigantic enterprises and with it a tendency to socialisation.' (Schumpeter, 1920/21:464). Relentless economising – 'Technologically and commercially it is progress' (Schumpeter, 1920/21:469) – punishes the economically maladapted with economic death. It has 'destroyed all peace and all certainty': 'It is a process of subjugation of men by machines and technology, a process which also brings democratisation, levelling and ... great insecurity.' (Schumpeter, 1920/21:464, 468).

Mobility, maximisation and world citizenship take the place of rootedness, blood and the time-honoured base: 'More and more temporary, rented utilisation is taking the place of a lasting relationship to the things around us.' (Schumpeter, 1920/21:470). The *splendor familiae* withers away because the family no longer has a firm or an estate that gives it a collective purpose or a multi-generational identity. The loss is a considerable one. In entrepreneurial capitalism the inter-generational impulse is 'one of the main reasons why people seek riches at all' (Schumpeter, 1920/21:470). The 'desire for personal and inheritable control over the means of production' (Schumpeter, 1920/21:471) is one of the richest seams of love and altruism in a high capitalist world which, psychologically and objectively, perpetuated lasting relationships even as it practised competitive under-cutting. Later capitalism is different. An ancestral castle is no longer 'the precondition for a cultivated life' (Schumpeter, 1920/21:470). A wall has gone up which separates the individual from the civil society in which he used to see his face reflected. Socialism then becomes the likely consequence. In 1920/21 as in 1942 Schumpeter was as clear as he was filled with regret. There was no alternative to State control.

In 1928, in Weimar Bonn, Schumpeter went back to the negation that could not be stopped. There he was saying, in the *Economic Journal*, that capitalism had a 'tendency towards self-destruction': 'trustified', 'organised', it was 'outgrowing its own frame' (Schumpeter, 1928:47, 48). In America, in 1936, he addressed the United States Department of Agriculture Graduate School in Washington on the topic 'Can capitalism survive?' He told them that because of amoral microeconomics and not because of unemployment and demand the fact was that it could not: 'The reason, the deepest reason, why I think that capitalism won't survive is the rationalizing effect the system has on our minds, the effect the system has of doing away with everything traditional.' (Schumpeter, 1936a:307).

Full employment restored through the Keynesianism of rearmament, Schumpeter gave a series of eight public lectures at the Lowell Institute in Boston in which he showed yet again that he remained profoundly concerned about the dynamics of domestic and international peace. Speaking in 1941 on the institutional underpinnings of modern capitalism and entitling his course 'An economic interpretation of our time', he told his listeners that exciting innovations were not guaranteed given the Marx-like concentration of capital and the Weber-like regimentation of mind that it brought about: 'Capitalist progress, embodying itself in larger units of control, would eventually produce a state of things in which private enterprise and the whole scheme of business action were becoming obsolete and amenable to wholesale bureaucratization.'

(Schumpeter, 1941:342). This sad acceptance of individual enterprise dried up – there was no sign of the expected exhaustion in America in 1941 – looks forward not only to *Capitalism, Socialism and Democracy* in 1942 but also to the Walgreen Lectures of 1950, never delivered as Schumpeter died immediately before: 'The free-enterprise system is not just a technical economic arrangement that can stand, or even requires, more or less control or regulation. It is a particular scheme of values and a particular way of life. These are rapidly vanishing from the American scene.' (Schumpeter, 1950a:443). Capitalism was under threat in 1950 as it had been under threat in 1918. Schumpeter throughout the whole of his academic career was predicting the end.

The pessimism is clear. More problematic is the confidence. Schumpeter says that capitalism goes out and central control comes in. Factually speaking, the prediction is without support: it was not market but command that experienced the recorded decline. In terms of the reasoning, moreover, the red tendency does not seem to emerge logically from the strict parameters of the Schumpeterian system. The entrepreneur loses out. Social values change. The State gets involved. It all adds up to something. But why should that something be central control?

11.1 SOCIETY

Marx emphasised the economic order. He concentrated on economic failings such as monopoly power, the falling rate of profit and the stagnation of total demand. The only economic problem that Schumpeter identified is the bureaucratisation of initiative, at once the 'inevitable complement' (Schumpeter, 1942a:206) of economic development and a parasite that gnaws away all vitality: 'The modern corporation, although the product of the capitalist process, socializes the bourgeois mind; it relentlessly narrows the scope of capitalist motivation; not only that, it will eventually kill its roots.' (Schumpeter, 1942a:156). Concentration was the basis, culture and interdependence the 'socio-psychological *superstructure*' (Schumpeter, 1942a:121). The majority of the contradictions Schumpeter detected in modern capitalism relate not to the economy per se but rather to 'a scheme of values, an attitude toward life, a civilization' (Schumpeter, 1950b:425). Schumpeter did not believe that performance per se had a tendency to self-destruct. Rather, given enough time, it would be perceptions and relationships that would negate the disequilibrium and produce something new.

Schumpeter's account of perceptions and relationships is selective and anecdotal. It is likely that he saw his *histoire raisonnée* as suggestive rather than exhaustive, an invitation to study dynamics with reference to groups and not a complete analysis of the historical process. Schumpeter does not indicate how comprehensive his coverage is intended to be. Nor does he convince the reader that the three social groupings he picks out as the most prominent do indeed undermine moral allegiance in the manner he describes.

11.1.1 The Aristocracy

The aristocracy, to Schumpeter as to Marx, is defeated by the bourgeoisie and subsequently marginalised into irrelevance. To Schumpeter this means the loss of cultural support for obedience and hierarchy. To his critics it will mean nothing of the sort. Hierarchy and self-restraint, some will say, are the product of the socialised super-ego that owes nothing to a hereditary class; while others will point out that capitalism creates its own past-dominated reverence through ongoing conventions and organisational memory. Social discipline is possible even without the museum-piece exemplar.

Feudal vestiges, moreover, can inhibit capitalism to the extent that they discourage critical thought. The aristocracy can be counter-productive where it leads the nation into the wasteful dead end of imperialism, chauvinism, protectionism or militarism. Landowners in less-developed countries are often so voracious but also so entrenched that a quasi-1789 would be needed even to open the door to the bourgeoisie. The Lords in bicameral polities defend Establishment privileges which get in the way of rapid growth. They hold no brief for social mobility which is a part of market capitalism. Schumpeter, one is tempted to say, is glamorising the fox hunters and the fourteenth earls while neglecting the fact that they were responsible for the Corn Laws, primogeniture and entailing as well.

Schumpeter's archetype is the European (especially the British) upper class. Living in the United States, it was a curious choice. The United States had no pre-feudal stratum on which it could depend for extra-economic support. It had no mixed economy of yesterday's classes in de facto alliance with those of today. The United States, in contrast to Europe, did not look back. Perhaps it was that very freedom from the past that enabled it to overtake Europe in the core Schumpeterian areas of fads, fashions, product development and built-in obsolescence.

11.1.2 The Intelligentsia

Too positive about the aristocracy, Schumpeter was too negative about the intelligentsia. There again his views were one-sided and unconvincing. Schumpeter makes no allowance for national differences in the status and influence of intellectuals; or for the way in which generalised prosperity reduces both discontentment and the plausibility of *critique*; or for the influence of right-wing intellectuals, pro-market and pro-military, who use the media to champion the cause of business. He does not explain why the intellectuals developed an obsession with the workers; or why the masses came under the spell of the minority; or why the unions neglected the entrepreneurial lead that the elite of ideas was able to usurp. Schumpeter does not answer the big question of whether the Vienna coffee-houses or the American muckrakers or the Depression-era New Dealers ever had the ability or even the wish to guide their society into State socialism. What he says, much more limited, is that intellectuals are insecure and resentful, desperately in need of external reassurance, 'panting with impatience to have their innings, longing to save the world from something or other, disgusted with textbooks of undescribable tedium, dissatisfied emotionally and intellectually' (Schumpeter, 1942a:47). No doubt there are unhappy people like that in every country. By itself, however, their existence is not an economics of socialist evolution but a simple reminder that not everyone can be equally happy every minute of every day.

Intellectuals like to think that they have power. Schumpeter takes their exaggerated self-importance at face value. A more realistic approach would be that intellectuals follow public opinion even as they lead it. If there was a 'Marxian revival' (Schumpeter, 1942a:3) in the 1930s, the reason is more likely to have been systemic de-legitimation through long-term unemployment than it was a 'well-defined group situation of proletarian hue', an alienated coterie that always expresses 'moral disapproval of the capitalist order' (Schumpeter, 1942a:153). Even in the 1930s the example of totalitarian Russia did not inspire the masses in Europe or America. Later on it was profoundly unattractive. Education and *embourgeoisement* increased the constituency with a stake in the system. Union-bashing and the taxpayers' revolt became defining characteristics of the working-class Conservative. Business studies inherited the popularity of left-wing sociology. The 'beardy-weirdy' agitator became something of a joke. Intellectuals, hostile or assimilated, have to sell to a public that likes high standards of living and is prepared to entrust poverty-relief to the invisible hand of full employment. America in the 1940s was not Austro-Hungary struggling with its industrial revolution. Even opinion leaders cannot lead opinion at will down roads that it does not wish to travel.

Schumpeter in any case underestimates the extent to which the opinion-leaders themselves are dependent on liberal democracy. Capitalism is a permissive system, unwilling and unable 'to control its intellectual sector effectively', all too aware that 'the freedom it disapproves cannot be crushed without also crushing the freedom it approves' (Schumpeter, 1942a:150, 151). Schumpeter writes that a tolerant system is not in a strong position to bring the confrontational to heel – and that the business class has an interest of its own in a hands-off State: 'In defending the intellectuals as a group ... the bourgeoisie defends itself and its scheme of life.' (Schumpeter, 1942a:150). What Schumpeter is forgetting is that the intellectuals, like the merchants, are dependent on the freedom of trade. It is not censorship and planning that give the dissident a forum but rather free speech and an open market. Especially will the freedom to persuade be of value to intellectuals where capitalism's deficiencies are not life-threatening and the reforms proposed only piecemeal and marginal. Many dissidents situate themselves on the middle ground. In favour of unemployment benefits and the protection of the environment but opposed to revolution or central control, such 'third way' thinkers will be strong supporters of liberal democracy precisely because of the opportunities it affords them for small advances made possible through debate.

Schumpeter fails to distinguish between the extremists and the moderates. He also fails to disaggregate the intelligentsia into its occupational sub-groupings. In particular, focusing as he does on journalists and media people, he assigns insufficient importance to the more measured proposals of the educational community that has figured so prominently in the work of 'post-industrial' thinkers like Galbraith. On the one hand, Galbraith has argued, knowledge-based business conjures up the educational and scientific estate quite explicitly because modern industry is dependent for its advance on a pool of trained manpower: 'In the mature corporation the decisive factor of production ... is the supply of qualified talent. A similar complex of educational institutions has similarly come into being to supply this need.' (Galbraith, 1967:286). On the other hand, Galbraith continues, the culture of producer-led demand and half-truth huckstering is doomed by the critical intelligence and the balanced perspective of the very class that without the technostructure would have remained in the shadows: 'Thus the paradox. The economy for its success requires organized public bamboozlement. At the same time it nurtures a growing class which feels itself superior to such bamboozlement and deplores it as intellectually corrupt.' (Galbraith, 1967:294).

Educators preach sensible reforms and press for moderate statism. Galbraith is confident that they will win. Schumpeter, in contrast, models his intelligentsia not on university teachers, learned and cautious, but on tabloid fault-finders who seldom listen to reason. Full socialism, he seems to be saying, will be the free gift of the over-heated and the out-of-control. When he does speak of the link between education and change, it is only to refer to the *over*-expansion of qualified manpower. It is clearly not technological progress in the sense of Galbraith but rather irrationality and error in the sense of the flat-earthers and the alchemists that he sees as the cause of the coming transformation. The argument is a curious one, that capitalism breeds socialism because it gets its forecasts wrong. It is a misuse of determinism to dissolve the complexities of the intelligentsia into a contention that graduates demand a post-capitalist system because the market economy cannot find them graduate jobs.

11.1.3 The Family

A similar flattening, a similar smoothing may be detected in Schumpeter's interpretation of the family. His reverse Malthusianism of fertility repressed and kinship stunted conceals the fact that, while the large family and the extended network probably have been eroded by economics, the nuclear family still remains a basic social fact. People still marry and they still have children. That is the essence of the matter. Even *one* child is enough for parents to save in order to hand on wealth. The corporate revolution provides a further reason for deferred gratification: unable to pass on a family business or even his own job, the executive must invest heavily in his children's education and their start in life. Childlessness itself can be a cause of thrift and self-restraint. While the State does act to temper the family failure, old age is expensive when there is no one there to help out.

Schumpeter has every right to lament the loss to society of Victorian kinship and the family seat. What he cannot do is to claim that the transformation of the family is breeding and forming the transition to the socialist future. Saving is safe. Investment is safe. Live-for-today citizens are less likely to demand State discipline than they are luxury holidays. Professional managers improve performance where they take over from substandard nepotists. Schumpeter says that the capitalist system is put under threat. A different perspective would be that the new-look family gives it a new lease of life.

11.2 ECONOMY

Schumpeter does not convincingly demonstrate that the social constituencies of aristocracy and family reinforce the capitalist order while the self-styled opinion leaders attack it from within. Nor does his account of the economic institutions of property and rationality add up to an unassailable proof that the age of the corporation is the last giant step on the road to the State. In the latter case as in the former, Schumpeter is describing his elephant as if it were the simple sum of its tusks and its tail.

11.2.1 Property

Much seems to hinge on the state of mind of the commercial classes.

Rightly or wrongly, they have come to think that they have had their day: 'The bourgeois order no longer makes any sense to the bourgeoisie itself.' (Schumpeter, 1942a:161). Lacking in self-confidence and convinced that he is unlovable, the typical bourgeois no longer believes that his bank or warehouse serves any useful purpose. Worse still, his values as well as his activities are coming under his own strict censure: 'The typical bourgeois is rapidly losing faith in his own creed.' (Schumpeter, 1942a:161). It is a serious diagnosis of low self-worth – but also one which the bourgeoisie itself might be completely unable to accept. Told that he hates himself for what he does, the executive replies that his production line makes possible an unprecedented democratisation of mass consumption. Told that he has lost faith in the business creed, the organisation man observes that individualism, achieved status, ambition, advancement, possession, independence, the work ethic remain as prominent in the present-day consensus as they were when the classical entrepreneur was the representative firm. The form in which the ideals find their embodiment has changed over time. The ideals themselves remain recognisably the same.

Private property has not disappeared despite the evolution of the joint-stock pool. Privateness itself is a desideratum and one with a high income elasticity of demand. People as they grow more prosperous expect to own their own homes, to go by car and not by bus, to have some protection against third-party pollution and neighbourhood-effect noise. In the case of private capital, small investors, holding their titles directly or through a unit trust or pension fund, continue to have a stake in their dividends and their capital-appreciation. That interest is none the less robust for being a share in a company rather the whole of the company purchased outright.

It is playing with words to say that the *share*-holders in a collective investment see themselves as collectivists who are rapidly losing faith in the capitalist creed. What is much more plausible is that they see themselves as private investors, as hostile as any family businessman to the socialist State that threatens their legal right to a way of life. It is arguably not socialism that the collective investment brings in its wake but rather a new-style capitalism in which every man is a conviction capitalist. One capitalist does *not* kill many. Bourgeois values become stronger, not weaker. Private ownership becomes a general expectation. It ceases to be the fenced-off property of a privileged few.

11.2.2 Rationality

Rationality too need not represent a threat to the survival of the system. Schumpeter says that it does, that there is a real danger from 'an attitude which spurns allegiance to extra-rational forces' (Schumpeter, 1942a:144).

Sociologically, the contention is that habits and rituals lose their power to constrain: if order presupposes the unthinking acceptance of *whatever is*, then a critical stance does go against the execution of unquestioning duty. Psychologically, the fear is that participants will use the system but that they will have no underlying commitment to its *ought-ness*: there is a need for an '*emotional* attachment to the social order' but this is 'the very thing capitalism is constitutionally unable to produce' (Schumpeter, 1942a:145). Both points are valid in themselves. Neither, however, makes due allowance for the continuity of convention that in the real world always dilutes the *Zweckrationalität* with a good measure of values and affects. Means–ends detachment is an ideal type. We today, however, are trapped with our means and our ends in a cultural matrix which tells us who we are.

Schumpeter in 'The crisis of the tax state' emphasised that even in capitalism the past marches alongside the future when the present sets out its stall: 'The bourgeois tax state of the present time does not exist anywhere as a pure type. Everywhere it is shot through with elements of the past, everywhere the shadows of future developments can more or less clearly be seen to fall upon it.' (Schumpeter, 1918:111). Time is absolutely continuous. Much that complements the goal-orientated is the direct result of socialisation and long usage. Even the moral standing of individualism and contract, of instrumental rationality itself, owes a great deal to the fact that these are social values, inherited and learned. They are group *ought-to-be*s that are shared within a community. A passport to the life in common, they have a momentum of their own which allows them to co-exist with problem-solving reason and to give it a rich normative context.

Schumpeter as a social conservative had a preference for change that followed the river bed of continuity: 'The bringing about of transitions from your social structure to other social structures with a minimum loss of human values, that is how I should define conservatism.' (Schumpeter, 1941:399). Schumpeter was right to say that rationality could prove a threat to conservatism. What a Durkheim would add is that conservatism provides normative reinforcement to rationality: 'The group thinks, feels, and acts quite differently from the way in which its members would were they isolated. If, then, we begin with the individual, we shall be able to understand nothing of what takes place in the group.' (Durkheim, 1895:104). Capitalism is circumscribed by its collective representations. That stock of institutions and memories provides a buffer against the normlessness of ideal-type calculativeness. Rationality itself is a *social* fact.

It is, moreover, open to the State to strengthen the loyalties. Military service, a national curriculum, citizen-based welfare, are three of the policy options it can explore in order to foster a social synthesis capable of countervailing the reductionism of reason. Regional policy to strengthen the social capital embedded in established communities is a fourth: 'The public peace ... is not kept primarily by the police, necessary as police are. It is kept primarily by an intricate, almost unconscious, network of voluntary controls and standards among the people themselves.' (Jacobs, 1961:41). Union discipline and the professionalisation of labour is a fifth: 'When the ... reflection with regard to the relation of his own republic to other republics is forced upon a man, when he discusses it with others and prepares for joint action with them upon it, he is receiving a training of the highest order.' (Marshall, 1875:366). Public support to ethical awareness and religious education is a sixth:

> In the Confucian societies, the erosion of ascription as a social principle has not implied the disappearance of the principle of *hierarchy* – of the idea that everybody, in the organizational context of each particular moment, has his proper *bun*, his proper role to play. The principles for the allocation of status have changed, but the importance attaching to status has been preserved. (Dore, 2001:207).

Public policy can do much to reinforce the conservatism. Even if *laissez-faire* does make us *homo homini lupus*, there is much that wise and thinking leadership can do to bend back the bent rod and make it straight again.

If, worst-case scenario, the system is actually at risk from cost–benefit agnosticism, then it is no less at risk from blind faith and visceral antipathy. Schumpeter says that no reasoned case in favour of capitalism will ever be enough to sway unfriendly public opinion that has made up its mind:

> Capitalism stands its trial before judges who have the sentence of death in their pockets. They are going to pass it, whatever the defense they may hear .... Utilitarian reason is in any case weak as a prime mover of group action. In no case is it a match for the extra-rational determinants of conduct. (Schumpeter, 1942a:144).

By that standard, capitalism cannot win. If there is unemployment and insecurity, ordinary people will blame the system because their non-rational short-termism blots out the long-term success. If there is full employment and growth, ordinary people will blame the system because they have been manipulated by intellectuals into an across-the-board rejection even of visible performance. Ignoring the balance sheet, it is stereotype and bias that will pre-filter the evidence. Capitalism in such a situation is put at risk not by a surplus of rationality but rather by a deficiency. More rationality and not less would presumably do much to convince the extra-capitalistic of the logic of the system.

11.3 POLITY

Schumpeter says that the capitalist State is active in ending the hegemony of the capitalist economy: 'The capitalist process produces a distribution of political power and a socio-psychological attitude ... that are hostile to it and ... will eventually prevent the capitalist engine from functioning.' (Schumpeter, 1942a:112). Public opinion pushes the government into a stifling interventionism. Intolerable controls bring the whole system down.

11.3.1 Taxing and Spending

Hayek would have been happy to accept that the road to serfdom begins with the social democrats and the social engineers: 'By the time Hitler came to power, liberalism was to all intents and purposes dead in Germany. And it was socialism that had killed it.' (Hayek, 1944:23). Marx and Engels arrived at a more complacent assessment: 'The executive of the modern State is but a committee for managing the common affairs of the whole bourgeoisie.' (Marx and Engels, 1848:82). It is easy enough to cite anecdotal evidence of laws which make it more difficult for businesses to make money. Examples would be high superannuation contributions, compulsory on-the-job training, extended maternity leave, restrictions on child labour, the exemption of the union closed shop from anti-monopoly legislation. The problem is that instances like these can just as easily be matched by countervailing illustrations such as infant-industry tariffs, exchange control, technical education, research subsidies, governmental joint ventures in risky lines of business, autarkist policies such as import-substitution and the 'buy local' campaign. Here it is the case that intervention strengthens the profit-seeking interest and does not undermine it. Schumpeter, like Hayek, reaches the conclusion that the bulk of the evidence more closely resembles the burdensome inspectorate than it does the tax exemption: this is the thrust of his assertion that private business, thwarted by a meddlesome State, 'will eventually cease to function' (Schumpeter, 1942a:156). Aware of the ways in which the mixed economy can strengthen capitalism and make it more lucrative, he reaches the conclusion that the complements are the exception, excess and drain the rule. Had he concentrated on the provision of infrastructure, the eradication of cholera, the interest-free loan, he might not have been so quick to say that the suffocation of the private sector was merely a matter of time.

The Schumpeterian vision is one of insidious and encroaching statism. A market failure is corrected by a guide price or a guaranteed sale: the result is 'capitalism in the oxygen tent – kept alive by artificial devices and paralyzed in all those functions that produced the successes of the past' (Schumpeter,

1943:185). A State-owned monopoly lacks the free market incentive to signal, adjust, adapt and compete: 'One of the causes of the efficiency of private business is that, unlike the politician or public officer, it has to pay for its mistakes.' (Schumpeter, 1939:II, 1040-41). Private business, meanwhile, becomes trapped in a web of nationalisations, licences, directives and restrictions so all-encompassing that it becomes de facto the puppet of the State: 'Unsocialized industries would cease to function simply because they would be prevented from functioning in their own way... . This would still be full socialization within our meaning of the term.' (Schumpeter, 1942a:228). Concentration of capital means that the giant corporations alone need to fall behind or to fail to bring down the whole edifice of interdependence: 'Any serious threat to the functioning of these will spread paralysis in the economic organism.' (Schumpeter, 1942a:II, 1044). Capitalist advance is a house of cards. The State has both the power and the propensity to blow the house down.

It will not happen soon: Schumpeter says that the whole process could take 50 or even 100 years. Nor will it happen all at once: 'Gradual socialization *within the framework of capitalism* is not only possible but even the most obvious thing to expect.' (Schumpeter, 1939:227). In the short run there might be the halfway-house of moderate social democracy. In the long run there will be regimentation precisely because, as Hayek puts it, only central direction can resolve the discordance that the Sorcerer's Apprentice has so clumsily conjured up: 'The rise of Fascism and Nazism was not a reaction against the socialist trends of the preceding period, but a necessary outcome of those tendencies.' (Hayek, 1944:3). Hayek at least believes that it is not too late to turn back: intellectual revulsion, determined privatisation, the de-control of enterprise can reverse the tendency before it has gone too far. Schumpeter is less optimistic about the power of free will. Evolution is taking its course. Sooner or later, the candle will go out.

11.3.2 Alternative Futures

The capitalist order will put itself out of business. Socialism will take its place. Schumpeter defines the unavoidable new equilibrium as 'public management of economic affairs and public control of all means of production' (Schumpeter, 1941:343). It is a political far more than an economic new world. Productive activity is transforming itself from decentralisation and plurality into government control and probably government ownership as well. Centralism is inevitable: 'The economic process tends to socialize *itself*.' (Schumpeter, 1942a:219). There is no other way.

Yet there is and Schumpeter acknowledges that there is. An interesting passage in *Business Cycles* refers to New Deal managed capitalism and implies that even a compromise can have a chance of survival: 'There is danger of a deadlock, by which we mean a situation in which neither capitalism nor its possible alternatives are workable. This is what, to a certain extent and presumably not yet for good, has happened in this country.' (Schumpeter, 1939:II, 1038). Words should not be allowed to obscure the content. The disparaging term 'deadlock' has the same meaning as the more neutral 'stable equilibrium'. The denial of the 'possible alternatives' conceals the fact that the 'deadlock' itself must be counted as an alternative. Still, however, the concession that there can be a compromise is an important one. The extremes not being 'workable', something else had to be found. Schumpeter expresses his opinion on the life span that he anticipates – 'presumably not yet for good'. It is just his opinion. A balance of forces is a position of rest. No one can know how long it will last or what new gravitational field will shock it into change.

Social democracy is one alternative to socialism. Fascism is another. Schumpeter was refining his insights on the future of capitalism against the backdrop not just of Stalin's Plan but of Hitler and Mussolini. Speaking of Nazi Germany in the 1930s, Schumpeter pointed out that it had done well on a mix of public control and public ownership: 'This is exactly the kind of performance that our model would have led us to expect from unfettered capitalism. Very obviously, however, capitalism was not unfettered.' (Schumpeter, 1939:II, 972). The Nazi model was a hybrid, part micro-market and part political lead. Not socialism, not capitalism, not even social democracy, the surprising fact is that it functioned reasonably well: 'The strength of the "fascist" state as against group interests, and its fundamental attitude to economic life – which for it is not an end in itself but a subordinate servant of extra-economic national goals – in this case facilitated a behavior in accordance with the rules of long-run economic rationality.' (Schumpeter, 1939:II, 976).

Central planning functions reasonably well. Fascism functions reasonably well. Fettered capitalism functions adequately even if not reasonably well. Then there is the socialism that acts on ideals and goes beyond mere expediency. Schumpeter said that socialism was culturally neutral: whereas capitalism has normative traits like contract and rationality which for it are indispensable links between mind and matter, socialism can think as it likes so long as it is centrally controlled. Intellectually speaking, his account is incomplete. Many socialists, it is true, have made material throughput their meta-objective, the State their ultimate tool. Other socialists, however, have concentrated on solidarity, cohesion, compassion and social justice, and have called for guilds, syndicalism and small-scale commune-ism as an alternative to the rat-race struggle for value-added. These non-economic, non-statist strands in the broad socialist tradition all deserve their day in court. Their emphasis on ethics over efficiency, deontology over consequentialism, would at the very least explain the appeal of socialism to Schumpeter's intellectuals. Socialism to Schumpeter was about productivity. Engineers might find this exciting. Intellectuals, on the other hand, will hardly risk their lives and livelihoods for a new social order that, culturally speaking, they are likely to regard as pedestrian, plodding and profoundly dull. The acknowledgement of value-based socialism as a valid alternative would extend society's freedom to choose. It would show why the intellectuals have chosen as they did.

There is a range of forms that the future can take. Schumpeter describes one path. There are others, some technical, some value-based. That is why, given the indeterminacy, there is an unintended irony in his repeated emphasis on 'the *certainty* that the economic process of capitalist society will eventually turn into something fundamentally different' (Schumpeter, 1939:II, 984). Evolution being the restless creature that it is, changes are undoubtedly taking their course. What is unclear is why all roads must lead to socialism and to socialism alone. The problem arises because Schumpeter treats the blue tendency as inseparable from the red tendency which must inherit its throne. Blue is the name for red when it is still young. Red is the name for blue when it has matured into itself. Somehow it is all too convenient and all too simplistic.

On the one hand there is the culture of capitalism. Public opinion does not like it and is glad to see it go: 'Capitalism produces by its mere working a social atmosphere – a moral code, if the reader prefer – that is hostile to it, and this atmosphere, in turn, produces policies which do not allow it to function.' (Schumpeter, 1939:II, 1038). On the other hand there is the new socialist way. Ordinary people feel satisfied because it gives them what they need: 'The socialist order presumably will command that moral allegiance which is being increasingly refused to capitalism.' (Schumpeter, 1942a:211). The Marxian materialism of falling profit-rates and desperate underconsumption leaves nothing to chance. Schumpeter's push of disappointing capitalism, pull of socialist promise, is much more a hostage to fortune. Schumpeter, saying that the decay of the blue system will engender 'allegiance' to the red one, is taking a risk by imputing sensations and perceptions which are far less predictable than Marx's matter in the course of fulfilling its fate. Schumpeter's theory of continuity and change may or may not be a theory of how capitalism will end. What it is not is a theory of what comes next. It cannot be more than half a theory. It is a grin without a cat.

12. The macroeconomics of success

Marx's macroeconomics is about unemployment and under-achievement, about capital accumulation that drives down the rate of profit and decennial crises, each one more severe than the crisis before. It is the macroeconomics of failure, the story of internal contradictions that must and will bring an illogical system to a close. It is a world away from Schumpeter's repeated denial that it was the macroeconomic integument that would put an end to the capitalist interregnum: 'There are no *purely economic* reasons why capitalism should not have another successful run.' (Schumpeter, 1942a:163n).

Robert Heilbroner was too quick to take Schumpeter's '*purely economic*' at face value. Heilbroner felt that socialism to Marx presupposed a complete breakdown in the system but that the transition to Schumpeter could only be the product of a social-philosophical choice:

> The socialist finale of Schumpeter's drama therefore rests wholly on extraeconomic factors .... There is no clear chain of causality or even of consistency leading from the economic to the political. Indeed, the very success that Schumpeter predicts for capitalism would seem to incline the outcome in another direction. ... This leaves unanswered why Schumpeter came to such a perverse conclusion. ... Assuredly it also makes clear that Schumpeter's political economy does not emerge inexorably from his economics. (Heilbroner, 1984:258).

The superstructure had all the answers. The economy by itself could not transform an economic order.

Heilbroner, taking the economics to be the macroeconomics was, of course, forgetting that it was the microeconomics of stifled entrepreneurship that in Schumpeter's perspective represented the real threat: 'Capitalist institutions, deprived of their impetus of incessant expansion which used to make them function, have now become bars to economic progress and are henceforth bound to produce political as well as economic deadlock.' (Schumpeter, 1944:162). Microeconomics would one day make the whole giant machine grind to a halt. Macroeconomics, '*purely economic*', was less likely to interrupt the unprecedented run of an institutional order that had proven itself to be a popular success.

This chapter concedes that the micro-market might retard the pace of innovation in the post-entrepreneurial age but shows that the macro-market is a reliable mechanism that never lets the team down. It is divided into three sections: Growth and development, Savings and investment, and Employment and prices. It reaches the conclusion that Schumpeter, try as he might to classify himself with 'those of us who accept the Marxian theory of the social process' (Schumpeter, 1939:I, 7), was as much an optimist about the macroeconomics of capitalism as he was a pessimist about its chances of survival.

12.1 GROWTH AND DEVELOPMENT

Science and technology have immeasurably improved the product: the modern workman enjoys a quality of dentistry that was not on offer at the court of Louis XIV. Mass production and rising incomes have ensured that excellence has been democratised through steady trickle down. 'Queen Elizabeth owned silk stockings. The capitalist achievement does not typically consist in providing more silk stockings for queens but in bringing them within the reach of factory girls in return for steadily decreasing amounts of effort.' (Schumpeter, 1942a:67). It is in the nature of capitalist development that it empowers even the classical manual class to secure a stake in chemical synthetics, electrical appliances, private transport and all the other innovations and novelties of the high-consumption society. Growth is good because it moves everyone up: 'The capitalist process ... progressively raises the standard of life of the masses.' (Schumpeter, 1942a:68).

Out goes intolerable deprivation and Dickensian squalor. In comes rising expectations satisfied by material advance: 'The real income and the social weight of the working class rise in this process.' (Schumpeter, 1942a:310). Purchasing power buys cultural approximation through conspicuous *embourgeoisement*: the result is a decline in divisive class consciousness certified by the class-based mode of self-presentation. The prospect of betterment means social harmony in place of labour–capital conflict: a revolution by spontaneous combustion is not likely where even the intellectuals cannot goad the workers into a solidarity which they rank far below their shopping. The relationship between the shop floor and the bosses is, 'in normal times, primarily one of cooperation' (Schumpeter, 1942a:19). Growth ensures that the social partners have good reason to keep the peace.

Growth has meant a pluralisation of prizes and of chances to make good: 'Business achievement is obviously not everywhere the only avenue to social eminence.' (Schumpeter, 1942a:18). Growth has opened up new opportunities for social and occupational mobility: whereas Marx had assumed that people born in the proletariat would stay in the proletariat, Schumpeter said that there was no reason in the flux of capitalism for ambition and ability to feel disheartened or crushed down. Inclusion and integration, in short, take the edge off the hunger for socialism. Socialism is still inevitable, but not because the ownership of the means of production has produced a social bifurcation that only the classless economy can resolve. Socialism and social class are not one topic but two separate topics. (Schumpeter, 1942a:19). Sociologically speaking, capitalism could last forever. It is the giant corporation and not the two-class dialectic that makes the change of system only a matter of time.

Growth is an across-the-board dividend. It does not affect the distribution of the national product. Schumpeter cites evidence to show that both the pyramid of incomes and the respective shares of labour and capital tend to be remarkably stable despite the dramatic evolution in the economy: 'Distribution, as is shown particularly by studies in England, is remarkably constant for all countries and as far back in history as we can go. It always follows the law commonly described as Pareto's Line. Even war and inflation have not altered it.' (Schumpeter, 1926/27a:60). Pareto's constancy strikes at the heart of Marxian impoverishment, if also at the catch-up thesis which predicts that the less affluent will become more affluent relative to the already-established. They will not. Growth and development can deliver a range of benefits. What they cannot do is to narrow – or to widen – the gap.

Relative deprivation is not growth-sensitive. Absolute deprivation is another matter: 'If capitalism repeated its past performance for another half century, starting with 1928, this would do away with anything that according to present standards could be called poverty ... pathological cases alone excepted.' (Schumpeter, 1942a:66). Schumpeter set the year at 1978. Anthony Crosland said in 1956 that, the helpless *residuum* alone excepted, 'such primary poverty as remains will disappear within a decade, given our present rate of economic growth' (Crosland, 1956:105). Either way, 1978 or 1966, it is beefsteak and not gruel that awaits the lower earning groups once the moving staircase of growth has moved all the classes up.

An escalator has a clearly-defined top step or final destination. Economic growth, on the other hand, has no upper bound or buffer. Schumpeter said it was 'one of the safest predictions that in the calculable future we shall live in an *embarras de richesse* of both foodstuffs and raw materials' (Schumpeter, 1942a:116). Looking to the future, Schumpeter did not anticipate a supply-side constraint on sustainable progress. Not a Malthusian in fear of the niggardliness of nature, not an environmentalist convinced that the dismal science was irresponsibly depleting irreplaceable reserves, Schumpeter postulated an *embarras de richesse* in the area of natural resources. This meant that economic growth need never run out of the inputs that it requires.

As with the supply of input, so with the demand for output. Keynes in 1930, in 'Economic possibilities for our grandchildren', had looked forward only

100 years to the 'freedom from pressing economic cares' that all but the stranded and the dependent would be able to enjoy: 'This means that the economic problem is not – if we look into the future – *the permanent problem of the human race*.' (Keynes, 1930:326, 328). Galbraith in 1958, in *The Affluent Society*, was to report that, in the United States at least, the end of unsatisfied needs could already be proclaimed: 'We may say that the marginal utility of present aggregate output, ex advertising and salesmanship, is zero.' (Galbraith, 1958:137). Both Keynes and Galbraith predicted that scarcity and economising would gradually take on the patina of the museum piece that recalled a bygone age. Schumpeter, in contrast, was more in tune with the obsessive acquisitiveness of ordinary consumers who refuse to call it a day: 'Such a state of satiety is no doubt very far off even if we keep within the present scheme of wants; and if we take account of the fact that, as higher standards of life are attained, these wants automatically expand and new wants emerge or are created, satiety becomes a flying goal.' (Schumpeter, 1942a:131).

The more we have of the old things, the more we want of the new ones. If supply moves forward, then so does demand. There is unlikely to exist a point of saturation beyond which there will not be enough dissatisfaction on the part of the consumer to validate the self-sustaining process of entrepreneur-led expansion.

12.2 SAVINGS AND INVESTMENT

Economists from Smith and Ricardo to Marshall and Cassels had accepted the reassuring proposition known as Say's Law that had ruled out any secular tendency towards excessive savings, inadequate investment: 'Demand *must* correspond to supply, supply to demand. The one must always call forth the other. That is why there cannot normally, and for a long time, be general overproduction .... *Overproduction in some sectors is necessarily under-production in others*.' (Schumpeter, 1926/27b:154). The Keynesian consumption function shattered the quiet confidence that 'what is annually saved is as regularly consumed as what is annually spent, and nearly in the same time too' (Smith, 1776:I, 359): 'We take it as a fundamental psychological rule of any modern community that, when its real income is increased, it will not increase its consumption by an equal *absolute* amount, so that a greater absolute amount must be saved.' (Keynes, 1936:97). Keynes believed that the average propensity to save had a tendency to increase steadily over time. Unless the average propensity to invest were simultaneously to capital-deepen demand by an equivalent amount, excess supply and idle capacity would be on the cards. The reason is that Keynesian theory predicts an irreversible downward trend in the pressure of households on the national stock of goods and services.

Keynes and secular stagnationists such as Hansen were in the tradition of recessionary over-savers like Malthus, Lauderdale and Hobson, in the spirit of the Marxian underconsumptionists like Lenin and Rosa Luxemburg who had counted on inadequate demand for the internal contradiction that would negate an intolerable negation. It was an intellectual position which Schumpeter went out of his way to reject. Schumpeter was attracted by the macroeconomic thermostat of self-equilibrating Say's Law. He did not see why the ultimate cause of decreasing prosperity would turn out to be achieved purchasing potential itself.

12.2.1 Macroeconomic Stabilisation

The Keynesian 'psychological rule' takes current saving to be a stable function of current real income. Schumpeter as early as 1908 had decided that the unfounded a priori had no intuitive appeal: 'Saving is without doubt not a function of income.' (Schumpeter, 1908:308). The more people have, the less people will want to have more. Retentiveness at the margin is bound to give way to hedonism at the margin as people lay in an ever-greater stock of gratification deferred: 'Savings as well is subject to the law of diminishing marginal utility. Here too any further increase is valued less than the directly preceding increment of equal magnitude.' (Schumpeter, 1908:303).

As incomes rise, so people think first of consuming more: 'If ... wages rise, the marginal utility of money for the worker inevitably falls, and that means the extension of his demand to less important consumer goods.' (Schumpeter, 1908:472). New consumables open up new wants even as *ceteris paribus* non-satiety presumes that spenders will buy more by means of short-run small increments. Besides that, there is the societal interdependence of conspicuous consumption and the ratchet effect of remembered habit that significantly reduce the incentive to bury pecuniary success in the anonymity of a savings account: 'Higher social position and accustomed luxury – a higher standard of life – generally more than balance out the size of income. People with high incomes ... save less intensively than people with low incomes, many of them not at all.' (Schumpeter, 1908:308). Miserly Keynesians are obsessed with security and stockpiled assets. Most people, Schumpeter clearly believes, become saturated with self-denial beyond a point.

The primary cause of incremental abstinence is not incremental earnings but marginal utility. That being the case, anxious pessimists who extrapolate demand deficiency from increasing affluence are in effect falling victim to a behaviourally-impoverished simplification of the decision-making process. People do not save for the sake of saving. Instead they save because they want to secure a return: 'The decision to invest precedes as a rule, and the act of investing precedes very often, the decision to save.' (Schumpeter, 1942a:395). Decision makers will not normally cut back on current consumption unless the investment opportunities constitute a sufficient temptation. Where they do, however, the withdrawals will be matched by the re-injections and the possibility of over-saving will therefore be extremely low: 'There is nothing to fear from people's propensity to save.' (Schumpeter, 1942a:398).

Because investment is the primary reason for saving, the Keynesians have done wrong to headline the income-elasticity while footnoting the pecuniary incentive: 'The stagnation thesis cannot be based upon the element of saving.' (Schumpeter, 1942a:396n). People save because they have a 'specific investment purpose in mind' (Schumpeter, 1942a:395). They do not save without it. Business saving – 'the greater part of total saving' (Schumpeter, 1942a:395) – is particularly outcome-orientated: 'Decisions to save depend upon and presuppose decisions to invest.' (Schumpeter, 1942a:396). High incomes probably are the necessary condition for high savings: people cannot put aside what they do not possess. What Schumpeter is emphasising is that high incomes cannot be the sufficient condition as well. People save in order to tap into an opportunity. Should investment outlets decrease, so too *pari passu* would savings. Rational and entrepreneurial, people would no longer have the same incentive to put the future first.

The exception is the absolute trough: 'Saving without investment occurs only in deep depressions.' (Schumpeter, 1954:1144). In a deep depression the posted returns are low and good investments are hard to find. Saving, however, actually increases on the part of those who fear business losses or redundancy. The 'paradox of thrift' is the consequence of the downswing and cannot therefore be its original cause. Firms, meanwhile, defer investment projects in order to make a speculative gain from the anticipated disinflation. At the very time when households are crying out for additional openings, the business demand for loanable savings goes into hibernation until current conditions improve.

The absolute trough of the Juglar cycle (and perhaps of the long-term Kondratieff as well) occurred, Schumpeter believed, in 1930. It was the exceptional equilibrium of that absolute trough that led Keynes to formulate the theory of saving that he did: 'It yields a psychological explanation of the Keynesian psychological law.' (Schumpeter, 1942a:395). Keynesian economics is Great Depression economics. It is no more than the atypical codification of a moment in time when capitalism was singularly down on its luck: 'The psychological law and the theory of hoarding that is based upon it are simply generalizations from that experience.' (Schumpeter, 1942a:395). No theorist of saving has much to learn from the Keynesians on an absolute trough that is the exception and not the rule.

Schumpeter's account of saving is imbued with calculative rationality. It is also an evolutionary theory, situated in time and resistant to change. Schumpeter knows that saving takes place not just because of marginal costs and benefits but because of 'a habit which once formed may outlive its rationale as may any other habit' (Schumpeter, 1942a:396). In the long run adaptation will occur and economics will push out such saving reflexes as have lost their function: 'The vanishing of investment opportunities ... would render those habits irrational.' (Schumpeter, 1942a:396n). In the short run, however, past practices will act as frictions that buffer the incursion of the present day. Adaptation, like Marshall's glacier, is a 'slow process' (Schumpeter, 1942a:396n) – and we start from here.

It might be possible to derive a theory of over-saving from learned responses that pay little heed to present-day stimuli. What is interesting is that Schumpeter, having recognised the possibility, himself showed little or no interest in pattern-maintenance as a cause of dysfunctional frugality.

Schumpeter knew that people save in order to enjoy a cushion of security, or to provide for their old age, or to leave a legacy for the next generation. He acknowledged with Marshall that the payoff to savings is not exclusively the pecuniary return, current and calculative. Even so, he clearly regarded the extra-economic bedrock of social conventions and psychological impulses as no imminent cause of an income-elasticity that would make spending on strike into an early reason for a recession or even for something worse. Perhaps this is indicative of a belief that, in modern conditions, insurance, social insurance, the decline of the family business, all make the precautionary motive to stockpile assets that much less urgent as the best-attainable means to the end.

As with the *Zweckrational* means to the end, so with the *Wertrational* end in itself. Schumpeter was familiar with Max Weber's socially-inculcated Puritanism that teaches the moral value of thrift. He knew that the Protestant Ethic once put a premium on consumption foregone that transcended any expectation of a lucrative new investment. It would have been easy for him to derive macroeconomic stagnation from so ascetic a pre-capitalistic legitimation. The fact is that he did not do so. Rationality to Schumpeter was the corrosive that would eventually dislodge the sentimentality. Given enough time, economic logic would drive the religious out of the marketplace and back into the Sunday schools.

Over-saving, moreover, would be counterbalanced by the new permissiveness. In the Keynesian 1930s birth rates were declining and European populations were contracting. Smaller families could have meant more household saving. In fact it was consumption that obtained the lion's share of the benefit: 'The desire to expand alternative demands is the very motive of childlessness.' (Schumpeter, 1942a:114). Sectors like agriculture which are numbers-dependent might be demand-constrained. Sectors like consumer durables which can harness entrepreneurial innovativeness to exploit what Marshall calls 'new wants, and new and more expensive ways of gratifying them' (Marshall, 1890a:185) will face no such limit. In the past, frugality and modesty were collective values that mounted a challenge to aggregate demand. We today are able to benefit from the upward shift in the consumption function that occurs when a self-indulgent new ethos frees up income for spending that might otherwise have been over-saved. Thus does economic growth generate the markets that it needs to keep itself in business.

Just as saving is unlikely to be excessive, so investment is unlikely to be deficient. Schumpeter was a theorist of creative destruction. He was committed to the idea that 'nothing in the social world can ever be *aere perennius*' (Schumpeter, 1942a:112). He could not simultaneously share the expectation that investment outlets would vanish, the economic frontier close for all time, growth-rates plateau in the stationary state of the status quo. The early stagnationists had failed to appreciate the new opportunities that were opening up before their very eyes: 'Those writers lived at the threshold of the most spectacular economic developments ever witnessed .... Nevertheless, they saw nothing but cramped economies, struggling with ever-decreasing success for their daily bread.' (Schumpeter, 1954:571). The twentieth-century saturationists shared with their classical forebears the 'complete lack of imagination' (Schumpeter, 1954:571) that made them think of investment as a vessel that was inexorably becoming full. Schumpeter was sharply critical of this myopia. The truth is unceasing endeavour. It is not the mindless inertia of more of the same.

Schumpeter's refutation of the stagnationists and the saturationists is encapsulated in the single word 'new'. New technologies crowd out old plant: 'Hence the task of providing equipment can never be solved once for all .... This is particularly clear where the new methods of production are embodied in new industries; obviously the automobile plants were not financed from the depreciation accounts of railroads.' (Schumpeter, 1942a:119). New imaginings refresh the diminishing returns Ricardianism of marginal deserts, inaccessible jungles and infertile mountain tops: 'The conquest of the air may well be more important than the conquest of India was – we must not confuse geographical frontiers with economic ones.' (Schumpeter, 1942a:117). Profit rates can indeed decline to zero in an innovation-less economy where the evolutionary process has ground to a halt. In an ever-changing environment, however, ambitious entrepreneurs continually shake the kaleidoscope. They introduce intellectual renewal into what otherwise would have been replacement investment as usual.

Over-saving relative to the demand for capital is evidently not a problem save in the temporary trough of a cycle that is bound to bounce back: 'We may put some trust in the ability of the capitalist engine to find or create ever new opportunities since it is geared to this very purpose.' (Schumpeter, 1942a:117). Schumpeter as an Austrian subjectivist had to admit that 'technological possibilities are an uncharted sea' (Schumpeter, 1942a:118). As an evolutionist and a futurologist, however, he clearly took the view that one wave of novelty would follow on from the pole position before. There would never be any reason to expect a ceiling, an exhaustion or a physical limit. Ricardo believed that the best would be used up first. Schumpeter felt that the radical and the unpredictable were forever in the process of emerging from the white heat of quest.

Always assuming, however, that the business sector remains enterprising and on the edge. Schumpeter's microeconomics of owner-operators and large corporations is here of direct relevance to his macroeconomics of expansion and advance. As was seen in Chapters 4 and 5, there is an undeniable tension between his view that teamwork can be entrepreneurial and his fear that the organisation will turn protective. Choosing the more dynamic scenario, his position seems to have been that innovation proceeds and the void is averted precisely because the large firm is more likely than the small one to conduct extensive R & D and to invest in new product-lines. Restrictive practices, price rigidities, oligopolistic understandings, far from being an impediment to progress, provide the security that makes possible the permanent disequilibrium of sustained experimentation. Top-heavy bureaucracies afraid to take risks would be a more serious cause for concern. A (microeconomic) loss of nerve could in such circumstances lead directly to a (macroeconomic) lack of demand. Schumpeter does not explain why giant corporations dozing their way to socialism may reliably be counted on to re-invest realised savings back into the flow.

Investment in any case is not exclusively business investment. Government investment is an important source of total demand. Schumpeter gives the example of growing involvement in parks and docks, a long-term trend and not a Keynesian shock absorber. It would have been possible to build on the income elasticity of public goods to make the increasing pressure for public supply yet another reason for the move into socialism. Schumpeter, characteristically, resists the temptation to treat social democracy as the macroeconomics of last resort. Public works are simply not needed to provide a permanent bulwark against the lethargy of mature affluence. Given time for adjustment and a market-clearing interest rate, desired investment will match the whole of desired savings and Say's Law will prove that the Keynesians were wrong.

12.2.2 Schumpeter and Keynes

The *General Theory* was published in 1936. By 1937 Schumpeter was beginning to think that the debate had passed him by: 'Keynes is Allah', he said privately, adding that 'the majority of our very best young people are almost fanatically for Mr Keynes' book' (cited in Swedberg, 1991:118). The English translation of the *Theory of Economic Development* had appeared in 1934: its message of entrepreneurship, markets, unemployment as the refreshing short break that repositions the troops meant that it appealed as little to public opinion as it did to university economists grappling with the Great Depression. In 1939 the massive *Business Cycles* came out. Schumpeter must have known that it failed to attract any serious interest: 'By this time', Swedberg writes, 'another world war was starting in Europe and Keynesianism had already swept the Harvard department of economics .... No one that counted thought that *Business Cycles* was a major work or on a par with *General Theory*.' (Swedberg, 1991:119). It was not the first time that Schumpeter had been well and truly upstaged by his rival for standing and influence. In 1930 the *Treatise on Money* had led Schumpeter to put aside his own manuscript on monetary economics.

Schumpeter and Keynes were almost exact contemporaries. They were born in 1883, the year of Marx's death. They died within four months of one another, in 1950 and 1949 respectively. More than just contemporaries, however, they were also close in their choice of topics and in the philosophical purposiveness that put mission into their investigations. Both were ideologically committed to the exchange economy. Both acknowledged that capitalism could fall short of its productive potential. Both had read widely, synthesized eclectically, trespassed into political economy because supply and demand told only a part of the story. Each was a social elitist, confident about leadership but mistrustful of the masses. Each went beyond the fiction of perfect information to acknowledge the ubiquity of speculation, uncertainty, expectation and the unintended outcome. Each took a policy-shaper's interest in the macroeconomic paralysis of the inter-war years. A sprinter is unlikely to be compared to a footballer. Schumpeter and Keynes were compared, and compared themselves, for the very reason that they were believed to be contenders in a single sport.

Keynes does not show much more interest in Schumpeter than high-profile Mozart probably showed in worthy, assiduous Salieri. There is no mention of Schumpeter in the *General Theory* and only a passing reference in the *Treatise* to Schumpeter's economics of innovation. Schumpeter, on the other hand, took great pains to spell out the differences that in his opinion put clear water between himself and his British counterpart. He did so in particular in his

History of Economic Analysis, in *Capitalism, Socialism and Democracy*, in the historic review – an 'unfavourable review' (Schumpeter, 1936b:160) – of the *General Theory* which appeared in the *Journal of the American Statistical Association*, and in the long appreciation (reprinted in *Ten Great Economists*) which Schumpeter wrote for the *American Economic Review* at the time of Keynes's death.

The obituary, as one would expect, speaks well of the deceased. Keynes showed 'brilliance in the forging of individual tools of analysis' (Schumpeter, 1952a:287). Keynes had a 'vivid appreciation' (Schumpeter, 1952a:265) of economic variables. Keynes was a 'formidable conversationalist' (Schumpeter, 1952a:264). Keynes provided 'sound advice added to sound analysis' (Schumpeter, 1952a:266) when drifting Britain desperately needed his *Economic Consequences of the Peace*. Many good things could clearly be said about Keynes. That did not mean, however, that his economics could normally be trusted or that his system would be of any real-world value: 'As with Marx, it is possible to admire Keynes even though one may consider his social vision to be wrong and every one of his propositions to be misleading.' (Schumpeter, 1952a:291). As with Marx, it is possible to learn from Keynes so long as one remembers that the economics one is learning will not be very relevant or especially useful in a world that wants to eliminate underperformance and not merely to theorise about it.

Keynes asserted that his theory was a *general* one. That was the nub of Schumpeter's critique. Keynes's economics, Schumpeter said, was not general at all but disappointingly specific. Circumscribed and bounded, the assistance it could provide was of necessity rather limited: 'A fruit knife is an excellent instrument for peeling a pear. He who uses it to attack a steak has only himself to blame for unsatisfactory results.' (Schumpeter, 1952a:287).

The Keynesian system is weighted down by the narrow specificity of time and place. Keynes, hungry as he was to be all-encompassing, was in his essence an Englishman of the inter-war years: 'He was surprisingly insular, even in philosophy, but nowhere so much as in economics.' (Schumpeter, 1952a:274). One illustration of his lack of a comparative perspective would be his neglect of the unique banking environment that made the Depression in the United States particularly severe. In the United States, because of irrational fears of monopoly finance, there was a multiplicity of small independents, 'Lilliput banks', inefficient and poorly managed: 'It is no wonder that these banks died in shoals.' (Schumpeter, 1941:352). There is nothing in the *General Theory* about the domino effect of failing banks. Britain had the Big Five. Concentration was one reason why as early as 1932 she was moving towards recovery – and the United States was not.

Keynes, moreover, taking seriously his own quip '*In the long-run* we are all dead' (Keynes, 1923:80), confined his system to a single Kitchin of at most 40 months. Output in the Marshallian short run is necessarily a function of variable inputs such as labour while the capital stock is assumed to be constant. The result is a model which is 'closer to macrostatics than macrodynamics, limiting it to the range of short-run phenomena' (Schumpeter, 1952a:282). Long-run analysis would have allowed Keynes to explore the investment multiplier in a setting in which the capital stock is not assumed to be fixed. As it is, his theory cannot explain what it is that actually *determines* income. It is a biased theory, a theory of 'special cases' (Schumpeter, 1952a:286). It is not a *general* theory at all.

The absence of investment of the Marshallian long run is exacerbated by the absence of innovation of the Marshallian secular period. In 1830 people invested in cotton mills but not in railways. In 1880 people invested in railways but not in motor cars. Schumpeter sees capitalism as new products and new techniques. He reproaches Keynes for concentrating on output-equilibrium and the simplifying *ceteris paribus* when the economic reality is development, discovery, entrepreneurship and creative destruction: '*All the phenomena incident to the creation and change* in this apparatus, that is to say, the phenomena that dominate the capitalist processes, are thus excluded from consideration.' (Schumpeter, 1952a:283).

To Schumpeter production functions 'are being incessantly revolutionized' whereas to Keynes, fundamentally, they are 'invariant' (Schumpeter, 1936b:162). The reaction to involuntary unemployment was bound to be different. Ups and downs, cyclical and transitory, are to Schumpeter an investment in the 'recurrent rejuvenation of the productive apparatus' (Schumpeter, 1942a:68). They will in the fullness of time convert current bankruptcy into future prosperity. Observed misalignment to Keynes is a sign of illness and not of health. It is assumed to be a stable state. If self-correcting novelty were just past the painful weeding out, Keynes would not have had to call for fiscal intervention to rescue income and employment from indefinite statics. In failing to distinguish between temporary unemployment in the transition and a long-term state of affairs that has no endogenous turning point, Keynes showed that his theory was limited and that it was not *general*.

Keynes, besides that, reasoned deductively from ad hoc *let-us-assume*s when a truly *general* theory would have incorporated the never-ending dialogue between conjecture and evidence. Keynes, 'in the worst style of a bygone age', makes extensive use of 'artificial definitions', 'specialized assumptions', 'treacherous generality' to produce 'paradoxical-looking tautologies' (Schumpeter, 1936b:161, 162) like the liquidity trap and the fallacy of composition of thrift which are totally unsupported by real-world experience. Keynes then draws upon his falsely-specified presumptions – 'It is Ricardo all over again' – to pyramid policy recommendations upon a base of unproven assertions that are packaged as science but in truth are value judgement and reform: 'Everywhere he really pleads for a definite policy.' (Schumpeter, 1936b:160). Schumpeter felt that the academic economist had a duty to be detached and impartial: 'What our time needs most and lacks most is the understanding of the process which people are passionately resolved to control. To supply this understanding ... is the only service the scientific worker is, as such, qualified to render.' (Schumpeter, 1939:I, vi). He had little time for Keynes who, in his view, was twisting the evidence in order to exaggerate his own case for macro-management and the sensible State.

Keynes, Schumpeter objected, derived his savings function from his 'fundamental psychological rule' which had no grounding save in his own personal introspection. Keynes used his consumption function to infer a widening gap between desired thrift and desired plant which no statistician had ever observed. Keynes deduced dysfunctional under-employment from the recessionary gap, public expenditure from idle capacity, egalitarian redistribution from the supposition that the rich save more. Questionable recommendations teetering on dubious selectivity, Schumpeter complained that Keynesian economics was the 'Ricardian Vice' all over again of seeing logic and calling it society. Schumpeter calls Keynes 'the father of modern stagnation' (Schumpeter, 1954:1172). He also implies that Keynes would have been the father of something far less discouraging if Keynes had lived up to his own avowed intent of writing a *general* theory that was founded on the facts.

Schumpeter did not recognise (or perhaps did not want to see) that there were unmistakeable similarities between his vision of economics and that of Keynes. His interpretation of entrepreneurial conquest as a non-rational drive recalls Keynes's 'animal spirits', that 'spontaneous urge to action rather than inaction' which makes the economic market considerably less tidy than the 'weighted average of quantitative benefits multiplied by quantitative probabilities' (Keynes, 1936:161). His prediction that interest rates would tend to zero because endogenous entrepreneurship would *ceteris paribus* go back into its shell is similar to Keynes's prediction that the 'euthanasia of the rentier', the 'euthanasia of the cumulative oppressive power of the capitalist' (Keynes, 1936:376), would *ceteris paribus* be the consequence of high endogenous savings and the low marginal efficiency of capital. There is a twitchy dimension in Keynes's market theory which parallels Schumpeter's own expectation of disequilibrium and dynamics: 'Economists set themselves too easy, too useless a task if in tempestuous seasons they can only tell us that when the storm is long past the ocean is flat again.' (Keynes, 1923:80). There is an evolutionary dimension in Keynes's invocation of memory, expectations, normal values, traditional differentials, which is a counterpart to Schumpeter's appeal to sociology and history to flesh out the subjectivity of his methodological individualism: 'It might be more accurate, perhaps, to say that the rate of interest is a highly conventional, rather than a highly psychological, phenomenon .... *Any* level of interest which is accepted with sufficient conviction as *likely* to be durable *will* be durable.' (Keynes, 1936:203). There is common ground even in the distanced instrumentalism which guided both of the socially-concerned pro-marketeers in their results-based assessment of the balance-wheel State.

Schumpeter looked mainly to the long run. He had a preference for *laissez-faire* because of his confident expectation that the entrepreneur would provide. When stating that 'I recommend no policy and propose no plan' (Schumpeter, 1939:I, vi), what he was in fact saying was that letting the disease run its course was his preferred prescription for a cure. Keynes, stranded in the short run at a station that he knew he did not like, turned instead to hands-on intervention because the market had no internal defences against the cycle. Schumpeter, Scitovsky observed (he was writing at a time when activists believed that the issue had been definitively resolved), 'failed to foresee the success of Keynesian macro policies in stabilizing the free-enterprise economy without making it less free and less enterprising' (Scitovsky, 1980:8). The common ground lies not in the instruments but in the legitimacy. Success was the ultimate standard of *ought-ness* that was employed by both Schumpeter and Keynes in their assessment of the balance-wheel State. Schumpeter was flexible enough to countenance welfare transfers and even a budget deficit once the other options had been exhausted. Committed to the pragmatic test of results, Schumpeter could easily have become a Keynesian if he had convinced himself, with Hansen, Samuelson and Galbraith, that public works and not wait-and-see had the better chance of breaking the log jam of the *Grapes of Wrath* and the tragedy of Jarrow.

Schumpeter, jealous of Keynes, played down the possibility of a synthesis. History has taken a similar view. Both long dead, Keynes on under-consumption is discussed at length in the macroeconomics text while Schumpeter on innovation is normally not mentioned at all. Partly the overlap has been lost because Keynes's disciples translated his qualified verbalisations into the simplified abstractions of graphs and mathematics: Schumpeter had no disciples and his culture of entrepreneurship cannot realistically be quantified with the precision of the IS–LM. Mainly, however, Keynes has scored well and the synthesis has been neglected because Schumpeter counselled patience whereas the Keynesians seemed able to correct the multiplying errors that were the market failures of automaticity's delay. In the long run we are all dead. The unemployed preferred Keynes to Schumpeter because Keynes at least gave them hope.

12.3 EMPLOYMENT AND PRICES

Aggregate demand is the means. Full employment with stable prices is the end. Schumpeter recognised that involuntary unemployment and intolerable inflation would badly tarnish the reputation of the capitalist order. He believed at the same time that the probability of macroeconomic failure was very low. State correctives were unlikely to be needed to keep the performance of the economy on course:

> The capitalist system *as such* needs neither regulation nor planning, in a depression or outside of a depression, in order to function .... It operates on its own, and with results unprecedented in economic history. The logical solution for a series of serious shortcomings would not be an increase but a reduction in State intervention. (Schumpeter, 1931/32:208).

Fine tuning, indeed, would more likely than not make any transitory imbalance worse.

12.3.1 Unemployment

The reserve army plays no part in Schumpeter's theory of the collapse of capitalism. In contrast to the Marxians (who had inherited technological displacement from Barton and Ricardo), in contrast to the Keynesians (who had built on a century of doubt as to whether Say's Law meant bliss), Schumpeter denied that the market system had sooner or later to put men out of work: 'I ... do not think that there is any tendency for the unemployment percentage to increase in the long run.' (Schumpeter, 1942a:69). Not increasing, presumably not falling, Schumpeter's unemployment seems in the long run to gravitate to a natural rate and to settle where it has always made its home.

The long run is stable. The short run, however, is exposed to the shocks. A national emergency like a war temporarily interrupts the normal mechanisms: 'Great unemployment is only the consequence of non-economic events.' (Schumpeter, 1912b:67). Creative destruction, endogenous and economic, is similar to a war in that it dislocates an established equilibrium in the transition to something new: 'Cyclical unemployment *is* technological unemployment.' (Schumpeter, 1939:II, 515). Innovation is of the essence but no adaptation is ever instantaneous. Only a moratorium on newness would be able to eradicate the frictional unemployment that is the immediate concomitant of economic progress. Schumpeter writes that, in whirlwind capitalism, 'revolution in existing industrial and commercial patterns is the permanent state of things' (Schumpeter, 1946c:407). A society that wants the secular improvement must be prepared to countenance the 'ephemeral' joblessness that is the price.

Interventionists said that public policy was indispensable to get market breakdown through its healing crisis. Schumpeter was more optimistic about a self-correcting mechanism that would automatically reverse the downswing once the dead wood of the past had given way to the new growths of the future. The market alone could ensure an upswing that would be sustainable: 'Recovery is sound only if it does come of itself.' (cited in Swedberg, 1991:148). Public policy was more likely to have the perverse effect of turning a transitory readjustment into a full-blown Depression. This it had done in the troubled 1930s: 'The subnormal recovery to 1935, the subnormal prosperity to 1937 and the slump after that are easily accounted for by the difficulties incident to the adaptation to a new fiscal policy, new labor legislation and a general change in the attitude of government to private enterprise.' (Schumpeter, 1942a:64). Neither 'an unprecedented catastrophe nor a symptom of decreased vitality of the system' (Schumpeter, 1941:352), the supernormal joblessness of the 1930s could easily have been contained had the policy makers effectively allowed the bad times to run their course. Intervening, they managed instead to make their own favoured cure into an independent cause of uncorrected ill-health.

The experience of the 1930s provides instance after instance of the harm that democracy can do. There were wage policies that fixed pay rates above the market-clearing level: 'Everywhere wages are higher than is compatible with full employment.' (Schumpeter, 1931b:98). There were union monopolies which had the charter to price the unemployed out of work: 'As long as the unions succeed in keeping wages above the level of a free labour market – as they wish to do – unemployment is inevitable.' (Schumpeter, 1926/27b:135). There were protective tariffs which both reduced the total volume of world trade and perpetuated domestic collusion to keep supply short: 'When firms collude, explicitly or implicitly, rather than competing with each other, the pressure is lost to extend production up to the point at which there is full employment.' (Schumpeter, 1926/27b:156). There were central bankers who leaned against the prevailing winds until in the end 'the great spring cleaning' (Schumpeter, 1941:352) was frustrated to a halt. There were fiscal egalitarians whose high taxes on high savers inadvertently reduced the pool of job vacancies that capital creation would have provided. There were bossy planners whose restrictions on mobility and prices undermined the ability of the market to transmit reliable signals. Public policy, in short, had, in case after case, had the unintended effect of blocking the access of the unemployed to the jobs that, intervention but taken away, they would have been all too eager to accept.

Adding the mistakes to the oversights to the missed opportunities, Schumpeter drew the inference that job-seekers had little to fear from a shortfall in total demand but 'plenty to fear from other factors' (Schumpeter,

1942a:398): 'The unemployment figure has been increased by anti-capitalist policies beyond what it need have been.' (Schumpeter, 1942a:71). The market would have stimulated the supply side to produce more jobs. New Economics and New Deal only ensured that a minor correction became an ingrained fact of life. Adam Smith on the threshold of modern capitalism had said that he had 'never known much good done by those who affected to trade for the public good' (Smith, 1776:I, 478). Milton Friedman, like Schumpeter before him, saw in the troubled 1930s the prolonged disruption that proved Smith right: 'The fact is that the Great Depression, like most other periods of severe unemployment, was produced by government mismanagement rather than by any inherent instability of the private economy.' (Friedman, 1962:38). To arrive at full employment, what was most needed was not more government macro-management but rather less.

Schumpeter at heart was always a Walrasian, suspicious of macroeconomic aggregates since it was microeconomic pricing that held the key, convinced that the State would not be needed so long as the auctioneer could allocate the supply. Yet he was never so doctrinaire as to reject the discretionary injection on principle where extreme circumstances made it essential for fiscal policy to pump in additional demand. Haberler believes that Schumpeter saw the sustained Great Depression as one such exception to the norm of the sound recovery that comes of itself:

> I don't think it is correct to say that he ruled out deficit financing altogether. In 1932 he recommended a gigantic expenditure program. I don't think he published it anywhere but he told me about it himself. I think the figure he mentioned was $9 billion which surely was quite a lot for that time. (cited in Wright, 1950:39).

Allen summarises the unpublished evidence from the 1930s in the following words: 'Colleagues remember that Schumpeter in those days proposed emergency spending in the billions of dollars, more than that proposed by other economists. But he was always careful to point out that these expenditures were one-time emergency projects.' (Allen, 1991:II, 33n). One-time or continuous, the proposal is hardly the hands-off recovery that is the ideal of the consistent free-marketeer. In the decade of Keynes and Roosevelt, even Schumpeter was not prepared to rely entirely on the invisible hand.

In the second (1946) edition of *Capitalism, Socialism and Democracy*, Schumpeter added a section which clarified his position. There he wrote that he had no objection to 'income-generating government expenditure in emergencies once they have arisen', only to 'policies that create the emergencies in which such expenditure imposes itself' (Schumpeter, 1942a:398). He also stated that he was in full agreement even with a budget deficit. This, he said, would be an 'efficient remedy' in a 'vicious spiral' where 'prices fall because they have fallen', 'unemployment feeds upon itself' and the danger is real of a 'downward cumulative process' (Schumpeter, 1942a:397). Schumpeter late in life appears to have developed a tendency towards Keynesianism. The criterion, however, was the urgency of the need. The manipulation of total demand was only justifiable where the depression was so deep that the market unaided could not be expected to ensure a speedy recovery. Unemployment satisfactorily reversed, the mending and the managing would have to stop since discretion would no longer have an economic function to fulfil.

Productive potential is being wasted when unemployed labour is not adding value. Schumpeter saw that idleness is an economic loss. Unusual among economists, he also recognised that it is a personal and a private tragedy. Schumpeter was sensitive to 'the suffering and degradation', 'the destruction of human values' (Schumpeter, 1942a:70) that blighted the lives of conscientious workmen whose jobs had disappeared. He called in the circumstances for government benefits to be paid to the able-bodied and not just the unemployable until such a time as trustworthy dynamism had created new work for them to do.

Public opinion, not in favour of doles and handouts that are 'lax and wasteful', is 'alive to the duty' (Schumpeter, 1942a:71) of providing a safety net for fellow citizens who have fallen on hard times. Compassion and the moral sentiments play a role, but so does the notion of fair play. The innovatory cycle of creative destruction is a source of welfare to the whole but of diswelfare to the part. It is not the 'fault' of the redundant that their industries are superseded by progress. Nor is it the 'fault' of the out-of-work that monopoly capital makes restricted capacity a fact of business life. Nowadays, Schumpeter wrote just before Wall Street went down, 'competition is admirable but dead' – and that in all fairness means the State: 'Support to the unemployed is an all but inevitable element in our economic system.' (Schumpeter, 1926/27b:159, 160).

The State has the duty of 'providing adequately for the unemployed' (Schumpeter, 1942a:70). It must do so, needless to say, '*without impairing the conditions of further economic development*' (Schumpeter, 1942a:70). Growth is the end that makes the short-run dislocation worthwhile. Growth, importantly, is also the means that makes the welfare transfers 'not only a tolerable but a light burden' (Schumpeter, 1942a:69). Social benefits were evidently not to be so generous as to constitute a disincentive to search, so open-ended as to postpone the long-term return to growth-enhancing work. Given a welfare system that does not put a jinx on future affluence, however, the welfare State can reliably depend on the incremental dividend to ensure that 'adequate provision can be made for the unemployed' (Schumpeter,

1942a:383n). So long as the welfare buffer is there to cushion the fall, no full employment policy is needed save economic growth itself.

12.3.2 Inflation

Schumpeter had been a witness to the hyperinflations of the 1920s that had called into question the viability both of the market order and of liberal democracy. He was in no doubt that rising prices could cause great harm: 'A state of perennial inflationary pressure will have, qualitatively, all the effects of weakening the social framework of society and of strengthening subversive tendencies.' (Schumpeter, 1950b:428). Lenin said that there was no surer way to destabilise a country than to debauch its currency. Schumpeter too acknowledged that rising prices could cause the ultimate collapse: 'Nothing undermines the framework of a society as does inflation.' (Schumpeter, 1950b:427). It is a sobering thought in a market economy where demand-pull and cost-push must forever bite the hand that frees them.

Capitalism thrives because the banks are willing to lend. New money adds value precisely because it papers private property into productivity and advance: 'Credit is essentially the creation of purchasing power for the purpose of transferring it to the entrepreneur.' (Schumpeter, 1912b:107). Finance allows new firms to enter and new experiments to be tried. It facilitates the quick formation of capital without new savings having first to be accumulated out of new incomes in the slow, laborious sense of Keynes.

Schumpeter, like Hilferding and other Central Europeans, saw the investment banker as a modern missionary who unblocks the channels of action. In the words of Eduard März:

> The investment banks played a decisive role in the genesis of capitalism during the last decades before World War I. Hilferding regards the dominance of finance capital as characteristic only of a certain stage of historical development; Schumpeter, on the other hand, sees it as a general social category. For him, bank credit created out of thin air is the demiurge of economic progress. (März, 1991:23).

A demiurge, certainly, but also a threat. All factors fully employed, prices thereupon rise since the money supply is demand-led by competition and speculation that tirelessly seek to bid away scarce inputs which cannot be increased.

The price revolution of the fifteenth and sixteenth centuries had shown how feudal society as well as orderly exchange could be subverted from within by the influx of gold and silver and the consequent expansion in the demand for goods. Speaking in the Austrian National Assembly in 1919, Schumpeter warned that it could all happen again: 'The problem of inflation brought about by banknotes is a very serious one. This is the main cause of our high level of prices. Manipulative profiteering is only a minor occurrence, which is only possible because people's pockets are full of money.' (Schumpeter, 1919:328). Writing as he did that rising prices had become a 'part of the mechanism' (Schumpeter, 1939:II, 449), one would have expected him to inveigh strongly against the money-on-demand permissiveness of credit-created capitalism that contained in its very logic the seeds of systemic distortion and decomposition. In fact, and while fully aware of the threat, Schumpeter was surprisingly determined to play down its immediacy.

There was the cycle: prices rise in the upswing but fall in the recession. There was the reflux: borrowing, because it must be repaid, means autodeflation in the backwash to any rise. There were scale economies and the productivity trend: 'The fall in prices is a symptom of the achievements of development.' (Schumpeter, 1912a:501). There was innovation itself: improved technology ensures that unit cost goes down and output expands. If there is more demand, then there is more supply as well. Plausible as they are, none of these reasons accounts for a genuine turning point. Schumpeter does not take up the big topic of a money-supply ceiling. He seems to be confounding the factors that can contain the rate of change with the credit control that alone can bring money-fuelled inflation to a halt.

There is, however, a conspicuous exception to his general complacency. This is the 'inflationary financing of government expenditure' (Schumpeter, 1939:I, 261). Where easy credit and unlimited paper are used to fund a permanent deficit, there the irresponsible and excessive burden of public spending paid for without compensating withdrawals must necessarily unleash an unjustifiable rise in price. The politicians become addicted to painless public finance. The share of the State ratchets up as downswing benefits harden into secular entitlements. It would clearly be a mistake, blaming borrowing for the rise, to 'throw away the baby with the bath' (Schumpeter, 1939:I, 295). Paper per se is not at fault. Inflation may be a monetary phenomenon but it is a political failure as well.

Demand-pull is not the whole of the story. Inflation can also be the consequence of cost-push. The trade unions of today have wholeheartedly absorbed the capitalist ethos of power and gain despite their protestations that they have 'renounced allegiance to the scheme of values of the private-property economy' (Schumpeter, 1950b:426). Full employment (whether the consequence of rapid growth or of contra-cyclical policies) means that their demands are likely to be approved: businesses are in competition for labour and are prepared to concede the scarcity rate. In a buoyant economy there is in any case no pressing need to dig in their heels: higher pay can be passed on as higher prices without any lasting fall in the profit margin. Rising interest rates and stringent money-supply controls would keep within limits the overheating that gives the unions and the employers the opportunity to make their upward revisions. Yet macroeconomic restraints can also be a cause of unemployment and slower growth. Wages and prices being inflexible downwards, the burden falls on real variables and the democratic consensus is put at risk. Weak government and not the private sector, here as before, is the ultimate cause of the inflation. Even so, it is the unions that cast the first stone.

Just as the government caves in to macro-monetary validation, so it is too timid to launch a direct assault on the sectionalism that lies behind the push. The unions, on their own or in alliance with other redistributive coalitions, resist any threat to their market dominance: 'The power of labor is almost strong enough in itself ... to prevent any reversal which goes beyond an occasional scaling off of rough edges.' (Schumpeter, 1950b:426). A government would have to be very strong indeed to rise to the challenge of industrial discipline. Labour being 'of all things the most difficult to socialize', Schumpeter observes, 'the road to solution may be tortuous and long' (Schumpeter, 1942a:379).

Schumpeter does not say what form the requisite compromises and restrictions would take, only that in the right circumstances it would probably prove possible to bend union power to the public interest. In England, 'the chances for successful solution by the political method of democracy are greater than they are anywhere else' (Schumpeter, 1942a:379). In less consensual societies, the State will have to fall back upon the dictatorial method of compulsion. The Soviets could not have nationalised their industry or planned their economy if they had not first mounted an attack on free credit markets, free collective bargaining and an unreformed union movement which had no reason not to push for pay.

Rising prices are 'unavoidable in the present political pattern' (Schumpeter, 1942a:374). Economics teaches that monetary and fiscal prudence on the demand side, liberalisation of restrictive union cartels on the side of supply, can slow down or arrest altogether the upward drift in price. The techniques and the tools are not the problem. The problem is the political will. Long-run health presupposes short-run dislocation: 'Nobody can counteract threatening inflation without also interfering with production.' (Schumpeter, 1942a:392). Politicians, forever focused on the upcoming vote-value, cannot afford to take the risk.

Inflation is not a monetary problem so much as it is a problem of the people who control the money. The political reality is that 'all really effective measures are unpopular' (Schumpeter, 1948:242). No politician in the democratic market can speculate in short-term unpopularity even if the curative recession would maximise his long-term standing: 'Nobody has attained political maturity who does not understand that policy is politics. Economists are particularly apt to ignore these truths.' (Schumpeter, 1950a:441). The result is that 'inflation runs on by common consent' (Schumpeter, 1948:242). Rising prices, historically speaking, 'were not stopped because the people who counted politically did not *want* to stop them': 'Each cabinet felt that this task might be more fitly undertaken by its successors who were welcome to spoil their electoral chances by doing so.' (Schumpeter, 1948:241, 242). Each cabinet was absolutely clear that the cat had to be belled. No cabinet, however, was prepared to commit political suicide and do the belling for itself.

Rising prices on the one hand, government failure on the other – profit fixing and wage fixing become the desperate last resort of party politicians afraid that monetary ceilings combined with union-bashing legislation will precipitately close down their shop: 'Perennial inflationary pressure can play an important part in the eventual conquest of the private-enterprise system by the bureaucracy.' (Schumpeter, 1950b:430). Schumpeter had observed with serious reservations the attempts of the Office of Price Administration – it was run by his young Harvard colleague J.K. Galbraith – to pull values out of the air in the over-bureaucratised political culture of the Second World War. Economics by fiat, he informed the self-styled philosopher-rulers, could only distort market signals and ultimately paralyse the confused.

A body such as the OPA necessarily wastes scarce time on negotiations and debates. Its edicts 'require, in order to produce their result, experience and ability that I do not see' (Schumpeter, 1942a:392). Directives are an 'obstacle to the expansion of output' (Schumpeter, 1942a:387). Reducing 'the degree of economic efficiency of the system' (Schumpeter, 1942a:387), they reduce the amount of public spending that can be funded through growth. Pay floors curtail job opportunities. They also encourage firms to pass on the supra-competitive chalice: 'Inflation comes through the payroll.' (Schumpeter, 1942a:391). It should surprise no one that a body such as the OPA will inevitably become 'highly unpopular' (Schumpeter, 1942a:392). It will become highly unpopular because it damages the prospects for the real sector but does nothing to prevent the nominal sector from one day bursting through its banks.

Controls impair the performance of the free enterprise economy: 'The business organism cannot function according to design when its most important "parameters of action" – wages, prices, interest – are transferred to the political sphere and there dealt with according to the requirements of the political game.' (Schumpeter, 1942a:386). Demand management will fail because price stabilisation is incompatible with the full employment guarantee. Direct controls will fail because they 'upset apple carts' and represent 'some half-baked socialism' (Schumpeter, 1942a:392). As one makeshift fails, so the next stop-gap is tried. Gradually but assuredly, the market is crowded out and State directive becomes the rule: 'In other words, price control may result in a surrender of private enterprise to public authority, that is, in a big stride toward the perfectly planned economy.' (Schumpeter, 1950b:430). Symbolically, perhaps, those were the last words that Schumpeter ever wrote. A few hours later he was dead.

High incomes are taxed – the wealthy, well-stocked with savings, simply continue to consume. The currency is devalued – expensive imports push up the cost of living. Rising prices de facto expropriate the *rentier* – the State itself has to provide the funds for investment. The frictions caused by one regulation lead to a demand for another regulation. That regulation in turn will spring another leak. The road leads to serfdom. At the end is the State: 'A situation may well emerge in which most people consider complete planning as the smallest of possible evils.' (Schumpeter, 1950b:430).

People lose faith in capitalism. They demand a stable order in which inflation will not redistribute or disrupt. What they fail to understand is that it is not the market which is responsible for the falling value of their money. Rather, it is the politicians, because the planners refuse with Canute to respect the unbuckable logic of the macroeconomic flow. The leaders should invest in the social fabric by keeping fiduciary money within the strict limits set by total transactions. Instead they over-expand and then try to control. Inflation is not a cause of socialism. Politicians are, since they refuse to trust the market that would have kept unwarranted rises in check.

13. The cycle

A number of economists in the 1920s and 1930s were seeking to explain the fluctuations that were as troubling as the trend was good. These included Spiethoff, Pigou, Myrdal, Ohlin, Cassel, Robertson, the ubiquitous Hayek and Mises, Wesley Clair Mitchell, building on earlier authors like Marx, Jevons, Marshall, Bagehot and Tugan-Baranowsky. Economic statistics were becoming available, allowing investigators to support their analyses with facts. The downturn after the post-war restocking boom, closely followed by the Wall Street Crash in 1929, lent urgency to the possibility that dynamics could turn malign. Schumpeter knew that great issues were at stake when he entered into the debate.

Schumpeter had touched on cycles in 1910 in his article on 'Das Wesen der Wirtschaftskrisen' and in 1911 in his *Theory of Economic Development*. He was still touching on cycles in his late works *Capitalism, Socialism and Democracy* and *History of Economic Analysis*. In 1927 there had been the article in *Economica* on 'The explanation of the business cycle'. In 1939 there was *Business Cycles*. Published in two volumes and over 1000 pages in length, it was Schumpeter's first book in a quarter of a century of papers. It was destined to become a classic that nobody read. The *General Theory* in 1936 (rapidly dynamised into a growth-model by Harrod and Domar) had captured the imagination of the younger generation, while the outbreak of the Second World War (much as Sarajevo had done for his earlier *Economic Development*) meant that the economics of moving disequilibrium had effectively been eclipsed by the bullets and the shells.

Cycles are not *obiter dicta* hovering like uninvited frictions around a straight-line trend. As far as Schumpeter is concerned, it is steady expansion that is the exception, the contours and the turnings that are the very essence of the capitalist way: 'Cycles are not like tonsils, separable things that might be treated by themselves, but are, like the beat of the heart, of the essence of the organism that displays them.' (Schumpeter, 1939:I, v). Cycles are not the attending midwife who helps things to happen. Rather, they are the main event, the very birth of wealth itself.

Cycles, superficially a disruption, are in truth the roller-coaster ride that economic prosperity is obliged to take: 'The cyclical process is not an incident but the whole of what is specifically capitalistic in economic life.' (Schumpeter, 1939:I, 405n). This chapter, the penultimate chapter in this book, probes into the origins and functions of the progress-bringing ups and downs. Section 1, Evolution in waves, shows that the Kitchins, the Juglars and the Kondratieffs are turned loose by entrepreneurship and made possible by credit. Section 2, Peaks and troughs, explains that the wealth of nations grows at an uneven pace because it is in the nature of the venturesome that they do not innovate to fixed meal times or live by the clock. Section 3, Continuity and breach, amplifies Schumpeter's vision of cycles as enterprise to show that even in the turmoil of disequilibrium there survives a still harbour of memories and artefacts. Conservatism is possible even in a changing world. In its essence, however, the sequence of permutations is the *stets verneint* that questions all the answers. Enterprise through market is evolution. In the absence of microeconomic restlessness even macroeconomic instability will not make any sense.

13.1 EVOLUTION IN WAVES

Marshall's evolution is the adaptive marginalism of small changes and Darwinian incrementalism: 'Economic evolution is gradual .... Its forward movements are never sudden.' (Marshall, 1890a:xi). Schumpeter's evolution is a herd of elephants that recycles the marginal progressiveness into the permanent revolution: 'Evolution is lopsided, discontinuous, disharmonious by nature .... The history of capitalism is studded with violent bursts and catastrophes.' (Schumpeter, 1939:I, 102). Marshall's evolution is slow and steady, an English summer's journey in the direction of a decent cup of tea. Schumpeter's evolution is a catalogue of upsets, a four-stage succession of prosperity, recession, depression, recovery that is the blessing and curse of nations that make development and not statics their quest.

Cycles are what capitalism does and is: 'Analyzing business cycles means neither more nor less than analyzing the economic process of the capitalist era.' (Schumpeter, 1939:I, v). The subtitle of *Business Cycles* proclaims where in comparative institutions its author expected his economics to begin and end: 'A theoretical, historical and statistical analysis of the capitalist process'. Schumpeter as late as 1937 was thinking of entitling his big book on white-knuckle advance *The Waves of Capitalist Evolution* (Stolper, 1994:58n).

13.1.1 Expectations and Outturns

Schumpeter always insisted on a continuing dialogue between the theory and the fact, the conjecture and the observation. Pure deduction without the support of evidence is, he said, only a skeleton without flesh; while raw data, unfocused and unfiltered, must forever be a 'meaningless jumble' where the

'Nonsense Induction' (Schumpeter, 1939:I, 30, 32) is not first given an *ex ante* or a lens. A two-way process was indispensable if the recorded swings in capitalism's uneven development were properly to be documented and understood.

In *Economic Development* Schumpeter had already ventured into the logic. In *Business Cycles* he sought to quantify and depict. Tracing his time series through 150 years from the British 'Industrial Revolution' in the 1780s to his own 1930s in the deep valley of its trough, he made it his objective to pinpoint the highs and the lows in order to explain why modern capitalism was also the age of fluctuation: 'It is obvious that only detailed historic knowledge can definitively answer most of the questions of individual causation and mechanism and without it the study of time series must remain inconclusive, and theoretical analysis empty.' (Schumpeter, 1939:I, 220). Each discrete observation was a whole unto itself. Given well-researched recurrences, however, it would still prove possible to generalise from the patterns and to pick out the regularities.

The detail is impressive, all the more so because Schumpeter was working without a team of assistants. Ironically, however, there is a sense in which the coverage is too restricted to be satisfying. A full account would have to track the mutations in property rights, business rules, lasting networks, social attitudes, fiscal policy, tariff protection, trade unionism, the Welfare State. It would have to distinguish inter-temporally between competitive capitalism and its corporate successor that so greatly altered the action and reaction times over a century and a half of transition and discontinuity. It would have to distinguish inter-spatially between the experience of countries as different as Britain, the United States and Germany in order to sift through the socio-political heterogeneities, to draw clear inferences from the unquestionably shared. Schumpeter said that the empirics of cycles had no need to bring in 'the entire range of the economics and sociology of capitalism' (Schumpeter, 1939:I, 279n). Even with his *ceteris paribus*, he said, it would still be possible to explain the periodicity and predict the amplitude. Other economists will not be convinced that the institutional foliage can so easily be pruned away from the productive fundamentals. A theory of the cycle which concentrates on the impact of sunspots or the disproportionality of plant might plausibly be in a position to abstract pure economics from its anthropocentric packaging. A theory which says that cycles are the envelope of thinking people making novel choices is less likely to be able to do so.

His evidence collected, Schumpeter found that *the* business cycle was in fact a nest of *three* business cycles, interlocked and overlapping. The first is the Kitchin, largely an inventory cycle, of 40 months. The second is the Juglar (comparable to Marx's 'decennial cycle'), with a median value of 9–10 years.

The third is the long-wave Kondratieff (beginning, historically, in 1789 with steam, in 1842 with the railways, in 1898 with electricity, the telephone and the motor car). Each Kondratieff has a circuit of 50–60 years. One Kondratieff lasts for six Juglars. One Juglar encompasses three Kitchins. Eighteen Kitchins add up to one Kondratieff. The recurrence is stable, rhythmic and predictable: Keynes too, referring to good and bad years, insists that it is the 'regularity of time-sequence and of duration which justifies us in calling it a *cycle*' (Keynes, 1936:313). The ratios between the nested cycles obtain 'not as an average but in every individual case' (Schumpeter, 1939:I, 174). Although there had been only three Kondratieffs since the world began, Schumpeter was certain that his sample yielded a good impression of the population that was to come. He was convinced that his facts meant what they said.

The confidence itself should set the alarm bells ringing. Schumpeter as a theoretician was the ultimate prophet of surprise, the high priest of creative destruction whose most representative thesis ought in all fairness to have been the following footnote: 'Cycles are an irregular phenomenon playing in an environment disturbed by additional irregularities.' (Schumpeter, 1939:I, 174n). Schumpeter as a statistician, however, was the undoubting Thomas, the well-documented scientist who could show that under capitalism even randomness arrives on time. The latter Schumpeter could predict the uniformity in length of each kind of cycle on the basis that his facts do not lie. The former Schumpeter had to question the very possibility of prediction. Cycles result from innovations. Flashes of insight seldom occur to plan.

Intuitively, there is something in the dialogue that does not sound right. Different departures require different time-spans to work themselves through the system. Different technologies have different capital–labour ratios. Discontinuities and kinks come from extra-cyclical exogeneities such as wars, gold discoveries, the globalisation of know-how, imitation through liberalised trade, intra-firm networks within multinational conglomerates, improved communications that speed up the transmission of novelty and shorten the feedback loop. Differences and externalities abound. Strangely, they seem to make no dent at all in the data. The invisibility of the trend-setting should set the alarm bells ringing. Schumpeter the theoretician lacks the tools to explain the recurrences that Schumpeter the statistician had managed to quantify.

Schumpeter cannot account for the uniform length of the measured cycles. Nor can he say how imbalance in a Kitchin and/or a Kondratieff can coexist with a general (not merely a partial) equilibrium in a Kondratieff and/or a Juglar that is superimposed on top. Clemence and Doody are hardly alone when they declare themselves thoroughly mystified: 'Statistical difficulties are associated with identifying different orders of equilibrium. Each type of cycle is supposed to arise out of a neighborhood of equilibrium. How can one, let alone three, equilibrium neighborhoods be identified, statistically or otherwise?' (Clemence and Doody, 1950:76). Tichy says that he simply cannot imagine what would be happening in an oil-plus-water economy where Juglar people were satisfied with their stock control but Kondratieff people were actively experimenting with product development: 'What should the system of market-clearing prices look like under such conditions?' (Tichy, 1984:80–81). The data-set is over-determined. Using the same explanation for the 60 years that it does for the 40 months, the underlying theory is just the reverse. Monocausal explanations come apart when the facts, which do not lie, speak only in a whisper, and only in Albanian, and only on Tuesdays by invitation or appointment only.

13.1.2 Innovation and Instability

Economists agree that trade cycles are a fact. Economists do not agree on the fundamental reason why saw-tooth always goes with growth. Cycles might be caused by exogenous shocks such as earthquakes, floods or droughts bringing about fluctuations in price-inelastic agricultural produce. They might be caused by gain-seeking banks pushing monetary interest below the real rate in order to expand their supply of credit. Cycles could be the consequence of replacement and reordering; of inter-sectoral mismatch; of inflexibilities and bottlenecks. Cycles could be the result of an excess or a deficiency in current real savings; or of sudden switches in consumer loyalties and demands; or of lemming-like herd instincts that act while the acting is hot; or of investment lags magnified into centrifugal misapprehension through multiplier overshooting. There are in truth as many theories of the cycle as there are learned journals that thin out the trees. Few of them have much in common with Schumpeter's vision of aggregative fluctuations as microeconomic initiative. Cycles come from the presence or absence of 'new combinations' and 'doing things differently' (Schumpeter, 1939:I, 84). Cycles come from imaginative entrepreneurship that, acting as the prime mover, is responsible for the oscillations even as it brings about the progress.

Invention is not the cause: discovery and execution are 'two entirely different things' (Schumpeter, 1939:I, 85). The trigger is not *ab initio* investigation but rather the industrial application of science and technology: 'The pure new idea is not adequate by itself to lead to implementation .... It must be taken up by a strong character and implemented through his influence.' (Schumpeter, 1912a:543). It is not the power of ideas but the power of power that gets things done.

Schumpeter does not construct a sophisticated sociology of creativity to explain where basic science comes from. That in itself provides an interesting insight into his theory of motivation. As far as he was concerned, investigators become excited to find out why sodium nitrite turns blue for the same reason that explorers risk their lives on a peak because it's there. Leaving Bonn in 1932, he left behind the message that *Fragelust* – 'the search for that which we call truth' – was not a means to an end but the nature of the beast: 'The development of science only began when scientific questions were asked out of a desire to inquire, out of an interest in the game of asking questions.' (Schumpeter, 1932:599). One man liked to watch Jenny spinning and another man was fascinated by the steam from his teapot. In the one case as in the other, what happened next owed little or nothing to the desire to make his fortune and very much to what Adam Smith calls 'Wonder', the instinctual surprise of the once-tranquil mind when confronted by something 'new and singular', unrecognisable and unclassified: 'We remain still uncertain and undetermined where to place it, or what to think of it .... What sort of thing can that be? What is that like? are the questions which, upon such an occasion, we are all naturally disposed to ask.' (Smith, 1795:37–8). Schumpeter shared the insight of Adam Smith that inquiry is curiosity long before it becomes use. Watt investigating the kettle was pushing back the frontiers first and foremost because he was Watt: 'Nothing of significance results in private or public life, in the arts or the sciences, that is not an absolute value for the acting individual.' (Schumpeter, 1932:599). So long as men and women lie awake scheming to get to Mars because Mars is more of a challenge even than a good game of chess, so long will science be the unintended outcome of disinterested probing because that is what the explorer does. An impatient concern with profit and loss is another way of saying that mankind will never get out of the caves and move upwards and onwards with Arkwright and Watt: 'We should still be without most of the conveniences of modern life if physicists had been as eager for immediate "application" as most economists.' (Schumpeter, 1933:101).

Schumpeter does not regard it as important for a theory of the cycle to be able to explain why steam power, nuclear power, microelectronics, jet engines happened to emerge at the precise moment in time that they did. What matters exclusively to him is the adoption phase that translates the exogenous breakthrough into the marketable product and sentences left-behind know-how to unanticipated obsolescence: 'A new idea will virtually never be taken notice of without the action of a recognised leader.' (Schumpeter, 1912a:544). Discoveries – 'Gold discoveries did little to help the discoverers' – are stillborn in the absence of the 'leaderly personality' who can rescue them from the shadows of neglect: 'Without people who can fulfill the role of leader these inventions would die a natural death.' (Schumpeter, 1912a:480, 487, 544). Science by itself is only latent potential in the absence of the entrepreneur who breathes life into the inert: 'The individual acts of realization and not the possibilities themselves are what concern us.' (Schumpeter, 1939:I, 9).

Innovation is what makes science into commerce. The entrepreneur is the genius who makes the drawing board into a subsequent boom. As for discovery itself, invention per se is merely the platform that gives the endogenous the freedom to aim high.

Invention typically runs ahead of innovation: 'New discoveries are continuously being added to the existing store of knowledge.' (Schumpeter, 1912b:79). An application 'need by no means be founded upon a discovery scientifically new' (Schumpeter, 1912b:66) in a public-goods paradise where 'preexisting knowledge is made use of' (Schumpeter, 1939:I, 85) and there is consequently no rush to create new possibilities: 'Knowledge – scientific and other – is always far in advance of actual practice.' (Schumpeter, 1927b:27). The entrepreneur need never be discouraged by the lack of something to do. Nor need he ever become an inventor himself lest otherwise his business lack the know-how that it needs.

Invention is possible without the extra-industrial shock of a sudden new demand. Not only is it possible, it is probable as well: 'The stock of technical knowledge increases independently. That would happen even in a static economy.' (Schumpeter, 1912a:479–80). New test tubes are not really the prerequisite where old test tubes have already made available the technology. Schumpeter, as Oakley writes, 'saw potential entrepreneurial agents as facing a more or less given and unlimited "pool" of inventions and relevant knowledge' (Oakley, 1990:127). Some new discoveries will become history-shaping innovations before the ink is dry. Most, however, will only be adopted after a lag: 'A new possibility, despite being widely understood, can lead a fruitless and shadowy existence for centuries without having any outside impact.' (Schumpeter, 1912a:544). New possibilities will be taken from a stock so stable that its inflows cannot account for a cyclical swing. The storehouse of the past, here as elsewhere, makes possible the free-wheeling new speculation.

The point is an important one. Development is jerky 'exclusively *because the new combinations are not, as one would expect according to general principles of probability, evenly distributed through time*' (Schumpeter, 1912b:223). Development is jerky because new things are bunched and new initiatives concentrated. The unevenness is a fact of modern life. What must be emphasized is that the see-saw has little to do with science and everything to do with adoption. Invention makes a valuable contribution to well-being through adding some serendipity at the margin to an ongoing pool. Innovation, however, makes a greater contribution still. Innovation alone determines which fish will be taken out of the common darkness. Innovation alone dictates what potential will be commercialised into a tradeable for sale: 'As soon ... as an innovation is put into business practice, we have a process which arises from, and is an element of, the economic life of its time, and not something that acts on it from without. In no case, therefore, is invention an external factor.' (Schumpeter, 1939:I, 9). It is not discovery but its exploitation that pipes the tune to which the succeeding cycles dance.

13.1.3 Credit

The cycle is about fishing. It is also about banks. While Schumpeter does in places acknowledge that 'the power to accumulate reserves' (Schumpeter, 1928:70) reduces the gate-keeper importance of credit-creation, he never correlates past profits, internally generated, with a new cycle's investment or suggests that venture capital is supply-constrained by savings. He has no need to do so. The ability to develop promising projects, Schumpeter argues, will never be blocked by a lack of finance precisely because the capitalist economy is normally able to rely upon demand-led lending. It is 'the *monetary complement* of innovation' (Schumpeter, 1939:I, 111).

The commercial banks must meet the reserve requirements of the central bank. Those ratios make an 'elastic' magnitude into a 'definite' one (Schumpeter, 1912b:114). Below that ceiling, not fully loaned up, they can create as many spendable claims as they can market. Schumpeter had himself lived through the Continental hyperinflations of the 1920s when dishoarding, falling real balances, accelerating velocity, recourse to money-substitutes had together conspired to bring the market order to its knees. The worst-case experience seems not to have convinced him that escalating credit will normally be enough to convert a boom into a bust.

If anything, the banks to Schumpeter were a force for macroeconomic stability. Lenders, taking on the risk of loss, have a pecuniary incentive not to give in too easily to the 'get-rich-quick morals' (Schumpeter, 1939:I, 150) of bubble-economy speculators. Also, the banks themselves fulfil an entrepreneurial function in that it is they who must recognise potential talent without a track record: just as the final consumer will ultimately do *ex post*, they must select *ex ante* the new combinations most likely to produce good results. Banks hold back on loans where they fear that over-expansion will leave their asset-liability position unprotected. Banks put up interest rates when they observe that prices rise in the boom. Banks, in short, exercise a moderating influence in the cycle. Entrepreneurs demand money to spend themselves into the upswing. It is the task of the bankers, demonstrating prudence, to know when to turn them down.

Credit is correlated with growth. Money is fully neutral neither in the downswing nor in the boom.

In the recession, bank lending expands real output since there is spare capacity in plant and labour. Paper originating outside the circular flow here leans effectively against the prevailing winds. In the boom, moreover, the banks can provide loanable funds that make possible productivity gains. Full employment need not buffer an end to growth. Bank money can pay for the taking in of slack.

Sooner or later, of course, the scarcity of physical inputs must mean that the crowding in of one project will necessarily spell the crowding out of another. All excess used up, the businessman can only 'withdraw the producers' goods which he needs from their previous employments': 'No goods and certainly no new goods correspond to the newly created purchasing power.' (Schumpeter, 1912b:106, 109). Even in the non-Keynesian case, however, where new combinations in presuppose old combinations out, the banks can still play an active part in raising the rate of growth. It is they who reallocate the funds: they in that way have the chance to back the winners in the zero-sum race. Besides that, their continued lending causes price rises in excess of wage rises. Forced savings is *de facto* redistribution of the national product in favour of the profit recipients who are the most likely to go for investment – and, through investment, for growth.

13.2 PEAKS AND TROUGHS

Schumpeter's cycle is traced out by the changes in the national product. It is a feature not simply of the Marshallian long run (the time frame in which fixed plant becomes explicitly variable) but *a fortiori* of the Marshallian secular period (the self-transcending phase in which innovation replaces old know-how with new). Because, in contrast to Keynesian short-termism, neither the capital stock nor the production function is a constant, Schumpeter's cycle cannot be said to be traced out by changes in the pool of jobs. There is no expectation that employment will move in step with value added: 'There is no unique or simple relation between employment (number of hours worked per week) and output.' (Schumpeter, 1939:I, 510). This is not to say that employment will never vary over the cycle, only that proportionality cannot be predicted. Just as there can be jobless growth, so there can be job-neutral fluctuations.

Schumpeter's cycle is an aggregative series. Although single-industry innovations are the trigger and the spark, the real focus is on epoch-making developments that administer a shock to the macroeconomy as a whole. Every cycle originates in place, not just in time: 'The boom is never general at first, but centres in one branch or a few branches of industry, leaving the other areas undisturbed, and subsequently only affects the latter in a different, and secondary, manner.' (Schumpeter, 1912b:233). The cycle originates in a leading sector and not in a historical invisibility. An innovation in pins will not make the economy spring into life. Railways, steel, motor cars, electricity will be the more powerful catalyst. Innovation must be a major change, a fundamental change. It cannot be an unpromising triviality that affects only the trailblazer and his family.

13.2.1 From Trough to Peak

Schumpeter's cycle begins in the tranquil equilibrium either of steady-state *stasis* or of repeat-order growth occasioned by additional inputs blended according to the well-established best practice. The basepoint is a circular flow that is happy with things as they are. Because there is no innovation and no entrepreneurship, there is no profit and no interest. Nor is there any doubt that the future will be other than the past carried on.

It is into this placid lake that the nonconformist casts a stone. Excited by new possibilities and not discouraged by social resistance, the business leader deviates from the norm and commits the initial act of discontinuity. Going against the 'done thing', unafraid to strike out into something new, he is the first mover in an economy where before him there was no mover at all. Should he succeed, he will reap the short-run windfall that is the pioneer's prize.

He will do so, moreover, without any risk to such assets as he may own. The initial innovator, 'a debtor by the nature of his economic function' (Schumpeter, 1912b:103), borrows from the banks in order to try new experiments. Presumably there was saving even in the equilibrium state: repeat-order investment could itself have created the income which made available, Keynes-like, the loanable funds. Possibly it is money creation that pays for the transformation: while it is not clear why banks would supply the *primum mobile* at zero interest, perhaps the reason is that they are already lending for final utility and automatically apply the consumption rate. Whatever the source, the seed corn is forthcoming and the new idea is made into a fact.

In the experimentation phase potential competitors will be afraid to chance the gamble. In the medium term, success once demonstrated, they will follow the leader and invest in imitation: 'The swarm-like appearance of entrepreneurs ... is the only cause of the boom.' (Schumpeter, 1912b:231). In the medium term the early entrants – there are 'crowds of them, which is what the boom consists in' (Schumpeter, 1927b:33) – will be able to secure a share in the pioneer's super-normal profit. Their acumen in backing the winner is proof that even mimicry is an entrepreneurial act. It is entrepreneurial to decide whether to conduct R & D in-house or whether to copy another firm's new initiative: 'An essential aspect of real Schumpeterian competition is that firms do not know *ex ante* whether it pays to try to be an innovator or an imitator.' (Nelson and Winter, 1982:286). It is entrepreneurial to know *what* product-line to enter; to *which* learning-by-doing to assign priority; *how* to interpret market signals where monopolistic competition makes brands qualitatively different; *whether* to imitate the best practice or merely the average practice in a heterogeneous industry where different firms reach the same end differently. It is entrepreneurial to recognise *when* it is safe to move in. It is entrepreneurial to act quickly *when* it is time to get out. Being entrepreneurial in the sense of copying is not precisely the same as being entrepreneurial in the sense of *new* combinations. Stranded between Kirzner and Schumpeter as it may well be, there is no mistaking the entrepreneurial contribution that intelligent emulation makes to the theory of the cycle. In the medium term the imitator receives a share in the monopoly rent. He does so because he has spotted a market niche and moved his productive assets into the void.

The medium term does not last forever. Sooner or later the hog cycle and the fallacy of composition must put paid to the super-normal prize: 'The individual entrepreneur, interested only in planning his own enterprise, takes no account of the swarm-like following of others, and so comes to grief.' (Schumpeter, 1912b:231). What one can do, all cannot. The first mimics score a valuable return. The subsequent clusters, bidding up the input and over-producing the output, spoil things for all. It is evidently the time-lag between the original experiment and the mass-produced copy that accounts for the upswing: 'The average time which must elapse before the new products appear ... fundamentally explains the length of the boom.' (Schumpeter, 1912b:233). The boom is about speed. It is about the willingness to adapt.

13.2.2 From Peak to Trough

The boom is powered by balance sheets and not by mass psychology. Followers in the upswing are inspired not by the unthinking herd instinct in the sense of Bagehot but by the pecuniary lure of proven profit that attracts new blood to a tried-and-tested gold field. The upper turning point occurs when the volume of entry simply exhausts the choice set. The over-supply of output, expanded too rapidly to be absorbed, then triggers off a deflation as rivals undersell and the panic-stricken seek to salvage what they can.

Speculators liquidate stocks and cause values to spiral down: 'Prices fall because they have fallen.' (Schumpeter, 1941:350). Past loans mature and must be repaid: the reflux contracts the money supply and, augmenting the over-shooting, puts further pressure on prices. Firms which incurred debts at prosperity prices must sell at contracts below cost: trading with borrowed money, they have no reserves or guarantees to shield them from bankruptcy.

As the knock-ons knock down the dominoes and the failures (including the bank failures) spread, so the reason becomes clear why Schumpeter was so much in sympathy with Clément Juglar's dictum 'La cause unique de la dépression, c'est la prosperité' (cited in Schumpeter, 1927b:29). Optimism, as Marshall says, breeds optimism in the boom: 'Confidence by growing would cause itself to grow.' (Marshall, 1879:155). It cannot continue growing for all time. The upper turning point reached, the market becomes overcrowded and the laughter must give way to tears.

Easy money in good times means '*over*indebtedness' (Schumpeter, 1939:I, 147) in the crisis. Banks – 'frightened banks' (Schumpeter, 1927b:41) – call in loans and reinforce pessimistic expectations. It is not difficult in the circumstances to conclude, in Haberler's words, that the upper turning point is always and everywhere a monetary phenomenon: 'The proximate cause for the breakdown of the boom is almost invariably the inability or unwillingness of the banking system to continue the expansion.' (Haberler, 1937:47). Schumpeter, like Haberler, recognises the importance of liquidity in the cycle. Even so, he is enough of a microeconomist to be reluctant to blame the ups and downs on the banks. Lending may be the 'heart', he writes, but it can never be the 'brain' (Schumpeter, 1939:I, 127). The initiator of the credit relationship is not the financier but the innovator. It is the borrower, not the lender, who in good times stimulates prosperity through 'brisk expenditure' and who in bad times falls victim to the 'elimination of antiquated elements of the industrial structure' (Schumpeter, 1942a:68). It is the demand for money, not the supply of money that, taking the active lead, makes the cycle go round.

Microeconomic bullishness is the cause. Microeconomic efficiency is the consequence. Schumpeter believed that the trough that followed the peak ought sensibly to be seen as the visit to the doctor that was the downswing's great contribution to the macroeconomy's good health. Recession is a process that fills a function, 'a time of harvesting the results of preceding innovation' (Schumpeter, 1939:I, 143). Not a misfortune but an investment in growth to come, the 'complete destruction' of the 'hopelessly unadapted' (Schumpeter, 1912b:253) was a necessary weeding-out that is another name for what capitalism does: 'Capitalism is not gentle to the capitalist.' (Schumpeter, 1941:351). Creative destruction is not gentle to yesterday's dead volcanoes: 'Like human beings, firms are constantly being born that cannot live.' (Schumpeter, 1939:I, 95). Over-shooting and bankruptcy is the real-world version of the Walrasian auction. The winding up of the conspicuously less-fit is Darwinian natural selection unleashed in the High Street. Jumps and disruptions are inevitable in an economic system that is guided by incomplete information. The market has its costs as well as its benefits. In the case of the downswing they are one and the same.

13.2.3 State and Cycle

Logically speaking, Schumpeter should have left it to free markets to put the economy back on its feet. Surprisingly, perhaps, there is throughout his work a guarded defence of macroeconomic policy to smooth out the birth-pangs of the new. American free enterprisers are often strident in their defence of 'don't tread on me'. Schumpeter, like many European liberals, was more willing to make pragmatic use of the State in cases like the cyclical downturn where the market cure would take too long or cut too deep.

Thus, in *Economic Development*, 25 years before Keynes, he was calling for public and private spending to be fine-tuned into the phase of greatest slack: 'The postponement of new construction by government enterprises or by great combines to periods of depression appears ... as an effective means of alleviating the cyclical movement and the danger of crises.' (Schumpeter, 1912b:253). In *Business Cycles*, similarly, he was recommending pump-priming and discretionary reflation when the healing cull was believed to be exacting too high a toll: 'The case for government action in depression ... remains, independently of humanitarian considerations, incomparably stronger than it is in recession.' (Schumpeter, 1939:I, 155). In normal circumstances, like a cough that simply goes away, the process of growth will eventually resume as if guided by an invisible hand that has decided to make new ideas into economic commodities. In extreme circumstances, there will be market failure and with it a need for the State.

In *Business Cycles* Schumpeter also says that wise leaders even under capitalism might be able to even out the cycle through getting the timing right: 'Given sufficient power and insight in a central authority, innovation may of course be planned for in such a way as to minimize disturbances.' (Schumpeter, 1939:II, 697). In *Capitalism, Socialism and Democracy*, he once again turns to the State to manage and civilise the process of economic transformation. Stating that he sees 'no point in trying to conserve obsolescent industries indefinitely', he immediately adds that he wants 'to avoid their coming down with a crash', 'to turn a rout, which may become a center of cumulative depressive effects, into orderly retreat' (Schumpeter, 1942a:90). In the short run the entrepreneurs will be fettered and contained. In the long run they will be free to choose. It is a compromise solution that shows just how much Schumpeter was a (moderate) statist even within the broad rubric of the freedom of exchange.

13.2.4 Innovations and Tautologies

The weeding out of the recession completed, the economy settles into the depression equilibrium. There it will slumber until such a time as the kiss of the entrepreneur will be able to awaken it. It is that moment of revival which constitutes the lower turning point. Behind it lies the apathy of repetition. Before it extends the vista of recovery and prosperity. Each cycle is distinct and independent. No cycle is merely a continuation of the cycle before. What all cycles have in common is that each must start at the lower turning point – and that the economy must slumber in equilibrium forever in the absence of the entrepreneur who shakes things up.

Schumpeter's theory states that the entrepreneur produces an upswing (when he acts) followed by a downswing (when he does not). The obsession with the new combiner leaves the model seriously under-determined: neglectful both of objective magnitudes like the lifespan of capital and of subjective expectations like the *whys* that elucidate the *whens*, monocausal explanations must inevitably be over-simplified and one-dimensional. A more fundamental objection is, however, that of Simon Kuznets, that Schumpeter's theory is not a falsifiable proposition at all but merely 'an obvious tautology': 'An entrepreneur *sui generis* is one who by definition introduces innovations that by definition result in a two-phase cycle.' (Kuznets, 1940:112). An entrepreneur by definition is one who first disturbs a placid accommodation and then refrains from doing so. Since the full-employment phase is effectively an abstention phase, there is in fact only a single active phase in the whole of Schumpeter's cycle: the other three are merely the working out of the new departure's ripple-like consequences. Two phases or four phases or one phase, Kuznets argues, the crucial point is that Schumpeter is not advancing a hypothesis but simply borrowing from the dictionary. The economy takes off because a disturber disturbs. The statement will be true but it hardly sheds much light on the proximate causes, the amplitude and the periodicity.

Schumpeter predicts that innovation will be concentrated in the depression phase. In insisting on equilibrium, he seems to be confusing his methodological baseline with a real-world state which, as Tichy points out, is more the deviation than the norm: 'That every cycle swings out into a state of equilibrium is neither theoretically nor empirically cogent.' (Tichy, 1984:82). It is not in the nature of restless entrepreneurs, motivated by money or driven by sport, to allow such self-perpetuating changelessness ever to emerge. Defeatism and passivity are not in the identikit. Rather than allowing their business to sink into the zero-profit range, entrepreneurs will take corrective action to search and switch, diversify and change. Under-performance equilibrium need never become a fact.

Even if the depression phase did indeed set in, still there is no reason to think that it will be the powerhouse of prosperity. Of course innovation will be valued in bad times: entrepreneurs will be under pressure to spring themselves from the stagnationary trap and will be impelled by survival itself to try out any novelty that might pay its way. Crucially, however, innovation will be valued in good times as well: then profits are high, internally-generated funds are plentiful, expectations are bullish, effective demand is buoyant, imitators are crowding in. Schumpeter predicts that innovations will be concentrated in the nadir. *A priori* makes it at least as likely that they will be clustered at the zenith instead.

Schumpeter's zenith, curiously, is precisely the point at which he predicted that hard-pressed businessmen would quietly give up the ghost. Tichy is right to suggest that dynamic entrepreneurs at the upper turning point might in fact decide to fight: 'That the innovation may be exhausted after a while is plausible. But why don't the innovative entrepreneurs look for other ones? Why do they repay bank-loans and so start the auto-deflation?' (Tichy, 1984:84). Their capital is excessive relative to the demand for the good – why don't they move into a neighbouring product? Their prices are falling as their market fills up – isn't it time to pioneer a new frontier? The seeds sown in prosperity *can* be reaped in prosperity. So long as there is entrepreneurship, there is no logical need for a downswing to rescue the national income from an upper turning point that will never occur. A more worrying possibility is that an investment boom will refuse to be buffered at the peak when resources are tight. Novelty and imitation will then struggle against full employment and minimal slack; and inflation with zero growth will be the undesirable result. It is a result, price change rather than quantity change, that is all but unanticipated in Schumpeter's theory of the cycle.

On the one hand there is the upswing, the downswing, the equilibrium peak and the equilibrium trough. On the other hand there is the never-satisfied iconoclast, daring, open-minded and born to roam. Schumpeter traces the cycle back to the entrepreneur. There is a sense in which not strength but weakness would yield the better predictions. Perhaps the cycle is the footprint not of world-class leaderliness but of second-rate talent that is too timid to fly.

World-class acumen does not react meekly to present-day conditions. Rather, it is perpetually planning ahead for an unknowable future that it hopes to turn into coin of the realm. The spirit of challenge, as Kuznets insists, is not something that fits easily into a four-stage cycle, and least of all into two changeless states: 'Given an infinite supply of possible innovations (inventions and other new combinations), why need entrepreneurial genius defer the next pioneering step until his preceding one has been so imitated and expanded that the upsetting of the equilibrium stops even him in his tracks?' (Kuznets, 1940:111). More in keeping with the personality of the eternal explorer, Kuznets is implying, would be the prospect of unceasing disturbance without pronounced peaks and troughs. Not waiting for old innovations to be driven into gluts and discounts by knee-jerk new imitators, the true entrepreneur proactively and seamlessly shifts his enterprise as soon as he senses a chance. Cycles in such a scenario would be the distinguishing feature not of successful capitalism but of an inability to dream.

Haberler correctly identifies not new knowledge but its bunched introduction as the core characteristic of the cycle: 'There is no reason why inventions should not be distributed more or less evenly in time; but there are good reasons for believing that, in practice, new methods come into use in a mass.' (Haberler, 1937:82). What he does not say is why the mass crowds in rather than starting new hares and pluralising the chase. Haberler knows that Schumpeter's own 'good reasons' had much to do with the footprint of the second-rate. He also knows that Schumpeter's conspicuous reservations make it extremely difficult to take his mediocrities at face value.

Discontinuity in Schumpeter's economics cannot be explained by invention: the pool is huge, discovery itself seldom clustered. Nor, however, can it be explained by the limited supply of bottleneck capacity: the ability to grind the untried and the unproven into lateral thinking is 'distributed in the population according to the Gaussian ... law, and should not be thought of as confined to a few exceptional cases' (Schumpeter, 1939:I, 99). Just as new openings are available in elastic supply, so the entrepreneurs able to do justice to them are not 'particularly rare birds': 'That ability is distributed as unequally as others are.' (Schumpeter, 1939:I, 130). Elastic supplies and Gaussian laws make it extremely difficult to bend an economic theory around the contours of the peaks and the troughs. Possibly the true Schumpeterian cannot do so at all.

If inventions were intermittent and entrepreneurs scarce, the dramatic ups and downs would make some sense. One giant would then be unleashing a mass of copies. Since, however, the scope for new departures is vast and leadership potential normally distributed, it is hard to derive the cycle from Schumpeter's theory of the entrepreneur. Whatever else may be said about his micro-based macro, it provides no convincing explanation of the Kitchin, the Juglar and the Kondratieff that Schumpeter the statistician was so eager to document. Schumpeter wanted to be both inductive and deductive. The problem is that he produced a theory that does not march to the rhythm of the facts.

13.3 CONTINUITY AND BREACH

The cycle is about new means and new ends. It is also about the bedrock of structure and the anchor of convention. Adaptation would be different if the cycle were exclusively about fresh choices and written-off bygones forever forgotten. The truth is, however, that even fluctuations have a base in time and vibrate within a realm that was laid out in the past. We start from *here*. Yet *here* starts from *there*. This section is about the conservative constants that circumscribe the entrepreneurial wild card.

13.3.1 Evolution and Revolution

Technological breakthroughs, Schumpeter writes, are 'of the very essence of capitalistic enterprise and hence cannot be divorced from it' (Schumpeter, 1939:I, 10). Technology in this context means more than the machinery and the chemicals alone. Schumpeter's 'new combinations' extend to organisation, location, salesmanship, even politics. The precondition is the newness. Capitalism is a comes-and-goes order. Change is in the air.

Change, however, need not mean a radically new start or a surgically different charter. Schumpeter exaggerates his case when in places he implies that it does: 'We will simply define innovation as the setting up of a new production function.' (Schumpeter, 1939:I, 87). Sometimes a new production function will indeed be the quantum leap that delivers the revolution. At least as often an established production function, refined and retuned, will be more than sufficient for the evolution in hand.

Nathan Rosenberg, concentrating specifically on the D of R & D, makes the point well:

> Most Development activities at any time are not devoted to the introduction of entirely new products, but rather to the improvement and modification of existing products .... Existing technologies commonly throw off signals and focusing devices indicating specific directions in which technological efforts can be usefully exercised .... In this respect, present activities are powerfully shaped by technological knowledge inherited from the past. (Rosenberg, 1994:14).

Gradualism is in the air. Thus do the marginal and the incremental ensure that the historical endowment will enjoy a protected lease of life.

The past is present in all five of the 'new combinations' that make up Schumpeter's taxonomy. Sometimes implicit, sometimes explicit, middle-aged realities, set in a rut, are the inseparable travelling partner of innovations and surprises, fresh and impetuous. They damp down the cycle. They make the revolution less.

The first of the five 'combinations' relates to 'the introduction of a new good ... one with which consumers are not yet familiar' (Schumpeter, 1912b:66). Change, Schumpeter believed, was only exceptionally demand-led: it is 'the producer who as a rule initiates change, and consumers are educated by him if necessary' (Schumpeter, 1912b:65). Even the 'need' for the private motor car, historically speaking, had to be want-created from nothing by the industry that also manufactured the cars: 'Any "need" for them that may have existed was certainly subconscious and not an element in the then existing system of economic values.' (Schumpeter, 1939:I, 85n). Schumpeter is convinced that product development is supplier-led, that new tastes will have to be inculcated in order to validate the production plans of industry. Economics, however, teaches a more conservative lesson. Rather than making the marketing of the implausible into an innovative act, cost-conscious producers would be well advised to target their novelty at a latent want (Marshall gives the example of the typewriter which satisfies a felt need for legible script) or at an ongoing lifestyle (consider the consumer durables and the frozen meals that followed but did not create the trend towards the two-career family). Change in such a scenario is evolutionary. It is not a sudden lurch into an explosive new upswing.

The second of the 'combinations' refers to 'a new method of production ... one not yet tested by experience in the branch of manufacture concerned' (Schumpeter, 1912b:66). Output ('the branch of manufacture') is constrained within boundaries. Input alone ('a new method of production') is permitted to explore unknown avenues. A new entrant, unencumbered by existing plant, premises and procedures, will clearly be in a good position to do this. A multi-period corporation, on the other hand, will be weighed down by the sheer endogeneity of its specialist technostructure and its long-term plan. A flash of inspiration is less likely to frighten the horses where it must fit in not just with the 'branch' but with the 'method' that went before.

Combination 3, 'the opening of a new market' (Schumpeter, 1912b:66), is the experience of a going concern that wishes to penetrate an untapped subset using the knowledge and techniques that made its core business a success. *Natura non facit saltum* revels in the news that a Burger King is being opened in Chengdu. It dances in the streets when Ikea sells its Harpsinfjörd in a Moscow mega-mall. Entrepreneurship in combination 3 may mean the slight modification of an established product in line with local conditions. What it will not mean is a radical breach with a historical continuity that has stood the test of time.

Combination 4, 'the conquest of a new source of supply of raw materials or half-manufactured goods' (Schumpeter, 1912b:66), describes what happens when Saudi crude is replaced by Nigerian crude while the power stations, only affected at the margin, see no reason to trade in their capital for wind. Prices may be lower and quantities may be more secure but still the pattern of economic life will go on very much as before.

Combination 5, 'the carrying out of the new organisation of any industry' (Schumpeter, 1912b:68), is the story of forward integration into retailing, the creation (or breaking up) of a monopoly position, the privatisation of steel, the nationalisation of water. Competition will not be the same and the economy will notice the difference. The change is visible. It is also small. Especially where the industry is an insignificant as sea salt and not as history-shaping as electricity, the knock-on ramifications of the innovation are most unlikely to produce a full-blown cycle. Perhaps they will not even produce a measureable deviation from a past-dominated trend.

13.3.2 Imperfect Competition

Schumpeter's *Business Cycles* is a work of economic history. It uses data to map fluctuations. Different statisticians might have plotted different patterns. They might in particular have been able to account for the breaks and the watersheds that Schumpeter's microeconomics had anticipated and that Schumpeter's evidence had been unable to identify. Wars, urbanisation, different types of investment with different sector-specificities, reconfigurations in the relative price of capital and labour – dummy-variable discontinuities such as these seem not to have troubled the *ceteris paribus* consistency of an auto-parroting data-set. Schumpeter himself was unable to explain the stability: 'Why innovations which differ so much in period of gestation and in the time it takes to absorb them into the system should always produce cycles of respectively somewhat less than 60 years, somewhat less than 10 years, and somewhat less than 40 months, is indeed difficult to see.' (Schumpeter, 1939:I, 174). Most of all is it difficult to see when one concentrates on changes in business organisation and entrepreneurial capacity which are at the heart of Schumpeter's theory of development alongside growth.

In *Capitalism, Socialism and Democracy* Schumpeter presented a vision of inter-temporal competition in which large corporations are the innovators and monopoly power is a synonym for progress. In *Business Cycles*, referring to the half-century that had framed the new realities of the 'octopus' and the 'robber barons', Judge Gary and Standard Oil, E.H. Chamberlin and Joan Robinson, he said that the market was more or less what it had been when Walras still walked the earth: 'There is little reason to believe that ... stability or rigidity has been on the increase during the last fifty years.' (Schumpeter, 1939:II, 536). Schumpeter in his book of 1942 said much about imperfect competition but little about cycles. Schumpeter in his book of 1939 said much about cycles but little about market share. Yet he was working on both books simultaneously in the late 1930s.

Schumpeter as a theoretician knew that flexprice and fixprice send out different signals and that oligopolistic strategies work against equilibrium corrections: 'It has been proved of late that in important respects imperfect or monopolistic competition will produce exactly the opposite of those results which might be expected from free competition in the theoretic sense.' (Schumpeter, 1934:122). One would in the circumstances have expected a different kind of cycle in a *Capitalism* world of corporations, cartels and concentration from that which would obtain in *Economic Development* atomism where price takers are not burdened with excess capacity, profit recipients and not their hired staffs make the crucial decisions, and new entrants react *ab initio* without getting into a rut. Schumpeter recognised that long-lived businesses could hoard patents and in that way delay or block the 'swarming' of which the cycle is made: 'A few big concerns ... can and will fight progress itself.' (Schumpeter, 1942a:96). The discovery did not lead him to make impeded adjustment and super-normal windfalls a part of his theory of the cycle: 'The circular flow is a model of a purely competitive system ... Professor Schumpeter has assumed away the monopolistic restrictions and market imperfections that form a large part of both the actual world and theories that are designed to explain it.' (Clemence and Doody, 1950:24).

Administered prices are not the same as auction-sale prices. Nor is collective action by a club the same as decentralised action by the numerous and the weak. The implications for the peaks and troughs are clear enough. As industry becomes more trustified, as entry becomes more difficult, logic suggests that the macroeconomy will be less and less susceptible to violent swings that take off and crash down. In one place in *Business Cycles* Schumpeter does indicate that he knew precisely what he was choosing not to unpack. The monopolisation of industry, he writes there, rather 'mitigates than intensifies cyclical difficulties' (Schumpeter, 1939:II, 539). More usually in *Business Cycles* he reaches the conclusion that monopoly power is 'as yet not great enough to dominate the picture in any country' (Schumpeter, 1939:I, 97). Society might one day evolve into predictable gradualism as if guided by the corporate planning of Schumpeter's *Capitalism*. Perhaps it might; but it is not there 'as yet'.

There is a lot of ruin in a convenient 'as yet'. Appealing as they do to history-to-come to produce the evidence that existing statistics do not reveal, the words are what Oakley perceptively calls an 'escape route' that in the case of Schumpeter 'allowed an opportunity to raise the standards of non-competitive analysis to pass him by' (Oakley, 1990:35, 213). Competition among the few 'never became part of his own theory of the cycle' (Oakley, 1990:215). The theory in *Capitalism* meant that it ought to be included: declaring himself 'unconvinced' by the convention that the microeconomics textbook should teach frictionless passivity first, Schumpeter wrote in his review of Stigler's new *Theory of Price* that 'the deviations from the perfectly competitive schema are themselves of the essence of capitalism and the source of phenomena that would be completely absent in perfectly competitive conditions' (Schumpeter, 1942b:847). The evidence in *Business Cycles* showed, however, that a break or rupture in the data-set could not, 'as yet', be identified. Schumpeter, Oakley observes, did not sufficiently appreciate the need for a 'radical reconstruction of his theoretical framework': 'Schumpeter's inclination was, in general, to portray the implications of monopoly power for business-cycle analysis as being of minimal concern.' (Oakley, 1990:209, 212). That, a good Schumpeterian would say, was not ambitious enough.

13.3.3 Habits and Heuristics

Schumpeter in his *Economic Development* tended to treat rejuvenation through innovation as the achievement of the new entrepreneur path-breaking the new business (Schumpeter, 1912b:66). Even in his late work on *Business Cycles* he was still expressing the opinion that it is the new tree in the forest that does the most good (Schumpeter, 1939:I, 96). Marshall, not very sympathetic to the 'great man' theory, concluded that the captain of industry is normally 'found on inquiry to have done little more than bring to a head a broad constructive movement which had long been in preparation' (Marshall, 1890a:xi–xii). Schumpeter, on the other hand, was obsessed with the world-historical Napoleon, the ultimate 'external factor' (Schumpeter, 1939:I, 255), who has it in his make-up to destroy through creation, to cut a swathe through the self-reproducing complacency of unthinking routine.

Yet the stable routine is there and it is a part of the cycle. Schumpeter was a conservative who knew that even when innovation becomes attractive, there are limits beyond which the entrepreneur will not go: 'Even if the external conditions change, it is never a question of doing something completely new, but only of adapting what was previously done to the new conditions. The value system once established and the combinations once given are always the starting point for every new economic period and have so to speak a presumption in their favor.' (Schumpeter, 1912b:40). We start from here. We also start from there. The economy fluctuates from boom to bust. The economy also retains a remembered past which gives it an anchor but also restricts its sovereignty.

Schumpeter knew that he was arguing for the recognition of the mixed mentality. He knew precisely what he was doing. The past, he said, does not evaporate simply because the new economy is steadily evolving out of the ruins of the old: 'Unbeknown to us, the past always sits in judgement over the present.' (Schumpeter, 1912a:535). The past has not gone away: 'Past economic periods govern the activity of the individual.' (Schumpeter, 1912b:6). Bygones may be forever bygone but reality sees the shard and the remnant in quite a different light: 'The economic system will not change capriciously on its own initiative but will be at all times connected with the preceding state of affairs.' (Schumpeter, 1912b:9). As far as Schumpeter was concerned, the continuity was not merely a fact of life but also a structural necessity: 'This stability is indispensable.' (Schumpeter, 1912b:40). Schumpeter's cycle is a mix of the constitutional and the in-period, of procedural rationality with means–ends calculativeness. That is why the economy may oscillate but it never spins out of control.

Even in his early work on *Economic Development*, Schumpeter was acknowledging that stable routines, 'normally transmitted almost without friction by inheritance, teaching, upbringing, pressure of environment' (Schumpeter, 1912b:84), are a complement to optimising and maximising in the ordinary course of business life: 'The field of individual choice is always, though in very different ways and to very different degrees, fenced in by social habits or conventions and the like.' (Schumpeter, 1912b:91). One would have expected him to emphasise the lessons of experience and the survival of knee-jerk in *Capitalism, Socialism and Democracy*: its theme, after all, is the primacy of structure. One is struck by the emphasis he places on past learning even in *Economic Development* which is ostensibly the story of the broken spell: 'New businesses are continually arising under the impulse of the alluring profit.' (Schumpeter, 1912b:131). New businesses are doing new things. In spite of that they are hardening their arteries through old things because they believe the retentiveness to be the necessary complement to the destruction.

The businessman is a path-breaker when, unafraid, he does the non-normal and throws his comforting prejudices to the winds. The businessman is also a path-follower who locks himself into habits and heuristics because uncertainty and unknowledge keep him awake at night. The duality between challenge and conservatism is a real one even in Schumpeter's adventurous early work on enterprise as 'the fundamental phenomenon of economic development' (Schumpeter, 1912b:74). In favour of change is the open-minded independence that goes beyond the 'seen and experienced' to act on the basis of intuition, hunch, vision and 'imagination' (Schumpeter, 1912b:85). In favour of consolidation is, however, acquired 'knowledge and habit', 'automatic', 'accustomed' and 'subconscious', 'as firmly rooted in ourselves as a railway embankment in the earth' (Schumpeter, 1912b:84). Locking-in through acculturation is fiercely protective not just of an existing production function but of precedent-driven management's rent of tranquillity: 'Every man would have to be a giant of wisdom and will, if he had in every case to create anew all the rules by which he guides his everyday conduct.' (Schumpeter, 1912b:83). External reality, now and to come, is unbounded and unknown. It is the great attraction of 'fixed habits of thought' that they at least have an 'energy-saving function' (Schumpeter, 1912b:86) that restores the business titan's peace of mind.

A 'giant of wisdom and will' could rely exclusively on 'conscious and rational effort' (Schumpeter, 1912b:10) to produce a green-field and an unencumbered response. Most people, lacking the intelligence and the time, make their choices from a strictly bounded set: 'The individual is never equally conscious of all parts of this value system; rather at any moment the greater part of it lies beneath the threshold of consciousness.' (Schumpeter, 1912b:39). In making his prediction, the individual deliberately rejects the full set of facts in order to concentrate his search on a sub-set of priority observations. He does so because trial and error have taught him that the common-practice prism is unlikely to leave him in the lurch: 'He acts in the ordinary daily round according to general custom and experience.' (Schumpeter, 1912b:39). Walras never anticipated that his *tâtonnement* would be cut short by the repetition of entrenched resistances. Schumpeter, embedding the *tâtonnement* in an ongoing circular flow that knows what it remembers, was more realistic about the extent to which current adaptation is refracted through past experience.

Herbert Simon says that what is happening is necessarily 'satisficing' quite simply because the mind of man finds textbook economising too steep a slope: 'One could postulate that the decision maker had formed some *aspiration* as to how good an alternative he should find. As soon as he discovered an alternative for choice meeting his level of aspiration, he would terminate the search and choose that alternative.' (Simon, 1979:503). Schumpeter's *Economic Development* looks forward to Simon's relied-upon rule of thumb. Even in the young firm, Schumpeter reflects, the familiar norm has the attraction that it keeps the innovator sane. Impressed that the behavioural rigidities have 'stood the test of experience', people decide that inherited standards have satisfied reasonable aspirations and that 'on the whole they cannot do better than go on acting according to them' (Schumpeter, 1912b:40): 'There may be rational *conduct* even in the absence of rational *motive*.' (Schumpeter, 1912b:91). Prospective developments are unknown and unknowable. Lacking the data that he needs, the creative destroyer has no alternative but to use the decision-making rules that he has learned.

Of course there is a cost: the selective standard of yesterday's 'good enough' is by its very function the filter and the channel that focuses business practice on a prominent adaptation to the exclusion of all the other variations that mind without mindset might have made into superior gains from trade. The entrepreneur's sunk capital and business connections 'hold him in iron fetters fast in his tracks' (Schumpeter, 1912b:6). The businessman's strongly-held prejudgements, causing him to dismiss contradictory evidence as a statistical aberration, 'become drag-chains when they have outlived their usefulness' (Schumpeter, 1912b:86). Undoubtedly things can go wrong.

Useful deviance might be sacrificed to the passive reproduction of tried-and-tested rules that reflect the everyday circumstances of the past.

Being constructive, however, it is Schumpeter's contention that evolution is unlikely to have perpetuated a random routine which is conspicuously unequal to the economic imperative: 'The assumption that conduct is prompt and rational is in all cases a fiction. But it proves to be sufficiently near to reality, if things have time to hammer logic into men.' (Schumpeter, 1912b:80). Learned repetitiveness delivers the goods. Simon's 'satisficing' gives even the pioneer a frame of reference. It is too burdensome to recalculate all expectations from the untouched *tabula rasa* each time that a new venture is being planned: individuals 'could not, in by far the majority of the cases, do the mental labor necessary' (Schumpeter, 1912b:40). Extrapolation from recent experience is a reasonable port in the storm. Habit and heuristic make possible an 'enormous economy of force, in the race and the individual' (Schumpeter, 1912b:84). One implication is that the businessman is thereby freed to concentrate his attention on radical uncertainties which no theoretical schema can ever encode.

Schumpeter in *Economic Development* presented the duality of challenge together with conservatism as a temporal sequence of personal attributes: 'Everyone is an entrepreneur only when he actually "carries out new combinations", and loses that character as soon as he has built up his business, when he settles down to running it.' (Schumpeter, 1912b:78). The early stage is doing the unthinkable. The later stage is pipe and slippers. It is also the stage of competition from interlopers that brings the brand-name's life cycle to a close.

Schumpeter in *Business Cycles* returned to the duality of present within past. There, however, he described the accelerator together with the brake not so much as the sequence of traits as the coexistence of skills: 'Every businessman realizes that running his plant in the customary way, going through all the motions of daily business routine, is one thing and that setting up the plant or changing its setup is another. He approaches these tasks with attitudes which differ characteristically from each other.' (Schumpeter, 1939:I, 37). Corporate capitalism is a mixed economy. Every businessman realises that he is obliged to be traditional even as he is obliged to be thrusting if his business is to be a multi-period success.

The businessman in *Economic Development* had travelled through aggressiveness until he reached inertia and then on to oblivion. The businessman in *Business Cycles* was obliged to reunite in his own character the very different talents of managing organisational breakthrough and perpetuating non-transferable specificities. The older Schumpeter like the older Marshall had become aware that the trees in the forest will normally wither but need not invariably die. Clearly, the rush into creative destruction – 'Economic progress, in capitalist society, means turmoil' (Schumpeter, 1942a:32) – is only a part of the story. The other part is the standard procedure. It is reference points, ordinary routines, the 'rules by which businessmen [form] their judgement about existing business situations and the changes to be expected' (Schumpeter, 1939:I, 6).

A firm with a past is a firm with a bias. The sheer momentum of convention acts as an institutional second string to the market-clearing integer that is ground out by supply and demand. The economic market, Schumpeter says, does not grope its way to equilibrium through a frictionless hedonism of its own free choice. Rather, it has a home in the *done thing* which weighs down its spontaneity with the drag-chains of remembered retention.

Exchange works well, Schumpeter writes, but only if '*all actions and reactions are performed within the bounds of familiar practice that has evolved from long experience and frequent repetition*' (Schumpeter, 1939:I, 47). Trial and error in periods past have produced the club good of a corporate culture that the free spirit would do well to protect and enhance. Entrepreneurship is essential for development. So is *natura non facit saltum*. Schumpeter writes of desired endstates that 'the extent and nature of the change ... can only be learned from experience' (Schumpeter, 1912b:238). By then, however, it will be too late to rethink the options. The replication of a previous choice that has been seen to work is better than a stab in the dark.

Nelson and Winter, reflecting on cumulative causality and path dependence, emphasise that practical knowledge is stored in organisational memory and that embedded practices do not quickly go away: 'We claim that organizations *remember* by *doing*.' (Nelson and Winter, 1982:99). They praise Schumpeter, along with Alfred North Whitehead, for his recognition that surviving patterns can be the precondition for economic survival itself: 'Neither Schumpeter nor Whitehead, we think, would deny the role of genius or luck, or argue that systematic differences in innovative competence do not exist. But their views are quite compatible with the proposition that organizations have well-defined routines for the support of their innovative efforts.' (Nelson and Winter, 1982:133–4). Nelson and Winter are right to assert that decision-making rules provide 'support and direction' to innovative departures in the institutional economics of Joseph Schumpeter. The older Schumpeter in particular, acknowledging the self-perpetuating nature of the going concern, had to accept that it was not just physical, social and human capital but intellectual capital too that had an inter-temporal identity.

Long-lived businesses, Schumpeter wrote, are held back by their lags even as they are pushed on by the market: 'Their action is subject to additional restrictions that proceed from the situations they have created for themselves by their past decisions.' (Schumpeter, 1954:973). The new entrant is not yet the beneficiary-victim of the conditioned reflex. Established incumbents, on the other hand, are likely to use a seasoned rubric to mould and shape the 'expectations they entertain about the future course of prices' (Schumpeter, 1954:973). Economists, value-free, have to say *what is* and not *what ought to be*. The older Schumpeter criticised his contemporaries for exaggerating the significance of the small and the flexible: 'The owner-managed firm survived much better in economic theory than it did in actual life.' (Schumpeter, 1954:892). The truth, Schumpeter said, is that long-lived businesses are more and more taking the place of Smith's quick foxes that nip in and take: 'Competition is as good as never "free".' (Schumpeter, 1908:309). As life becomes long, so procedures become entrenched. If capitalism is challenge, then so too is it conservatism.

Schumpeter by temperament was a conservative. In *Economic Doctrine and Method*, published when he was 31, he made clear that he had a holist's doubts about the atom cut loose from the *Volksgeist*: 'In every nation there exists a common fund of ideas, feelings, dispositions, etc., which is as unshakeable as are the mountains of its country.' (Schumpeter, 1914:99). In the *History of Economic Analysis*, published posthumously in 1954, he stated that making sense can never be *ab ovo* and that today's thinkers effectively perceive that which they have been schooled down to see: 'Since history is an important source – though not the only one – of the economist's material and since, moreover, the economist himself is a product of his own *and all preceding* time, economic analysis and its results are certainly affected by historical relativity.' (Schumpeter, 1954:13). Schumpeter was sensitive to horizontal and lateral standardisation, the group mind and the belief-system bequeathed. In *Economic Development* and in *Business Cycles*, he applied the same conservatism to his interpretation of growth and the fluctuations of which it is made.

Bounded rationality might damp down the amplitude of the cycle. This would happen where potential experiments were pre-selected by multi-period standards. Newness, not out-of-the-blue but an element in the corporate plan, would then form part of a 'continuing stream' (Kuznets, 1940:111). Schumpeter, in an essay on 'The entrepreneur in the modern economy', went so far as to describe the giant corporation as 'a kind of business-orientated planned economy', a source of 'stabilisation through conscious, planned action' (Schumpeter, 1929:245). It was the direct consequence of advanced capitalism and a sound reason not to bring in the State. Looking to the future, and abstracting from wars and emergencies, he expressed the view that 'the waves of the economic cycle are becoming milder and milder and that what was called in the nineteenth century a "crash" hardly ever happens now' (Schumpeter, 1929:245). An essay written just before Wall Street and in the public domain just after was unlikely to have the same appeal that it would have had a year earlier. The message, however, is pure Schumpeter through and through. Fixed costs and fixed procedures mean that the past steadies the present and that nature does not make leaps.

The corporate plan will intendedly ensure that novelties occur as the concomitant of an ongoing process. The search being uninterrupted, there is no reason to think that the successes will be bunched. Swarming itself will be less explosive where significant entry barriers and oligopolistic mutual insurance ensure that the imitator is not an untested outsider but a familiar player who knows the game. An existing supplier has local knowledge. That knowledge acts as a built-in stabiliser and smooths out the process of technology transfer.

Habits and heuristics can damp down the amplitude. They can, however, also exacerbate the violence of the swings. A distorting lens can obscure a copying opportunity pioneered by a genuine leader until gradual adjustment is left behind by the error-correcting mad dash. Obsolete schemata can delay the recognition of first-best technology and exaggerate the random fluke into a wonder-drug panacea. Capricious fashions and consumer resistance can lead to the dumping of unsaleable stocks. Embedded networks can blunt the cutting edge. Inter-temporal cautiousness can dam up the moving equilibrium until not a *tâtonnement* but a flood becomes the only way to only way to restore the balance.

Conservatism can clearly account for the violent cycle even as it can account for the damped one. What it cannot explain is the clock-time predictability of a data-set oscillating to a fixed timetable. As with his theory of the new, so with his theory of the continuing: Schumpeter on the Kitchins, the Juglars and the Kondratieffs had no hypothesis that would enable him to put his evidence into a context.

14. Conclusion

The devil is in the details. There is hardly a prediction or a conjecture in the whole of Schumpeter's economics that can be bought at face value. The small firm is not disappearing. Bank credit is not essential for business initiative. The large firm is not necessarily the mould-breaking innovator. Oligopoly is not monopoly but a form of competition. Large organisations have U-shaped costs that display scale diseconomies after a point. Zero interest makes no sense save in the arid and inconceivable stationary state. The bourgeois class is not dependent on its entrepreneurial segment for its status or survival. Entrepreneurship within the organisation means that the *individual* entrepreneur is not indispensable for economic advance.

Corporate shareholders need not prove functionless or passive. Calculativeness can complement personality and need not stunt it. Rationality is as compatible with the corporation as it is with the plan. Citizens can vote down the socialist dystopia in favour of the capitalist status quo. Productive efficiency through social discipline is another name for a police State that frightens out creative destruction. Ideals in socialism can produce devolved new lifestyles that challenge the dominance of central control. Market socialism with commanded quantities leads to unacceptable rents and unexplained inefficiencies. Social democracy can be a viable halfway-house. A State bureaucracy does not face the same pressures from the top that discipline the office-holders in private business.

The intelligentsia is not anti-capitalist and not very powerful. Unemployment and cycles can be perceived as macroeconomic threats to uncoordinated exchange. Evolution into control may occur because it is the economy and not the society that happens to self-destruct. As thesis after thesis falls under suspicion, so the reader begins to think that Schumpeter, like Marx, did not fully understand the economic technicalities of markets on the move. Perhaps he did not really care. There are political economists like that. We meet them every day.

The individual hypotheses are always debatable and frequently suspect. As Daniel Bell puts it so tactfully: 'Schumpeter's insights are of limited help.' (Bell, 1965:84). The broad synthesis is, however, a different matter. The analysis of process is more than the sum of the contentions. It is the greatest of Schumpeter's contributions that he recognised the need for each tree to be properly situated in the forest to which it belongs. No actor, no action, can ever be a *ceteris paribus* outside.

As an economic philosopher, Schumpeter understood that all of human life is a struggle for scarce concepts. He used the interdependent constructs of market, enterprise and evolution to make sense of the core economic functionalities of production, consumption, distribution and exchange. Defining capitalism and socialism, inquiring into the legitimacy of property and contract, he was unprepared to let the *why* questions fall by the wayside merely because business-minded undergraduates demand reductionist *how to*s that might make them rich but will seldom make them wise. This is not to say that Schumpeter disparaged the practitioner's tool-kit, only to suggest that without the intellectual's comprehensive overview, the hewer of tools will not know *which* tools to hew or *why* they should be hewed at all.

As an economic sociologist, Schumpeter wanted to put people back in. There are the inter-personal affiliations of class and family that weave the selfish monads into a seamless web. There is the changing power-structure that replaces the profit recipient with the cog in the wheel. There is the attitudinal capital that makes the ambitious hungry to get on and the loyal determined to fit in. There are the business heuristics, the national idiosyncrasies, the social conventions that make the wealth of nations a conservative compromise. Efficiency is the economist's maximand *because* it is a consensual aspiration. Entrepreneurship is eulogised and not stigmatised *because* the community questions the sacredness of its sacred cows. Schumpeter's economics is not the physics of goods and services. Instead it is the human-centred study of interlocking identities when common institutions come together to buy and sell.

As an economic historian, Schumpeter knew that matter was in motion and that the future was the descendant of the past. He looked backward in order to look forward. At all times he was sensitive to survivals like the aristocracy but also to innovations which crossed the Rubicon. Interested in change and aware that choice is unknowledge, he was not in sympathy with general-equilibrium modelling that buried uncharted search in the comfort-zone of time-less, place-less mathematics. Statics is a fine subject for people who have lost their link to the system. Disequilibrium, however, is what is out there in the world. There is no point in shutting economic science off from the being-created truth.

History has been the record of enterprise working through the market to produce evolution. Schumpeter tried to get a purchase on the momentum. He found it a sad fact of life that even the economy had to grow old. His predictions are sombre and they may be wrong. The devil is in the details. Schumpeter was a man of breadth and vision whose real contribution lay in the holist's search for a framework and the organicist's refusal to remove the part from the whole.

References

Allen, R.L. (1991), *Opening Doors: The Life and Work of Joseph Schumpeter,* 2 vols, New Brunswick: Transaction Publishers.

Aréna, R. and C. Dangel-Hagnauer (2002), 'Introduction' to R. Aréna and C. Dangel-Hagnauer (eds), *The Contribution of Joseph Schumpeter to Economics: Economic Development and Institutional Change,* London: Routledge.

Barone, E. (1908), 'The ministry of production in the collectivist state', *Giornale degli Economisti*, English translation in F.A. Hayek (ed.) (1935a), *Collectivist Economic Planning: Critical Studies on the Possibilities of Socialism*, London: Routledge and Kegan Paul.

Bell, D. (1965), *The End of Ideology*, revised edn, Cambridge, MA: Harvard University Press, 1988.

Berle, A.A., Jr. and G.C. Means (1932), *The Modern Corporation and Private Property,* London: Macmillan.

Bottomore, T. (1992), *Between Marginalism and Marxism: The Economic Sociology of J.A. Schumpeter,* Hemel Hempstead: Harvester Wheatsheaf.

Bukharin, N. (1917), *Imperialism and World Economy*, London: Merlin, 1972.

Chandler, A.D., Jr. (1977), *The Visible Hand: The Managerial Revolution in American Business,* Cambridge, MA: Belknap.

Clemence, R.V. and F.S. Doody (1950), *The Schumpeterian System,* New York: Augustus M. Kelley, 1966.

Coe, R.D. and C.K. Wilber (eds) (1985), *Capitalism and Democracy: Schumpeter Revisited,* Notre Dame: University of Notre Dame Press.

Crosland, C.A.R. (1956), *The Future of Socialism*, revised edn, London: Jonathan Cape, 1964.

Crosland, C.A.R. (1971), *A Social-Democratic Britain*, Fabian Tract 404, in his *Socialism Now*, ed. by D. Leonard, London: Jonathan Cape, 1974.

Dore, R. (2001), *Social Evolution, Economic Development and Culture*, ed. by D.H. Whittaker, Cheltenham UK and Northampton, MA, USA: Edward Elgar.

Durkheim, E. (1895), *The Rules of Sociological Method*, trans. by S.A. Solovay and J.H. Mueller, New York: The Free Press, 1938.

Friedman, M. (1962), *Capitalism and Freedom,* Chicago: University of Chicago Press.

Frisch, H. (ed.) (1982), *Schumpeterian Economics,* New York: Praeger.

Galbraith, J.K. (1952), *American Capitalism*, revised edn, New Brunswick: Transaction Publishers, 1993.

Galbraith, J.K. (1958), *The Affluent Society*, Harmondsworth: Penguin Books, 1962.

Galbraith, J.K. (1960), 'The nature of social nostalgia', in his *The Liberal Hour*, Harmondsworth: Penguin Books.

Galbraith, J.K. (1965), *Economic Development,* Cambridge, MA: Harvard University Press.

Galbraith, J.K. (1967), *The New Industrial State*, revised edn, Harmondsworth: Penguin Books.

Galbraith, J.K. (1973), *Economics and the Public Purpose*, Harmondsworth: Penguin Books, 1975.

Galbraith, J.K. (1974), 'Perfecting the corporation: what comes after General Motors', *The New Republic*, 2 November, in his *Annals of an Abiding Liberal,* Boston: Houghton Mifflin, 1979.

Galbraith, J.K. (1977a), 'Near or far right' (review of *Capitalism, Socialism and Democracy*), *New Society*, Vol. 758, 14 April.

Galbraith, J.K. (1977b), *The Age of Uncertainty*, London: British Broadcasting Corporation and André Deutsch.

Galbraith, J.K. (1981), *A Life in Our Times: Memoirs,* Boston: Houghton Mifflin.

Goldscheid, R. (1925), 'A sociological approach to problems of public finance', English translation in R.A. Musgrave and A.T. Peacock (eds), *Classics in the Theory of Public Finance,* London: Macmillan, 1958.

Haberler, G. (1937), *Prosperity and Depression*, 3rd edn, London: George Allen and Unwin, 1958.

Haberler, G. (1951), 'Joseph Alois Schumpeter, 1883–1950', *Quarterly Journal of Economics*, Vol. 64, in S.E. Harris (ed.), *Schumpeter, Social Scientist*, Cambridge, MA: Harvard University Press.

Haberler, G. (1981), 'Schumpeter's *Capitalism, Socialism and Democracy* after Forty Years', in A. Heertje (ed.), *Schumpeter's Vision*, New York: Praeger.

Hanusch, H. (ed.) (1988), *Evolutionary Economics: Applications of Schumpeter's Ideas,* Cambridge: Cambridge University Press.

Harris, S.E. (ed.) (1951), *Schumpeter, Social Scientist*, Cambridge, MA: Harvard University Press.

Hayek, F.A. (ed.) (1935a), *Collectivist Economic Planning: Critical Studies on the Possibilities of Socialism,* London: Routledge and Kegan Paul.

Hayek, F.A. (1935b), 'The present state of the debate', in F.A. Hayek (ed.), *Collectivist Economic Planning: Critical Studies on the Possibilities of Socialism*, London: Routledge and Kegan Paul.

Hayek, F.A. (1944), *The Road to Serfdom,* London: Routledge and Kegan Paul, 1976.

Hayek, F.A. (1949), *Individualism and Economic Order*, London: Routledge and Kegan Paul.

Hayek, F.A. (1988), *The Fatal Conceit*, London: Routledge and Kegan Paul.

Heertje, A. (ed.) (1981), *Schumpeter's Vision*, New York: Praeger.

Heilbroner, R.L. (1984), 'Economics and political economy: Marx, Keynes, and Schumpeter', *Journal of Economic Issues*, Vol. 18, in J.C. Wood (ed.) (1991), *Joseph A. Schumpeter: Critical Assessments*, Vol. IV, London: Routledge.

Hilferding, R. (1910), *Finance Capital: A Study of the Latest Phase of Capitalist Development*, trans. by M. Watnik and S. Gordon and ed. by T. Bottomore, London: Routledge and Kegan Paul, 1981.

Hobson, J.A. (1902), *Imperialism: A Study*, 3rd edn, London: George Allen and Unwin, 1938.

Jacobs, J. (1961), *The Death and Life of Great American Cities*, Harmondsworth: Penguin Books, 1964.

Jewkes, J., D. Sawers and R. Stillerman (1969), *The Sources of Invention*, London: Macmillan.

Kamien, M.I. and N.L. Schwartz (1982), *Market Structure and Innovation*, Cambridge: Cambridge University Press.

Keynes, J.M. (1923), *A Tract on Monetary Reform*, London: Macmillan.

Keynes, J.M. (1930), 'Economic possibilities for our grandchildren', in *The Collected Writings of John Maynard Keynes*, Vol. IX: *Essays in Persuasion*, London: Macmillan, 1972.

Keynes, J.M. (1936), *The General Theory of Employment, Interest and Money*, London: Macmillan, 1973.

Kirzner, I.M. (1973), *Competition and Entrepreneurship*, Chicago: University of Chicago Press.

Kirzner, I.M. (1979), *Perception, Opportunity and Profit: Studies in the Theory of Entrepreneurship,* Chicago: University of Chicago Press.

Kuznets, S.S. (1940), 'Schumpeter's *Business Cycles*', *American Economic Review*, Vol. 30, in his *Economic Change,* London: William Heinemann, 1954.

Lange, O. (1936/37), 'On the economic theory of socialism', in O. Lange and F.M. Taylor, *On the Economic Theory of Socialism*, Minneapolis: University of Minnesota Press, 1938.

Lenin, V.I. (1917), *Imperialism, the Highest Stage of Capitalism*, Moscow: Foreign Languages Publishing House, 1950.

Leo XIII (1891), *Rerum Novarum*, in G.C. Treacy (ed.) (1939), *Five Great Encyclicals*, New York: Paulist Press.

Leontief, W.W. (1950), 'Joseph A. Schumpeter (1883–1950)', *Econometrica*, Vol. 18, No. 2, pp. 103–10.

Luxemburg, R. (1913), *The Accumulation of Capital*, London: Routledge and Kegan Paul, 1951.

Marshall, A. (1875), 'Some features of American industry', in J.K. Whitaker (ed.), *The Early Economic Writings of Alfred Marshall, 1867–1890*, London: Macmillan, 1975, Vol. 2.

Marshall, A. (1879), *The Economics of Industry*, 2nd edn, London: Macmillan, 1881 (with Mary Paley Marshall).

Marshall, A. (1890a), *Principles of Economics*, 8th edn (1920), London: Macmillan, 1949.

Marshall, A (1890b), 'Some aspects of competition', in A.C. Pigou (ed.) (1925), *Memorials of Alfred Marshall*, New York: Augustus M. Kelley, 1966.

Marshall, A. (1897a), 'The old generation of economists and the new', *Quarterly Journal of Economics*, Vol. 11, in A.C. Pigou (ed.) (1925), *Memorials of Alfred Marshall*, New York: Augustus M. Kelley, 1966.

Marshall, A. (1897b), Letter to Edward Caird dated 5 December, in A.C. Pigou (ed.) (1925), *Memorials of Alfred Marshall*, New York: Augustus M. Kelley, 1996.

Marshall, A. (1907), 'Social possibilities of economic chivalry', in A.C. Pigou (ed.) (1925), *Memorials of Alfred Marshall*, New York: Augustus M. Kelley, 1966.

Marshall, A. (1919), *Industry and Trade*, 4th edn, London: Macmillan, 1923.

Marshall, A. (1923), *Money Credit and Commerce*, London: Macmillan.

Marx, K. (1859), Preface to *A Contribution to the Critique of Political Economy*, in L. Colletti (ed.), *Karl Marx: Early Writings*, Harmondsworth: Penguin Books, 1975.

Marx, K. (1867), *Capital*, Vol. I, New York: International Publishers, 1967.

Marx, K. (1884), *Capital*, Vol. III, New York: International Publishers, 1967.

Marx, K. and F. Engels (1848), *The Communist Manifesto*, Harmondsworth: Penguin, 1967.

März, E. (1991), *Joseph Schumpeter: Scholar, Teacher and Politician*, New Haven: Yale University Press.

Mayhew, A. (1980), 'Schumpeterian capitalism versus the "Schumpeterian Thesis"', *Journal of Economic Issues*, Vol. 14, in J.C. Wood (ed.) (1991), *Joseph A. Schumpeter: Critical Assessments*, Vol. III, London: Routledge.

Medearis, J. (2001), *Joseph Schumpeter's Two Theories of Democracy*, Cambridge, MA: Harvard University Press.

Menger, C. (1871), *Principles of Economics*, trans. by J. Dingwall and B.F. Hoselitz, New York: New York University Press, 1981.

Mises, L. von (1922), *Socialism: An Economic and Sociological Analysis*, 2nd edn, trans. by J. Kahane, London: Jonathan Cape, 1936.

Mises, L. von (1949), *Human Action*, 3rd edn, Chicago: Contemporary Books, 1966.

Mises, L. von (1962), *The Ultimate Foundations of Economic Science*, 2nd edn, Kansas City: Sheed Andrews and McMeel, 1978.

Mitchell, W.C. (1984), 'Schumpeter and public choice, Part I', *Public Choice*, Vol. 42, in J.C. Wood (ed.) (1991), *Joseph A. Schumpeter: Critical Assessments*, Vol. IV, London: Routledge.

Morishima, M. and G. Catephores (1988), 'Anti-Say's Law versus Say's Law: a change in paradigm', in H. Hanusch (ed.), *Evolutionary Economics*, Applications of Schumpeter's Ideas, Cambridge: Cambridge University Press.

Nelson, R.R. and S.G. Winter (1982), *An Evolutionary Theory of Economic Change*, Cambridge, MA: Harvard University Press.

O'Connor, J. (1973), *The Fiscal Crisis of the State*, New York: St. Martin's Press.

Oakley, A. (1990), *Schumpeter's Theory of Capitalist Motion*, Aldershot, UK and Brookfield, USA: Edward Elgar.

Pius XI (1931), *Quadragesimo Anno*, in G.C. Treacy (ed.) (1939), *Five Great Encyclicals*, New York: Paulist Press.

Robinson, J. (1943), review of *Capitalism, Socialism and Democracy*, *Economic Journal*, Vol. 53, No. 212, pp. 381–3.

Rosenberg, N. (1994), *Exploring the Black Box: Technology, Economics and History*, Cambridge: Cambridge University Press.

Rostow, W.W. (1991), Foreword to R.L. Allen, *Opening Doors: The Life and Work of Joseph Schumpeter*, Vol. I, New Brunswick: Transaction Publishers.

Rothschild, K.W. (1986), 'Capitalists and entrepreneurs: prototypes and roles', in H.-J. Wagener and J.W. Drukker (eds), *The Economic Law of Motion of Modern Society: A Marx–Keynes–Schumpeter Centennial*, Cambridge: Cambridge University Press.

Samuels, W.J. (1985), 'A Critique of *Capitalism, Socialism and Democracy*', in R.D. Coe and C.K. Wilber (eds), *Capitalism and Democracy: Schumpeter Revisited*, Notre Dame: University of Notre Dame Press.

Samuelson, P. (1951), 'Schumpeter as a teacher and economic theorist', in S.E. Harris (ed.), *Schumpeter, Social Scientist*, Cambridge, MA: Harvard University Press.

Scherer, F.M. (1965), 'Firm size, market structure, opportunity, and the output of patented inventions', *American Economic Review*, Vol. 55, in his *Innovation and Growth: Schumpeterian Perspectives*, Cambridge, MA: MIT Press, 1984.

Scherer, F.M. (1967), 'Market structure and the employment of scientists and engineers', *American Economic Review*, Vol. 57, in his *Innovation and Growth: Schumpeterian Perspectives*, Cambridge, MA: MIT Press.

Scherer, F.M. (1970), *Industrial Market Structure and Economic Performance*, Boston: Houghton Mifflin.

Scherer, F.M. (1984), *Innovation and Growth: Schumpeterian Perspectives*, Cambridge, MA: MIT Press.

Scherer, F.M. and M. Perlman (1992) (eds), *Entrepreneurship, Technological Innovation and Economic Growth: Studies in the Schumpeterian Tradition*, Ann Arbor: University of Michigan Press.

Schumpeter, E.B. (1954), Editor's Introduction to J.A. Schumpeter, *History of Economic Analysis*, London: George Allen and Unwin.

Schumpeter, J.A. (1906), 'Über die Mathematische Methode der Theoretischen Ökonomie', *Zeitschrift für Volkswirtschaft, Sozialpolitik und Verwaltung*, Vol. 15, in *Aufsätze zur Ökonomischen Theorie* (Schumpeter, 1952b).

Schumpeter, J.A. (1907), 'Das Rentenprinzip in der Verteilungslehre, I', *Schmollers Jahrbuch*, Vol. 31, in *Aufsätze zur Ökonomischen Theorie* (Schumpeter, 1952b).

Schumpeter, J.A. (1908), *Das Wesen und der Hauptinhalt der theoretischen Nationalökonomie*, Leipzig: Duncker und Humblot .

Schumpeter, J.A. (1912a), *Theorie der Wirtschaftlichen Entwicklung*, Leipzig: Duncker und Humblot.

Schumpeter, J.A. (1912b), *The Theory of Economic Development*, trans. by R. Opie from the 1926 (revised) edition of *Theorie der Wirtschaftlichen Entwicklung*, London: Oxford University Press, 1961.

Schumpeter, J.A. (1913), 'Eine "dynamische" Theorie des Kapitalzinses: Eine Entgegnung', *Zeitschrift für Volkswirtschaft, Sozialpolitik und Verwaltung*, Vol. 22, in *Aufsätze zur Ökonomischen Theorie* (Schumpeter, 1952b).

Schumpeter, J.A. (1914), *Economic Doctrine and Method*, trans. by R. Aris, London: George Allen and Unwin, 1954.

Schumpeter, J.A. (1915), 'Wie studiert man Sozialwissenschaft?', *Schriften des Sozialwissenschaftlichen Vereins in Czernowitz*, No. 2, in *Aufsätze zur Ökonomischen Theorie* (Schumpeter, 1952b).

Schumpeter, J.A. (1917/18), 'Das Sozialprodukt und die Rechenpfennige: Glossen und Beiträge zur Geldtheorie von Heute', *Archiv für Sozialwissenschaft und Sozialpolitik*, Vol. 44, in *Aufsätze zur Ökonomischen Theorie* (Schumpeter, 1952b). An English translation (by A.W. Marget) has been published as 'Money and the Social Product', *International Economic Papers*, Vol. 6, 1956.

Schumpeter, J.A. (1918), 'The crisis of the tax state', in *Economics and Sociology* (Schumpeter, 1991).

Schumpeter, J.A. (1918/19), 'The sociology of imperialisms', *Archiv für Sozialwissenschaft und Sozialpolitik*, Vol. 46, in *Economics and Sociology* (Schumpeter, 1991).

Schumpeter, J.A. (1919), Speech to the 24th session of the Austrian National Assembly, 4 July, in *Aufsätze zur Wirtschaftspolitik* (Schumpeter, 1985).

Schumpeter, J.A. (1920/21), 'Sozialistische Möglichkeiten von Heute', *Archiv für Sozialwissenschaft und Sozialpolitik*, Vol. 48, in *Aufsätze zur Ökonomischen Theorie* (Schumpeter, 1952b).

Schumpeter, J.A. (1926/27a), 'Steuerkraft und nationale Zukunft', *Der Deutsche Volkswirt*, Vol. 1, in *Aufsätze zur Wirtschaftspolitik* (Schumpeter, 1985).

Schumpeter, J.A. (1926/27b), 'Die Arbeitslosigkeit', *Der Deutsche Volkswirt*, Vol. 1, in *Aufsätze zur Wirtschaftspolitik* (Schumpeter, 1985).

Schumpeter, J.A. (1927a), 'Social classes in an ethnically homogeneous environment', in *Economics and Sociology* (Schumpeter, 1991).

Schumpeter, J.A. (1927b), 'The explanation of the business cycle', *Economica*, Vol. 7, in *Essays* (Schumpeter, 1951).

Schumpeter, J.A. (1927c), 'Unternehmerfunktion und Arbeiterinteresse', *Der Arbeitgeber*, Vol. 17, in *Aufsätze zur Wirtschaftspolitik* (Schumpeter, 1985).

Schumpeter, J.A. (1928), 'The instability of capitalism', *Economic Journal*, Vol. 38, in *Essays* (Schumpeter, 1951).

Schumpeter, J.A. (1929), 'Der Unternehmer in der Volkswirtschaft von Heute', in B. Harms (ed.), *Strukturwandlungen der Deutschen Volkswirtschaft*, reprinted in *Aufsätze zur Wirtschaftspolitik* (Schumpeter, 1985).

Schumpeter, J.A. (1929/30a), 'Wenn die Finanzreform misslingt', *Der Deutsche Volkswirt*, Vol. 4, in *Aufsätze zur Wirtschaftspolitik* (Schumpeter, 1985).

Schumpeter, J.A. (1929/30b), 'Ökonomie und Soziologie der Einkommensteuer', *Der Deutsche Volkswirt*, Vol. 4, in *Aufsätze zur Wirtschaftspolitik* (Schumpeter, 1985).

Schumpeter, J.A. (1931a), 'Recent developments in political economy', manuscript of a lecture, probably delivered in Japan, in *Economics and Sociology* (Schumpeter, 1991).

Schumpeter, J.A. (1931b), 'The present world depression: a tentative diagnosis', *American Economic Review*, Vol. 21, in *Essays* (Schumpeter, 1951).

Schumpeter, J.A. (1931/32), 'Dauerkrise', *Der Deutsche Volkswirt*, Vol. 6, in *Aufsätze zur Wirtschaftspolitik* (Schumpeter, 1985).

Schumpeter, J.A. (1932), 'Das Woher und Wohin unserer Wissenschaft', in *Aufsätze zur Ökonomischen Theorie* (Schumpeter, 1952b).

Schumpeter, J.A. (1933), 'The common sense of econometrics', *Econometrica*, Vol. 1, in *Essays* (Schumpeter, 1951).

Schumpeter, J.A. (1934), 'The nature and necessity of a price system', in Columbia University Commission, *Economic Reconstruction*, reprinted in *Essays* (Schumpeter, 1951).

Schumpeter, J.A. (1935), 'The analysis of economic change', *Review of Economic Statistics*, Vol. 17, in *Essays* (Schumpeter, 1951).

Schumpeter, J.A. (1936a), 'Can capitalism survive?', in *Economics and Sociology* (Schumpeter, 1991).

Schumpeter, J.A. (1936b), 'Review of Keynes's *General Theory*', *Journal of the American Statistical Association*, Vol. 31, in *Essays* (Schumpeter, 1951).

Schumpeter, J.A. (1937), Preface to the Japanese edition of *The Theory of Economic Development*, in *Essays* (Schumpeter, 1951).

Schumpeter, J.A. (1939), *Business Cycles: A Theoretical, Historical and Statistical Analysis of the Capitalist Process*, 2 vols, New York: McGraw-Hill.

Schumpeter, J.A. (1941), *An Economic Interpretation of Our Time* (the Lowell Lectures), in *Economics and Sociology* (Schumpeter, 1991).

Schumpeter, J.A. (1942a), *Capitalism, Socialism and Democracy*, 3rd edn, London: George Allen and Unwin, 1976 .

Schumpeter, J.A. (1942b), review of G.J. Stigler, *The Theory of Competitive Price*, *American Economic Review*, Vol. 32, No. 4, pp. 844–7.

Schumpeter, J.A. (1943), 'Capitalism in the postwar world', in S.E. Harris (ed.), *Postwar Economic Problems*, in *Essays* (Schumpeter, 1951).

Schumpeter, J.A. (1944), review of H.J. Laski, *Reflections on the Revolution of Our Time*, *American Economic Review*, Vol. 34, No.1, pp. 161–4.

Schumpeter, J.A. (1946a), 'The future of private enterprise in the face of modern socialistic tendencies', English translation of 'L'avenir de l'entreprise privée devant les tendances socialistes modernes', in Association Professionelle des Industriels, *Premier Congrès Patronal*, English translation in *Economics and Sociology* (Schumpeter, 1991).

Schumpeter, J.A. (1946b), review of F.A. Hayek, *The Road to Serfdom*, *Journal of Political Economy*, Vol. 54, No. 3, pp. 269–70.

Schumpeter, J.A. (1946c), 'Comments on a plan for the study of entrepreneurship', unabridged text of 'The creative response in economic history', *Journal of Economic History*, Vol. 7, 1947, in *Economics and Sociology* (Schumpeter, 1991).

Schumpeter, J.A. (1947), 'Theoretical problems of economic growth', *Journal of Economic History*, Vol. 7, in *Essays* (Schumpeter, 1951).

Schumpeter, J.A. (1948), 'There is still time to stop inflation', *Nation's Business*, Vol. 36, in *Essays* (Schumpeter, 1951).

Schumpeter, J.A. (1949a), 'Science and ideology', *American Economic Review*, Vol. 39, in *Essays* (Schumpeter, 1951).

Schumpeter, J.A. (1949b), 'Economic theory and entrepreneurial history', in *Change and the Entrepreneur*, reprinted in *Essays* (Schumpeter, 1951).

Schumpeter, J.A. (1949c), 'The Communist Manifesto in sociology and economics', *Journal of Political Economy*, Vol. 57, in *Essays* (Schumpeter, 1951).

Schumpeter, J.A. (1949d), 'English economists and the state-managed economy', *Journal of Political Economy*, Vol. 57, in *Essays* (Schumpeter, 1951).

Schumpeter, J.A. (1950a), 'American institutions and economic progress' (the Walgreen Lectures, uncompleted), in *Economics and Sociology* (Schumpeter, 1991).

Schumpeter, J.A. (1950b), 'The march into socialism', *American Economic Review*, Vol. 40, in *Capitalism, Socialism and Democracy* (Schumpeter, 1942a).

Schumpeter, J.A. (1951), *Essays on Entrepreneurs, Innovations, Business Cycles, and the Evolution of Capitalism*, ed. by R.V. Clemence, Brunswick, NJ: Transaction Publishers, 1989.

Schumpeter, J.A. (1952a), *Ten Great Economists*, London: Routledge, 1997.

Schumpeter, J.A. (1952b), *Aufsätze zur Ökonomischen Theorie*, ed. by E. Schneider and A. Spiethoff, Tübingen: J.C.B. Mohr.

Schumpeter, J.A. (1954), *History of Economic Analysis*, London: George Allen and Unwin.

Schumpeter, J.A. (1985), *Aufsätze zur Wirtschaftspolitik*, ed. by W.F. Stolper and C. Seidl, Tübingen: J.C.B. Mohr.

Schumpeter, J.A. (1991), *The Economics and Sociology of Capitalism*, ed. by R. Swedberg, Princeton: Princeton University Press.

Scitovsky, T. (1980). 'Can capitalism survive – an old question in a new setting', *American Economic Review* (Papers and Proceedings), Vol. 70, No. 2, pp. 1–9.

Seidl, C. (ed.) (1984), *Lectures on Schumpeterian Economics*, Berlin: Springer.

Shackle, G.L.S. (1972), *Epistemics and Economics*, Cambridge: Cambridge University Press.

Shionoya, Y. (1992), 'Taking Schumpeter's methodology seriously', in F.M. Scherer and M. Perlman (eds), *Entrepreneurship, Technological Innovation and Economic Growth: Studies in the Schumpeterian Tradition*, Ann Arbor: University of Michigan Press.

Simon, H.A. (1957), *Models of Man*, New York: John Wiley and Sons.

Simon, H.A. (1979), 'Rational decision making in business organizations', *American Economic Review*, Vol. 69, No. 4, pp. 493–513.

Smith, A. (1776), *The Wealth of Nations*, ed. by E. Cannan, 2 vols, London: Methuen, 1961.

Smith, A. (1795), 'The history of astronomy', in *Essays on Philosophical Subjects*, reprinted in J. Ralph Lindgren (ed.), *The Early Writings of Adam Smith*, New York: Augustus M. Kelley, 1967.

Stolper, W.F. (1951), 'Reflections on Schumpeter's writings', in S.E. Harris (ed.), *Schumpeter, Social Scientist*, Cambridge, MA: Harvard University Press.

Stolper, W.F. (1994), *Joseph Alois Schumpeter: The Public Life of a Private Man*, Princeton: Princeton University Press.

Streissler, E. (1982), 'Schumpeter's Vienna and the role of credit in innovation', in H. Frisch (ed.), *Schumpeterian Economics*, New York: Praeger.

Swedberg, R. (1991), *Joseph A. Schumpeter: His Life and Work*, Cambridge: Polity Press.

Swedberg, R. (1998), *Max Weber and the Idea of Economic Sociology*, Princeton: Princeton University Press.

Sweezy, P.M. (1951), 'Schumpeter on *Imperialism and Social Classes*', in S.E. Harris (ed.), *Schumpeter, Social Scientist*, Cambridge, MA: Harvard University Press.

Tawney, R.H. (1921), *The Acquisitive Society*, London: Collins, 1961.

Tawney, R.H. (1931), *Equality*, 4th edn, London: George Allen and Unwin, 1964.

Tichy, G. (1984), 'Schumpeter's business cycle theory: its importance for our time', in C. Seidl (ed.), *Lectures on Schumpeterian Economics*, Berlin: Springer.

Titmuss, R.M. (1970), 'The evolution of social policy', unpublished lecture at the Civil Service College, London, 23 November 1970, in the papers of Richard Titmuss, British Library of Political and Economic Science, London School of Economics, Box 3/370.

Treacy, G.C. (ed.) (1939), *Five Great Encyclicals*, New York: Paulist Press.

Veblen, T.B. (1899), *The Theory of the Leisure Class*, London: George Allen and Unwin, 1970.

Wagener, H.-J. and J.W. Drukker (eds) (1986), *The Economic Law of Motion of Modern Society: A Marx–Keynes–Schumpeter Centennial*, Cambridge: Cambridge University Press.

Weber, M. (1922/23), 'The social psychology of the world religions', in H.H. Gerth and C.W. Mills (eds), *From Max Weber: Essays in Sociology*, London: Routledge and Kegan Paul, 1948.

Weber, M. (1948), 'Bureaucracy', in H.H. Gerth and C.W. Mills (eds), *From Max Weber: Essays in Sociology*, London: Routledge and Kegan Paul.

Wiles, P. (1981), 'A Sovietological view', in A. Heertje (ed.), *Schumpeter's Vision*, New York: Praeger.

Wood, J.C. (ed.) (1991), *J.A. Schumpeter: Critical Assessments*, 4 vols, London: Routledge.

Wright, D. M. (1950), 'Schumpeter and Keynes', *Weltwirtschaftliches Archiv*, Vol. 65, in J.C. Wood (ed.), *Joseph A. Schumpeter: Critical Assessments*, Vol. I, London: Routledge, 1991.

Index